Cultural Competence for Public Managers

Managing Diversity in Today's World

Cultural Competence
for Public Managers

Managing Diversity in Today's World

Espiridion Borrego
Richard Greggory Johnson III

CRC Press
Taylor & Francis Group
Boca Raton London New York

CRC Press is an imprint of the
Taylor & Francis Group, an **informa** business

CRC Press
Taylor & Francis Group
6000 Broken Sound Parkway NW, Suite 300
Boca Raton, FL 33487-2742

© 2012 by Taylor & Francis Group, LLC
CRC Press is an imprint of Taylor & Francis Group, an Informa business

Printed in the United States of America on acid-free paper
Version Date: 20110706

International Standard Book Number: 978-1-4398-2807-6 (Hardback)

Visit the Taylor & Francis Web site at
http://www.taylorandfrancis.com

and the CRC Press Web site at
http://www.crcpress.com

Contents

PART V: WHERE DO WE GO FROM HERE?

Supplemental Material and Templates

The DVD provides additional information. The 15 minute video on the Seattle Office for Civil Rights's Race and Social Justice Initiative (RSJI) describes the experiences and reasons for developing the RSJI. In A, employees from Seattle describe the lessons learned from the RSJI and contain contact information for the employees. There are many communities experiencing similar demographic changes who can benefit from Seattle's experience. The rest are templates created so they can be copied and used.

Video: The Seattle Office for Civil Rights' Race & Social Justice Initiative Training Video

Preface

Cultural Competence for Public Managers gives busy professionals a guide to becoming leaders in developing cultural competence in their organizations. It provides a conceptual foundation and successful examples for developing cultural competence, including competencies for international collaborations.

In this increasingly globalized society in which we live, the need for a higher level of sophistication in working cross-culturally and internationally is demanded of local governments, state governments, tribal corporations, nonprofit organizations, and others, as well as at the federal levels of government. This book discusses positive and negative real-world examples from universities; local, state, and federal governments; health care service providers; and nonprofit organizations. It includes examples from Europe and Asia as well as the United States.

This book describes the rapidly changing worldwide population demographics that are bringing new cultures into many countries and societies. The transition from a predominately monocultural society into a multicultural society is requiring managers to become culturally competent to successfully manage the cultural diversity of employees in today's workplace. The issues that the culturally diverse landscape is creating in the United States, Asia, Europe, Africa, and Latin America are discussed. There is a description of the obstacles and several major personal and social barriers to success that stand in the way of becoming culturally competent. Definitions of polychronic and monochronic time are given. The differences between the assimilationist and the multicultural viewpoints are discussed. Cultural competence is not only an attainable personal attribute; it also can be built into the knowledge, skills, and performance measures for the public sector leadership pipeline. Cultural competence is grounded in solid management practices that are adapted for today's culturally diverse workplace by the relevant theoretical research on cultural competence. Some of the examples illustrate purely management practices that are then extended into the relevant cultural context. In some ways, cultural competence can be seen as developing a cultural intelligence that helps managers manage a diverse and multicultural workforce where many cross-cultural interactions occur.

The term *cultural competence* is defined as managing diversity in all its forms. The focus is on the managers and employees in the workplace. Cultural competence will encompass race and ethnicity, gender, social class, sexual orientation, and cultural characteristics that are becoming increasingly more important in the workplace. There are other forms of diversity that are important in the workplace, among them generational differences, religion, politics, and technology. These various forms are mentioned whenever it is appropriate and informative to do so. Race and ethnicity, gender, sexual orientation, social class, and cultural differences seem to be more difficult to bridge in the workplace.

In the beginning chapters, the authors clearly define terms and provide their own cultural competence model that will add significantly to the current field. The book provides actual examples of cultural missteps and positive examples along with cultural competencies that have worked in practice. Practical and useful standards and performance measures are provided along with proven coaching and mentoring guides. Cultural competencies have been designed for implementation at the executive level, the middle-manager level, and the employee level.

This book fills a critical missing gap in the current research and literature on cultural competence. What has been missing is the application of reality-based cultural competencies for people working in complex organizations in ways that positively empower them to be leaders in very diverse work settings. Organized thematically, the book defines the scope of cultural competencies, highlights best practices, and describes variations in responsibility for administering cultural competence for executives, managers, supervisors, and employees. The authors give expert advice for building a culturally competent organization and troubleshooting cultural competence issues.

Cultural Competence for Public Managers uses a format and style that is readable to busy practitioners. The book is peppered with liberal uses of real-life examples, templates, checklists, exercises, and guides.

The book also comes with a DVD that contains the Seattle Office for Civil Rights' Race & Social Justice Initiative training video. The DVD also has a Word document that contains a report by three City of Seattle employees describing the Race & Social Justice Initiative. The rest of the Word document contains mentoring and coaching templates, self-assessments, cultural competence orientation outline, international meeting checklist, and a variety of measures for cultural competence.

Let the adventures begin!

Espiridion (Al) Borrego
Richard Greggory Johnson III

Acknowledgments

We would like to thank Lara Zoble for her impeccable knowledge regarding the process for getting this book completed and for her timely and sage advice.

Thanks go to Dr. Vicky J. Borrego for her patience and unwavering support of this critical project.

We would especially like to thank Elliott Bronstein, Glenn Harris, and Julie Nelson from the City of Seattle for their description of the Seattle Race and Social Justice Initiative (RSJI), which is included in the DVD Appendix A. They have included their contact information for anyone who would like to learn more about the RSJI.

Authors

Espiridion (Al) Borrego is an associate professor in the Public Administration Program at the University of Texas–Pan American. He has served on President Barack Obama's transition team. He has been a senior consultant and lead business partner at Alignment Strategies, Inc. (ALS). He served as the assistant secretary for veterans' employment and training at the U.S. Department of Labor. He was the dean of the School of Business and Public Administration, University of Alaska, and an associate professor of public administration. He was also a
presidential management intern at NASA, Office of the Comptroller, and a Ford Foundation fellow. He holds a PhD and an MPA in public administration from the University of Southern California.

Richard Greggory Johnson III is an associate professor in the Masters of Public Administration Program, School of Management, University of San Francisco. He has published several refereed journal articles in addition to publishing several books including *A Twenty-First Century Approach to Teaching Social Justice: Educating for Both Advocacy and Action* (Peter Lang Publishing, 2009). His research centers on social justice/human rights and public policy. He holds a PhD in Public Administration and Policy from Golden Gate University and
masters degrees from DePaul University and Georgetown University. He is also a Fulbright Scholar Alumnus (Hong Kong, 2010 to 2011).

INTRODUCTION TO CULTURAL COMPETENCE: DO I REALLY NEED TO BE CULTURALLY COMPETENT?

1

Chapter 1

Why Cultural Competence Is Important

If a man be gracious and courteous to strangers, it shows he is a citizen of the world, and that his heart is no island cut off from other lands, but a continent that joins them.

Sir Francis Bacon

Example 1.1: I'll Do Exactly What You Ask Me to Do

Ana was the daughter of immigrant parents and was a first-generation college student. She competed for and was selected as Presidential Management Intern (PMI), which is now the Presidential Management Fellows (PMF). She went to work for the Comptroller's Office in NASA, where she was a program analyst for the physics and astronomy missions. She and her immigrant parents came from a very family-oriented culture where the parents and all figures of authority are treated with the utmost respect and never questioned. She had been working there for about one and one-half years when one morning Charles, the deputy comptroller, asked her to come into his office. He told Ana he wanted her to take a closer look at the system engineering of one of the astronomy missions that was beginning to experience some problems that could lead to schedule delays. He wanted a better understanding of the issues. She agreed and returned to her office. She worked late into the evening and then came in very early the next morning to finish her report. The following afternoon, she went in to see Charles to give him her report. Charles read it and then looked up at her.

Charles: This is not what I need.
Ana: I know that, sir.

Charles: Then, why did you give it to me?

Ana: Sir, it is what you asked me to do.

Charles: I know, but it is not what I need.

Ana: Actually the problems are with the fabrication of two of the instruments that the scientists are building, and until those problems get fixed, system engineering is on hold.

Charles: This is what I need. Why didn't you tell me that in the first place?

Ana: That is not what you asked me to do, sir.

Charles: Okay, just finish this and get it back to me.

1.1 Introduction to and Short History of Cultural Competence

Ana's experience with Charles can be a typical situation. Many employees from family-oriented cultures will not question figures of authority and will do what is literally asked of them. They may not use their experience and insight to produce the best work product. They will follow orders and direction diligently. Not all such conversations end as well as this one did. Strictly following orders and waiting to be told what to do are not what most managers expect from good employees. Doing so hurts the careers of otherwise excellent employees, as well. Cultural competence would have helped both Charles and Ana.

In discussing cultural competence, a short history of how we got to this point is useful and informative, as is a brief review of relevant terms and concepts. The terms, concepts, and models mentioned here are described and cited in much greater detail in Chapter 3 and the Appendix. This chapter is intended only as a brief introduction and background.

The United States, Europe, and some Asian countries are experiencing aging populations with low birthrates and unprecedented levels of immigration. Many countries that had been predominately monocultural now have significant multicultural communities, which create cultural changes in the country. The cultural changes have generated many discussions of assimilation versus multiculturalism. Much of that debate has been acrimonious. The demographics are driving a cultural change that will continue into the future.

Since the passage of the Civil Rights Act, many terms have come into the lexicon, for example, *affirmative action, representative bureaucracy, diversity, reverse discrimination, social equity, managing diversity,* and *cultural competence.* A short history of how the United States got to this point is helpful in understanding the terms and concepts.

The Civil Rights Act of 1964 banned discrimination against women and minorities. Women and minorities were classification terms of gender, race, and ethnicity. Culture and cultural characteristics were not a concern at that time. In broad terms it may be said that an organization does not discriminate when the race, ethnicity, and gender of employees reflect their proportion in the communities the organization serves. The employees of a representative bureaucracy are proportionally representative of their numbers in the community. When the Civil Rights Act passed, the employees of most organizations were not representative of the communities they served. Affirmative action became a way to overcome past discrimination and to increase the proportion of women and minorities in organizations. More women and minorities were hired into organizations. Some questioned whether these were the most qualified for the positions for which there were hired, and with that question came the concept of reverse discrimination. Were more qualified white men being discriminated against when women and minorities who might be less qualified were hired or promoted, instead of the white male? Diversity, at that time, meant how representative an organization was in terms of minorities and women. A diverse organization more closely reflected the community it served. The next step was when some individuals questioned whether a minority from a wealthy family should be given preference over someone who is white and poor. The concept of equity or fairness was brought into the equation. Social equity broadened the concept of diversity to include race/ethnicity, gender, social class, sexual orientation, and disabilities.

In 1964 when the Civil Rights Act passed, the proportion of minorities was small in the United States. The two main groups the act affected were women and minorities. Minorities are people of color or nonwhites. Heavy immigration began after the 1980s, and increased the proportion of people of color in the country. The top four countries that have the largest number of U.S. immigrant workers are Mexico, China, India, and the Philippines (Sum, Harrington, and Khatiwada 2005). The U.S. Census Bureau (2010) lists the five countries of origin for the U.S. foreign-born population as Mexico, China, Philippines, India, and El Salvador.

In 2011, the situation is very different. Now, about one of every three Americans is a minority and about one in eight people in the United States was born in another country (Day n.d.; Morello and Keating 2009; Ortman and Guarneri 2009). This year more minority births are expected than white births (Yen 2010). Census Bureau projections show that in the 2040s, there will be no racial or ethnic majority in the United States (Day n.d.; Ortman and Guarneri 2009). There are many immigrant and minority communities in parts of the country that had been predominately white. These immigrant and minority communities retain many of the cultural characteristics of their country of origin. Thus the United States is shifting very quickly from a monocultural country into a multicultural country. The cultural changes are making some people unsettled and uncomfortable. This provides a different cultural context for understanding cultural competence and managing diversity.

Immigrant and minority communities were suffering disparities in health care. Many such communities retained their original cultures and languages, and these diverse cultural characteristics were creating problems in the delivery of adequate health care. The Western medical model did not always translate well into an immigrant or minority community's cultural views of health care. Further, the different cultural characteristics and languages brought about a host of problems. The federal government mandated the delivery of culturally competent health care to these communities. Cultural competence, in this context, means the delivery of health care services in a culturally relevant manner. Funding enabled research into cultural competence. The concept of diversity now includes cultural diversity, or different cultures with different cultural characteristics. Cultural diversity becomes an important concept. To make matters a bit confusing, the term *diversity* is still used when describing a representative bureaucracy. For example, *diverse organization* is the term still used to describe the proportional representation of the various employee categories within an organization.

Research into the culturally competent delivery of health services to immigrant and minority communities was incorporated into the concept of cultural competence in public administration. Cultural competence, in an organizational context, is the ability to manage the different employee cultural characteristics (i.e., employees' diversity or cultural diversity) to build an effective organization. Where earlier the emphasis had been on classification—for example, race and gender—that emphasis began shifting to culture and cultural characteristics. It was the cultural difference between the Western European (or U.S.) cultural delivery of health care services to communities with a different cultural concept of health care that was creating misunderstandings and problems. These misunderstandings were creating disparities in the delivery of health care.

Cultural competence was perceived as the way to overcome or bridge the cultural differences to provide culturally relevant health care. To be effective, health care services were to be provided in a way that would be culturally relevant to the immigrant and minority communities. That meant learning and understanding the culture, cultural characteristics, and language of the immigrant and minority communities. Organizations were now expected to have employees who understood the culture and language of the communities they served. The easiest place to find people familiar with the culture and language of these client communities was within the communities themselves. As members of the communities were hired, they brought their own cultural characteristics into the organization. Some of the cultural characteristics differed from the Western European cultural traits found in most U.S. organizations.

In the same way that the different cultural characteristics were creating misunderstandings and problems in the delivery of health care services; employee cultural misunderstandings and problems began to surface in organizations. The research then led to organizational requirements for cultural understanding within the organization.

Public administration research on cultural competence draws heavily from the research on the delivery of health care services to immigrant community. Many of the same terms and concepts are used, but now in an organizational context. People from the immigrant communities are employed in organizations. They may be legal residents or children of recent immigrants. These immigrants come from almost every country in the world. They retain many of the cultural characteristics of their country of origin. Some of these cultural characteristics are different than the more common Western European cultural characteristics. The cultural differences (cultural diversity) of the employees can create cross-cultural misunderstandings in the organization. The concept of diversity is also changing. In the past, the term *diversity* referred to such classifications as race and gender and whether their representation in the workforce was similar to their proportions in the population. The term is still used by some authors in this way. The research on cultural competence expanded the meaning of diversity to include cultural diversity (employees with different cultural characteristics). Sometimes the term diversity is used interchangeably for race and gender classification and cultural diversity, which can be confusing. The research on cultural competence shows the importance for managers and employees to understand the different cultural characteristics of their organization's culturally diverse employees.

The first tenet of almost all the research on cultural competence is respect for and understanding of the culture of the immigrant and minority communities. For example, respect for understanding of other cultures is incorporated into the public administration literature. Respect does not mean that a manager has to learn about the Korean culture when hiring an employee who is Korean. It does mean that to be effective, a manager has to understand how those cultural characteristics can create cross-cultural misunderstandings. Cultural competence is the ability to manage cultural diversity (different cultural characteristics) in a way that allows diversity to contribute to the effectiveness of an organization rather than create misunderstandings and conflict. Cultural diversity can indeed contribute to the effectiveness of an organization, but it can also create misunderstandings and conflict in an organization. Culturally competent managers can create effective cross-cultural work teams and prevent an organization from becoming dysfunctional.

There is extensive research literature on the culturally competent delivery of health care services to immigrant and minority communities. The public administration literature brings in the same cultural competence concepts. There is very little research and literature, however, on how a manager or employee can be culturally competent or how a manager can manage a diverse workforce of employees who have many different cultural characteristics.

Managing a culturally diverse workforce requires a more limited set of cultural competencies than does delivering services to culturally different communities. For example, government employees are expected to speak English. Learning another language is not required. On the other hand, a manager needs a quick way to learn enough about many different cultural characteristics to manage a culturally diverse workforce. A manager does not have to manage in a way that is culturally relevant to each employee. Instead, an effective manager has to create a common ground or shared culture where culturally diverse employees can work effectively together.

The research on culturally competent delivery of services to immigrant and minority communities also resulted in cultural competence organizational requirements. The organizational requirements can be summarized as follows:

1. A mission statement incorporating cultural competence
2. Policies and procedures that incorporate cultural competence
3. A diverse organization—using the broader definition of diversity to include race, ethnicity, gender, sexual orientation, social class, disabilities, culture, and cultural characteristics—and culturally competent workforce
4. Position descriptions that include cultural competence skills

Cultural competence as described above came from research on delivering services to immigrant and minority communities that retained much of the culture and language of their countries or origin. Each community had it own culture and language. Respecting and understanding other cultures in this case meant learning about one or two different cultures and languages.

Demographics are driving the next step in cultural competence. The baby boomers are beginning to retire. By 2012, about one third of the Senior Executive Service is projected to retire along with 27% of all federal supervisors (Klingner, Nalbandian, and Llorens 2010). Some state and local governments are facing similar demographics. The replacement pool for the retiring baby boomers is more culturally diverse. Currently almost one in three people in the United States is a minority, and one in eight was born in another country. The proportion of people of color in the United States will continue to increase. The replacements for the baby boomers will come from this culturally diverse pool. Employees will have cultural roots in many different countries. Intermarriage and adoptions from other countries are creating a large number of biracial, multicultural people. Managers will thus be required to manage employees with many different cultural characteristics. Employees will have to work effectively with other culturally different employees. The lessons from the research on delivering culturally competent services to communities whose members have different cultural characteristics show that problems can frequently arise. Cultural misunderstandings complicate the public manager's ability to manage culturally diverse employees and to create effective cross-cultural work teams.

There is also a shift in perspective. After the Civil Rights Act, it was assumed that whites were accommodating minorities and women, that is, that white men were taking steps to overcome the negative effects of past discrimination. In the emerging world of increasingly multicultural organizations, discrimination must remain a thing of the past, for every manager and employee will need to be culturally competent. Regardless of the culture to which an employee belongs, there will be many other employees who are culturally different. To be effective, every employee will have to be culturally competent, even employees of color.

The next step in the evolution of cultural competence is adapting the research on cultural competence and extending it to making it useful to a public manager dealing with a very culturally diverse workforce. Employees will need to understand how to navigate the organizational culture to be successful in their careers.

Whereas cultural competence was an approach developed to resolve health care disparities in the delivery of health care services to immigrant and minority communities, the new context for cultural competence is the culturally diverse organization. European and American organizational culture reflects the cultural characteristics of Western Europe. The cultural characteristics of employees whose families are from Asian, African, and Latin American countries differ from the cultural characteristics of employees with origins in Western Europe. These cultural disparities can lead to misunderstandings and conflict in the same way that the delivery of health care services by government agencies steeped in Western European culture created disparities in the delivery of health care services to culturally different communities.

This short history is intended to provide a quick understanding of the terms that are used. The rest of the book discusses these terms, concepts, models, and competencies in much greater detail and with the appropriate citations.

1.2 Why Public Managers Need to Be Culturally Competent

In 2008, Barack Obama, an African American with a biracial background, was elected president of the United States. In 2009, he nominated the first Latina, Sonia Sotomayor, to a vacancy on the U.S. Supreme Court. This nomination generated discussion regarding the progress of minorities in the United States. Clearly, there has been much progress. Whether there has been enough progress to eliminate race as a future issue is another question. The nomination hearing for Sotomayor brought the issue of race to the forefront, however, when she commented, "I would hope that a wise Latina, with the richness of her experiences, would more often than not reach a better conclusion than a white male who hasn't lived that life" (Savage 2009). Discussing race can still be a sensitive and difficult process containing many cultural landmines, but the demographic reality is that both of these individuals reflect the changing face of the United States. There are similar demographic dynamics in European and other industrialized countries.

Organizations are the confluence of all the different racial and ethnic groups, reflecting the diversity in their respective societies. What makes discussing race difficult is bridging the varied histories, experiences, and perspectives that members from each group bring to the discussion. Social perceptions come into play, and sometimes people have general negative stereotypes of other groups. Interactions are filtered through the lens of those negative social perceptions. Misunderstandings then serve to reinforce those negative social perceptions and can then further create social distance among the groups. The first author (Borrego 2009) analyzed a survey of 4,000 college students approximately split into four similarly sized groups of Asian, black, Latino, and white students. Each racial or ethnic group had negative social perceptions of the other groups (see Tables 1.1 through 1.4, which show the percentage of whites, blacks, Hispanics, and Asians, respectively, perceiving other racial or ethnic groups as dishonest, violent, and lazy). Such perceptions can lead to various levels of racialized workplaces where there is considerable tension among the various racial and ethnic groups.

The good news is that the majority of students in the study had neutral or more positive perceptions of the other group. But there remains a relatively large percentage of students with negative perceptions of all the other racial and ethnic groups. Negative social perceptions of other groups may predispose individuals to validate their own negative perceptions when they see in the other group cultural characteristics they do not understand. Approximately 74% of the students indicated that both cultural identities should be equal. About 83% of the Asians indicated that both identities should be equal. About 75% of the Hispanics agreed with this view. About 68% of the whites agreed that both identities should be equal (Johnson and Borrego 2009). This is a large percentage of the students willing to be accepting of multiculturalism. There may be generational differences with the older generation of whites being less accepting of the multicultural perspective.

Johnson and Rivera (2007) surveyed University of Vermont students in human resource management classes on their stereotypes of multicultural men and women. The survey included social class. In looking at the stereotypes, it is worthwhile understanding that they may or may not have a kernel of truth, but the stereotypes can also be distorted generalizations that are not always true and can harm individuals (see Table 1.5).

There remain many negative stereotypes that cross racial, ethnic, gender, and social class lines. These negative social perceptions and stereotypes also play out in the workplace. It is understandable how these negative perceptions and stereotypes can result in racial, ethnic, gender, and social class divisions. As more multicultural and women employees enter the workforce to replace white and male employees, such perceptions can create organizational fault lines. For an easy test to see if your organization is culturally competent, look at the cafeteria or lunchroom. Are the employees gathered according to their various racial or ethnic groups, or are the groupings more mixed?

How do we accept and productively embrace the differences employees bring into an organization and still have members of the company feel they are all being treated equally? How do we bring people who disagree on such issues as same-sex marriage to work together as a team? What do we expect of immigrants? Should they assimilate totally, or is it okay if they maintain many aspects of their original cultures? Managing diversity and developing cultural competence will not always happen in a supportive environment; more than likely, cultural competence skills will be required in the midst of these sometimes-contentious informal discussions.

Table 1.1 Whites' Perception of Other Racial and Ethnic Groups: Percentage of Whites Perceiving Other Groups as Dishonest, Violent, and Lazy

	Dishonest	*Violent*	*Lazy*
Blacks	40.3	40.4	14.1
Asians	39.2	6.2	8.1
Hispanics	25.4	29.4	17.6

Table 1.2 Blacks' Perception of Other Racial and Ethnic Groups: Percentage of Blacks Perceiving Other Groups as Dishonest, Violent, and Lazy

	Dishonest	*Violent*	*Lazy*
Whites	16.6	37.7	19.8
Asians	18.0	4.9	10.2
Hispanics	20.5	35.9	15.7

Table 1.3 Asians' Perception of Other Racial and Ethnic Groups: Percentage of Asians Perceiving Other Groups as Dishonest, Violent, and Lazy

	Dishonest	*Violent*	*Lazy*
Whites	37.1	14.3	15.6
Blacks	40.3	43.3	21.6
Hispanics	28.5	32.7	23.1

Table 1.4 Hispanics' Perception of Other Racial and Ethnic Groups: Percentage of Hispanics Perceiving Other Groups as Dishonest, Violent, and Lazy

	Dishonest	*Violent*	*Lazy*
Whites	28.4	18.0	10.7
Blacks	31.5	44.5	12.5
Asians	41.0	5.0	8.5

Table 1.5 Stereotypes of Multicultural Men and Women, Including Social Class

	Men	Women
African American	Criminals, Whores, Athletic, Rappers	Many Children, Loud, Good Cooks, Strong, Sexy
Asian	Intelligent, Quiet, Small, Autocratic	Intelligent, Quiet, Small, Subservient
Hispanic	Macho, Uneducated, High Sex Drive, Greasy	Loud, Curvy, Good Dancers, Many Children
Native American	Drunks, Spiritual, Uneducated, Violent	Nurturing, Spiritual, Absent from America's Landscape
White	CEOs, Leaders, Cheaters, Privileged	Catty, Ambitious, "Barbie Dolls," Smart
Working Class	Large Family, Underachievers, City Residents, Uneducated	Born That Way, Absent Fathers, Live in Trailer Parks

Source: Adapted from Johnson III, R., and Rivera, M., *Journal of Public Affairs Education*, 13 (1), 21, 2007.

If managing diversity can be this difficult, why is it worthwhile to become culturally competent? As societies become more diverse, organizations are also becoming more diverse. In the United States and in many countries in Europe, the dominant populations have low birthrates and are rapidly aging, and so their numbers in the workforce will need to be replenished. Benevolent immigration and family reunification policies have led European societies, as well as the United States, to accept large numbers of immigrants. Meanwhile, in the United States the 78 million baby boomers, those born between 1946 and 1964 (U.S. Census Bureau 2006), are beginning to face retirement. The leading edge of that wave turns 65 in 2011, becoming eligible for Medicare. The trend will continue for 18 years. The Census Bureau report (2004) projects that as early as 2042, there will be no racial or ethnic majority in the United States. The replacements for the baby boomers will be more diverse than the boomers are.

Organizations are reflecting this diversity, and the long-term demographic trends mean they will become even more diverse in the future. Immigrants and their children are usually closer to and retain their culture more than do fifth- or sixth-generation children. They will bring their cultural characteristics into the organization when they become employees, and these cultural characteristics will not always be in sync with the organizational culture. Consequently, misunderstandings can quickly arise.

Example 1.2: Cultural Competence Can Help

Bill is a manager who attends his organization's multicultural and diversity leadership program. His organizational unit is extremely diverse.

Bill: I had not realized how the employees and I saw the work environment so differently. They had not been complaining about anything and I thought they were all happy. I had not realized that over half of the employees would leave at the first opportunity. I thought they were happy with their work and was not asking them how they saw their involvement in the organization. They did not feel they were given assignments where they could contribute and did not feel a part of the organization. They did not like the way they were treated. I thought that they liked my management style; they did not.

I have learned to listen differently. I now know how to talk with the employees without being overly sensitive that I would say the wrong word or be misinterpreted. Working with employees on long-term career plans has given them a long-term investment in the organization. Discussing their careers makes it easier to compliment their strengths and to really focus on the shortcomings in their performance and the relationships they need to build. Yeah, there are cultural differences, but now I am learning about their cultures and they are learning about mine. It made it easier to talk and we are all a better team now. I am using what I learned with everyone. We are becoming the go-to people for new projects.

What skills are needed to bridge the differences Bill mentions and to successfully manage and work with diverse and multicultural employees and colleagues? Cultural competence is the ability to effectively work and interact with other people of different cultures and other types of diversity. Cultural competency has also been described as managing diversity. Diversity also includes gender, social orientation, social class, and cultural characteristics. The rest of the book will discuss defining and acquiring cultural competence.

1.3 Obstacles to Cultural Competence

Respecting and understanding other cultures are the first steps in becoming culturally competent. For many of us, there are numerous obstacles to our understanding other cultures. Recognizing the roadblocks to understanding the cultural characteristics of diverse employees can help us overcome those obstacles. How well we deal with other aspects of cultural competence—communication, misunderstandings and conflict, and leader–follower dynamics—depends on our understanding others' cultural characteristics and how they differ from our own.

Consider the following questions asked of one of the authors of this text. What do they reveal about the questioner?

- "How many igloos did you see when you lived in Alaska?" (There are no igloos in Alaska.)
- "What form of currency do they take in Alaska?"

Many of us are notorious for our lack of understanding about cultures other than our own, as well as for our poor knowledge of world geography. Before we can engage in any thoughtful dialogue about how public managers can be the change agents to transform their organizations into ones that are culturally competent, we must address concerns about certain patterns that we all exhibit.

Richard Bucher (2010), in his book *Diversity Consciousness*, describes six personal and social barriers to success in overcoming prejudice and discrimination:

1. Limited perceptions
2. Ethnocentrism
3. Stereotypes
4. Prejudice
5. Prejudice plus power
6. Discrimination

Numerous psychological studies have been conducted on how we perceive people, places, things, and the world around us. Research has shown us that to organize and store information into categories, we can experience and understand only portions of the sights, sounds, feelings, and other external stimuli that constantly bombard us. We take many shortcuts in order to process all this information. In taking these shortcuts, it is important to understand, we may be creating additional barriers for ourselves by constructing stereotypes and developing prejudice.

Ethnocentrism is a widespread and deep-seated belief that "ours is better than yours." The Pew Global Attitude Project (2007) found that more than 70% of the people in 47 countries agreed with the statement, "Our people are not perfect, but our culture is superior to others." Only in Germany, France, Britain, and Sweden did more than half the people surveyed disagree with this statement.

Another obstacle to cultural competence is stereotyping by race, gender, sexual orientation, ethnic origin, social class, and the like. Stereotyping can be defined as an unproven and oversimplified generalization about an entire group (Bucher 2010). Stereotyping behavior revolves around every dimension of diversity, including job position, job function, race, ethnicity, religion, social class, language, learning styles, and sexual orientation (Bucher 2010). It is essential that public managers realize that putting people into one-size-fits-all mental boxes severely limits their ability to relate effectively to employees and supervisors alike in increasingly more diverse organizations.

Stereotypical thinking gives rise to prejudice, which may be defined as "an irrational and inflexible opinion formed on the basis of limited and insufficient knowledge" (Bucher 2010, 79). This major obstacle to success in achieving cultural competence is so troubling because rigid prejudgment is made before any encounter or communication takes place. We have seen and perhaps personally experienced many examples of prejudice. One recent and vivid illustration is the treatment of Muslims or anyone that appeared to be Muslim after the terrorist attacks on the United States on September 11, 2001. Sikhs, whose religious practice requires them to grow beards and wear turbans, were especially singled out after the 9/11 attacks, even though their religious practice differs from those of Muslims. Bucher notes that the treatment of Muslims, or people mistaken as followers of Islam, was quite different than what occurred after the Oklahoma City bombings, in which the perpetrators happened to be fair-skinned Christian army veterans. Religious and racial profiling are also examples of prejudice that seriously hamper our ability to create a culturally competent workplace and an opportunity to transform ourselves, learn from each other, and, ultimately, solve the kinds of complex problems and issues we are facing in this global community.

Prejudice plus power leads to the various "isms" that are at work, with the most volatile being racism. Bucher describes this obstacle to success as including institutional racism and the belief that one race is superior to another. Even leaders considered to be more enlightened and culturally sensitive than most can succumb to this obstacle to building cultural competence. Desmond Tutu, the recipient of a Nobel Peace Prize for his long history of work in ending apartheid in South Africa, describes the insidiousness of racism. During his first trip to Nigeria and upon encountering severe turbulence, he recounts his immediate reaction:

> I found I was saying to myself, "I really am bothered that there's no white man in the cockpit. Can these blacks manage to navigate us out of this horrible experience?" It was all involuntary and spontaneous. I would never have believed that I had in fact been so radically brainwashed. I would have denied it vigorously because I prided myself on being an exponent of black consciousness, but in a crisis something deeper had emerged. I had accepted a white definition of existence, that whites were somehow superior to and more competent than blacks. Of course those black pilots were able to land the plane quite competently. (Tutu 1999, 252)

From his experience, Tutu had learned the importance of forgiveness in the face of racism.

The authors would add a seventh personal and social barrier to success in overcoming prejudice and discrimination, and that would be a sentiment held by some and called *white entitlement*. To many people, there is no such thing as discrimination in the United States, where everyone has the ability to receive a slice of the American pie. All that is required is hard work, delayed gratification, and loyalty to one's employer. The notion of the self-made person who makes good despite all odds remains very much alive in the United States, and there are enough examples to support this belief. Some people who cling to this belief do not want to discuss the issue of race and its effects on society.

Peggy McIntosh (1988, 7) describes some of the privileges of being white as her "invisible, weightless knapsack of special provisions, assurances, tools, maps, guides." She continues to discuss these privileges, asserting, "I am never asked to speak for all the people of my racial group," and "I can be pretty sure that if I ask to talk to 'the person in charge,' I will be facing a person of my race." Perhaps white entitlement also allows people to not have to think about race as a factor in their lives or as part of their success. Such interviews as those conducted by Feagin and Vera (1995) found that race tended to be considered a factor when a person of color committed a crime or became a movie star, for example. The same experience was more individualized when a white was involved, with the person's race not being seen as relevant.

The world is a mosaic of wildly different cultures and customs, colloquial expressions, and definitions of even the concepts of time and space itself. The importance for public managers operating from a well-defined foundation of cultural competence has never been greater in that the world is truly one global society. The economic, human, and natural resources management issues facing contemporary public managers require a working definition of how to work with vastly divergent groups. These examples will be broad brushstrokes of the more pronounced differences and similarities.

People from different cultures encode and decode messages differently, increasing the chances of misunderstanding, so the safety-first consequence of recognizing cultural differences should be to assume that everyone's thoughts and actions are not just like ours. Such assumptions stem from potentially devastating ignorance and can lead to much frustration for members of both cultures. Entering a different culture than your own with such ethnocentrism is another by-product of ignorance and cultural misunderstanding.

1.4 Cultural Characteristics

In order to become culturally competent, public managers will find a discussion of the major cultural differences between the West and East particularly helpful. Not understanding the cultural characteristics of culturally diverse employees can lead to accepting stereotypes and creating workplace cultural misunderstandings. Most organizations in the United States have a Western European culture, and some even favor a male orientation. There are still discussions about whether men and women manage and lead in the same way. Being seen as having leadership qualities is important to the career success of managers and employees. In one organization, white co-workers perceived employees of color to be very hardworking and nice, but not as having leadership qualities. Yet the employees of color were among the top-performing employees. Viewed through the lens of Western

European culture, some of their cultural characteristics were being misinterpreted. It is worthwhile for managers and employees alike to understand that different cultures have differing cultural characteristics. Understanding other cultures, their general cultural characteristics, is the first step in the cultural competence model. How Eastern cultural characteristics manifest themselves in organizations is explored in later chapters.

Hall (1959) was the first to develop the concept of polychronic and monochronic cultures depending on how they organize their time. According to Hall, time is conceptualized as a silent language that can communicate meaning and order activities. Northern Europe, the United States, and Canada are considered to be monochronic. Latin America, the Middle East, and Africa are considered polychronic (Hall 1983). Lindquist and Kaufman-Scarborough (2007) see information technology, both at home and at work, as creating more polychronic environments.

The very notion of how time is perceived, fate versus determinism, the role of the individual versus a group orientation, nonverbal cues and communication, and the leader–follower relationship in organizations are a few of the major differences between the East and West. East and West are used to create a general conceptual framework. Hall's work (1959, 1983) is not just a comparison of Asian countries with the United States and European countries, for there are many countries that reflect a combination of these two perspectives. Some Latin American countries may reflect many Eastern perspectives. Conversely, globalization, and the need to compete for a country's industrial base, has brought some Western perspectives into several industrialized Asian nations.

Albrecht (2001) describes one way of contrasting managing in the East with managing in the West as the difference between the Judeo-Christian tradition of the Ten Commandments with the Confucian and Taoist traditions of the East. She writes that the absolute values of "thou shalt" or "thou shalt not" found in the West differ vastly from the Eastern philosophy of observing the order of the universe and changing behaviors appropriate to the circumstances of the moment.

1.5 Perceptions of Time

Meetings in organizations are scheduled for a certain time, and it is expected that the invited employees will be there at the appointed time. When a meeting is scheduled and some employees do not arrive on time, it is not unusual for Asian, Latino, or Native Americans to ask, "Are we on Asian time, or are we on Latino time, or are we on Indian time?" This query may seem to be simply about clock time, but in reality it points to vast cultural differences in the way people from non-Western cultures perceive the world; it goes much deeper than looking at a clock.

Our understanding of time has undergone several revolutionary changes in how we perceive the universe and our places in it. The idea of an unchanging and absolute universe has been replaced by the understanding that space and time are affected by everything that happens in the universe; they are dynamic and expanding (Hawking 1998). When referring to time and space as perceived by different cultures, the authors are essentially describing how individuals perceive their place in the universe and how their behavior and actions change as a result of their perception.

Time is one of the most central differences that separate cultures and cultural ways of doing things in the East and the West. In the West, time tends to be seen, not as a dynamic quantity as described by Hawking, but as a linear quantity that can be measured. This measurement of time is usually focused on one event or interaction at a time, as in the expression "the march of time." This Western approach to time is often called monochronic in that events are dealt with in a linear way with a focus on following procedures—using such methods as Robert's Rules of Order, for example—to promote efficiency in reaching decisions and adhering to plans.

Eastern countries, along with Native American tribes, First Nations of Canada, parts of Latin America, Mexico, and India, view time in more polychronic terms. Time is seen not in absolutes but, rather, as an aesthetic almost too intricate and vast for the human mind to comprehend. Time seems to have an unlimited continuity that contains both the culture's ancestry and the generations yet to be born. Time is a dynamic process in which the past, present, and future influence each event or decision to be made. By contrasting the two types of perceptions, Table 1.6 illustrates the difference between a monochronic and a polychronic view of time.

One can see from Table 1.6 that the Western or monochronic perception of time is the organizational culture in the United States. The Eastern or polychronic perception of time reflects cultural differences that can lead to cross-cultural misunderstandings.

Table 1.6 Two Perceptions of Time

Western: Monochronic	Eastern: Polychronic
Measured as benchmarks toward a goal.	Has unlimited continuity that unravels, then reconnects.
Tackles one major goal at a time.	Works on several things at the same time.
The job comes first.	People and relationships come first.
Tend to perceive less, but see more detail.	View is more panoramic.
The individual is the starting point.	The group is the starting point.

Source: Data from Hall, E., *The Silent Language*, Doubleday, New York, 1959; Hall, E., *The Dance of Life: The Other Dimension of Time*, Doubleday/Anchor, New York, 1983; Hall. E., and M. Hall, *Hidden Differences: Doing Business with the Japanese*, Doubleday/Anchor, New York, 1987.

The difference between a polychronic and a monochronic perception of time can be illustrated in a very dramatic example that was told to one of the authors when he was a faculty member of the University of Alaska system. As part of the Alaska Native Land Claims Settlement Act of 1971, officials from a variety of state, federal, local, and Alaskan Native tribal organizations met in Anchorage, Alaska, for the purpose of signing the final agreements. Many months of negotiations and hard work had already taken place, leading to this final face-to-face meeting of the principals involved. The Settlement Act extinguished Alaskan Natives' claim for the entire state of Alaska in exchange for one-ninth of the land plus monies from the federal treasury and oil revenue, along with the creation of 13 Alaskan Native corporations. Representatives from the tribal organizations were first on the agenda and began by discussing the spirit of the land, explaining their sacred connection to it, and honoring their past ancestors and the generations to follow that would be the beneficiaries of this significant transfer of land. They spoke in stories and about their subsistence lifestyle supporting their cultural beliefs and values, and how their yet unborn relatives would be protectors and guardians of their faith. The stories were woven between past, present, and future themes. When they concluded after several hours, it was up to the federal officials to make their presentation. Out came the visual aids, complete with timelines exhibiting the dates and milestones by which their duties would be discharged. The presentation was brief and to the point; it lasted less than one hour. Their presentation concluded with their pro-posed action steps, and they waited politely to receive approval and concurrence from the Alaskan Native tribal representatives. The meeting adjourned, leaving the government officials frustrated and unsure about what to do next and what had taken place at the meeting.

This may seem to be a quaint example about Alaska and Native Alaskans. In reality, it points to important cultural differences. Employees with polychronic per-ceptions of time see relationships as important. Many polychronic cultures also involve storytelling to establish a context and to be seen as respectful (establish a relationship first). Organizations in the United States usually have monochromic organizational cultures and tend to be more bottom-line oriented. If an employee with polychronic cultural characteristics is making a presentation, he may begin by telling a story. He is being respectful. Employees with monochronic cultural char-acteristics may be listening and thinking, "When will this guy get to the point?" The polychronic employee may consequently be seen as not very competent. In fact, he may be. A Native Alaskan MPA student commented that he knew what changes his Native Alaskan organization needed to make, but he was not going to contra-dict his elders. This perspective frequently continues when polychronic employees work in organizations.

It is the disconnection between organizational monochronic cultural expecta-tions and the polychronic cultural characteristics of some employees that is creating a cultural misunderstanding. A manager who understands such cultural differences (diversity) can be in better position to mentor or guide the polychronic employee.

The manager who can look past the cultural characteristics to see the talent and capabilities of the polychronic employee is in a position to capitalize on the talents of culturally different employees.

New brain research has found that cultural differences affect people at basic levels of how they experience the world. People from Western societies, including America and European countries, who think of themselves as highly independent entities, focus on central objects and see more detail. People from the East, which includes Japan, Korea, and China, tend to remember more about the background or context of a scene rather than the details themselves. Eastern cultures generally tend to stress interdependence. The research suggests that cultural differences are so profound at a fundamental level that people are not even aware of them.

1.6 Other Dimensions of Culture

It is seldom that a researcher has the opportunity to control variables when undertaking large-scale studies across countries in order to identify and classify cultural differences. One researcher, however, was able to study differences among the various components of the IBM Corporation in the 1970s.

In one of the most extensive organizational studies ever undertaken, Geert Hofstede (1980) was able to identify and validate five independent dimensions of national cultural differences among 64 countries. Much of what the study produced has been internationally recognized as a standard from which cultural differences can be contrasted. Northouse (2007, 305) sees the work of Hofstede as "probably being the most referenced on cultural dimensions and for setting the benchmarks for most of the research on world cultures."

The cultural dimensions Hofstede described in his 1980 study may be useful in understanding differences between people's workplace values in the public organization. They are power distance, individualism, masculinity, uncertainty avoidance, and short-term versus long-term orientation. These five dimensions, combined with the perception of time and the specific organizational culture that one is working in, are useful for understanding cultural differences as they are played out in individual behavior within the workplace. An example of this dynamic comes from Albrecht (2001) when she describes Asians, who speak the least in meetings but may have the most to contribute, as they interact with Americans.

1.6.1 Power Distance

The power distance dimension in the Hofstede model is the degree to which inequality both exists and is accepted among people without power. A high power distance score would indicate that there is within a country an unequal distribution of power and the people tend to accept this and understand their place in society. Low scores would indicate that people felt more or less equal in their societal role.

Countries with high power distance scores tend to exhibit centralized companies with strong hierarchies. There would be large gaps in compensation, authority, and respect. Power distance scores are high for Latin, Asian, and African countries, smaller for Germanic countries. Power distance is one of the cultural characteristics that influence the way leaders and followers relate to each other (leader–follower dynamics). The example at the beginning of this chapter illustrates the differences in power distance and how they affect the manager–employee relationship.

1.6.2 *Individualism*

The cultural dimension described in Hofstede's model as individualism represents the degree to which people are integrated into groups. Some societies are highly individualistic and expect people to look after themselves. Only six of the countries surveyed score high on the individualistic scale. They were, in priority order, the United States, Australia, the United Kingdom, the Netherlands, Canada, and Italy. The other side of this dimension is the group with strong interpersonal relationships and family ties. Countries with low scores on this scale include Panama and Guatemala. I-oriented employees may be seen as more productive and having leadership potential than we-oriented employees. In I-oriented culture, the individual is given credit for successes. In we-oriented cultures, it is hard to see which individual should get the credit for the success. Many U.S. and European organizations tend to be more individualistic in culture.

1.6.3 *Masculinity*

Hofstede compared countries on a scale of masculinity versus femininity to represent the distribution of roles between the genders in this IBM study. Scores also indicate the extent to which traditional male and female roles in society are followed. At the time of this study, Japan rated a high masculine score, as did some European countries, including Germany, Austria, and Switzerland, as well as moderately high scores in the Anglo countries. Sweden had the lowest score for masculinity, as did many of the Nordic countries and the Netherlands. Latin and Asian countries, as well as France, Spain, and Thailand, all had moderately low scores on this dimension.

1.6.4 *Uncertainty Avoidance*

Uncertainty avoidance deals with the degree to which a society can tolerate uncertainty and ambiguity and whether its members feel uncomfortable or comfortable in unstructured situations. Hofstede describes this dimension as having to do ultimately with humankind's search for Truth and whether our culture believes members of society are attaining this truth in absolute terms.

Scores for uncertainty avoidance were higher in Latin American countries, Japan, and German-speaking countries. Chinese, Nordic, and Anglo countries had lower uncertainty avoidance scores. This may seem to be an esoteric and philo-sophical discussion. In practice, employees avoid uncertainty by waiting to be told what to do. It is not that they do not know what needs to be done. They are cultur-ally trained to avoid uncertainty. The ability to deal with ambiguity is considered by some to be a leadership trait. One can see how different cultural characteristics can prevent a manager from utilizing the full talents and capabilities of a culturally different employee.

1.6.5 Long-Term versus Short-Term Orientation

The cultural dimension of long-term versus short-term orientation was included when one of Hofstede's colleagues collected data from students in 23 countries. Long-term orientation is the degree to which the society esteems its traditions and values or tends not to some degree. A low score on this dimension would indicate that change and innovation may occur more rapidly, since adherence to long-stand-ing traditions is not an impediment. Countries with a high score on this dimension are concerned with "saving face" and valuing traditions and social obligations. The Asian countries, including China, Hong Kong, Japan, and South Korea, exhibit long-term orientations.

Long-term orientation in this context is different than the long-term planning used in many organizations. In this context, long-term means an adherence to maintaining tradition and is usually accompanied by a respect for figures or author-ity or elders. Western managers may see employees with these cultural characteris-tics as passive. As one employee with such cultural characteristics said, "I will work as hard as I can and when I'm finished, I'm ready to do what you want me to do, but I won't do anything to change the system" (pers. comm.*). The ability to see how to change the system can be seen as a leadership trait. It is not that these employees do not know how the system needs to be changed. They are culturally trained not to change the system, for doing so can be seen as disrespectful in their culture. A culturally competent manager can coach polychronic employees to understand the monochronic expectations of the organizational culture. Having employees who are more productive rewards the manager.

The cultural characteristic of "saving face" merits greater understanding as a major difference between deep-seated value systems in the West and East. The West's short-term orientation often results in a brash, opinionated, highly maver-ick, and individualistic leadership style that clashes with the subtle sense of com-munal duty found primarily in Asian countries. Kelts (2010) described Toyota's president Akio Toyoda's recent testimony to Congress, in which he apologized for his company's massive recall of defective automobiles, as a classic example of the many misunderstandings that can occur between cultures. Toyoda first declined

---

* Students in focus groups on cultural learned helplessness conducted by the first author in 2006 at the University of Texas Pan-American were promised confidentiality.

an invitation by a U.S. congressional committee to discuss and apologize for the recall, leaving it instead to Toyota's U.S. division. A sign of successful corporate leadership in Japan requires top executives to remain virtually invisible in order to maintain maximum harmony and save face for all members of the corporation, especially if there has been a major error made. When Toyoda changed his mind after the congressional committee made a second request—formally and respect-fully written—he first came across to the American public as aloof and arrogant. Members of the congressional committee displayed typical Western communica-tion styles that highly prize transparency, openness, and direct responses, examples of the short-term orientation. Finally, after saying he would have to reflect deeply on one of the committee member's skepticism about his sincerity in apologizing, Toyoda said, "All the Toyota vehicles bear my name. For me, when the cars are damaged, it is as though I am as well" (Kelts 2010, 2).

1.6.6 Other Aspects of Culture

It is worthwhile exploring other aspects of culture to provide a more complete pic-ture of areas where cross-cultural misunderstandings may occur in organizations. Different people have defined culture in a variety of ways, but there are common components. Some of these commonalities include language, food, history, reli-gion and spirituality, and social class and education (Oldfield and Johnson 2008). Relatively new to the definition of cultures is self-esteem. Akande Adebowale (2009) argues that scholars who study culture have missed self-esteem as key com-ponent. Adebowale suggest that self-esteem is a value aspect of any culture because of its implications for gender and age. For example, a fair amount of discussion has surrounded the wearing of headgear by women living in the Middle East and other Muslim countries around the world. Westerners generally believe that such adornment lowers a women's self-esteem and denies her basic freedoms as a human being. If asked, however, many of these same women would suggest that they feel empowered and safe wearing their headdresses or even full-dress wear. This response becomes important as immigrants and children of immigrants become employees. They may wear clothing that is familiar to their cultures, but not familiar to the U.S. expectations of professional dress.

Religion can become closely intertwined with culture and in some cases may seem inseparable. Even religions that are broadly classified as one type—for exam-ple, as Christian, Muslim, Jewish, or Buddhist—may be comprised of individual members who may be very conservative or very liberal in their interpretations. The differences among the members of one religious group may seem as large as the differences between the religions. Various religions may be more prescriptive of the relationships between men and women than others. When employees bring such diversity into an organization, the potential exists for workplace cultural clashes. In organizational settings, communicating inclusiveness is almost always a good practice. Feeling included and a valued member of the organization can be a great motivator. Yet some citizens may characterize the country itself as a certain religion. For example, there are people who consider the United States a Christian country. The Civil Rights Act prohibits discrimination based on religion. How does a manager handle an employee who persists in wishing employees who are Buddhist, Hindu, or Muslim Merry Christmas and Happy Easter?

Personal space is also a cultural value. Some cultures value closeness and physical contact when they converse. People conversing with each other will stand close to each other, and there will be frequent touching of the other person's arm or shoulder. Other cultures prefer more physical distance in their meetings and conversations. Shaking hands with others for many is an acceptable practice. Indeed, many multicultural students are given the advice that when interviewing and networking, they should use a firm handshake and look the interviewer directly in the eye. Left open are suggestions on how many times to shake hands and how long to hold the handshake, especially when shaking hands across gender lines. When does shaking hands become holding hands? What different messages do shaking hands and holding hands convey? What someone from a culture unused to shaking hands firmly and looking directly at someone's eyes interprets as being correct may instead be viewed as a limp handshake and a shifty look simply because after looking directly at the interviewer's eyes, the person then looked away, uncomfortable looking directly at someone. Someone from a culture more comfortable with close physical contact may use two hands for the handshake; he or she may sometimes use one hand for the handshake while the other is placed on the recipient's arm or shoulder while warmly looking that person in the eyes. Across gender lines, this gesture of warmth and friendliness can easily be interpreted as uncomfortable and unwelcome. Being neutral in the interaction and letting the other person establish the personal space is a way to create a more comfortable and conducive environment. This approach requires that managers and employee be adaptable and flexible about an employee's preference for personal space.

1.7 Questions That Need to Be Asked about Cultural Competence

Sue (2006, 38) raises at least three important questions about cultural competence:

1. What characteristics constitute cultural competency?
2. If cultural knowledge is important, is it possible to "know" all cultures?
3. How much knowledge is necessary, and what are the contents of this knowledge?

In the United States, race and ethnicity are classified in broad categories. Among the categories are African Americans, who include people who have been in the United States for many years as well as recent immigrants from many countries in Africa; Asians and Pacific Islanders, who come from countries as diverse as

China, Korea, Japan, Thailand, the Philippines, and India; Hispanics or Latinos and Latinas, who can be of any race, have origins in countries from the Caribbean, Central America, and South America; and whites, who also come from many different countries. The broad classifications mask the many different countries with different cultures within each broad classification. This issue of classification is further complicated when gender, social class, and sexual orientation are included as part of cultural competence. Can we really understand all cultures and diversity in contemporary public organizations, or do we need to develop cultural competencies that do not require an in-depth knowledge of each culture and diversity?

The literature on cultural competence contains conceptual definitions, which are general and, many times, abstract. Missing are specific cultural competencies for executives, middle managers, supervisors, and employees. This book addresses these questions and the competencies for executives, middle managers, supervisors, and employees by complementing the conceptual definitions of cultural competence with proven practices, which work in contemporary multicultural and diverse organizations and will advance theory and practice in cultural competence.

1.8 Why a New Cultural Competence Model Is Needed

The most extensive work on cultural competence has been in the delivery of government services to minority and immigrant communities (Johnson, Lenartowicz, and Apud 2006). Much of the research on cultural competence focuses on respecting and understanding the culture of the immigrant community and on using linguistically appropriate communications. Public managers, in their function as managers of employees, face a requirement for cultural competence that is different than what is necessary for delivering services to one or a small number of immigrant communities. Managers will be managing very diverse and multicultural organizations. Employees advance, retire, and move to other job opportunities. Employees may have origins in countries with different cultures. It thus becomes extremely difficult to learn, in depth, the culture and language of each employee. Cultural competencies for managers and employees must meet management needs and be adapted to facilitate working with many diverse cultural, racial, and ethnic groups. A basic set of cultural competencies serves as the foundation for interactions with employees and other managers who are themselves diverse and multicultural.

The establishment of cultural competencies for organizations and human resources means embedding the policies and practices that support leveraging diversity and developing culturally competent employees, managers, and executives into organizational structures and human resource practices. The extensive definitions in the literature are adapted here to be useful to practicing managers.

Cultural competence opens another door. Globalization facilitates international collaborations and interactions. Many federal agencies engage in international collaborations, not just the U.S. Department of State. The North American

Free Trade Agreement (NAFTA) has labor and environmental agreements. The U.S. Department of Labor (DOL) administers the labor agreements with Canada and Mexico. The DOL also has labor attaches in many countries. Numerous local governments create sister-city relationships with cities in other countries. Some states send economic delegations to other countries and work at developing long-term relationships. University and college faculty travel to other countries for presentations, and some faculty members are involved in research collaborations with faculty in other countries. Some faculty get teaching opportunities at universities in other countries, and many university and college administrators travel abroad to visit universities. In addition, many students take advantage of studying abroad.

Cultural competence can facilitate international collaborations. To be the most effective, cultural competence has to be supplemented by elements of international diplomacy, which has evolved protocols to develop good relationships with other countries and to resolve difficult issues. Diplomats represent their respective countries and organizations. The addition of the three elements of international diplomacy—developing good relationships, establishing protocols for resolving difficult issues, and viewing oneself as a representative—fills the cultural competence toolbox for managers.

1.9 What Public Managers Need to Know about Cultural Competence as a Leadership Competence

Managing diversity, which now includes cultural diversity, is an important leadership competency. The federal government addresses managing diversity through the U.S. Office of Personnel Management's (OPM) Senior Executive Service (SES) leadership requirements. OPM describes the leadership requirements for working with multicultural people through the "leveraging diversity" competency in the "Leading People" executive core qualifications. According to OPM (2010a), leveraging diversity "fosters an inclusive workplace where diversity and individual differences are valued and leveraged to achieve the vision and mission of the organization" (p. 33). In a less direct manner, OPM also addresses this leadership skill in the fundamental SES competencies. In "interpersonal skills" OPM (2010a) states, "Treats others with courtesy, sensitivity, and respect. Considers and responds appropriately to the needs and feelings of different people in different situations" (p. 32). Because part of meeting the requirements for the Senior Executive Service requires applicants to describe how they meet these qualifications, diversity competencies can be demonstrated and measured. Agencies submit their best candidates to the OPM Qualifications Review Board (QRB) for certification.

Change does not always come easily, and the same can be said of managing the increasing diversity in public organizations, nonprofit organizations, universities, and even the private sector. The demographic changes, along with such other diversities as gender and sexual orientation, can also be accompanied by contentious discussions. The increasing multicultural demographic changes are accompanied by discussions on assimilation versus multiculturalism. In an analysis of the social perceptions of 4,000 college students divided into almost equal numbers of Asians, blacks, Hispanics, and whites, 3 of 4 students were comfortable with multiculturalism. Multiculturalism means that people identify with their country of origin and also identify themselves as American. Only 1 of 6 supported the assimilationist viewpoint that everyone should identify himself or herself as only American. From this group, compared with multicultural students, twice as many whites supported the assimilationist perspective (Borrego 2009). Yet with the large number of students supporting multiculturalism, large numbers of students saw the other groups as being dishonest and violent. Blacks and Hispanics were perceived more negatively. Asians were perceived the most positively, followed by whites (Johnson and Borrego 2009). Surveys of students in human resource management classes also showed negative stereotypes of multicultural people, working-class people, and women (Johnson and Rivera 2007). Managing diversity, while important, will not always occur in a supportive and welcoming environment.

Managing diversity has been discussed in many ways, yet cultural competence as a concept is a relatively recent phenomenon. The field of public administration has discussed cultural competence primarily in terms of social equity, diversity, race, ethnicity, and multiculturalism. The initial concern in public administration was the underrepresentation of racial and ethnic minorities in organizations. Dolan and Rosenbloom (2003) see many scholars concerned with the extent to which women and racial minorities were integrated into the public bureaucracies. In discussing the state of social equity in U.S. public administration, Frederickson (2005) sees the early development of social equity as focused on race and gender in employment, democratic representation, and service delivery. He also describes multiculturalism and diversity as suggesting a broader definition of social equity. Diversity has many aspects, including race, differences in ethnic norms and behavior, gender identity, sexual orientation, and technology and that diversity brings its own challenges (Johnson, Reyes, and Smith 2009; White and Rice 2005). Cultural competence is a developmental process that evolves over an extended period. Both individuals and organizations are at various levels of awareness, knowledge, and skills along the cultural competence continuum (adapted from Cross et al. 1989).

1.10 Top 10 Reasons Why Cultural Competence Is Important

1. The reality of global labor demographics will require public managers to be culturally competent. There will no longer be any clear cultural or ethnic majorities, and leaders in public organizations and managers will be required to exhibit superior cross-cultural skills in order for the mission to be accomplished.

2. Cultural competence is transformative. It requires people from different cultures to create a common ground or shared culture to create effective organizations.
3. Cultural competence promotes understanding and interactive communication resulting in better solutions to complex organizational problems and achievement of organizational goals and objectives.
4. Cultural competence puts cultural tools in a manager's toolbox.
5. The culturally competent organization is more flexible and adaptable, making it better at responding to such unforeseen events as crises.
6. The culturally competent organization exhibits more innovation and adaptability, better communication, and the ability to recruit and retain the best employees; it is more productive; and it has less likelihood of incurring the costs of discrimination.
7. Being culturally competent results in one's ability to network and learn from everyone and anyone.
8. Cultural competence leads to more creativity and innovation.
9. The public manager must learn how to manage diversity as the world continues to reflect the reality of demographic changes leading to a globalized society. Employees will more likely retain aspects of their cultural identity and bring those cultural characteristics into the workplace.
10. In order to progress up the leadership pipeline, public managers will be evaluated on their cultural competence as a leadership standard in public organizations.

1.11 Summary and Conclusion

Demographic shifts have changed the social and cultural landscapes of the United States and Europe. In the United States, the demographic shifts have moved beyond the tipping point. Immigrants have much higher birthrates than whites, so the demographic shifts will continue inexorably to the point that in the 2040s, there will be no racial or ethnic majority, even if no new immigrants are allowed into the United States. In Europe, the percentage of immigrants is lower, but the contrasts seem greater. Europe is also struggling with the low birthrates and the need for new entrants into the labor market. Cross-cultural negative social perceptions and stereotypes continue to persist and complicate the integration of diverse peoples into society and organizations. While the media and pundits discuss assimilation versus multiculturalism, the reality lies somewhere between these two poles. The real question is, how do we all work together in a way that moves society forward during the times of great global challenges? Together we succeed and divided we fail.

For societies to continue being successful, they must have successful institutions and organizations. In a multicultural society, multicultural employees will staff institutions and organizations. The avenue to managing such diversity in the workplace is cultural competence. The following chapters contain a cultural competence model with the elements necessary to manage diversity. Managerial cultural competencies are developed from the cultural competence model for executives, managers, supervisors, and employees. Performance standards are developed. Extensive examples from real life, both positive and negative, are used to illustrate the concepts. Cultural competence in health administration, higher education, and international collaborations will be discussed. Human resources can be a helpful resource, and so its role is discussed.

Chapter 2

How Globalization and Immigration Are Changing the World

2.1 Introduction

Globalization is commonly described as a greater interconnectedness among the countries of the world along several dimensions: economic, political, trade, and cultural. Many barriers have been eliminated or lowered. Global economies are now intermixed. A trip to the grocery store in the United States shows fruits and vegetables grown in countries such as Mexico, Ecuador, and South Africa. Medical tourism, where patients go to different countries for medical care, is flourishing. Technology makes it easier to communicate across the world. The Internet and computer-based communications such as Skype can instantly connect people across the world, helping to create a global community.

Immigration has increased in many countries with asylum and family reunification programs and the flow of undocumented immigrants seeking better lives. It is now easier for immigrants to maintain communication and cultural ties with their families and friends who remain in their countries of origin. When immigrant communities become larger, stores and restaurants having the foods and other commodities they are familiar with begin appearing. This development recreates communities of their native culture embedded in the larger culture of their host country, making it easier for immigrants to maintain their native culture and customs. There are immigrant communities in the United States where the residents do not need to speak or understand English to thrive. This phenomenon makes assimilation less necessary for immigrants.

The impact of less assimilated communities on the United States can be described in the following ways. In the last 30 years or so, immigrants have been coming from many other parts of the world. Numbers do not adequately show the diversity of the communities these immigrants establish. Driving through any large city truly shows the richness of this diversity. There will be several different immigrant communities. Each of these communities will have shops and restaurants that cater to the immigrants. The experience of driving through is almost like stepping into another country. For those individuals who enjoy diversity, the experience is truly a cornucopia of riches. For those who are uncomfortable with diversity, it can be very disconcerting.

This diversity has brought with it discussions about what immigration means for the country. As a result, several important questions arise when thinking about the increase of diverse communities. Here are just a few of the questions:

■ Should immigrants totally assimilate and acquire all the cultural characteristics of their new culture?
■ Is a multicultural perspective, which allows immigrants to maintain many of the customs of their countries of origin, including language, a better approach?
■ Does the multicultural perspective cause more division and conflict in our society, or is it more important that assimilation of new immigrants help create a more nationalistic and unified society?

The discussion concerning diversity can be contentious and is reflected in the media coverage of immigration. Sometimes the conversation uses instances of undocumented immigrants to paint the whole ethnic group in an unflattering picture. Media stories focus on the benefits that immigrants receive and do not focus on their contributions. These discussions find their way into the workplace in informal conversations. Employees who are recent immigrants or children of immigrants are sensitive to these conversations and may perceive that they are unwelcome in the organization. We are not discussing the pros and cons of assimilation versus multiculturalism, but simply detailing what is happening and what historically tends to happen as immigrant communities evolve.

2.2 The United States

The United States is a country of immigrants aside from the hundreds of tribes of indigenous peoples that were reduced in population and rounded up to reside in sovereign reservations across the country. In the early years the immigrants came mostly from Europe. On the southern border, many states were part of Mexico and then became part of the United States. These states had large populations of

Latinos with many ties to Mexico. Many of these immigrants would go to western states such as Washington to work on farms. They would go to Michigan and Wisconsin for the same reasons. Over the last few years, they also have been going to the Southeast and the Midwest to work in factories and construction. There have been many immigrants from Vietnam, Cambodia, Somalia, Iran, Ethiopia, and Russia, as well as many other countries. Each group brings its own culture into the United States, and many immigrants and their children become employees in organizations.

Currently, one in eight people in the United States was born in another country. The foreign-born population of the city of Seattle, for example, has increased from 11% in 1980 to 20% in 2010 (City of Seattle Race and Social Justice Initiative 2008). This jump mirrors increases in immigrant communities in other locations. A report prepared for the U.S. Congressional House Subcommittee on Immigration, Border Security and Claims (Sum, Harrington, and Khatiwada 2005) describes foreign immigration into the United States as "one of the most powerful demographic, social, and economic forces in the nation over the past two decades" (p. 2). The analysis of the 2000 Census of Population and Housing showed that of the increase in the nation's civilian labor force between 1990 and 2000, 47% came from new foreign immigrants. The findings show that in 2004, 92 of 100 new immigrants actively participating in the labor force were able to find employment and that in 2004, new immigrants were 15% of the labor force. Mexico, India, El Salvador, the Philippines, and China were the top five countries of origin of the new immigrants (Sum, Harrington, and Khatiwada 2005). Recent immigrants and their children are more likely to be closer to their native cultures than are fourth or fifth generations. Furthermore, these recent immigrants and their children are more likely to bring those cultural characteristics into the workplace.

Table 2.1 summarizes current and demographic changes the United States is projected to go through by 2050. The population is aging and there are fewer replacement workers, and those replacement workers will be more diverse. In 2005, almost one in three people in the United States can be considered minorities or nonwhite. The greatest growth will be in Asians and Hispanics; indeed, change from 2000 to 2005 shows the growth already beginning. The foreign-born will increase from one in eight to one in five residents.

The numbers show a statistical picture of the demographic changes. However, the percentages fail to show how truly diverse the changes are. Each broad category includes people from many different countries. Some of these countries may have similar languages, as do countries categorized as Hispanic or Latino. A common language does not mean the same culture, of course. Many of these countries can be characterized in much the same way as are England and the United States, described by some people as "two countries separated by a common language." The same dynamics are at work here as well. Many of the countries, in the same broad characterization, may have very different languages as well as cultures. Common to all, however, is having pride in their countries of origin and not wanting to be

Table 2.1 Percentages of Racial and Ethnic Groups in the United States

	% in 2000	% in 2005	% in 2050 (projected)
African Americans	12.7	13.0	13.0
Asian	3.8	5.0	9.0
Hispanic	12.6	14.0	29.0
White (non-Hispanic)	69.4	67.0	46.0
Foreign-born		12.0	19.0
Working Age (18–64)		63.0	58.0
65 and older		12.0	19.0

Source: Data from Pew Hispanic Center, *Pew Hispanic Center Tabulations of 2000 Census and 2005 American Community Survey,* http://pewhispanic.org/ reports/middecade/, 2006; U.S. Census Bureau, *Census Bureau Projects Tripling of Hispanic and Asian Populations in 50 Years; Non-Hispanic Whites May Drop to Half of Total Population,* http://www.census.gov/Press-Release/ www/releases/archives/population/001720.html, 2004; U.S. Census Bureau, *Selected Characteristics of Baby Boomers 42 to 60 Years Old in 2006* (PowerPoint), U.S. Census Bureau, Population Estimates as of July 1, 2006, Age and Special Populations Branch, Population Division, U.S. Census Bureau, Washington, DC, http://www.census.gov/population/socdemo/age/ 2006%Baby%Boomers.pdf, 2006.

classified as being from a different country or culture. People from all these coun-tries are converging as employees in today's organizations. Managers have to blend the resulting diversities into effective organizations. Employees have to work effec-tively with other colleagues from different cultures as well.

Cultural competence seems to imply an emphasis on race and ethnicity. Cultural competence, in the broadest sense of the term, also includes other diversities, among them gender, sexual orientation, and social class and cultural characteristics. The emphasis on other diversities is increasing as well. Five states have legalized same-sex marriage, for example, and in other states there are efforts for legalization as well as resistance to these efforts. In late 2010, President Obama signed the repeal of the ban on openly gay members serving in the military. This, in effect, ends the "don't ask, don't tell" policy. The policy ends after Pentagon officials complete plans and the President, Secretary of Defense, and the Chairman of the Joint Chiefs certify that combat readiness will not be affected (Associated Press 2010). Top mili-tary officials told the House Armed Services Committee that the "don't ask, don't tell" repeal training was going better than expected and that the training would be complete by June 2011 (Mianecki 2011). In contrast, many other industrialized countries already openly accept gays into the military. Women, another minority group, have come a long way; but there is still much progress to be made. These changes are being reflected in public organizations as well. Organizations are becoming more diverse as they reflect the changing demographics and offices of human resource management find ways to offer benefits to same-sex couples.

The retirement of the baby boomers (born between 1946 and 1964), 78 million strong, has begun, and an increasingly diverse population will replace them (Day n.d.; Ortman and Guarneri 2009; U.S. Census Bureau 2006). The leading edge of the baby boomers turns 65 in 2011. Baby boomers born in 1946 became eligible for early Social Security in 2008. The baby boom is an 18-year phenomenon, with almost 20 million baby boomers born between 1946 and 1950 alone (Baby Boomer Headquarters n.d.). As this population, an "elephant in the snake," as has been characterized by some, enters retirement, there will be fewer people to replace this demographic bubble. Furthermore, the replacements will be a much more diverse group than the baby boomers.

The effects of the aging of baby boomers are being felt now, with 30% of federal government employees becoming retirement-eligible in the next five years. This estimate doubles in the next 10 years. As of 2008, the number of workers aged 45 and over will be 40% of the workforce (Dohm 2000). Public administration has larger proportions of older workers (Dohm 2000). In 2006, Linda Springer, director of the U.S. Office of Personnel Management, said the federal government would be facing a retirement tsunami. She said 60% of federal white-collar employees, numbering about 1.6 million, and 5,400 federal executives would be eligible for retirement in the next 10 years (Barr 2006). There are comparable demographics at the state and local levels of governments as well as in the quasi-public and nonprofit sectors. The 2008 recession and subsequent struggling economy may, however, mean fewer retirement-eligible employees actually do retire. Despite the approximately 15 million people unemployed in the United States as a result of the recession, the long-term trend indicates a wave of retirements will still be taking place. It is well to remember that the replacement pool for the retiring baby boomers will be smaller and more multicultural.

Universities will also be affected by the changing demographics. Women attending college already outnumber male students. It is projected that by 2020, students of color will be 46% of the total student population in the United States. Many of these individuals will be first-generation college students and immigrants whose first language is not English (Seurkamp 2007). This characteristic will present a challenge for many universities and will affect both faculty and university administrators. Being a first-generation college student and having parents who do not have a high school education are considered risk factors for educational achievement (Arbona 2005). The changing college population also highlights that public and nonprofit organizations will be recruiting from a very diverse and multicultural population to fill the openings created by retiring baby boomers.

The demographic future for the United States is one of organizations that will more closely reflect the racial and ethnic diversity of the population. Public organizations deliver services to these immigrant communities. To be effective in delivering services, managers will have to understand the different cultures of their employees and client populations. Employees will be more diverse, and their cultural differences will show up in the daily interactions. Diversity can bring in different perspectives, which can enrich the operations of any organizations. Diversity is also a fertile ground for misunderstandings. Other diversities such as sexual orientation and same-sex marriage can create contentious discussions in the work environment that may create awkward and sometimes hostile working conditions. Cultural competence is a way to bridge these divides that invariably occur.

The most extensive work on cultural competency to date has been in the delivery of public health and social services to minority and new immigrant communities. The National Association for Social Workers (NASW) has developed a definition and standards for cultural competence in social work practice. Pope-Davis and Coleman (1997) address requirements by the American Counseling Association to mandate cultural counseling competencies. The Georgetown National Center for Cultural Competence has done extensive work on defining a set of values and principles that enable health care and social service providers the structures that enable them to work effectively cross-culturally. What has been missing in all these endeavors and is the substance of *Cultural Competence for Public Managers* is how public managers can operationalize cultural competencies into a leadership pipeline for public and nonprofit organizations.

2.3 Europe

Europe is experiencing similar dynamics to those occurring in the United States. The original populations of many European countries have birthrates below replacement levels. The low birthrates of the original populations and the high immigration rates in European countries are changing many countries' national or ethnic characteristics, with the long-term prospect that their original populations will become the minority. Immigration has increased to fill the need for labor. While immigration to meet labor shortages has slowed since the 1970s, family reunification and foreign-born people seeking asylum have increased the numbers of the foreign-born in Europe (Hall 2000). According to workpermit.com (2008), which dispenses advice on immigration, the demographic composition of Europe is changing, and Europe will need 56 million immigrant workers by 2050. Godoy estimated there were 11 million legalized immigrants and several million more illegal immigrants in Europe in 2002 (Delgado Godoy 2002). The ethnic mix in England, similar to that in other European countries, is also changing, driven by high rates of net immigration (Johnston 2005). Over the long term, immigrants and their children create the prospect of the original population becoming the minority. Coleman (2006) characterized this shift as a third demographic transition.

Several articles by Adrian Michaels (2008) and Christopher Hope (2009) in *The Telegraph* discuss the demographic changes that Britain and the European Union are undergoing. Accordingly, immigration is changing the culture and society of Europe. A low white birthrate and migrants with higher birthrates are driving the demographic change. The articles mention that Spain had a foreign-born population of 3.2% in 1998, which more than quadrupled to 13.4% by 2007, and that 28% of the children born in England and Wales had at least one immigrant parent. The demographic changes are bringing to the forefront the concern about how immigrants integrate into European societies; in other words, discussions concern assimilation versus multiculturalism. This debate in some ways mirrors the discussion in the United States on the integration of immigrants and whether they should assimilate or retain their cultural and linguistic heritage.

2.3.1 Cultural and Diversity Issues for European Countries

Yazid Sabeg, France's commissioner for diversity and equality, predicted that his country was heading toward an apartheid system and possible social warfare if diversity issues were not addressed soon. In some French neighborhoods comprised mostly of immigrants from former French colonies in northern and central Africa, the unemployment rate for young people is above 50%. France experienced urban riots in Paris in 2005, leading to rapid political change along with the creation of a national diversity plan government initiative. According to a diversity readiness index, the Society for Human Resource Management (SHRM, 2010), implemented by *The Economist* Intelligence Unit, France placed 10th among 11 Western European countries rated in their ability to deal with diversity issues. The index rated 47 countries on 39 indicators, including national diversity, workplace diversity, social inclusion, government inclusion, and legal framework. France was ranked third among Western European nations, yet the country was ranked near the bottom in the region for diversity issues such as workplace and social inclusion. The fear is that without a diversity plan that includes recruiting young professionals from communities troubled with strife, there will be serious consequences.

There are other diversity issues affecting France and being taken up by politicians and the media alike. President Nicolas Sarkozy has launched a national debate on a national identity that some see as anti-Islamist (Crumley 2010). There has been anguish about the removal of bacon burgers from the several of the French affiliates of the Franco-Belgian fast-food chain Quick. Members of the conservative Union for a Popular Majority see this as undermining France's "secular, integrationist social model" as expressed by ruling Conservative Party spokesperson Secretary General Xavier Bertrand (Crumley 2010). France has banned the wearing of face veils in public, and women wearing the niqab or burqa can be fined (Reuters 2011).

A niqab is the face-covering veil worn by only a few hundred Muslim women in France and the burqa is the loose outer garment. French police arrested two women wearing veils. The police claimed they arrested the women for being part of an unauthorized protest (CNN Wire Staff 2011).

Voters in five European states were recently found to be in favor of supporting a ban on the *burka*, the heavy felt dress that covers the female body from head to toe. The countries were France, Britain, Italy, Spain, and Germany (Blitz 2010). Of all respondents, 70% in France supported the move, followed by Spain and Italy; and then approximately 50% of the voters in the United Kingdom and Germany were in favor. This issue is less strong in the United States, where only 33% of voters queried were in support of the *burka* ban.

A recent news item suggests that France is "demonstrating what looks like a neurotic obsession with Islam—if not outright Islamophobia—as it frets over the halal hamburgers that are sold in a handful of the 362 French affiliates of Franco-Belgian fast-food chain Quick" (Crumley 2010). Halal hamburgers were the result of removing bacon burgers from the menu and replacing them with beef handled humanely and processed using principles of Islamic law and with a slice of smoked turkey. Claiming discrimination against non-Muslim customers, officials from the northern city of Roubaix filed charges with justice authorities against Quick for "prejudicial religious catering" (Crumley 2010). It should be noted that this menu change was made in many other French cities, which provoked no problems or debate. As suggested by Crumley, perhaps it is "time for France to take a deep breath."

Italy is experiencing a similar situation in that communities made up of predominantly one ethnic group are on the rise. Roberto Maroni, Italy's interior minister, warns against using a social model where "ghettos" are formed and occupied by members of only one ethnic group. A ghetto refers to a typically slum area in a city in which one ethnic group resides, usually out of economic hardship or racial or ethnic discrimination. In addition, Italy has experienced violence as a result of the stabbing death of an Egyptian youth blamed on Peruvian and Ecuadorian gang members. Minister Maroni added that Italy should find ways to better integrate legal foreigners to the country rather than relegating them to urban ghettos and increasing the likelihood of more racial and ethnic tension.

Southern Italy has also been embroiled in racial violence against African immigrants (Jones 2010). Race riots in the southern Calabrian town of Rosarno were compared to the 1960s racial violence in the United States. Jones's article (2010) states that about 8,000 illegal immigrants, primarily from sub-Saharan Africa, are in Italy on a temporary basis to pick fruit and vegetables. Citing an 18% unemployment rate in the region, politicians have been arguing that the jobs should go to Italians and not illegal immigrants. The immigrants live in abandoned factories with no running water or electricity.

The anti-immigrant sentiment is also part of the public debate in the Netherlands, especially in the form of anti-Islam movements. Making up only about 6% of the Dutch population, Muslims have been described as a presence that threatens the Dutch way of life, states Tony Sterling of the Associated Press (2010). Anti-immigrant politicians have been gaining public sentiment, according to the article. "It's not too much to ask that people who come here share our values," states one of the members of the public interviewed by the reporter.

2.4 Asia

In Asia, cross-cultural competence or managing diversity varies by country. Cultural competence or workforce diversity initiatives are part of many multinational corporations' human resource practices. For many countries' organizations it is gender that is becoming the priority in managing diversity. In countries that have multicultural citizens, managing multiculturalism becomes the priority. Malaysia is comprised of Malay, Chinese, and Indian cultures, and so managing multiculturalism there is challenge. As is the case with Singapore, with around 75% of its population being ethnically Chinese and 15% being Malay or Indian Muslim, Southeast Asia is more diverse than Japan, Korea, and China.

Thailand's diversity issues are not pronounced in the areas of ethnic and religious division, according to Lawler (1996). The biggest diversity issue is centered on the role of women in Thai society, especially within the labor market. Thailand tends to reinforce the traditional roles of men and women in their society, and there are few restrictions on discriminatory behavior.

2.4.1 Cultural and Diversity Issues in Asia

There are deep differences between the values and beliefs of people living in the Eastern regions of the world and the populations of the Western Hemisphere. Because the East and the West are at opposite ends of the planet Earth, if not literally then culturally, the cultural differences that determine the context from which managers and leaders operate in the modern complex organization need to be understood. The Western nations, including North America and the European continent, conduct government and private business in a fast-paced, no-nonsense, linear and rational manner, which can be interpreted as offensive and brusque to other nations, including those found on the Eastern continents, for Eastern traditions emphasize building trust and relationships over a period of time before business is conducted.

Reuters news service recently reported that the famous fast-food chain restaurant McDonald's operating in Singapore had to apologize for substituting a cupid stuffed toy for a pig as part of a promotion honoring the Chinese zodiac signs. Not wanting to offend its Malay patrons who, as Muslims, do not eat pork or pig products, their Chinese customers became incensed that they could not complete their zodiac collection with their birth animal. Apologizing through a half-page ad in a local newspaper, the restaurant learned that not wanting to offend one ethnic group in Singapore, they upset another. Multiracial Singapore has been successful in avoiding racial tension since riots occurred in the 1960s, yet the government considers race to be a major diversity issue facing the country.

2.5 Central and Latin America

Central and Latin American countries have many similarities and just as many differences. In common are the influences of the Spanish and Portuguese who colonized these countries. The treatment of the indigenous peoples varies by country, but many of the indigenous peoples are finding their voice. The rights of the indigenous population are getting more attention. Mestizos—people of mixed blood—bridge the European and indigenous cultures. Many of the countries have immigrants from England, Germany, Italy, and other European countries. The influence of the Catholic Church is an undercurrent in many countries.

Diversity issues can vary in kind and intensity from the more cosmopolitan cities to the rural regions. Women have made strides, but there is still much of the paternalistic culture in evidence. Women make up less than 30% of the administrative and managerial positions. They are only about 3% of the senior executives. Gender is thus very much a diversity issue.

Social class, sometimes determined by ethnic origin, shapes the relationships of people. The global reach of corporations that stress diversity management is bringing an oasis of sensitivity to diversity issues, however. Globalization of commerce is also illuminating a light on the importance of diversity management. Central and Latin American countries face diversity issues similar to those of the rest of the world.

2.6 Africa

In a 2005 study directed by Sameena Nazir under the auspices of Freedom House, a Washington-based monitoring group, violence against women and spousal abuse in the form of "honor killings" continue to be a major problem in many of the Middle Eastern and North African countries. Honor killings are the slaying of women for such perceived slights to their families' honor as infidelity. According to the study, Tunisia and Morocco rate the highest (p. 11). Tunisia and Morocco also received high scores in the category of Economic Rights & Equal Opportunity for women (p. 12). This category looks at the rights of women to land, property, inheritance, education, employment, and labor protection (Freedom House 2005).

In selecting volunteers, the Peace Corps is making a special effort to reflect the richness of the diversity of the United States. The organization's wiki Web site has an exceptional section on diversity and cross-cultural issues for each country in which it has volunteers. The Web site lists diversity and cultural issues for female volunteers, volunteers of color, senior volunteers, and gay, lesbian, or bisexual volunteers; possible religious issues for all volunteers; disability issues for volunteers with disabilities; and possible issues for married volunteers. An excellent resource for those who wish to learn about the diversity and cultural issues, the Peace Corps Web site can be accessed at http://www.peacecorpswiki.org. The diversity and cross-cultural section can be accessed by putting "diversity and cross-cultural issues" in the search box. The following sections are summaries from selected African countries of the diversity and cross-cultural section of the Peace Corp Web site, which is updated by volunteers and reflects their experiences.

2.6.1 Kenya

As in other African countries, the people in rural areas have not had the exposure to people of other cultures and races that residents of large cities have experienced. Women are expected to perform the traditional roles of housework and to be deferential to men. It is common for women to experience unwanted sexual comments. People of color who travel with white companions may be viewed as prostitutes. Seniors are shown great respect. Homosexuality is considered illegal in Kenya, and the penalties for homosexuality can be prison or deportation. People who are physically challenged are treated with the same dignity as other people.

2.6.2 Botswana

While the country has constitutional protection for women, in the rural areas less-educated women have less power and responsibility than men. Seniors are accorded much respect. Homosexuality is illegal and considered immoral.

2.6.3 Cameroon

Cameroon culture is patriarchal. It is not uncommon for women to receive unwanted sexual advances. Men consider women who look into their eyes as propositioning them regardless of what the women are saying. A man propositions a woman by scratching the palm of her hand when they shake hands. Seniors are treated with deference. It is common for any Asian to be considered Chinese and to know the martial arts. Kung fu movies are global phenomena. Cameroon considers homosexuality to be illegal, and the topic is not discussed in public.

2.6.4 Madagascar

Madagascar was populated by people from various countries and has racial and ethnic diversity. As sometimes happens when people from different cultures populate a country, there can be an underlying tension among the various ethnic and racial groups. Women have more traditional roles in rural areas than in the city. Seniors are given great respect. There is a cultural taboo against homosexuality although it is tolerated in foreigners.

2.6.5 Mozambique

The Mozambique constitution sees men and women as equal, but the reality is that women reflect the more traditional roles. Asians are seen as being either Japanese or Chinese and are stereotyped as knowing the martial arts. Hispanics are thought to be either Cuban or Portuguese. Homosexuality is not illegal, but it is not accepted. People with disabilities are not accorded the dignity of others and may experience prejudice.

2.6.6 South Africa

South African culture is patriarchal, and the racial divisions still linger. Races are classified into four categories: white, colored, Asian, or black. People are treated according to their classification. South Africans are conservative and many deny that homosexuality exists in their culture.

2.6.7 Tanzania

Gender relations are traditional, with the man being the head of the household. He speaks for the other members of the household. Many Tanzanians are not familiar with people from other countries. The culture is conservative, and many citizens deny that homosexuality exists in their country.

2.6.8 Uganda

Gender roles are distinct, and each has its own set of responsibilities. Skin color, rather than race or ethnicity, is used to differentiate among people. Homosexuality is illegal, and sentences for people convicted of homosexuality can range from 17 years to life in prison. Same-sex public displays of affection are discouraged.

2.6.9 Zambia

Zambian culture is paternalistic, and women are treated as seriously as men. The rural populations are not as familiar with other races and ethnicities as are residents of the cities. Homosexuality is illegal, though not actively prosecuted. It is seen as immoral. Seniors, as throughout much of Africa, are treated with great respect.

2.7 Additional Commentary on Generational Issues

An interesting observation when reading about cultural issues regarding the way seniors are treated in Africa is the generational divide in the Peace Corps volunteers. Seniors are given great respect in Africa. The "senior cultural issues" reside with younger volunteers. The generational cultural divide is greater among the volunteers than among the residents of African countries and U.S. senior volunteers. This dichotomy speaks to the generational divide in the United States.

2.8 Additional Commentary on International Cultural Issues

In a discussion of cultural competence in various countries, a colleague of the authors, who has extensive international experience, commented that he had observed that countries colonized by Latin-based countries such as Spain and Portugal showed less overt racism, but more graft and corruption. On the other hand, countries colonized by Britain showed more overt racism, but less graft and corruption.

There seems to have been more intermarriage between the Portuguese and Spanish occupiers with the indigenous populations than between British colonizers and indigenous populations. This intermarriage led to a blended ethnicity, the mestizo race that is common from the United States through Central America and into South America. Mestizo is a combination of the Spanish or Portuguese and the indigenous peoples. The Spanish, Portuguese, and indigenous cultures contain many aspects of polychromic time and are family and relationship oriented. Latin-based countries typically are more family and relationship oriented. It is common in many countries that when a request is made, a gift is given. The gift may be a bottle of wine or, in some cases, money. The same tradition can exist when seeking help from government officials.

When employees from these cultures enter organizations, they may continue this practice and offer gifts to supervisors. Because most, if not all, public organizations have ethics regulations about receiving gifts, it is wise to be careful about accepting or, better yet, not accepting gifts from employees. Refusing gifts should, however, be done with the cultural understanding of the gesture. A gift can be refused with an explanation of the ethics regulations. It is worthwhile, while refusing the gift, to acknowledge the sentiment in which the employee offered the gift.

There seems to have been less intermarriage between the British, who colonized many countries, and the residents of those countries. The distinction between being British and being a resident of the country in question was more clearly defined in these circumstances. British culture is monochronic, whereas many of the cultures Britain came to dominate can be considered to be polychronic. The cultural distances can thus be considered greater between Britain and the people of the countries they occupied as compared with the divide between the Spanish and Portuguese colonizers and the indigenous peoples with whom they intermarried. With the British being the occupiers, the power distance between the cultures was great, making overt racism more likely to be a cultural by-product. With no mestizo culture to act as a bridge in this situation, the divide remained large.

We leave the reader to draw his or her own conclusions on these observations.

2.9 Summary and Conclusion

Demographic changes are driving a cultural change in the United States and many European countries. The United States and Europe have aging populations and low birthrates. Globalization and immigration, illegal as well as legal, are creating cultural change in many of these countries. Countries that were once predominately monocultural are now multicultural. Some people in previously monocultural countries are not welcoming the cultural changes. Acrimonious discussions about the role of legal and illegal immigration and the cultural changes it brings are common in these countries. Some critics are espousing limits on legal immigration and increased efforts to completely stop illegal immigration. Harsh language becomes more common. Yet the reality is that the demographics will continue to drive cultural change. Transitions are not always easy.

Chapter 3

Defining Cultural Competence for Public Managers

If we cannot end our differences, at least we can help make the world safe for diversity.

For in the final analysis, our most basic common link is that we all inhabit this small planet. We all breathe the same air. We all cherish our children's futures. And we are all mortal.

John Fitzgerald Kennedy
American University Commencement Address, 1963

3.1 Introduction

The U.S. federal government has provided much of the impetus for research on cultural competence (Bailey 2005). The federal government has also required delivery of culturally competent services to immigrant and minority communities. Culturally competent linguistic services are required, for example, for delivery of services to communities whose members have limited English proficiency. In addition, the federal government has supported research into cultural competence. The research has led to various definitions of cultural competence, and those definitions have been incorporated into the research of cultural competence in public administration (Johnson, Lenartowicz, and Apud 2006). The research also lays out organizational requirements for cultural competence.

International businesses use cultural intelligence as their version of cultural competence. The business perspective examines the dynamics of business management of international companies with a mix of managers from different countries. People from different countries and backgrounds are working together, and the different cultural characteristics can frequently clash. Because the aspect of employees of different backgrounds working together is missing in the research on cultural competence, the research from business adds a valuable perspective for public managers.

The international business perspective brings forward two ideas that provide insights for public managers. The first is the concept of cultural intelligence. Cultural competence can be seen as form of cultural intelligence. Thomas and Inkson (2004) define cultural intelligence as the capability to deal effectively with people from different cultural backgrounds. Cultural intelligence consists of cultural knowledge, the practice of mindfulness, and behavioral skills. Goleman (2000) developed the concept of emotional intelligence and brought to the forefront an emphasis on the contribution of understanding our emotions and the way they affect our personal and social relationships. Emotional intelligence is a requisite for career success. Later Goleman (2000) brought in diversity as part of emotional intelligence but did not fully explore the dynamics. (Emotional intelligence and its role in resolving difficult employee issues is discussed in Chapter 14.) The second idea that the business use of cultural intelligence contributes is a study of the cultural characteristics of managers and employees from different countries. Many of the large number of immigrants and first-generation employees and managers in the United States and Europe retain and exhibit those same cultural characteristics.

Sociology contributes the concept of diversity consciousness as described by Bucher (2010). Diversity consciousness is the nexus of diversity awareness, understanding diversity, and diversity skills.

3.2 Research on Cultural Competence

Federal legislation fueled the development of cultural competence by requiring cultural competence as a condition of receiving federal assistance funds (Bailey 2005). The 1965 Social Security Act that established Medicare and Medicaid mandated that Medicaid recipients receive culturally and linguistically appropriate services. The 1990 Disadvantaged Minority Health Improvement Act required the Office of Minority Health (OMH) to address the cultural and linguistic barriers to health care. The OMH funded research to understand how the cultural and linguistic differences were creating disparities. Johnson, Lenartowicz, and Apud (2006), in their literature review of cultural competence, find that cultural competence is widely used in the United States in the fields of health care, medicine, psychology, and education in the context of minorities and governmental agencies and systems. Cultural competence is also used in the context of workforce diversity referring to cultural subgroups classifieds by gender, ethnic origin, religion, sexual orientation, and age.

A very dramatic example of why cultural competence in the delivery of health care services, especially for newly arrived immigrant communities to countries not of their origin, is so essential is shown in the book *The Spirit Catches You and You Fall Down: A Hmong Child, Her American Doctors, and the Collision of Two Cultures* by Anne Fadiman (1998), a winner of the National Critics Circle Award. The book describes what happened when Lia Lee entered the U.S. medical system diagnosed as an epileptic. Her story became a tragic case history of cultural miscommunication. Three-month-old Lia Lee and her parents were members of a large Hmong community that had recently immigrated to California. A chain of events was set in motion when the baby arrived at the emergency room in Merced from which she, her parents, and the doctors would never recover.

The Hmong were recruited in the 1960s by the U.S. Central Intelligence Agency to fight the "secret war" in Laos against communist forces. They fought for the United States to block supply lines and rescue downed U.S. pilots. When they were singled out for retribution, tens of thousands fled to Thailand, with the largest number of the Hmong people eventually becoming repatriated in the United States; traditionally a close-knit and fierce people, the Hmong have been less amenable to assimilation than most immigrants, adhering steadfastly to the rituals and beliefs of their ancestors. Lia's pediatricians held just as strongly to another tradition: that of Western medicine. Parents and doctors both wanted the best for Lia, but their ideas about the causes of her illness and its treatment could hardly have been more different. The Hmong see illness and healing as spiritual matters linked to virtually everything in the universe, whereas the Western medical community marks a division between body and soul and concerns itself almost exclusively with the former. Lia's doctors attributed her seizures to the misfiring of her cerebral neurons; her parents called her illness "*qaug dab peg*"—the spirit catches you and you fall down—and ascribed it to the wandering of her soul. The doctors prescribed anticonvulsants; her parents preferred animal sacrifices. For the Hmong, illness may also occur as a result of an intense emotional experience, as felt through a frightening or upsetting event. Thankfully, the medical community has now experienced and published information that includes the need for demonstrating culturally sensitive care.

A cultural factor rarely discussed in cultural competency is the role that spiritualism plays in many cultures. It is clearly relevant when delivering health care services to immigrant communities, as *The Spirit Catches You and You Fall Down* so eloquently describes. Spiritualism exists in many cultures and is a belief that is retained by many children of immigrants. While there are many articles in anthropology about the spiritual practices of several cultures, such readings are not usually mainstream reading. Spiritual practices that may seem odd or steeped in superstition to many people in the United States and other European countries are culturally embedded and very real in many cultures. A lawyer who is Mexican American was talking to one of the authors about regular conversations she has with her father, who had died many years before. She described the conversations with her deceased father and the answers she has received to questions she has had. Without the cultural understanding that ancestral worship is part of many cultures, her behavior could be considered as odd or even crazy.

Another Mexican American couple, where the husband has a PhD and the wife is a lawyer, described the cleansings they gave their son when he had nightmares or anxieties. They used a chicken egg. Such cultural beliefs are often given short shrift by individuals whose background is more rational, scientific, and Western. However, the beliefs are very real to many people. Many public employees come from cultures where such beliefs are part of their cosmological worldview. Although such beliefs are personal, they may be articulated in the workplace. One can imagine the reaction if an employee is overheard discussing her conversations with deceased relatives.

There is extensive literature on cultural competence in the delivery of services to minority and immigrant communities (Assemi, Mutha, and Hudmon 2007; Carpenter-Song, Schwallie, and Longhofer 2007; Dana and Allen 2008; Lecca 1998; Pope-Davis and Coleman 1997; Reimann et al. 2004; Rouson et al. 2009). Much of the literature focuses on the delivery of different types of government services to segmented minority and immigrant communities. The topics include, for example, delivering culturally competent social services to elderly Latinos (Applewhite 1998); incorporating cultural competency training in psychiatry (Qureshi et al. 2008); achieving cultural competence for clients and workers in a multicultural society (Bonder, Martin, and Miracle 2001); providing cultural competency training for staff serving Hispanic families with a child in psychiatric crisis (Zayas et al. 1997); establishing cultural competence in nursing homes (Parker and Geron 2007); and developing culturally competent mental health services and incorporating cultural competence in the criminal justice system (Primm, Osher, and Gomez 2005).

Tombros, Jordan, and Monterroso (2007), commenting from an international perspective on cultural competence and global health disparities based on race, ethnicity, and socioeconomic disparities, stated, "Cultural competence is not simply a matter of social pleasantries; rather it has real-life consequences for health outcomes" (p. 325). They see cultural competence affecting institutional policies and procedures, as well as the interactions between health providers and patients. For them, globalization is increasing diversity across the world and with this diversity comes a continuing need for cultural competence. They cite a study showing that 68% of U.S. medical schools are providing some form of formal training in cultural competence. Another 14% are seen as planning to provide training in cultural competence.

3.3 Definitions of Cultural Competence

The research on delivery of services to immigrant and migrant communities has yielded several definitions of cultural competence. One definition is incorporated in the 1994 Developmental Disabilities Assistance and Bill of Rights Act. The Center for Mental Health Services of the Department of Health and Human Services, Substance Abuse and Mental Health Services Administration, also defines cultural competence. Various other researchers have likewise defined cultural competence.

The 1994 Developmental Disabilities Assistance and Bill of Rights Act defines cultural competence as "services, supports or other assistance that are provided in a manner that is responsive to the beliefs, interpersonal styles, attitudes, language and behaviors of individuals who are receiving services, and in a manner that has the greatest likelihood of ensuring their maximum participation in the program" (Bailey 2010, 175). The legislation provided a legislative definition of cultural competence. In effect, the 1994 Disabilities Act legislates the delivery of services in a culturally relevant manner. The services are to be delivered in a manner consistent with the culture of the recipient.

On its Web site, the Center for Mental Health Services of the Department of Health and Human Services (2009) defines cultural and linguistic competence as "an integrated pattern of human behavior that includes thoughts, communications, languages, practices, beliefs, values, customs, courtesies, rituals, manners of interacting, roles, relationships and expected behaviors of a racial, ethnic, religious or social group; the ability to transmit the above to succeeding generations is dynamic in nature."

The 1994 Developmental Disabilities Assistance and Bill of Rights Act was not the first attempt to define cultural competence. Cross and colleagues (1989) of the Georgetown University Child Development Center published *Towards a Culturally Competent System of Care*. They define cultural competence as a "set of cultural behaviors and attitudes integrated into the practice methods of a system, agency, or its professionals that enables them to work effectively in cross cultural situations" (Cross et al. 1989, 2). For Cross et al., cultural competency is a cultural development process that has a negative to positive continuum. They list six stages:

1. Cultural destructiveness
2. Cultural incapacity
3. Cultural blindness
4. Cultural pre-competence
5. Cultural competency
6. Cultural proficiency (1989, 6–8)

The definition of cultural competence used by the National Center for Cultural Competence, Georgetown University, was adapted from the work of Cross et al. (1989).

Gallegos (1982) wrote "The Ethnic Competence Model for Social Work Education" in B. W. White's *Color in a White Society*. Gallegos sees ethnic competence as the acquiring of a culturally relevant understanding of the problems of minorities that can be used to deliver culturally appropriate interventions. The

National Association of Social Workers (NASW 2007, 10) defines culture as "the integrated pattern of human behavior that includes thoughts, communications, actions, customs, and institutions of a racial, ethnic, religious, or social group." This definition is consistent with the definition of cultural competence in the 1994 legislation.

Sue (2006) and Sue, Ivey, and Pedersen (1996) define cultural competence for mental health providers as follows:

1. Cultural awareness and beliefs: Provider's sensitivity to his or her own personal values and how these may influence perceptions of the client, client's problem, and the counseling relationship
2. Cultural knowledge: Counselor's knowledge of the client's culture, worldview, and expectations for the counseling relationship
3. Cultural skills: Counselor's ability to intervene in a manner that is culturally sensitive and relevant (Sue 2006, 238)

This cultural competence framework was adopted by the American Psychological Association in its "Multicultural Guidelines" (Sue 2006).

Betancourt and colleagues (2003, 118) see a culturally competent health care system as "one that acknowledges and incorporates—at all levels—the importance of culture, assessment of cross-cultural relations vigilance toward the dynamics of cultural differences, expansion of cultural knowledge, and adaptation of services to meet culturally unique needs." They see three barriers to a culturally competent health care system:

1. Organizational barriers: The lack of minority representation in the leadership and workforce. The representation does not reflect the racial and ethnic composition of the population.
2. Structural barriers: The lack of cross-cultural communication capabilities. There is a lack of interpreter services or culturally and linguistically appropriate health education information.
3. Clinical barriers: Cross-cultural differences between client and provider. The cultural and linguistic barriers lead to poorer health outcomes.

Zayas and colleagues (1997, 406) define cultural competence as "the knowledge and interpersonal skills to understand, appreciate, and work with families from cultures other than one's own and using the knowledge and skills effectively to employ therapeutic techniques in achieving behavioral and emotional change."

Pope-Davis and Donald (1997) developed an operational definition of cultural competence that includes transforming the cultural knowledge into organizational standards, policies, practices, and attitudes to better serve culturally diverse clients. For them, competence includes learning new behaviors and using them appropriately.

Brach and Fraser (2000) see cultural competence in an organizational context of incorporating the appropriate practices and policies to address cultural diversity. Associations, university centers, and foundations also play a large role in defining cultural competence. The Cultural Institute of Canada defines cultural competency in an organizational context as the behaviors, attitudes, and policies that allow organizations to work with culturally diverse populations. Specifically, this institute defines cultural competence as being "a set of congruent behaviors, attitudes, and policies that enable the organization or agency to work effectively with various racial, ethnic, religious, and linguistic groups" (Cultural Diversity Institute of Canada 2000, 1).

Taylor (1994, 154) sees intercultural competence as "an adaptive capacity based on an inclusive and integrative world view which allows participants to effectively accommodate the demands of living in a host culture." Chang (2007) likewise sees cultural competence as integrative. He believes it is transformative and attained through the experience of internal discovery and external adjustment. In Chang's study of international humanitarian aid workers, their experience of cultural competence is divided into three levels:

1. Peripheral level: Encounter and recognize
2. Cognitive level: Familiarize and adjust
3. Reflective level: Transform and enlighten (2007, 193)

Cultural competence is defined in the context of delivery of government services to immigrant and minority communities. In summary, it can be said that cultural competence is derived from the delivery of services and has two perspectives, the personal and the organizational. The personal perspective focuses on acquiring cross-cultural knowledge and skills (Zayas et al. 1997) and a set of congruent behaviors and attitudes that come together among professionals and enable them to work effectively in cross-cultural situations (Cross et al. 1989; Cultural Diversity Institute of Canada 2000). The organizational aspect refers to the organizational capacity to have the linguistic capability to deliver services to communities whose members have a limited English proficiency. It also refers to organizations being diverse and reflecting the diversity of the community the organization serves.

3.4 Cultural Intelligence and Its Contribution to Cultural Competence

In the business community, cultural competence is also framed as cultural intelligence and is associated with international business (Johnson, Lenartowicz, and Apud 2006). The impetus for developing cultural competence or cultural intelligence in international business was the failure of U.S. expatriates working overseas and headquarters managers not understanding the challenges of working with other cultures (Farley and Ang 2003; Johnson, Lenartowicz, and Apud 2006; Thomas and Inkson 2004). These underlying dynamics are the same ones that exist for public managers, namely, effectively working with people of other cultures with different cultural characteristics. Cultural intelligence is helpful because of its focus on cross-cultural interactions with employees who are culturally different.

The perspective in business intelligence is working overseas with people from other cultures. The value of this perspective in public administration is twofold. One is for any public manager or employee who is involved in international initiatives. The other is that with the increased diversity of employees, there may be many employees who retain the cultural characteristics of their original cultures, as is reflected in the increasing workplace diversity.

Globalization is seen as increasing international business opportunities and collaborations. The definitions relevant to international business are similar to those applying to public administration (Cross et al. 1989; Hofstede 2001; Tan and Chua 2003). Black and Mendenhall (1990) found positive correlations for performance and cross-cultural training. Johnson, Lenartowicz, and Apud (2006) also found broad coverage in the literature on workplace diversity in the United States that they see as triggered by U.S. federal regulations for delivering public health and educational services to minority communities. This literature broadly defines cultural competence as the respect for and understanding of other cultures and includes other diversity factors similar to definitions of cultural competence in public administration.

Johnson, Lenartowicz, and Apud (2006) see many international business failures blamed on the practitioner's lack of cultural competence. They see globalization as increasing collaborative ventures with foreign firms. Many of the ventures do not succeed, for which they see two reasons emerging from the literature: the failure of expatriates and the inability of managers to understand the cultural challenges of working in other countries. Thomas and Inkson (2004) see the globalization of people creating new and major challenges because of the difficulty of bridging cultural boundaries.

In their literature review, Johnson and colleagues (2006) find that cultural competence is widely found in the United States in the fields of health care, medicine, psychology, and education in the context of minorities and governmental agencies and systems. Cultural competence is also used in the context of workforce diversity referring to cultural subgroups classified by gender, ethnic origin, religion, sexual orientation, and age. They see the definitions as specific but not applicable to international business. Earley (2002) and Earley and Ang (2003) introduced the concept of cultural intelligence, which is "a person's capability to adapt as s/he interacts with others from different cultural regions" (2002, 283).

Cultural intelligence is defined by Thomas and Inkson (2004, 14) as meaning "being skilled and flexible about understanding a culture, learning more about it from your ongoing interactions with it, and gradually reshaping your thinking to be more sympathetic to the culture and your behavior to be more skilled and appropriate when interacting with others from the culture." They define cultural intelligence as having three components:

1. Knowledge of the culture and principles of cross-cultural interactions
2. Mindfulness practice that pays attention to cross-cultural cues
3. Culturally correct behaviors

Tan (2004) suggests that cultural intelligence be viewed in the context of emotional or social intelligence. Emotional intelligence assumes that people use culturally familiar situations in interacting with others. Cultural intelligence involves interacting with others in unfamiliar situations. Tan defines three key parts of cultural intelligence:

1. Cultural strategic thinking—thinking and solving problems in particular ways
2. Motivational thinking—being energized and persistent in one's actions
3. Behavioral thinking—acting in certain ways

Kumar, Rose, and Subramaniam (2008, 320) define cultural intelligence as representing "an individual's capability for successful adaptation to new and unfamiliar cultural settings and ability to function easily and effectively in situations characterized by cultural diversity." They define cultural intelligence as comprised of three aspects:

1. Mental (metacognitive and cognitive)
2. Motivational
3. Behavioral

The mental aspect is the ability to conceptualize, acquire, and understand cultural knowledge. The motivational aspect is the willingness to interact with others and to adapt to others' cultures. The behavioral aspect is having the adaptive behaviors agree with the mental and motivational aspects.

Amiri, Moghimi, and Kazemi's study (2010) focused on the correlation between cultural intelligence and employee performance. The researchers see cultural diversity creating problems for individuals and organizations. Yet globalization has created a need for more culturally diverse organizations. Cultural intelligence is emerging as an important factor in an employee's performance inside and among various cultural environments (2010, 418). Their study found significant correlation between cultural intelligence (metacognitive, cognitive, and motivational aspects) and employee behavior.

The use of the concept of cultural intelligence brings an interesting perspective to the discussion. One way of looking at cultural competence in today's world is as a form of intelligence that in some ways has similarities to emotional intelligence. Gardner (1983) expanded the number of intelligences to eight. To the more traditional intelligences of verbal-linguistic and logical-mathematical he added spatial, bodily-kinesthetic, interpersonal, intrapersonal, musical, and environmental. Daniel Goleman (1995) added the concept of emotional intelligence to the lexicon. Goleman devoted a few pages to diversity, mainly in terms of discussing the dynamics of tolerance and prejudice.

In his book *Working with Emotional Intelligence* (1998), Goleman includes leveraging diversity as one of the competencies of the broad category of social competence. He identifies four characteristic ways of behaving that define this emotional-intelligence leveraging-diversity competency (1998, 54):

1. Respecting and relating well to people of different backgrounds
2. Understanding different perspectives and being sensitive to the differences of a group
3. Seeing diversity as opportunity
4. Challenging bias and intolerance

Writing from a sociological perspective, Richard Bucher (2010) speaks of a diversity consciousness. Bucher sees diversity consciousness as being at the center of three areas: understanding of diversity, diversity awareness, and diversity skills. For him, diversity is used in relationship to a changing cultural landscape. He sees diversity as being broader than race and gender. In a way, it encompasses the many ways in which we differ from each other. Diversity is thus becoming more complex than the categories of race, gender, sexual orientation, and social class. Which of these forms of diversity is more important to a first-generation Chinese female who is a lesbian and whose parents are poor? A person's personal appearance is fading as a predictor of cultural characteristics. An awareness of diversity can lead one to want to understand the differences. Diversity skills are interacting with each other in ways that value and respect those differences. This process can culminate in cultural competence.

3.5 Cultural Intelligence and Leadership

Cultural intelligence has been used in the context of leadership as well. The important element that cultural intelligence and leadership bring into the equation is managing a diverse workforce. Understanding the cultural characteristics of the employees is important in this regard. The work of Hofstede (covered in Chapter 1) is central to understanding cultural characteristics and differences in these works.

Northouse (2007) includes a chapter on culture and leadership in his book *Leadership: Theory and Practice*. It is interesting to note that his third edition, published in 2004, did not include the chapter on culture and leadership. The evolution of his work may be seen in the context of globalization and increasing diversity generating more interest in cultural intelligence and cultural competence. Northouse defines culture as the "learned beliefs, values, rules, norms, symbols, and traditions that are common to a people" (2007, 302). He views culture as being dynamic. He defines multiculturalism as taking more than one culture into account and also classifying by race, gender, ethnicity, sexual orientation, and age. Diversity encompasses different cultures or ethnicities within a group or organization. He sees the work of Hofstede (1980, 2001) as probably being the most referenced work on cultural dimensions and the benchmark for much of the research on world cultures. Analyzing the responses from 100,000 respondents in more than 50 countries, Hofstede identified five major dimensions where cultures differ: power distance, uncertainty avoidance, individualism-collectivism, masculinity-femininity, and long-term and short-term orientation. Northouse also cites the work of Hall (1976) on the primary characteristics of culture. Hall's work has been described in terms of polychromic and monochromic cultural characteristics (discussed in Chapter 1).

In the context of culture and leadership, Northouse references the work of House and others (2004) as offering the strongest findings. These studies, called the GLOBE studies, covered 62 societies. The GLOBE researchers used their own research as well as the work of other researchers (Hofstede 1980, 2001; Kluckhohn and Strodtbeck 1961; Triandis 1995). (These dimensions of culture are also discussed in Chapter 1.) The researchers identified nine dimensions of culture:

1. Uncertainty avoidance
2. Power distance
3. Institutional collectivism
4. In-group collectivism
5. Gender egalitarianism
6. Assertiveness
7. Future orientation
8. Performance orientation
9. Humane orientation

They also described leadership behaviors as they are viewed in different cultures. They enumerated six global leadership behaviors:

1. Charismatic or value-based leadership
2. Team-oriented leadership
3. Participative leadership
4. Humane-oriented leadership
5. Autonomous leadership
6. Self-protective leadership

Yukl (2002) includes a chapter on ethical leadership and diversity in his book *Leadership in Organizations*. He sees the importance of cross-cultural research on leadership because of increasing globalization. Similar to Northouse, he describes the works of Hofstede (1980, 1993) and the GLOBE Project as being important to cross-cultural leadership.

Thomas and Inkson (2004) include a chapter on leadership across cultures in their book *Cultural Intelligence.* They describe the leadership styles of several countries. They refer to leadership in Arab countries as a "sheikhocracy," a blend of personal autocracy and conformity to rules and regulation. The respect is for those who make the rules and not for the rationality of the rules themselves. Leadership in Japan is based on a combination of *amae*, defined as indulgent love with obligation and the moral obligation to pay the debt. Leadership in France is characterized as paternalistic and charismatic. Russian leaders are characterized as powerful autocrats. The value to public managers of these studies is understanding the expectations of employees who may be recent immigrants or children of immigrants from these countries. The expectations of these employees may differ according to the leadership style they have experienced in their countries of origin.

Thomas and Inkson (2004) see culturally intelligent leadership as focusing on the culture and expectations of the followers. They classify the cultural characteristics as either individualistic or collectivistic. Individualistic cultures expect the individual to make decisions. Collectivist cultures expect decisions to be made by consensus. They also use Hofstede's classifications: power distance, uncertainty avoidance, and masculinity and femininity.

Chin and Gaynier (2006) bring into the discussion of culture and leadership the concept of the organizational culture. They attribute to globalization an increasingly diverse workforce, and with the diversity, a more complex social environment within the organization. They argue that twenty-first century leaders need cultural intelligence in addition to intellectual intelligence and emotional intelligence. They attribute the lack of understanding of the organizational and ethnic cultures of the workplace as leading to the failure, confusion, and frustration of leaders. They see the Western value of color blindness as being well-meaning but misguided. For them, "managing cultural differences is a key factor in building and sustaining organizational competitiveness and vitality" (2006, 5). They discuss British, Japanese, Italian, and American corporate leaders as leveraging their cultural strengths to create competitive advantages. They also believe the process involves three characteristics:

1. Having a shared management philosophy
2. Creating a cultural environment
3. Developing human resource strategies that include cultural diversity

They see culturally intelligent leadership as creating a balance that includes the leader's style, the follower's expectations, and the situation. This balance creates an organizational common ground where the leader and the followers can be effective.

Reviewing the current literature on cultural competence reveals some important aspects of cultural competence in the various approaches. The key aspects can be summarized as follows:

1. All the approaches are responding to the increased cultural diversity driven by the demographic changes and the many different cultural characteristics that now exist in today's society and organizations.
2. The definition of diversity is being expanded beyond race, gender, sexual orientation, and social class.
3. Diversity can be seen as including cultural characteristics, generational differences, religion, regional differences, organizational roles, and technology.
4. The literature draws heavily from the research on the federally mandated delivery of services to immigrant and minority communities. (The next section of this chapter describes cultural competence from this perspective in more detail, making it easier to see the contribution of the research on immigrant and minority communities.)
5. Respect for and understanding of other cultures is the first concept in cultural competence.
6. Culturally competent communication is very important.
7. The work on cultural competence and cultural intelligence includes working with others who differ culturally and working with culturally diverse employees.
8. The work on cultural competence and leadership focuses on cultural differences and the different perspectives each culture brings to the organization.
9. The work on leadership also includes leader-follower dynamics and creating a common ground where the leadership style and cultural characteristics and expectations of the employees can meet.

The concepts of diversity consciousness and cultural intelligence bring in an interesting perspective. Many societies and organizations are transitioning from being monocultural to becoming multicultural. Having an awareness or consciousness of the changes created can lead to having a cultural intelligence similar to the concept of emotional intelligence. Emotional intelligence competencies when applied in a cross-cultural context can be helpful to culturally competent management practices. (The use of emotional intelligence competencies in cross-cultural settings is discussed more thoroughly in Chapter 14.)

3.6 Understanding Diversity, Social Equity, and Cultural Competence

Before a public organization can begin to implement cultural competency practices for its employees and its constituents, it is important that its managers understand the shifts that have occurred during the last 40 years. Knowing how society got to this point in multicultural relations helps illuminate many of the multicultural dynamics experienced in today's organizations. Many organizations continue to operate in a space where affirmative action policies lead. This means that enforcing a method of hiring a certain number of people of color is a continued mindset for many public mangers. The truth is that affirmative action has never been about quotas. The incorrect assumption about affirmative action is that it is a quota system referring to hiring a certain number of people of color and women for a certain number of open positions. For example, if an organization has four open positions, one may go to a person of color and one position may go to a woman. This faulty system has never worked for one main reason: Anytime there is a system built on preferential treatment, it will lead to resentment and feelings that persons receiving these benefits are not otherwise qualified to become employed.

The notion that people hired under an affirmative action policy are not otherwise qualified could easily be observed in the 2009 case in which a group of predominately white firefighters sued the city of New Haven, Connecticut, because they believed that their qualifications were overlooked when it was time for promotion. Instead of their being promoted, people of color, with lesser credentials, were hired. While it is true that this case was ruled in favor of the plaintiffs, it must also be noted that the plaintiffs showed an underlying sense of entitlement. In the documentary *Shattering the Silences* (Nelson and Pellett 1997), political scientist Neil Pinter makes the point very clear that many white people have the perception that they do not have to give up anything for anyone. Here, Pinter is referring to the fact that historically, white people have felt that they belong on top of the social ladder. While tensions around this issue persist, it is clear that well-meaning public organizations have caused more harm than good by relying on affirmative action as a quota system to equal the playing field in job opportunities.

Although many people believe that affirmative action has benefited people of color, it must also be noted that qualified people of color have benefited minimally by affirmative action policies. Research continues to indicate that white women are the true beneficiaries of affirmative action programs. This statement is not to pit one oppressed group against another but, rather, to illuminate the truth about who has historically gained more from affirmative action. Take, for example, Table 3.1, formulated by the deans at Golden Gate University (GGU) and the University of Vermont (UVM).

It is clear from the demographics of both institutions that deans of color make up significantly fewer positions than do their white female counterparts or white male counterparts. This finding is particularly true within GGU, where three of its four deans are white women. This is alarming considering that GGU is located in the downtown business district of San Francisco, where there are high concentrations of professionals of color. UVM is located in Burlington in Vermont, one of

Table 3.1 Comparison of People of Color, Women, and Men at Two Higher Education Institutions

Golden Gate University	Dean of Color	Women	Men
School of Law		X	
Ageno School of Business			X
School of Taxation		X	
School of Undergraduate Studies		X	
University of Vermont	Dean of Color	Women	Men
College of Agriculture and Life Sciences			X
College of Arts and Sciences		X	
College of Education and Social Services	X (female)		
College of Engineering and Mathematics			X
College of Medicine			X
College of Nursing and Health Sciences		X	
Continuing Education		X	
Graduate College			X
Honors College	X (male)		
Rubenstein School of Environment Natural Resources		X	
School of Business Administration			X

Source: Data from Golden Gate University, http://www.ggu.edu, 2010; University of Vermont, http://www.uvm.edu, 2010.

the most undiversified states in the United States. One might argue that people of color are not attracted to a state like Vermont, which is rural and substantially distant from most U.S. cities (Montreal, Canada, is 90 miles north of Burlington).

Common reasons given for not recruiting people of color as deans at UVM are unconvincing:

1. People of color would not want to work at UVM because the weather is too cold in Vermont.
2. There is too much snow in Vermont.

3. There are not enough other people of color in the state.
4. Search committees cannot find qualified faculty and administrators of color.

Search committees consistently cite the above reasons for not having a diverse applicant pool at UVM, even though deans and other senior-level positions are often recruited through national searches with large and reputable search firms. Therefore, attracting well-qualified people of color to the deanery should not be an issue for UVM.

Unfortunately, UVM has not had a good track record of hiring senior administrators of color. Chartered in 1791, UVM has had only one president who was not a white man. Dr. Judith Ramely will go down in history as being UVM's only female president. Her presidency lasted only a few years and was marred by such issues as her dress, her demeanor, and her style of leadership, issues that would not be mentioned about men.

In 2006, the university conducted a search for a new provost. The search committee was aggressively looking for diverse candidates, and the final pool of candidates resulted in two men of color, one white male, and one white female. One might argue that the pool was very diverse, and in fact it was at 75%. The Women's Caucus of UVM and the ALANA Coalition of Faculty and Staff of Color were both involved with the hiring process by attending the open forums for each of the four candidates. However, the new provost hired was the white male.

The rollback of affirmative action policies means that public managers must remain creative about how their organizations attract and retain a diverse workforce. Affirmative action was never on its own supposed to end employment discrimination. Through it, however, the U.S. Equal Employment Opportunity Commission (EEOC) did seek to monitor alleged discrimination (R. Johnson, pers. comm., 2011). Nonetheless, endless lawsuits would make *affirmative action* a negative term. As recently as 2009, the U.S. Supreme Court ruled that bypassing white firefighters for promotions was unconstitutional (Cooper 2009). This case demonstrates that while affirmative action is not over yet, it is on its way to becoming a set of antiquated policies with no authority and no power.

Example 3.1: Advancement for Faculty of Color

Yolanda is a first-generation Mexican American college graduate and holds a PhD from an Ivy League university. She is a tenured professor at an elite New England public university. Yolanda enjoys teaching her classes and conducting her groundbreaking research. In the past few years, Yolanda has been passed over for many administrative positions at the university, including as the director of the race and culture program. She believes that the hiring committee was unaware of her talents and that the committee did not see her as a professional. Many of her colleagues know nothing about her background and are not necessarily inclined to find out. Yolanda's office is adorned with artifacts from Mexico such as handmade dolls and colorful woven rugs and artwork. She has been in the same office for the last several years, and not one of her colleagues has asked about the meaning of her art, dolls, or rugs. Still, Yolanda is one of the foremost experts in her field of romance languages. When the hiring committee did not recommend Yolanda for the position, the hiring official followed suit. Their reasons were the following: First, the hiring official felt that Yolanda was unapproachable and that students and other colleagues would have difficulty relating to her because of her strong demeanor. Second, the committee believed that Yolanda's Spanish accent was very heavy and too thick. Therefore, students and other faculty could not understand what she was saying. This evaluation is ironic given that Yolanda has received outstanding student evaluations for the last 10 years while being employed at the university. Finally, the committee believed that Yolanda lacked the administrative experience to direct the program, despite the fact that non-faculty of color at her university were consistently put in administrative positions with little or no experience.

At UVM, diversity has been on the agenda for years. Many of the department chairs have linked performance of faculty to their ability to conduct research on diversity issues and involvement with diversity organizations. Measuring performance on diversity has been predominately limited to faculty. Very little is being done in other areas of the university. For example, out of 12 college and school deans, only 1 is a person of color. In 2007, there were a total of 68 faculty of color (tenure and tenure track), while there were 514 white and non-Hispanic faculty (University of Vermont 2009a). People of color seem to increasingly populate the custodial levels at UVM. Most of these individuals are Asian-born or from other countries.

The issue certainly becomes that the theory of cultural competencies is viewed as needed in theory. In practice, however, many organizations still do not reflect the diversity of the communities they serve. The underlying assumption in affirmative action and cultural competence is an equal distribution of groups at all levels of an organization, not just at the top or the bottom.

3.6.1 Social Equity

George Frederickson (2005) traces the evolution of social equity in public administration, drawing a line back to Henri Fayol's (1949) "Principles of Management." Equity for employees in an organization was one of Fayol's 14 principles. Frederickson describes an expansion of the definition of equity from employees to issues of race and class inequality in the 1960s and the use of "social equity" becoming a feature in public administration. Initially, social equity was based on justice, fairness, and equality being a part of public administration. Over time, public administration acknowledged that government services were not as efficient and effective for all citizens, and thus social equity became the third pillar of public administration, after efficiency and effectiveness. Frederickson further expands the definition of equity beyond race, gender, and ethnicity to now include sexual preference, certain mental and physical conditions, language, and variations in economic circumstances. He also uses multiculturalism and diversity as a broader definition of social equity. Frederickson's work brings in the concept of equity (justice, fairness, and equality) applied socially to employees and citizens. Social equity has come to encompass all the differences, or diversities, that distinguish us. Diversities bring much richness into the landscape of humankind, but they also create fault lines, which can divide us. There are still many negative social perceptions and stereotypes of people who are perceived as different from the mainstream.

3.6.2 Cultural Competence in Public Administration

The field of public administration has discussed cultural competency primarily in terms of social equity, diversity, race, ethnicity, and multiculturalism. The initial concern in public administration was the underrepresentation of racial and ethnic minorities into organizations. Dolan and Rosenbloom (2003) see many scholars concerned with the extent to which women and racial minorities have been integrated into the public bureaucracies. In discussing the state of social equity in U.S. public administration, Frederickson (2005) sees the early development of social equity as focused on race and gender in employment, democratic representation, and service delivery. He also describes multiculturalism and diversity as suggesting a broader definition of social equity. Diversity has many aspects—including race, differences in ethnic norms and behavior, gender identity, sexual orientation, and technology—and that diversity brings its own challenges (Johnson, Reyes, and Smith 2009; White and Rice 2005).

Being culturally competent assumes an understanding of and respect for different ethnic and cultural systems (Bush 2000). Sue (2006) sees cultural competence as the knowledge and skills of a particular culture and describes the conceptual framework of Sue, Ivey, and Petersen (1996), which includes cultural awareness and beliefs, cultural knowledge, and cultural skills. The Tilford Group (2004) at Kansas State University developed a model of diversity competencies to prepare students to live and work in a diverse world.

Cultural competence is a developmental process that evolves over an extended period. Both individuals and organizations are at various levels of awareness, knowledge, and skills along the cultural competence continuum (adapted from Cross et al. 1989). Cultural competencies also imply a focus on race and ethnicity. Diversity competencies broaden the definition to include other characteristics such as gender, sexual orientation, and social class that create differences and are also as important as racial and ethnic distinctions. This book uses both terms interchangeably, and both encompass a definition of diversity that includes race and ethnicity as well as gender, sexual orientation, and social class.

3.7 Toward Cultural Competence Standards: Where We Stand Today

The research on cultural competence began with the federal requirement for culturally competent delivery of health care to immigrant and minority communities. Health care and social service professional associations and university centers researching culturally competent delivery of health care developed models for the culturally competent delivery of health care. The work of the professional associations was incorporated into the research of cultural competence in public administration and adapted for organizations.

NASW has developed a definition and standards for cultural competence in social work practice (2007). Georgetown University's Center for Child and Human Development, which contains the National Center for Cultural Competence, has conceptual frameworks, models, guiding values, and principles for cultural competence. The work done by professional associations and university centers on cultural competence is a good starting point for developing cultural competence for public managers. Their definitions are more general, making them better suited for public managers, who face the full range of diversity and race and ethnic employees and issues. The following section lists the definitions, models, standards, and performance measures for cultural and diversity competence. Much of this effort is a result of the research of federally mandated health and social services to immigrant and minority communities. One can see more easily the roots of the current work on cultural competence in public administration.

3.7.1 National Association of Social Workers

NASW has developed standards for cultural competence in social work practice. Some of the standards are based on the work of Pope-Davis and Coleman (1997) and on selected papers from the NASW Conference titled *Color in a White Society* (White 1982). Pope-Davis and Coleman (1997) address American Counseling Association requirements to mandate cultural counseling competencies, and their edited book addresses race, ethnicity, gender, and sexual orientation. The following passages contain excerpts from the NASW Indicators for the Achievement of the NASW Standards for Cultural Competence in Social Work Practice (2007).

NASW (2007) clearly defines cultural competence: "Cultural competence refers to the process by which individuals and systems respond respectfully and effectively to people of all cultures, languages, classes, races, ethnic backgrounds, religions, and other diversity factors in a manner that recognizes, affirms, and values the worth of individuals, families, and communities and protects and preserves the dignity of each." NASW further operationalizes cultural competence: "Cultural competence is the integration and transformation of knowledge about individuals and groups of individuals into specific standards, policies, practices, and attitudes used in appropriate cultural settings to increase the quality of services, thereby producing better outcomes (Davis and Donald 1997). Competence in cross-cultural functioning means learning new patterns of behavior and effectively applying them in appropriate settings."

NASW defines the standards for cultural competence in social work practice as follows:

1. Ethics and values
2. Self-awareness
3. Cross-cultural knowledge
4. Cross-cultural skills
5. Service delivery
6. Empowerment and advocacy
7. Diverse workforce
8. Professional education
9. Language diversity
10. Cross-cultural leadership

3.7.2 National Center for Cultural Competence

Georgetown University's National Center for Cultural Competence has done extensive work on cultural competence. The center provides conceptual frameworks, models, guiding values and principles, definitions of cultural and linguistic competence, and policies to advance and sustain cultural and linguistic competence. The center defines cultural competence as requiring organizations to have the following specific characteristics:

1. Have a defined set of values and principles and demonstrate behaviors, attitudes, policies, and structures that enable them to work effectively cross-culturally
2. Have the capacity to
   a. Value diversity
   b. Conduct self-assessment
   c. Manage the dynamics of difference
   d. Acquire and institutionalize cultural knowledge
   e. Adapt to diversity and the cultural contexts of the communities they serve
3. Incorporate the above in all aspects of policy making, administration, practice, and service delivery and systematically involve consumers, key stakeholders, and communities

The center has developed a checklist for policy-shaping individuals at the federal, state, local, and program levels. The checklist facilitates policy making for culturally and linguistically competent primary health care services. Several of the items from the checklist, which are appropriate for public managers, are replicated in the following list.

A primary care system, organization, or program should have the following characteristics:

1. A mission statement that articulates its principles, rationale, and values for culturally and linguistically competent health and mental health care service delivery
2. Policies and procedures that support a practice model, which incorporates culture in the delivery of services to culturally and linguistically diverse groups
3. Processes to review policies and procedures systematically to assess their relevance for the delivery of culturally and linguistically diverse groups
4. Policies and procedures for staff recruitment, hiring, and retention that will achieve the goal of a diverse and culturally competent workforce
5. Policies and resources to support ongoing professional development and in-service training (at all levels) for awareness, knowledge, and skills in the area of cultural and linguistic competence
6. Position descriptions and personnel performance measures that include skill sets related to cultural and linguistic competence
7. Fiscal support and incentives for the improvement of cultural competence at the board, agency, program, and staff levels

3.7.3 The Tilford Group

The Tilford Group of Kansas State University (2004) has also developed diversity competencies, which they define as the attitudes, attributes, knowledge, and skills that college and university students need to live in a globalized society. The models were developed from an extensive literature review, evaluation of training programs, and focus groups (Johnson and Rivera 2007).

The Tilford Group's diversity competencies for college and university students include the following:

1. Knowledge: Awareness and understanding needed to live and work in a diverse world
2. Cultural self-awareness: Ability to understand one's ethnic self-identification
3. Diverse ethnic groups: Understanding different cultures and ethnic groups
4. Social, political, economic, and historical framework: Understanding how sociopolitical, economic, and historical factors and events affect racial groups around the world
5. Changing demographics: Understanding how changes affect race
6. Understanding of population dynamics related to ethnic minority and majority citizens

7. Personal attributes: Traits needed to live and work in a diverse world
   a. Flexibility: Adaptability to a changing world
   b. Respect: Appreciation for differences in others
   c. Empathy: Ability to respect another person's culture and perspective
8. Skills: Behaviors and performance tasks needed to live in a diverse world
   a. Cross-cultural communication: Verbal and nonverbal communications with different groups
   b. Teamwork: Ability to work with diverse groups toward a common goal
   c. Conflict resolution: Ability to resolve cultural conflicts
   d. Critical thinking: Ability to use inductive and deductive reasoning
   e. Language development: Ability to speak and write in more than one language
   f. Leadership development: Ability to provide diversity leadership

Siegel, Haugland, and Chambers (2003) have selected performance measures and benchmarks for assessing organizational cultural competency for health care delivery. They used an expert panel to gain agreement on performance measures and benchmarks. The performance measures and benchmarks appropriate for public mangers are shown in Table 3.2.

3.8 Summary and Conclusion

Cultural competence was defined in the context of delivery of government services to immigrant and minority communities. Some of these communities had members with limited English proficiency. There has been a series of legislation mandating culturally competent delivery of services. The federal government provided support for research of cultural competence. There are several aspects of the research and definition of cultural competence that are helpful to public managers:

1. Cultural competence is useful for cross-cultural interactions, and the culturally sensitive attitudes and behaviors are skills or competencies that can be learned.
2. Understanding the cultural characteristics and appreciating or respecting people from other cultures is the first part of cultural competence.
3. Culturally sensitive and relevant communication is important.

The business community frames cultural competence as cultural intelligence. The impetus for cultural intelligence arose from the failure of U.S. expatriates working in other countries to adjust to the cultural requirements of working overseas. Globalization has increased international business opportunities and led to more diverse organizations. The meaning of diversity is evolving into cultural diversity with the increasing cultural diversity brought about by the demographic

Table 3.2   Organizational Cultural Competence Performance Measures and Benchmarks

Measure	Benchmark
1. Cultural Competence as Part of the Mission Statement	Mission statement must include goal of achieving Cultural Competence.
2. Cultural Competence Plan of Organization	Cultural Competence must exist in the following components: 1. Objectives 2. Strategies 3. Implementation plan with lines of responsibility and a timetable 4. Dissemination plan 5. Oversight method 6. Management accountability
3. Cultural Competence Plan Requirement for Organizational Components	There must be a requirement for organizational components of the administrative entity to have a cultural component.
4. Responsibility for Cultural Components	A person or position responsible for Cultural Competence must be named and must be part of the management or leadership level.
5. Budget	There is an identifiable provision of monies earmarked for Cultural Competence activities.

Source: Based on Siegel, C., Haugland, G., and Chambers, E., *Administration and Policy in Mental Health,* 31 (2), 2003.

changes. The emphasis on intelligence and its relationship to emotional intelligence brings into the equation a mental and motivational aspect (Kumar, Rose, and Subramaniam 2008). Amiri, Moghimi, and Kazemi (2010) see cultural diversity in organizations creating problems for individuals and organizations. They found a significant correlation between cultural intelligence and employee behavior. The discussion on cultural intelligence expands cultural competence beyond the delivery of government services to immigrant and minority communities to include organizational diversity. It still includes the emphasis on learning about others' cultures and cultural characteristics. There is also an understanding that the lack of cultural competence can lead to misunderstandings and conflicts that lead to organizational failure (Farley and Ang 2003; Johnson et al. 2006; Thomas and

Inkson 2004). Goleman (2000) sees diversity as an opportunity to develop cultural competence or intelligence. Seeing the opportunity in diversity implies having the flexibility to adapt to changing demographics. This view adds to the earlier list two more aspects to consider:

1. Lack of understanding different cultures and cultural characteristics can lead to misunderstandings, and resulting conflict can lead to organizational failure.
2. Flexibility and adaptability are necessary to take advantage of the increasing diversity.

The work on cultural competence and leadership brings into the discussion the concept of leader–follower dynamics, with the cultural diversity of followers seen as being the different cultures and ethnicities at work (Northouse 2007). Thomas and Inkson (2004) see culturally intelligent leadership as focusing on the culture and expectations of the followers, as well as on the cultural characteristics of the followers. The cultural characteristics are described by Hall (1976) and Hofstede (1980, 2001). The emphasis is on effective cross-cultural interactions among people.

There are also organizational components to cultural competence. The organizational components are similar to those in any other program, except they are focused on cultural competence. The efforts require cultural competence to be part of the mission statement; it should involve a strategic plan, accountability, responsibility, and its own budget. To implement the organizational requirements of cultural competence is a management and leadership task. The leadership of an organization can develop a cultural competence initiative or program. The entire management chain is involved in the implementation, and each level will have a different level of responsibilities.

Chapter 4

Cultural Competencies

Peace is the respect for the rights of others.

Benito Juarez

Example 4.1: Creating a Team

Pablo is a faculty member in a university on the Texas–Mexico border. He has supervised students who have conducted research for the Mexican government and for nongovernmental officials and presented them with the results. Pablo is a Mexican American born and reared in Texas, and he does not speak Spanish very well. He is also not familiar with Mexican government protocols. At the first meeting and anytime he meets new officials he says, "I don't speak Spanish very well. I have been away in Texas for many years and did not get the chance to speak Spanish, and I also am not very familiar with Mexican government protocols." The Mexican officials always assure him the meeting can be conducted in English. Pablo responds, "Thank you, that is very kind and generous, but I really would like to learn to speak better Spanish, and I really need to learn Mexican protocols if my students are going to continue to do research in Mexico. I really would like your help. Would you help me with the words that I don't know and please let me know what protocols I need to know for these meetings and for any presentations?" All the Mexican officials agree to help.

When asked why he takes this approach, considering the meetings can be conducted in English, Pablo responded:

> I first started doing this because I needed to get better at speaking Spanish and I really needed to learn the protocols to create more opportunities for my students. This seemed like the quickest and easiest way for me to learn, and then I noticed something interesting was happening. We got along better, and we felt more like friends than business associates. There was a warmer feeling when the meetings ended; and by helping me, they had a

69

vested interest in seeing that I was successful. We had somehow become a team. If I made a mistake, it did not create an awkward moment, but a very friendly opportunity to demonstrate that this is the way that we do it. My Spanish is now much better, and I learned that the way we do a hug, or *abrazo*, when we meet in Texas is different from the way it is done in Mexico. You know, there is something very empowering for others when they help you learn something they know well. After the presentations or meetings, we can talk about our respective cultural differences because now it is an educational opportunity and not a divide.

By inviting the Mexican officials to participate and help, Pablo has created one group or team from two different groups and, thereby, a supportive environment for learning about other cultures. He learns from those who know best what he needs to be successful. By admitting that he is unfamiliar with their business culture, he can accept his own mistakes as a learning opportunity and not a moment of awkwardness. Pablo does not need to be defensive about what he does not know. His lack of knowledge is an opportunity for the others to help, which empowers them and involves them in the success of the presentations. They have a vested interest in seeing that Pablo is successful. As part of the discussion, Pablo can educate them about the way business is done in his own culture. At the end of the presentation, Pablo and the Mexican officials with whom he does business are one team, not two separate groups. The beginnings of a good professional relationship have been established.

4.1 Introduction

The research on cultural competence, as described in Chapter 3 and the Appendix, coupled with the concept of cultural intelligence and with culturally competent and intelligent leadership, shows the two aspects of cultural competence: the cross-cultural interactions with culturally diverse individuals and the culturally competent organization. This chapter focuses on the cross-cultural competencies necessary to interact successfully with and manage culturally diverse employees.

4.2 Developing the Foundation Cultural Competencies

The research on cultural competence has focused on the delivery of government services to a culturally different community. Whereas a public employee or manager can learn the culture of that community, managers of today's organizations face a more complicated challenge. Employees reflect the full diversity of the communities they serve, and so a manager will have to manage and work with employees from many different cultures as well as full range of diverse employees. Employees are mobile and move to other parts of the organization or to other organizations. Also, new employees join the organization, frequently bringing in new culturally diverse backgrounds. Thus, learning each culture and diversity that employees bring into an organization becomes extremely difficult and sometimes impossible.

The foundation cultural competencies are the competencies that a manager or employee would use when managing or interacting with other employees. These competencies assume that a manager is not familiar with the culture or diversity of the employee. When a manager does not know about an employee's culture or diversity background, it is important to understand that cultural differences exist and can affect the working relationship.

The foundation cultural competencies are derived from the research on culturally competent delivery of services complemented with the research on cultural intelligence from the business community and culturally competent leadership (described in Chapter 3). This approach uses concepts from the research that are appropriate for an organizational setting where managers supervise culturally diverse employees and teams are culturally diverse.

Cultural competency begins with understanding culture and the diverse cultural characteristics. Understanding culture is a core concept in cultural competence, cultural intelligence, and culturally competent leadership. This approach focuses on the cultural characteristics in cultural intelligence and culturally competent and intelligent leadership. The setting for cultural intelligence and culturally competent leadership is the organization. The cultural characteristics in question include monochronic and polychronic worldviews, studied by Hall (1976); Hofstede (1980, 2001), whose work on these cultural dimensions is most referenced; Northouse (2007); and the GLOBE studies (House et al. 2004).

Communication is the second cultural competency. Communication in the delivery of government services to culturally diverse communities usually refers to linguistic competency, or understanding the language of non-English speakers. The 1965 Social Security Act requires Medicaid to provide "culturally and linguistically appropriate services." The 1990 Disadvantaged Minority Health Improvement Act requires that health professionals address cultural and linguistic barriers to the delivery of health care. Linguistic competence is also included in the Georgetown University National Center for Cultural Competence and The Tilford Group diversity competencies. It can be assumed that most employees in the organization will speak English; it is also worthwhile to consider that cultural differences can arise out of the diverse cultural characteristics of employees. The cultural differences can create situations where culturally diverse employees can interpret the same communication in different ways, leading to misunderstandings.

From the research on culturally competent and intelligent leadership come pertinent lessons for managing multicultural employees. Thomas and Inkson (2004) see a common ground at the intersection of the leadership style, the cultural expectations of the followers, and the organizational norms. Chin and Gaynier (2006) also bring the organization into the discussion. They also see managing the cultural diversity of the workforce as a key factor in building and sustaining organizational integrity and competitiveness.

Being formal institutions with formal requirements, organizations create their own culture. The concept of an organizational culture—a concept that has been recognized for many years—can include both the formal and the informal organization. For example, Connolly (2008) explores whether the organizational culture is a plus or a minus for the organization. There may be employees of color who may not be familiar with the requirements for success in organizations. The organizational culture can be viewed as the common ground that brings together the leadership style of the manager and the diverse cultural characteristics of the employees.

The fourth foundation cultural competency is being adaptable and flexible. Taylor (1994, 154) considers intercultural competence as "an adaptive capacity based on an inclusive and integrative world view." Chang (2007) sees cultural competence as integrative and transformative and learned through the experience of internal discovery and adjustment. This notion is embodied in Chang's three levels: encounter and recognize, familiarize and adjust, and transform and enlighten. Being adaptive is part of cultural intelligence. Kumar, Rose, and Subramaniam (2008) see the adaptability as part of their motivational and behavioral aspects of cultural intelligence. Amiri, Moghimi, and Kazemi (2010) see cultural intelligence as having a significant correlation with effective employee behavior. Earley (2002) and Earley and Ang (2003, 283) have defined cultural intelligence as "a person's capability to adapt as s/he interacts with others from different cultural regions." The Georgetown University National Center for Cultural Competence also includes adaptability in its definition of cultural competence. There, researchers see adaptability as the ability to adjust to diversity and the cultural contexts of the communities to be served. Flexibility is one of the personal attributes of cultural competence as defined by The Tilford Group's diversity competencies (2004), in which flexibility is defined as the ability to adapt to a changing world. Adaptability and flexibility are also emotional intelligence competencies. These competencies will be required in the United States, which is certainly undergoing unprecedented demographic changes. The current shift from a monocultural to an increasingly multicultural workplace will create many new cross-cultural situations. Being flexible will allow managers and employees to adapt to the coming changes.

The fifth competency is being inclusive. Taylor (1994) sees intercultural competence as being inclusive and integrative. Thomas and Inkson (2004) open the door to inclusiveness as a cultural competency by including a focus on the culture and expectations of the followers. In a study of multicultural executives conducted in conjunction with Columbia Business School, Korn/Ferry International (1998) describes the discrimination faced by many of the executives of color. Employees of color and culturally diverse employees may experience the organization workplace differently than employees from the dominant culture. Barak and Levin (2002) examine the relationship between diversity characteristics, inclusion, fairness, stress, and social support and the outcome variables of job satisfaction and well-being of employees with diverse racial and ethnic backgrounds. Their findings indicate that women and employees who are racial and ethnic minorities are more likely to feel excluded and to feel lower levels of job satisfaction and well-being. Their research adds an important element to cultural competence in managing a diverse workforce and the importance of inclusion of those who are different from the organizational mainstream.

Inclusiveness is one of the foundation competencies because it can help foster the sense that we are all part of the same team. One can communicate inclusiveness by using words such as *we* and identifying the manager and the employee as members of the same team. Managers can also communicate inclusiveness by visiting the diverse employees and not just spending the majority of time with culturally similar managers and employees. Inviting culturally different employees to join one's social networks is also being inclusive. (Inclusiveness is discussed in other chapters as well.)

4.3 The Foundation Cultural Competencies

Many people will agree that a work group composed of very diverse people can be more effective than a work group where everyone is similar. Diversity can enrich a group, but it also brings in the possibilities of misunderstandings and discord. To make the diverse work group more effective, the group's cultural diversity has to be managed so that it contributes to the members' joint efforts, and doing that requires cultural competence or being cross-culturally socially adept.

The foundation cultural competencies are based on the assumption that the manager is not familiar with each employee's cultural characteristics. The manager should be aware that differences can exist that will affect the relationship between the employee and management. Each employee is the best person to educate the manager about his or her particular culture and background. The manager should know that focusing on developing a good working relationship comes first. Developing a safe and supportive environment cultivates a good relationship.

The foundation cultural competencies are designed to give a manager the skills to create a supportive environment where he or she learns from the situation and from each individual employee. The supportive environment then leads to good working relationships. The emphasis is on developing the communication skills to create the supportive environment and the good working relationships. Such skills are the foundation for bridging the differences that exist and allow co-workers to feel comfortable in discussing those differences. Any misunderstandings that may arise in these discussions are then easily resolved.

Developing standards creates a floor and ceiling to evaluate a manager's and an employee's effectiveness in achieving cultural competence. The minimum standards are designed to prevent problems and represent a starting point for the organization to move toward cultural competence. Successful standards are designed to create the culturally competent organization.

The foundation cultural competencies, shown in Table 4.1, are the core cultural competencies. They are used to develop a supportive environment to bridge differences. They create an environment where differences can be discussed in a way that brings people together rather than drives them apart. As basic competencies, they are used in any interactions with employees, other managers, community groups, and constituent groups and in international collaborations. The foundation cultural competencies do not assume one knows much about another person's culture or diversity. The competencies are designed to create a supportive and gracious environment for cross-cultural interactions. Once this supportive environment has been created, discussion about differences can bring the people together instead of creating differences and misunderstandings about the differences.

The relationships among the foundation cultural competencies can be seen in Figure 4.1. Communication is the central cultural competence, which ties the other competencies together. Communication expresses respect and creates common ground. Common ground focuses on areas that bring people together, not on areas that emphasize their differences. Inclusion brings others into work and informal

Table 4.1 Foundation Cultural Competencies

Cultural Competencies	Successful Standards	Minimum Standards
1. Respecting and understanding diverse employees	Seek to understand other cultures and other types of diversity	Acknowledge that there are different cultures
2. Communicating with diverse employees	Communicate respect, understanding, and inclusiveness	Understand that words, gestures, jokes, and expressions may mean something very different in another culture
3. Creating common ground or a shared culture	Use organizational culture to establish a common ground and shared culture	Solicit and listen to others' perspectives
4. Adaptability or flexibility	Institute changes for tomorrow's changing demographics	Respond to today's demographic changes
5. Inclusiveness as a way to create effective teams and collaboration	Include others in formal and informal organizational networks	Connect with other social and informal networks

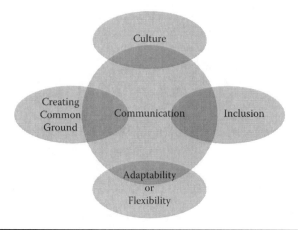

Figure 4.1 Foundation cultural competencies.

networks. Adaptability or flexibility prepares the organization for the increased demographic changes the future will bring.

4.4. Respecting and Understanding Culture

The research on cultural competence discussed in Chapter 3 shows the importance of understanding the culture and cultural characteristics of others. Culture is defined as learned beliefs, values, rules, norms, symbols, and traditions that a people hold in common (Northouse 2007). These qualities are shared and evolve over time. Culture is transmitted to other members of the group. Multiculturalism is the existence of multiple cultures in a society or system, and diversity is the existence within an organization or other system of different subcultures categorized by race, gender, ethnicity, sexual orientation, and age (Northouse 2007). For Yukl (2002), managing diversity increases creativity and leads to better decisions and better leaders who foster appreciation and tolerate for diversity. (Cultural characteristics or dimensions are discussed in Chapters 1 and 3.)

In the United States, with its long history of immigration, it is difficult to determine how closely employees relate to the culture of their country of origin. Individuals may be third generation with only a vague understanding of the culture of their country of origin. On the other hand, some employees may have strong ties and a clear understanding of the culture of their country of origin. Appearances and names are not good guides to how close employees are to their roots. It can be embarrassing to make the wrong assumption about how closely another employee is to his or her country of origin. Establishing a good working relationship can create the supportive environment to learn about the culture and cultural characteristics of employees.

In many cultures, business is conducted through the relationships created by individuals. Many organizations, though, place their emphasis on the business at hand or on the bottom line, not on personal relationships. For these organizations, relationships come second. Creating good professional relationships is worthwhile, however. When working with professionals from other cultures, creating a good working relationship is facilitated by first creating a good workplace cross-cultural relationship. The basis of the cross-cultural relationship is that employees bring their cultural selves into the workplace and that their cultural outlook may have a different value system than the organizational culture.

Cross-cultural respect also means providing multicultural employees tough challenges and expecting the best performance (Goleman 2000). Cross-cultural respect and understanding do not mean making excuses or expecting less from multicultural employees. A good cross-cultural relationship makes it much easier to work through difficult issues. The foundation for good cross-cultural working relationships is respect and understanding of the different cultural characteristics.

Table 4.2 lists cultural competencies for respecting and understanding other cultures. The cultural competencies are adapted from the research on cultural competence. The table is set up so that a manager can use it for a manager's performance evaluation.

A manager creates respect by showing that cultural diversity is valued and important for accomplishing the vision and mission of the organization. The standard for respect begins when the manager articulates how valuable cultural diversity is to the success of the organization. Many organizations have policies that express their value for diversity. The manager can then discuss how the organizational policy applies to the organizational unit for which the manager is responsible. Developing others is one of the competencies for OPM Executive Core Qualification (ECQ) 2 Leading People. Employee development contributes to the accomplishments of organizational goals and objectives and is provided by giving employees feedback and opportunities for formal and informal training. Where formal employee development plans are used, the manager will discuss how leveraging diversity or cultural competence is to become part of the employee's development; the manager will also reiterate how important cultural competence is to meeting organizational goals and objectives in line with the mission and vision of the organization.

Understanding how to develop respect for and a knowledge of other cultures begins with reexamining the golden rule: "I treat others in the way I want to be treated." Although an age-old adage we repeat without much thought, this rule makes sense on some level; if we treat others as well as we want to be treated, we will be treated well in return. This rule works well in a monocultural setting, where everyone is working within the same cultural framework. In a multicultural setting, where words, gestures, beliefs, and perspectives may have different meanings, this rule has an unintended consequence; it can send a message that my culture is better than yours. It can also create a frustrating situation where we believe we are doing what is right, but what we are doing is not being interpreted in the way in

Table 4.2 Measures for Respecting and Understanding Other Cultures

Measures the Manager Undertakes	Unsatisfactory	Satisfactory	Excellent	Outstanding
1. Has attended training on cultural competence and cultural diversity				
2. Articulates the value of cultural diversity to the success of the organizational unit				
3. Requires cultural competencies in employee development plans				
4. Provides feedback to employees on cultural competencies				
5. Gives employees opportunities to attend cultural competence and cultural diversity workshops				
6. Gives culturally diverse employees challenging assignments				
7. Makes an effort to hire culturally diverse employees				
8. Explains organizational culture to employees				
9. Understands the opportunities and challenges that cultural diversity can bring				
10. Mentors culturally diverse employees				
11. Successfully meets the other cultural competencies: communication, creating common ground or a shared culture, adaptability and flexibility, and inclusiveness				

which it was meant. A word or a gesture intended to show how well intentioned we are may, for example, have negative connotations in another culture. This miscommunication can lead to problems. If we are doing the right thing, as we believe, then the problem must be the other person. This is not the path to building good relationships.

4.4.1 Cautions

It is always wise to proceed with caution and understanding. When interacting with others, we interact with individuals who can vary widely within their broad classifications. It is common for many second- or third-generation children of immigrants not to speak the language of their parents. To assume they speak the language of their parents can make for an awkward and embarrassing situation. American culture especially as portrayed in music and television can level many cultural differences. Whether the diversity is race, ethnicity, gender, sexual orientation, or social class, it is better not to make assumptions about how individuals feel about it. A much better strategy is to include their help in guiding you through what is important to them. Never make or act on assumptions about others until you have checked with that person to see if your assumptions are accurate.

In the workplace, these different cultures and employees who bring other diversities into the workplace converge to become part of an organizational culture. While respect for others usually implies learning about fellow employees, it also suggests that employees who are part of the diversity may themselves need to learn how to navigate the organizational culture.

It is common for members of one culture not to fully understand the social cues of another culture. Being unable to read the nonverbal and even sometimes verbal cues of others makes communicating well difficult. As part of a leadership program for managing diversity, the participants, who were African American, were given 360-degree instruments, which measured their emotional competence and resiliency. The 360-degrees feedback refers to a circle in which feedback is provided by an individual's subordinates, peers, supervisors, and sometimes clients or customers to construct an in-depth assessment.

Five dimensions made up the instrument:

1. Emotional intelligence
2. Resilience
3. Organizational climate
4. Leadership style
5. Managerial style

The participants' peers, supervisors, and employees rated them as having difficulties reading others' emotional and nonverbal cues. They also rated the participants as having difficulty understanding other employees' perspectives. Nonverbal and emotional cues are interpreted differently across cultures, as well as across gender lines and social classes. Individuals interpret nonverbal and emotional cues based on the culture or social class with which they are familiar. This can easily lead to misunderstandings that can degenerate into manager–employee problems. It is not enough to learn about someone else's culture and the differences in that culture. Respect means helping others understand how the organizational culture may differ from their own culture. It helps them, and it helps the manager.

Example 4.2: Reading Cross-Cultural Cues

Alima is a General Schedule 15 (GS-15) in a federal agency. The daughter of immigrants from the Middle East, she had a reputation as being hard-charging, very knowledgeable, and always prepared. Alima was invited by the assistant secretary to make a presentation to the secretary and other assistant secretaries of the agency on a new project she had developed. After the presentation, her colleagues asked her, "How did it go?" "It was terrible," she answered. "I couldn't read them, and I just kept talking and talking. One assistant secretary told me that I had already convinced him, and if I kept talking he would withhold his support." When the assistant secretary who had invited Alima to make the presentation returned, Alima asked her, "How did it go?" The assistant secretary answered, "They said you had such a hard-charging reputation and that is why they agreed to hear your project, and they were surprised and disappointed that you wimped out." "I couldn't get a read on how they were reacting to my presentation," responded Alima, "and I got nervous."

Respecting other cultures implies a one-way interaction in which the dominant culture respects and learns about the other culture. True respect, however, using the cultural competence model, should include a two-way interaction. When two cultures meet, each culture should learn about and respect the other culture. In the workplace, doing so may mean helping someone unfamiliar with the organizational culture learn about it and understand it.

The traditional world of work reflects the cultural perspectives that are predominately male and Western European (Cook, Heppner, and O'Brien 2002; Worthington, Flores, and Navarro 2005). In this perspective, the role of work is more central and individualistic than in more family- and group-oriented cultures. In family-oriented cultures, the family and group are primary, so decisions revolve around the family first. Employees from family-oriented cultures, such as those found in many parts of Latin America and Asia, may be perceived as unfocused on their work. Others who come from cultures where negotiating is a way of life may negotiate for everything and be perceived as overbearing.

Organizations have unique cultures that blend their technical work with the social and cultural characteristics that employees bring into the organization. The accounting department can have a very different organizational culture than the public affairs department within that same organization. Helping an employee bridge the cultural or other diversity characteristics into the organizational culture communicates a message of inclusiveness to the employee. He or she is part of the organization, and the differences the employee brings into the organization are contributing to the effectiveness of his or her department.

Respect requires *empathy*, defined as "the identification with or vicarious experiencing of the feelings, thoughts, etc., of another" (*Random House Webster's College Dictionary* 1997, 428). When meeting people from a different culture, take a second to put yourself in their shoes. What are they experiencing, and what are their expectations? How can I make that person more comfortable with our interaction? How can I be gracious? Showing empathy can be as simple as making someone physically comfortable by creating a comfortable environment in which cross-cultural discussions can occur. Also helpful is understanding the impact of our words and actions on others who are culturally different. This understanding is especially important for managers, supervisors, and others in positions of authority. If you view yourself as a gracious host, you have gone a long way to show respect for others. Although playing gracious host may seem to be a great deal of effort and work, the payoff is in having not only better relationships and fewer problems but also more effective work groups. As someone once said, "If you don't have time to do it right the first time, where are you going to find the time to fix it?"

Universities value knowledge, and as commonly noted, "Knowledge is power." Thus it can be difficult to comprehend that starting with little knowledge can actually be helpful in developing multicultural relationships. Instead of proceeding based on what we think we know about someone else's culture, a better approach is expressing our interest in learning about that person's culture and perspective. A conversation using this approach would start with "I don't know much about your culture or background, and I would like to learn more. What do I need to know?" Using this approach lets others know you are unfamiliar with their culture, which makes it easier for them to forgive cultural missteps, since they have been made aware of your lack of knowledge. Pablo, in the example at the beginning of this chapter, provides a good example of this approach. Expressing interest in someone's culture is an expression of respect.

Different cultures handle personal and family questions quite differently. In some cultures, such questions are simply a way of developing good relationships. Other cultures view personal questions as intrusive and impolite. Using a question such as, "What do I need to know?" lets the other person determine the parameters of the discussion. It also validates and acknowledges the importance of the knowledge the other person brings to the discussion, another sign of respect. The same rules apply to diverse and multicultural managers and employees. In today's multicultural organizations, there can be many employees with varied diversities from differing cultures. Treating someone with respect does not mean that one agrees with his or her perspective. It means that one is acknowledging what is important to the other person.

Knowing and understanding an employee's cultural background and characteristics is just one part of a professional workplace relationship. Managers and employees are still expected to be knowledgeable about their profession and work.

4.5 Communicating with Culturally Diverse Employees

A safe environment is created by developing good working relationships, fostering good cross-cultural communication, and communicating that everyone is a part of a team working on a common purpose.

This approach has three purposes. The first purpose is to develop good working relationships and, consequently, good long-term relationships with employees, colleagues, and other managers. Such relationships are not necessarily friendships, though friendships can develop over time. The second purpose is to communicate what kind of person one is, that is, communicating in way that leaves a good impression and strengthens one's reputation and credibility. Managers can now work with diverse employees to modify any cultural characteristics that are holding an employee back. The third purpose is to communicate that you are a team working together for the mutual success of the team members. Creating good relationships creates the common ground to explore sensitive topics in a positive way. Measures for effective communication are shown in Table 4.3.

Culturally competent managers are sensitive to differences across gender lines, sexual orientation, and social class. Such managers are encouraged not to make assumptions. For example, many individuals consider themselves biracial, making it difficult to ascertain their culture or social background. In such cases, it is best not to assume an individual's identity. Racial and ethnic classifications are broad and include people with origins in diverse countries with cultures that may not be similar. Managers are encouraged to learn from each employee about his or her particular background. The employee is the best person to provide the information the manager needs. The manager lets the employee determine his or her own comfort level, which keeps the discussion in a comfortable and supportive environment, preventing any misunderstandings that may cause the conversation to degenerate into an awkward situation.

Example 4.3: Communicating Inclusiveness and Being Part of the Team

Kathleen walks into Bill's office and says, "Bill, I just got a call from Public Affairs and they need a response to a congressional inquiry. A Congresswoman who sits on our authorization committee is unhappy with the way our office treated one of her constituents. They need our response by tomorrow afternoon. What do you think is the best way to get this done in this timeframe, and what can I do to best help you in getting this done by tomorrow afternoon?"

What does Kathleen communicate in this scenario?

1. We are working on this together; we are a team.
2. I value your judgment and expertise. (She validates Bill's expertise.)
3. I am here to give you what you need to get it done. I have your back.

This seems simple and not worth mentioning, but many employees of color do not feel part of the organizational culture. Some may have had the experience

Table 4.3 Measures for Communication

Measures the Manager Undertakes	Unsatisfactory	Satisfactory	Excellent	Outstanding
1. Understands cross-cultural verbal and nonverbal communications				
2. Provides constructive feedback to culturally diverse employees				
3. Communicates a safe environment where culturally diverse employees feel comfortable sharing their cultural characteristics				
4. Communicates in a way that lets employees know they are each a valued member of the team				
5. Communicates the importance of cross-cultural relationships in creating effective work teams				
6. Understands how cross-cultural misunderstandings can be created				

of being promoted and having fellow employees tell them, for instance, "You only got promoted because you are woman or because you a minority" (Korn/Ferry International 1998). In other instances, many multicultural employees may be aware of the acrimonious discussions of immigration. For them, communicating inclusion—we are a team—has enormous motivational value. Providing validation and an expectation of excellent performance also communicate respect. Knowing that they have their manager's support also has great motivational value for multicultural employees.

Treating someone else with respect is always a good foundation for starting a conversation. One shows respect by understanding that another person's experiences are important to them. Respect means acknowledging that someone may experience a situation differently. Acknowledging someone else's experience does not necessarily invalidate one's own experience. Doing so simply means that multiple perceptions exist and are accepted. It may require flexibility on the part of the manager, however, to accept that there may be multiple perceptions at work and not just one. Respect means having the other person determine where his or her comfort level may be, given the specific situation. It also means that as important as it is to listen to what is said, it can be just as important to listen to what is not said. What is not said can help the listener understand where sensitive areas are likely to be.

Part of showing respect is making the other person comfortable. As a good working relationship develops, it will be easier to talk about previously uncomfortable topics. Inadvertent gaffes are less likely to occur. Asking directed and pointed questions can make some people uncomfortable. Letting the other person determine his or her comfort level is one way to create a more comfortable atmosphere. Listening to what is not said lets the listener know where uncomfortable areas may lie. Staying out of the uncomfortable areas keeps one from creating an awkward situation.

4.6 Creating Common Ground or a Shared Culture

As organizations reflect the increasing diversity of society, many employees will bring into the work situation the cultural characteristics they have acquired from their family's culture. Some of these characteristics will fit well into a work situation. Other cultural characteristics may create inaccurate perceptions of the employees. There are cultures where, for example, it is considered impolite to be direct and look directly at others. Some employees may seem more passive and expect to be told what to do. Other employees may be more assertive and sometimes even aggressive in their interactions with others. Although it is better to understand the cultural attributes that employees bring into an organization when there is a lot of diversity, doing so is not always possible. Creating common ground or a shared culture is a mechanism for working with diverse employees whether one knows their cultural attributes or not. In essence, creating common ground or a shared culture is using the organizational culture to create a miniculture with which all employees can identify.

As shown in Table 4.4 and explained in the paragraphs that follow, managers can take specific measures to create common ground and a shared organizational culture. From initial career planning to the establishment of cross-cultural mentoring arrangements, these measures help multicultural employees become valued and successful members of the organization.

Organizations are a good place to create common ground and a shared culture. As discussed previously, organizations already have their own cultures. Subunits within an organization can create their own organizational culture. The technical parts of the organization may have a different culture than the public affairs office. The organizational culture can become common ground to learn about others' diversities and cultures. Regardless of the organizational unit and its culture, the work can become the unifying common ground. The discussions on diversities revolve around how to be more effective in the workplace. The discussions are not about my culture versus your culture but, rather, about how we increase organizational effectiveness with everyone reaping the rewards of higher productivity.

Creating common ground or a shared culture is putting all assumptions on the table and making that strategy part of your everyday working style. Common ground provides everyone with the same cultural understanding and, therefore, creates a level playing field. Organizations typically have their own culture, which can vary from organization to organization. Common ground makes explicit the organizational culture and what is required of employees to succeed and thrive in it. The organizational culture becomes the unifying culture.

If you are a manager, an easy way to have this conversation is to make it part of helping an employee to create a long-term career plan. Creating a long-term career plan for an employee is the organization's and the manager's way of communicating that the employee is indeed a part of the long-term future of the organization. The career plan becomes the roadmap and the opportunity to discuss what is required for long-term success. By agreeing to the career plan, the employee agrees to be coached on what it takes to be successful. Working with employees on long-term careers has a secondary purpose: It lets the managers know what employees expect from the organization. Some employees may want to rise as high as they can in the organization. Others may be happy where they are. Now the manager knows what to expect from each employee. (A more detailed discussion on developing long-term career plans will be detailed in Chapter 8.)

Treating others with respect while communicating that you are a team that is working together helps to create common ground. Common ground is that area in which people are comfortable working together. It is that area where the participants work as a team to be successful. It is that area where we all agree to take the next step together. It is also that area where we are mutually supporting each other

Table 4.4 Measures for Creating Common Ground and a Shared Culture

Measures the Manager Undertakes	Unsatisfactory	Satisfactory	Excellent	Outstanding
1. Formulates formal career development plans for each employee				
2. Mentors employees (see sample mentoring agreement on DVD)				
3. Explains organizational requirements (e.g., the cultural characteristics) required for success				
4. Provides feedback to employee on how employee is viewed by others (part of mentoring agreement)				
5. Encourages feedback from employees				
6. Encourages employee to develop cross-functional relationships				
7. Encourages employee to have cross-cultural mentors				

and know what to expect from each other. Common ground is the result of the relationship that has been created.

4.7 Being Adaptable and Flexible

Flexibility and adaptability are recognized as key competencies for executives in today's changing world. Flexibility and adaptability are also key foundation cultural competencies. Adaptability is a key component of the emotional competence model developed by the Hay Group (2004a). The manager shows flexibility and adaptability by recognizing demographic and social changes and adapting his managerial style to the new reality by becoming culturally competent. The manager also adapts the organizational strategy appropriate to the organizational level for which he or she is responsible. Culturally competent managers undertake measures that reflect their organization's adaptability and flexibility (see Table 4.5). The managerial cultural competencies are designed to create a safe environment for this cultural exchange to happen and to lay the foundation for a good working relationship.

Cultural competence is easier to learn in an organizational or workplace context, where discussions are bounded by organizational and workplace etiquette and legal requirements about the working environment that is created. It is not the place to get into discussions about assimilation versus multiculturalism or about an individual's opinion of same-sex marriage. Such discussions are held outside the organizational framework. Cultural competence in the workplace happens in a more limited and bounded environment, but it creates a solid foundation that can be extended to international relations and interactions with multicultural communities.

Employees who have been doing the same job for many years tend to develop a set way of doing their work and fixed expectations of what they require from employees who report to them. If their approach is an effective style and has made them successful, such long-term employees will not see a reason to change. They would probably agree with the saying "If it is not broken, don't fix it." As long as the environment or the organization does not change, maintaining the status quo is effective. Change means extra effort and work. However, the environment is changing and in ways that require changes from employees. When an environment changes, what was successful in the past will not necessarily be successful in the new environment. Thus even long-term employees must be adaptable and flexible.

The first step in becoming adaptable or flexible is to accept that the environment has changed. Developing the flexibility to adapt to change begins with answering "Why do I have to change?" The answer is clear: because there has been a fundamental change and what worked before is not working now. New skills are needed. It is reasonable to expect employees to bring appropriate technical and professional skills into organizations. Employees will also bring their social and cultural selves into organizations, and with demographic changes come employees with different

Table 4.5   Measures for Adaptability and Flexibility

Measures the Manager Undertakes	Unsatisfactory	Satisfactory	Excellent	Outstanding
1. Articulates the demographic and cultural changes in the organization				
2. Formulates a long-term plan to adapt to the changing cultural environment				
3. Sends employees for cultural competence and cultural diversity training				
4. Develops cultural competence training for employees				
5. Actively seeks to understand the cultural characteristics of employees				
6. Is comfortable discussing his or her own cultural background				
7. Can effectively manage cross-cultural work teams				

cultural and social backgrounds. Effective organizations will be culturally competent in managing this diversity into effective work teams.

The demographic changes have begun, and organizations are beginning to reflect that diversity. The demographic changes are not equally distributed across the country, however. If you are in an organization with little diversity, you have the opportunity to become culturally competent before your organization becomes more diverse. You have, in other words, the time to adapt. Adaptability is the ability to alter, redefine, or reinvent the organizational mission or methods of conducting business. This cultural change will intensify and deepen as organizations reflect the increasing diversity.

Adaptability begins with accepting that the demographic change is here and will continue well into the future. This gives both a short-term and a long-term perspective to cultural competence. In the short term, individual employees at all levels develop individual cultural competence. With the understanding that comes with cultural competence, managers can create the culturally competent organization.

4.8 Inclusiveness as a Way to Create Effective Teams and Collaboration

Inclusiveness involves creating opportunities for employees to become part of the formal and informal networks in an organization. Inclusiveness in the formal structure means giving employees the opportunity to show their capabilities to higher levels of management, as well as other units in the organization. Informal networks will likely be multicultural. It is fairly common for employees with common cultures or diversities to create informal subcultures. Some organizations have affinity groups which are more formal organizational groups of employees with similar cultures or diversities (e.g., African Americans; Asians; Latinos; gay and lesbian employees; or bisexual and transgender employees). The groups arise to further the interests of their members. Inclusiveness should mean that all who are interested may become members of the group, not just those who identify with the group's major characteristics.

There is also research at the individual level, which is useful for public managers and adds to the definition of cultural competence. Barak and Levin (2002) examined the relationship between diversity characteristics, inclusion, fairness, stress, and social support and the outcome variables of job satisfaction and well-being of employees with diverse racial and ethnic backgrounds. Their findings indicate that women and employees who are racial and ethnic minorities are more likely to feel excluded and to feel lower levels of job satisfaction and well-being. Their research adds an important element to cultural competence in managing a diverse workforce and shows the importance of including those who differ from the organizational mainstream. Experiences from multicultural leadership programs show that multicultural employees tend to be well known only in their organizational subunits. They do not have wide visibility. Including multicultural and diverse employees in meetings with higher-level managers communicates inclusiveness. Culturally competent managers are mindful of the need to include multiculturally diverse employees in the organizational culture and take specific measures to do so (see Table 4.6).

Inclusiveness means including everyone. What is available to one should be available to all. There should not be a feeling that one group is getting special treatment that is not available to others. No one should feel excluded. Cultural competence is necessary for everyone, not just the dominant group. Because employees will work and interact with other employees from different cultures, genders, sexual orientations, and social classes, cultural competence is good for all employees.

Employee development plans are a good tool to manage inclusiveness. Employee plans should include what is required to make employees successful at their current job or position, as well as include developmental assignments that prepare employees for higher positions. The developmental aspects of the plan are optional, because some employees may be happy where they are and may not aspire to higher

Table 4.6 Measures for Inclusiveness

Measures the Manager Undertakes	Unsatisfactory	Satisfactory	Excellent	Outstanding
1. Meets with affinity groups				
2. Includes culturally diverse employees in his or her informal group				
3. Meets with culturally diverse individuals for informal conversations				
4. When appropriate, includes culturally diverse employees in meetings with other organizational units				
5. Interacts with culturally diverse employees equally				

positions. That is okay. They have had the opportunity to be included. The employees who seek upward mobility are not receiving opportunities unavailable to others. They are volunteering for additional developmental assignments.

Mentoring can be used to bring diverse employees into the formal and informal networks in an organization. When employees are doing well, giving them opportunities to showcase their work to higher level managers is a way of communicating inclusion. Inviting employees to one's workplace social or informal network is another way to communicate inclusiveness.

4.9 Summary and Conclusion

Understanding and using the cultural competencies will help prepare managers and employees for the demographic changes that are making organizations more diverse. The range of diverse cultural characteristics is becoming so large that it is very difficult for a manager or employee to fully understand the culture of each employee.

The five cultural competencies for public managers are keys to organizational success in a multicultural environment:

1. Respecting and understanding diverse employees
2. Communicating with diverse employees
3. Creating common ground or a shared culture
4. Being adaptable and flexible
5. Being inclusive

These cultural competencies are the foundation for interacting with other employees and managers. Successful and minimum standards are developed for each cultural competency. Performance measurements are established for each standard. The standards and performance measurements are useful for developing cultural competence training programs.

CULTURAL COMPETENCE FOR EXECUTIVES, MANAGERS, SUPERVISORS, AND EMPLOYEES

II

Chapter 5

Experiences from Successful Multicultural and Diversity Programs

> Diversity without unity makes about as much sense as dishing up flour, sugar, water, eggs, shortening, and baking powder on a plate and calling it a cake.
>
> **C. William Pollard**

5.1 Introduction

There are many successful multicultural and diversity-training programs in both the private and public sectors. The elements that make multicultural and diversity-training programs successful can enlighten managers in their efforts to create more culturally competent organizations. It is helpful for managers to understand the perspectives of multicultural employees. Multicultural and female employees frequently experience the workplace environment in different ways than do nonmulticultural or male employees (Korn/Ferry International 1998). Many of these different experiences arise from cultural differences. Managers who understand the cultural differences are in a much better position to overcome cultural barriers. Employees of color and women who understand the cultural differences between their cultural perspectives and those of the other employees can help managers reach across cultural barriers. This perspective adds to and illustrates the cultural characteristics or dimensions identified by Hall (1976) and Hofstede (1980, 2001).

The heart of any successful multicultural and diversity-training program is focusing on the manager–employee relationship and the cultural context of leader–follower relationships. The relationship between the employee and the supervisor is key to the future of the employee and the effectiveness of any organizational unit. It is the supervisor who conducts the performance review of the employee and has a major impact on the employee's career. Problems with supervisors are one of the most common reasons that employees suffer career setbacks. The foundation cultural competencies are fundamental to establishing a good relationship between a manager and an employee. Either the manager or the employee can initiate creating a good relationship. The supervisor–employee relationship is key to developing and sustaining culturally competent organizations.

5.2 Cross-Cultural Lessons

There may be individuals who question the applicability of lessons from the private sector, arguing that the public sector is different than the private sector. Yes, there are many differences, yet there are also many commonalities in public and private sector organizational structures. Corporations are seen by some as being structured around profit, whereas public organizations are structured around public service. The pursuit of profit, especially in a competitive arena, where more than one corporation is competing for the same customers, can serve to make the private sector organizations more sensitive to societal changes and changes in the demographics of their customers. Corporations that can better market their products to the emerging and very diverse communities, for example, as well as tap into the large purchasing power of the gay, lesbian, and transgender communities, will have a competitive edge. Multinational corporations already have experience working with different cultures. Some of the research conducted on cultural competence involves employees of multinational companies going from the United States to other countries. Cultural competence in this context is commonly referred to as cultural intelligence.

The insights gained from the multicultural leadership training can provide an understanding of how culturally diverse employees experience the organizational culture differently. The multicultural participants were the employees seen by their managers as the most productive. Many of the participants had polychronic cultural characteristics. Their managers and many of their co-workers had monochronic cultural characteristics. Cross-cultural misunderstandings and dissatisfaction were occurring across the cultural boundaries. Managers and fellow employees saw the multicultural employees—who were polychronic—as hard workers and very nice, but not as leaders. The managers and other employees had monochronic perceptions of leadership. When they did not see monochronic cultural characteristics in the multicultural employees, they assumed the employees were not leadership material.

Both the managers, with their monochronic cultural perspective, and the multicultural employees, whose cultural characteristics are polychronic, gained a cross-cultural understanding and appreciation, namely, respect. The managers and the multicultural employees learned the foundation cultural competencies. The result was improvement in the organization's return on its investment in the training and in the organization's bottom line. Many of the examples in this book are designed to teach managers and employees about polychronic cultural characteristics in the organization.

One multicultural leadership program focused on developing the manager–employee relationship to deliver better work results. In this case, about 95% of the supervisors were white and their employees who participated in the program were multicultural. Most of the managers and employees had good relationships, but the relationships were not translating into the development of the employees and better organizational results. The managers were not particularly adept at coaching their employees. In fact, the managers were reluctant to provide critical feedback, especially when the employee was of a different race, ethnicity, or gender.

Insights that are useful for organizational cultural competence initiatives came from a focus group of multicultural executives who participated in a multicultural leadership program that also included sexual orientation. Further insight was gained from multicultural leadership training involving a group of highly valued or high-performing African Americans at another corporation. This program involved a variety of instruments on emotional intelligence, resiliency, organizational climate, managerial styles, leadership styles, and workplace environments. The instruments provided 360-degree feedback. The participants were rated by their employees, peers, and supervisors, and where appropriate, by their customers. Both programs included further sessions between participants and their supervisors, along with executive coaching sessions. The employee–supervisor and executive sessions provided unique insights into the opportunities and challenges faced by multicultural employees. These feedback instruments provided a wealth of information. Based on the success of these training programs, the diversity initiatives were extended to all employees, including white males.

The participants saw themselves as facing several personal and leadership challenges. They saw their organizational experience as a lonely one. Some participants felt uncomfortable as executives. Their experience of the organization's culture as a lonely one springs from their perceiving themselves as outsiders, rather than as an integral part of the organizational culture. This perception was especially a concern where the participant was a member of a relatively small racial or ethnic minority. Gender was sometimes a factor, especially when female participants worked in areas that were predominately male environments. They articulated the same feelings of not being fully accepted members of the organizational culture.

In a focus group of Latino students at a university in the Texas Rio Grande Valley, very near the border with Mexico, a female graduate student enrolled in an undergraduate degree program far away from the Rio Grande Valley eloquently expressed the same sentiment expressed by the corporate employees. She said, "I went from an area where everyone looks like me to a university where only the janitors looked like me." In another illustration, a white female associate dean from a northeastern university was providing training for a group of faculty at a southwestern university. She told of her experiences as a doctoral student, assistant professor, associate professor, and now associate dean, describing feeling that she did not belong there, that she would be found out and asked to leave. This sentiment of not quite belonging expresses what may be a universal perspective for multicultural individuals who see themselves as different from the majority of employees in an organizational culture. It is this sentiment that makes inclusion a very important cultural competency. For managers, it is particularly important to inculcate employees with a strong sense that they are valued members of the team. Using the foundation communication cultural competencies, discussed in Chapter 4, will facilitate that task of communicating a sense of everyone being a part of the team.

Multicultural executives had a sense of selling themselves short yet still felt a lack of confidence, whereas the women were actually more likely to express their lack of confidence. Men were reluctant to talk about it, but when asked as part of executive coaching sessions, they would express the same sentiment. This phenomenon also occurs in many multicultural people in different settings. Respect for multicultural employees also means providing challenging assignments. Doing this shows respect for their abilities.

Example 5.1: I Don't Belong Here

A Latina graduate student talking about her undergraduate experiences at a highly ranked university said, "I know that I did just as well, if not better than, all the other students here to get accepted, but I get the feeling that I don't belong and that they will discover that I don't belong and they will ask me to leave." A high-level political Latina appointee, while waiting for the secretary of the department to arrive at a secretary's department meeting said something quite similar: "There are times that I'm sitting at one of these meetings and I get the feeling that I don't belong here and that they will find out I don't belong here and they will ask me to leave."

Managers chose highly valued, talented individuals or their best employees as participants in the multicultural leadership program. The participants were chosen because they were considered some of the best-performing employees. Their competence and performance were never an issue. Yet, many of these employees felt that they did not belong there. Communicating respect for the employees who bring diversity into an organization helps employees to overcome this fear.

Establishing common ground and a shared culture contributes to a good working relationship and can give all employees a sense of safety in taking risks and stretching their abilities. Staying in a zone where employees do not feel safe taking risks and possibly failing in a project makes it difficult for them to develop the skill set necessary to advance into the higher levels of the organization. These dynamics can, over a long period of time, lead to organizations where most multicultural employees are in the bottom half of the organizational pyramid, a situation that can serve to further reinforce the feelings of not belonging or being less competitive than other employees.

Example 5.2: Communicating Inclusiveness

Marissa, an executive coach, stepped into Robert's office and introduced herself. Robert is the supervisor of Shirley, a black female employee who uses leg braces and has difficulty walking. Marissa was conducting an executive coaching session with Shirley that included Robert.

Introducing herself, Marissa said, "Hi, Robert, I'm Marissa, and I'm here for the executive coaching session with you and Shirley."

"Hi, Marissa, glad to meet you," replied Robert. "Let's walk over to where Shirley works."

Marissa and Robert then walked to Shirley's office, where Robert said, "Hi, Shirley, Marissa is here for your executive coaching session. I thought we'd meet in your office to make it easier for you."

"Robert, I can walk over to your office," Shirley responded. "It may take me a little longer than the other employees, but not that much longer. I want to meet in your office where all the other employees meet with you."

Robert could have shown inclusiveness by including Shirley in the decision of where to hold the meeting.

As this scenario shows, even managers whose hearts are in the right place and who want to do the right thing can communicate the wrong message. Using the foundation communication cultural competencies can help managers avoid such awkward situations. When Marissa arrived in Robert's office, he could have called Shirley and said, "Hi, Shirley, Marissa is here for our executive coaching session. Where would you like to have the meeting?" Robert is communicating respect by including Shirley in the decision on where the meeting is to be held. The sense of being a working team is also reinforced, because Shirley gets to decide the location for the meeting. Enabling a member of a working team to make some of the decisions conveys the message that the individual is a valued team member.

Determining where the executive coaching session is to be held seems like a small, insignificant decision. In many ways it is, and yet, to employees from a minority or multicultural group, who may be feeling unsure of themselves or sense that they do not belong, being asked to make the decision is a symbolic act of great importance. It conveys respect, and this feeling of being respected can create a sense of confidence and can be very inspiring.

Also in common for many of these diverse employees was a trait of being very cautious and being very cognizant that they had obstacles to overcome to be accepted into the organizational culture. The cautiousness for these employees translated into a hesitancy in their communication. Their feeling of not quite being accepted or belonging translated into their expressing their opinions hesitantly and hedging the importance of their work. When an open question was directed at all the participants of a meeting, for example, they would hesitate to answer and let others go first, even when they knew more than the speaker did. When expressing their opinions, they would preface their ideas by saying, "I think that maybe this is a good idea, if everybody agrees if we...." In the same situation, the white employees would say, "I've looked at this, and I definitely think that this is what we should do." A manager hearing and observing the surface dynamics here could conclude that the multicultural employees, appearing less assertive than the white employees, may not have the leadership qualities required by the organization.

Many of these participants exhibited a protective pulling-back in their interactions with others and especially at business meetings. Some of this behavior can be attributed to their feeling of not belonging and what one participant expressed as "I almost feel like they will think I'm an imposter who is not supposed to be here. My performance is as good or better than theirs, but I still have this feeling." For others, especially African Americans, it was a desire not to be seen as the angry black male or angry black female. This protective pulling-back was creating social distance between them and other employees.

The protective pulling-back in the interactions with other employees was creating a perception that the multicultural employees were not leadership material. As one manager expressed this perception, "They just don't step up as leaders." This perception also held for Asians, who as a group were relatively well thought of. The common perception was that Asians are very smart and very competent technically, but they were not perceived as leadership candidates. Yet, their managers chose the participants precisely because they were some of their top performers.

Many people have the common perception that it is performance alone, especially great performance, that creates career advancement. This was the belief of many of the participants. As one participant expressed this belief, "If I just work hard, the company will take care of me." The experience of many of the multicultural employees, however, was that yes, while good performance is necessary for long-term career growth, their excellent performance was not getting them promoted.

Example 5.3: Stuck in the Comfort Zone

Marissa, an executive coach, found it common for supervisors, 95% of whom were white, to talk about the great performance of their multicultural employees. When Marissa would say, "From everything you are telling me, they are doing great and should get the next promotion when it becomes available," a common response from many of the supervisors was for them to pause, and then say, "They are good at their job. They get the highest performance bonuses, but they are just not ready for the demands of the next level." When Marissa would ask the supervisors to elaborate by naming some specific shortcomings, they would respond with a variation of another common response: "They keep to themselves and don't mix with other employees. They don't know a lot of people outside our organizational unit. I am not quite comfortable having them represent me at higher-level meetings yet. They don't step to the plate and take charge. They seem comfortable staying where they are."

The employees in question were diverse and multicultural—Marissa did not find this phenomenon when the supervisor and the employees were of the same racial or ethnic background. This was the case even though both the manager and the employees said they had good relationships and in the interviews they seemed quite comfortable with each other. The managers saw these interviewees as some of their best employees; nonetheless, there was something missing that was holding multicultural employees back. These were employees with polychronic cultural characteristics. Many of these employees were simply unaware of the monochronic organizational culture. Constructive feedback from their managers would have been productive for both managers and employees.

There was a cultural dissonance between the manager and the employees. The employees knew they were high performers. They also knew they had fewer promotional opportunities than the nonmulticultural employees. The managers were not as inclusive of them in their social networks as they were of employees who were of the same racial or ethnic background. Their excellent work performance or even good relationship with their manager was not enough to advance their careers. There were cultural factors that had to be overcome by both the managers and the employees.

Example 5.4: From Supporting Role to Headliner

The top executives were asked what they wanted to see before promoting employees into the top executive circles. One top executive, in a frank and blunt moment, said:

> Entry into the top executive ranks is by invitation only. We know whom we want by their reputation. What problems do other managers go to them to solve? How good is their credibility? How good are they at developing relationships with others inside and outside the company? Who can they bring to the table to help us be successful? We don't just want to know how good they are at their jobs; they're supposed to be good at their jobs. We want to know what difficult projects they have taken where it is hard to tell if they will be successful or not. We call them crucible roles. We want to know how they handle themselves under pressure and how they handle failure. If they don't fail at something, we know they just want to do what is safe and

not take risks. Before we invite them into the executive ranks, we need to see them perform. If we don't see them perform, we don't know how good they really are.

Interestingly enough, these are the same unspoken criteria used to select many, though not all, top political appointees and career SES (Senior Executive Service) candidates. Many multicultural employees believe that good performance is the only requirement for career success. Many believe that if their performance is excellent, their managers will take care of them. This is not always the case. The assessment of the multicultural programs showed that understanding what it takes to be successful is very motivating for employees.

One of the top-rated components of the multicultural leadership training programs was a symposium attended by the participants and their supervisors. The theme of the symposium was navigating the organizational waters or doing what is necessary to get ahead. The top executives talked about their leadership experiences and what was required of employees to advance, especially into the top executive ranks. Employees learned that besides performance, they had to develop their organizational reputation and credibility. They had to be seen as the go-to person for some skill needed by the organization. They needed relationships with others inside and outside the organization who could help them become more effective employees. They had to be visible to the top executives in the organization.

Multicultural executives were formed into teams and given real company problems to solve. They presented their solutions to the top leadership. Some of the teams' solutions were innovative enough that they were formed into real working company teams to solve the problems. They got an opportunity to develop relationships with other company executives whom they did not previously know. Their abilities were showcased to the top-tier executives of the company. One of the senior vice presidents was writing down the names of the employees making the presentation and the quality of their performance. She later contacted a few of the employees to ask them to consider positions where they could work for her. Successful executives and managers are always looking for effective employees.

Having opportunities to have senior managers and executives view an employee's capabilities and effectiveness is an important way to showcase an employee's talent. But as happens when someone steps on a stage, an employee had better be prepared. Such an opportune moment is a live performance with no retakes. When the bright lights are turned on, they illuminate the employee's entire performance: the good, the bad, and the ugly.

The participants frequently mentioned that they were not getting feedback from their supervisors. If they wanted feedback, they had to explicitly ask for it. In the executive coaching sessions, it became clear that many supervisors were reluctant to provide feedback, especially critical feedback, when the employees were of another race, ethnicity, or gender. Many female supervisors were just as reluctant as their male counterparts to provide feedback to their employees if they were of a different race or ethnicity, even if the employee was a female.

Example 5.5: Getting and Giving Critical Feedback

Sara, an executive coach, was meeting with Sam, a white manager in his early 50s, and his employee Gabriel, a young Hispanic male, to discuss the career development plan they had developed together. Sam and Gabriel traveled throughout the state working with several cities on a variety of policy issues. When they both walked into the conference room, Sara noticed the warm and comfortable relationship they had. They were chatting and gently teasing each other. She could sense their mutual warmth and sense of ease. The executive coaching session went extremely well. Sam and Gabriel had been working together for five years and had developed a great working relationship. They had great respect for each other. Sam and Gabriel were both very comfortable with the employee development plan they had developed. Sara was thinking that all the sessions should be this easy.

Just as they were getting ready to leave, Sara said, "I can see that both of you have a great relationship and that Gabriel is doing extremely well. Then there isn't any reason that Gabriel shouldn't get the next available promotion."

Sam paused, took a deep breath, and turned to Sara: "No, there is a problem. When we work with city councils and city administrators, Gabriel is great and very professional. But when we return to our company's offices in those cities, he starts joking around with the staff, and they think he is not very professional."

While Sam was talking, Gabriel was looking at him, eyes wide and mouth open in extreme surprise. Gabriel asked Sam, "Why didn't you tell me?"

Sam answered, "I wasn't comfortable saying anything."

Sara worked with the two men to determine how to fix this perception that Gabriel was not professional. The multicultural leadership program showed that many managers, even when they had great relationships, were uncomfortable giving critical feedback when employees were of a different race, ethnicity, gender, or sexual orientation. Gabriel comes from a culture in which joking with others is part of the social fabric. He did not understand that work was a different environment, one where social joking can be perceived as unprofessional. Not understanding this difference was hurting Gabriel's career.

Feedback is a critical component in developing excellent employees. Not getting feedback, especially critical feedback, can and has derailed many careers. It was evident that many of the managers in the training program were reluctant to provide feedback when their employees were of a different gender or racial or ethnic group. The multicultural employees felt a deep frustration at their difficulty in getting feedback. They knew their career success depended on frank and honest evaluations.

The multicultural executives saw their problems as coming not from the top executives but from the level right beneath the top executives. The implication is that diversity programs are easier to accept by top executives than by middle managers. Top executives with a long-term strategic and external social environment perspective understand how the organization must respond to a changing social environment and may be more aware of societal trends than are middle managers. Top executives also have more access to information from their strategic planning staff. Top executives of major corporations exist in a competitive environment. Changing societal demographics may affect their ability to market to many diverse multicultural markets. They know that having employees who reflect and understand these communities can be a competitive edge.

Middle managers may be more attuned to the day-to-day operational requirements of the organization and are therefore less likely to pay much attention to societal trends and the effect societal trends will have on the organization. There may be more pressure to meet and exceed organizational goals. The feedback from the employees indicates that successful diversity initiatives (as well as other organizational initiatives) depend on the willingness and capabilities of the middle managers. The middle managers manage other managers, and their organizational reach can expand exponentially depending on how many organizational levels exist beneath them.

The multicultural executives in the multicultural training programs discussed the difficulty in finding multicultural employees for any promotional opportunities. This problem was supported by workplace-environment surveys taken of all the participants. The participants consistently rated the organization's career development the lowest. As can happen when programs are targeted to specific groups, they did not want to be viewed as diversity hires or promotions. They wanted to be evaluated on the merits of their efforts. This sensitivity points to some of the difficulties in managing diversity. How do you work with identifiable groups without creating the sense that these groups are being singled out for special treatment? Organizational communication will have to be very open and clear for diversity programs to be successful.

It may be expected that the focus of multicultural programs is to make white managers culturally competent. It is equally important for all employees to be culturally competent. Cultural competence is especially important for multicultural employees, who bring into the organization their individual diversity characteristics. Managers may have social perceptions about other groups who are different. In today's climate, they may not publicly express their sentiments, but they may act on their social perceptions. The trainers who had developed the multicultural leadership training program discussed their findings with some of the top executives in their company. The trainers expressed the dissatisfaction of the Hispanic employees with the company's lack of career development for them. The Hispanic employees felt they were not receiving career advice and feedback and were not being given any developmental assignments. One of the executives responded, "We would like to give more developmental assignments to our Hispanic employees, but it means they will have to move. The Hispanics are so family-oriented that they won't move to take developmental assignments, even when they will lead to promotions." The other executives nodded in agreement.

One can easily form social perceptions of any group when the members of that group are not well known. Such perceptions can develop from interactions with just one or two employees, when they reinforce a perception of group characteristics. These perceptions can subsequently become entrenched. Managers will then act on these social perceptions. Employees can sometimes unconsciously reinforce inaccurate social perceptions.

Another issue that came up in the coaching sessions with multicultural employees was their feeling that being successful would cause them to lose their culture. Ari is the first-generation son of parents who had emigrated from a Middle Eastern country. He is close to his parents. When asked about his long-term career plans he said, "I don't want to be an executive. I don't want to give up my culture to be successful. My parents wouldn't like it." Variations of this theme were expressed by a sizable number of the multicultural employees. Children of recent immigrants, especially if they are close to their families, may have to live in two cultural worlds. Recent immigrants may have social perceptions of Americans that conflict with the values of their cultures. Children become caught between the conflicting cultural requirements of their families and their work colleagues. Stories are common of conflicts that arise when the children of immigrants become Americanized or take on many of the cultural characteristics of their host European country while still holding some of their parents' cultural values. They become caught between two worlds.

An employee faced with this situation may literally perceive himself or herself as living in two worlds. Cultural competence can help bridge those two cultural worlds. Employees caught in this predicament are in a situation that globalization—specifically international collaborations—has made more common. They can view themselves as individuals who are traveling back and forth between two very different cultures. Cultural competence shows employees how to respect whatever culture they are currently in.

Multicultural employees can also help other employees learn about them and their diverse cultures. It is helpful to understand that not all employees are culturally competent. They may not know how to approach a discussion or ask a question in a way that is appropriate in the organizational setting. They may ask a question based on the values of their own culture. Furthermore, some employees may not be socially adept in their own culture, much less in cross-cultural situations. There are employees who would like to understand others but do not know how to initiate a conversation. They know it is easy for a misunderstanding to occur. Some minority groups—such as female employees; gay, lesbian, and transgendered employees; and employees of color—may have experienced discrimination in the past. An employee's past experiences may make him or her more sensitive to perceived snubs or insults. By being culturally competent, however, that employee can help other employees learn about his or her culture. It is helpful to understand that communicating across cultural boundaries can at first be awkward for many employees. Being respectful of others and creating a safe common ground and shared culture to develop new relationships can be very helpful. If, for instance, someone says something in an awkward manner, one ought to try to makes the situation less awkward. One can always say, "I'm not quite sure I understand. Please tell me more."

5.2.1 Workplace Environment

Workplace-environment surveys were conducted in a large corporation. The surveys were part of a multicultural program that involved more than 400 participants and their supervisors. The program contained many of the success factors described by Rice and Arekere (2005) in their discussion of the Glass Ceiling 1995 fact-finding report "Good for Business: Making Full Use of the Nation's Human Capital" and the 1999 National Partnership for Reinventing Government benchmark study "Best Practices in Achieving Workforce Diversity." The top leadership and management were committed to the program, which was developed specifically for the organization and addressed preconceptions and stereotypes. The program began with Hispanic employees and was later extended to all groups, including white males.

The workplace survey asked questions about performance, achievements, being part of a team, support, communication, organizational climate, employee development plans, and employee–supervisor relationships. Supervisors were asked the same questions, but they were asked how they thought their employees would answer the questions. The supervisors were brought together with their employees during executive coaching sessions to discuss the results of the workplace-environment surveys.

The participants rated their relationships with their managers as being very good. They were satisfied with communication with their supervisors and the support they received from them. Women, while still rating their relationships with their supervisors as being good, rated their relationships lower than the men. This gender difference persisted throughout the survey. The managers consistently rated their employees as being more satisfied than the employees really were. Managers also consistently thought that their employees were less satisfied with their managers than they were.

There are some inherent dangers when managers perceive their employees to be more satisfied with their workplace environment than they really are. Having good relationships can deceive a manager into thinking or believing employees are happy and satisfied. Many of these employees who indicated that they had good relationships with their managers were actively looking to leave their organizational unit at the first opportunity. Losing good employees is often a setback for organizational effectiveness.

Ninety-five percent of the supervisors were white. Many were not comfortable relating to employees of color or employees with other diversities. The difficulty the managers were experiencing seems to come from two factors. One was a sensitivity in not wanting to say something that could be interpreted as derogatory or insulting. The other factor was they did not know how to communicate in a culturally competent manner. Once the managers had undergone training, they were much more confident in working with and relating to employees of color and other diverse employees. The employees recognized the difference in the way the managers related to their employees.

There has been much progress for women in the workplace. Yet, the surveys indicated that for these organizations, there is still a gender gap. Women tended to be less satisfied than the men on many elements of the workplace environment. Many managers, most of whom were white, were reluctant to provide critical feedback when their employees were of a different gender, race, or ethnicity. The managers and employees had good working relationships, yet the managers were hesitant to offer feedback. There was no reluctance, though, when the employees were of the same gender and race or ethnicity.

Overall, participants rated their inclusion in the social (informal) and informational networks in the middle of the range. These results are similar to findings of Barak and Levin (2002). The gap between women and men was large in this area, with women scoring lower. The scores for women were low enough that many of these women also expressed their concern in executive coaching sessions. The managers had more optimistic perceptions of the situation.

Social and informal networks are important to the career success of employees. Much work-related information is communicated through informal networks. Information not available through the official organizational structure almost becomes organizational capital that employees use to make their jobs easier for themselves and the other members of their informal networks. Work information is also communicated in social settings outside the organization. Employees meet for dinners and parties in each other's homes, for instance. Work is discussed in these situations.

Career development was the area rated the lowest by participants and their managers. Women rated it much lower than the men. The participants did not see themselves as being positioned for long-term careers and advancement into the top executive levels. There was a consistent lack of mentors and long-term career plans for the participants. Formal and informal mentors are especially critical to the career development of women and multicultural employees. A Korn/Ferry International study (1998) showed that 73% of the African American females who reported they had an informal mentor had faster salary and total compensation growth than did African American women who had no informal mentors. Informal mentors were critical in advocating for upward mobility and for teaching the informal rules of the organization.

The Korn/Ferry International study (1998) also reports the value of supportive superiors and co-workers. Hispanic women who reported having supportive superiors had faster salary growth than had Latinas without supportive superiors. African American males who had supportive co-workers also had faster salary growth than had African American males without supportive co-workers. The report states that the upward mobility of African American and Hispanic employees depends on the formal and informal mentoring they receive in the organization.

The efforts of the program on career development proved to be the most motivating for employees. The participants mentioned three elements of career development as being very helpful:

1. Long-term written career plans signed by the employee and the supervisor
2. The realization that great work performance was not enough to guarantee long-term career success
3. A career plan that identified each employee's responsibilities

An executive coach facilitated the long-term career planning in sessions attended by both employees and their supervisors. After several sessions with different employees, it became clear that many employees had not thought much about their long-term careers. Their supervisors had not completed long-term career plans for themselves either. Many employees had misguided notions about what was required for long-term career success. One female employee of color at one of the sessions was complaining that her supervisor would not let her prepare the budgets for their organizational unit, and she really wanted to learn budgeting. Her supervisor explained that budgeting for their organizational unit involved working with other units and that she did not have relationships with the other unit directors. When she developed working relationships with them, he explained, he would be delighted to have her prepare budgets. Developing those relationships became part of her career plan.

Many employees had the impression that their good performance was all that was required for success. Not so! The top executives explained that from their perspective, good performance and even great performance at their jobs was expected. Good performance only meant they were suited for the job they were doing, not that they were ready for a promotion. Good work performance is always necessary; but as an employee climbs higher on the organizational ladder, other factors become more important.

The top executives told the participants that by the time they meet a candidate for promotion into the executive ranks, they already know the candidate by the person's reputation and credibility. They asked the participants, "What are you the go-to person for? What do other employees go to you to help them with? What problems do others bring you to solve? When others depend on you, do you deliver? We already know you by reputation and your credibility before we meet you in person." Employees worked with their supervisors to see what types of expertise were valued in the company and, given their current positions, what special expertise would be worthwhile for them to develop. In many cases, employees volunteered to enter university programs, which the employees themselves would pay for. Sometimes the supervisors made provisions for the employees to attend company-sponsored training. The additional training and education became part of their career plan.

The relationships that employees developed inside and outside the company were very important to their long-term career success. A senior vice president told the participants, "We don't just look at how you handle the resources that are under your control. We look at the other resources that others control and that you bring to the table." Many of the career plans included others with whom it would be important for the employee to develop relationships. Employees were given cross-functional assignments where they could work with employees outside their organizational units. The employees were willing to take additional workloads because they now saw the value to their careers.

Many of the participants were well known and had good reputations inside their organizational units. However, they and their capabilities were not well known outside their immediate organizational unit. Gaining visibility outside their own work units would be beneficial to their careers. Giving visibility to employees is an area where managers can be extremely helpful. Employees willingly volunteered for projects where they could work with employees in other organizational units. They could present the results to others outside their area. In many cases, the supervisors agreed to have the employees represent them in company meetings. The first step was to have the employee accompany them to the meetings where they would be introduced. This allowed the employees to see how the meetings were conducted and who was attending the meetings. Thus employees were prepared well before they actually represented their supervisors.

Managers can play an important role for employees who come from polychronic backgrounds and are group oriented. Usually reluctant to claim individual credit for work they do, these employees will give credit to their team members rather than focus attention on their own contributions. A manager can say, "I know you don't like to talk about yourself and your accomplishments, but I would really like to tell my boss how good you really are. To be able to do that, I need to know your particular contributions to the success of your project. Help me tell my boss how proud I am of you by telling me what you have done." In this way, managers can create a buzz about their employees that the employees are uncomfortable creating for themselves.

The career planning sessions were for the benefit of the employees, but many of the supervisors used the sessions to develop a career plan for themselves. Once they felt comfortable with their plans, the supervisors discussed them with their managers.

The success of multicultural leadership programs was based on the precepts of cultural competency. The companies communicated respect for the benefits their diverse employees were bringing to the company. They became ambassadors to their communities, where they represented their respective companies. The participants saw that they now were integral team members whose contributions helped make the company successful. The career plans established a common ground and shared culture where the employees work with their managers for their combined success. Having learned how to communicate cross-culturally with other employees, the participants and their managers developed mutually improved relationships. They adapted to the changing cultural demographics their companies were facing.

The leadership program also included the four aspects of the cultural competence model: culture, communication, misunderstandings and conflict, and leader–follower relations. Employers and managers learned about the different cultural backgrounds that employees bring into an organization. They learned that many of their employees who come from family-oriented cultures are more reluctant to be more I-oriented and not likely to talk about how good they really are. Managers could then be the ones to create a buzz about their outstanding employees. Both managers and employees learned how to mentor others. Managers could now communicate in a manner that showed respect for diversity, acknowledging that their employees were valued and integral members of their team. Employees learned how to resolve problems with their managers and other employees in a way that strengthened their relationships. Many misunderstandings and conflicts that had existed in the past were now being prevented.

Especially important to the success of the leadership program was the emphasis on the leader–follower relationships. Improving the supervisor–employee relationships provided a return to the company's bottom line. Employees and in many cases the managers volunteered for additional assignments and projects. Employees enrolled in educational and training programs where they enhanced their professional skills.

Human resource offices developed diversity standards and performance measurements for their managers to assess the continuation of the success. Managers knew that their efforts were being assessed. The top executives demonstrated their ongoing commitment to diversity management through the diversity management performance standards.

5.3 The Multicultural Leadership Program

An online program assessment was designed and conducted to answer four questions:

1. What was the measurable impact to the company's bottom line?
2. What was the impact of the program on the participants?
3. What was the impact of the program on the managers of the participants?
4. What was the impact on the company's human resource policies and systems?

The assessment used both quantitative and qualitative data. The quantitative data included the results of the surveys on the workplace environment; the responses to the online assessment; and company employee data such as promotions, attrition rates, and employee movement. The qualitative data included the career development plans developed jointly by the participants and their supervisors, employee feedback, online assessment comments, comment forms filled out by the facilitators of discussions between the participants and their supervisors, and additional anecdotal information. Both the participants and their supervisors filled out the assessment instrument. The data included not only the participants' self-perceptions but also the supervisors' observations about the changes evident in their employees who participated in the program. When supervisors responded to their surveys, their employees were asked about the changes they observed in the managers.

The program was seen as driving business results through the increased contributions of the participants. Eighty-two percent of the participants saw themselves as increasing their contributions to the company. Seventy-five of their managers agreed that the participants had increased their contributions to the business. Eighty-four percent of the participants saw themselves as generating more solutions to business issues, and 79% of their supervisors agreed. Eighty-two percent of the participants reported that they were now bringing increased innovation to the company, and 79% of their supervisors agreed. The positive impact to the business was ranked in the top three positive impacts of the program.

The program accelerated the development and advancement of the employees. Twenty percent of the participants were promoted, and over 6% were on developmental assignments. Sixty-five percent of the first- and second-level managers were promoted, and over 7% were on developmental assignments.

The program enhanced the capability of the managers to manage and develop multicultural employees. Ninety-five percent of the managers were white. Eighty-eight percent of the managers said they had developed more committed partnerships with their employees. Eighty-five of their employees agreed. Eighty-four of the managers said they applied what they learned from the program to their other employees, and 72% of their employees agreed.

From the perspective of human resources, the program resulted in an increased commitment by the participants. Eighty-six percent of the employees reported that they were more committed to the company, and 81% of their supervisors agreed. Over a two-year period, the number of high-risk and moderately at-risk employees to leave their organizational units dropped from 81% to 42%. The number of employees being mentored increased by 28%. Human resource offices instituted diversity management performance standards based on the assessment of the programs.

The assessment showed that the multicultural leadership program had a hard bottom-line return for the organization. The assessment was conducted at the end of the second year, when it had been more than a year since many of the participants had completed the program. The effects of the program for these employees lasted more than a year. Cultural competence has a bottom-line payoff for organizations. Cultural competence training is effective and has a multiplier effect. More than 80% of the managers said they were applying what they learned to other employees. More than 70% of their employees agreed that they were applying what they learned to other employees. Knowing that they were valued members of the organizational team and that their diversity was seen in a positive light energized employees to take on additional assignments and projects and to further their education. Having long-term career plans showed the path to the career success each employee wanted to achieve.

5.4 Examples of Public Sector Initiatives

The following are two examples of diversity initiatives in the public sector. They provide lessons for managers. The City of Seattle incorporates many of the successful tenets of cultural competency. (More information can be found on the city's Web site: http://www.seattle.gov.) The University of Vermont (UVM) example shows that having a top-level desire for cultural competency is not always enough. Many impediments still have to be overcome.

5.4.1 The City of Seattle's Race and Social Justice Initiative

Seattle, like many other cities and communities, is becoming more diverse. Immigrants are expected to be 20% of the population of Seattle by 2010 (City of Seattle Race and Social Justice Initiative 2008). In the Seattle public schools, students speak more than 80 different languages. In 2006, 34% of Seattle's population was nonwhite. Many people of color felt they were not being well served by the city. By the early 2000s, efforts to address race-based disparities in social services evolved into the Race and Social Justice Initiative (RSJI).

The RSJI focused on institutional racism, which it defined as "organizational programs, policies, or procedures that work to the benefit of white people and to the detriment of people of color, usually unintentionally or inadvertently" (City of Seattle Race and Social Justice Initiative 2008). City departments created change teams to support the implementation of departmental work teams. The RSJI Coordinating Team identified five central concerns (City of Seattle Race and Social Justice Initiative 2008):

1. Workforce Equity: Improve diversity of workforce
2. Economic Equity: Change purchasing and contracting practices to increase participation by people of color
3. Immigrant and Refugee Services: Improve access to services for immigrant and refugee communities
4. Public Engagement: Improve access and influence of communities of color
5. Capacity Building: Increase the knowledge and tools used by city staff to achieve race and social justice

Specific departments took lead roles for each central concern. The Citywide Core Team was established and received intensive training on institutional racism, group facilitation, problem solving, and strategic action planning. The Citywide Core

Team members assist the change teams, department managers, and city staff to implement the Initiative.

These are some selected findings from an assessment of the RSJI's accomplishments from 2005 to the present and reported in the RSJI Report 2008: An efficient management structure has been developed, and most of the city departments are implementing the Initiative. Of special interest to other communities that would like to implement a similar initiative is the effort to develop capacity building. Change-team members and managers participated. The managers participated in four components:

1. A one-hour introductory orientation
2. An eight-hour training using the PBS documentary *Race: The Power of an Illusion* (2003)
3. An eight-hour antiracism curriculum
4. A four-hour follow-up skills-based training

A translation and interpretation policy was created in 2007, and the mayor issued an executive order requiring departments to implement the policy. The mayor also issued an executive order that instructed departments to designate a liaison to coordinate and implement public engagement processes and strategies.

In 2007, an analysis of workforce diversity conducted by the city's personnel department showed that employee diversity exceeded the diversity of the city's working-age population. The best effort at recruiting people of color was for entry-level positions with low barriers to entry (e.g., laborers and administrative assistants). Seattle has committed to develop policies to help employees with upward mobility and to create professional development opportunities for employees.

The RSJI has many of the elements of the successful private sector multicultural leadership training programs. The City of Seattle had a strong commitment from its mayor to support the effort. The city provided training on race and, by extension, cultural differences. The effort signaled a top-executive message of inclusion for employees. The city made a commitment to provide employees with the knowledge to advance their careers. There is a particularly powerful message of inclusion when employees can see a clear path to achieve their desired career ambitions.

Elliott Bronstein, Glenn Harris, and Julie Nelson from the City of Seattle detail the lessons learned in implementing the Seattle Race and Social Justice Initiative (see DVD Appendix A). They have included their contact information for anyone who would like to learn more about the RSJI.

5.4.2 University of Vermont

In 2005 UVM embarked on an ambitious plan to ensure that every undergraduate student received education in cultural competency. This goal was not accomplished without great effort at many levels. The following section provides a brief account of UVM's effort to institute a six-credit diversity requirement for its undergraduate students.

UVM is situated in Burlington, Vermont, the state's largest city, which has around 100,000 residents in the metro area. Vermont is still considered to be one the "whitest" states in the United States. Founded in 1797, UVM is reflective of the state, with less than 7% of its student body identifying as students of color. Seventy percent of its students are from out of state and affluent.

The "Waterman Takeover" occurred in 1988 and was a direct result of UVM students coming together to protest a lack of attention given to students of color and their issues at the university. This event resulted in the creation of the one-credit Race and Culture course, required for all students in all colleges and schools at UVM, except in the College of Arts and Sciences, which had been teaching its own diversity classes for many years prior to the Waterman Takeover. The period of the one-credit diversity requirement lasted from 1989 until 2005, when talks of the six-credit diversity requirement started to emerge. The Race and Culture course was funded by a grant, which expired in 2005. The grant expiration was the true impetus for a renewed interest in the introduction of the six-credit diversity requirement.

Diversity is a core value for UVM, as is shown by the following message on its Web site:

> The University of Vermont holds that diversity and academic excellence are inseparable. An excellent university, particularly one that is a public land grant, needs to actively seek to provide access to all students who can excel at the institution, without respect to their backgrounds and circumstances, including, among other differences, those of race, color, gender, gender identity or expression, sexual orientation, national and ethnic origin, socioeconomic status, cultural and/or geographic background, religious belief, age, and disability. There is, moreover, a compelling national interest in a higher education sector rich in diversity and opportunity, and a clear state interest in making the educational benefits of this diversity and opportunity accessible to all. (University of Vermont 2009b)

In 2008, the six-credit diversity requirement was implemented. Many faculty expressed concerns about the extra credits that would be needed for the requirement. Faculty also expressed resentment, as many faculty members were not educated to teach cultural competencies. The students were not especially concerned, nor did they protest the new requirement.

Currently, the six-credit diversity requirement remains an unfunded mandate with no additional financial or human resources. For example, in one of the largest colleges on campus, there is only one faculty member teaching the diversity requirement. His courses total 200 students per semester, whereas his colleagues teaching major classes have fewer than 25 students per semester. The six-credit diversity requirement is a reasonable solution to exposing UVM college students to differences. However, UVM expects the requirement to be continued without the appropriate resources to make it truly successful.

5.5 Learning from the Private Sector and Public Sector Initiatives

Both the private sector multicultural leadership program and the public sector initiatives at Seattle and UVM can contribute to public managers and employees understanding the organizational dynamics of cultural competence. The private sector provides a window into how diverse employees with different cultural characteristics can create innovation and organizational success and also highlights the pitfalls that can accompany diversity. It also shows that cultural competence has a real bottom-line payoff and return to the organization.

The initiatives from the public sector show that Seattle may be in the forefront in instituting its Race and Social Justice Initiative.

5.5.1 Learning from the Private Sector

There are several valuable lessons that can be learned from the private sector multicultural leadership program:

1. Employees with different cultural characteristics can have misunderstandings and problems.
2. Multicultural employees may be sensitive to negative social perceptions and may try to overcompensate.
3. The supervisor–employee relationship is a key relationship for cultural competence.
4. Supervisors of culturally different employees may be reluctant to provide constructive criticism.
5. Communication with multicultural employees is helped by understanding the cultural characteristics of the employees.
6. Employees with polychronic cultural characteristics may not be seen as having leadership potential.
7. Multicultural employees have difficulty reading another employee's social and emotional cues.
8. Great performance is not enough for career success.
9. An employee's reputation and credibility are also important and may be subject to cultural social perceptions.
10. Cultural characteristics and leader–follower dynamics (two aspects of the cultural competence model) can create misunderstandings and conflict.

11. Top executives are critical to the success of cultural competence.
12. The layer below the top executives may be the most resistant.
13. Cultural competence has a hard bottom-line payoff for organizations.

5.5.2 Learning from the Public Sector

Seattle is expected to have an immigrant community of about 20% this year. Seattle public school students speak 80 different languages. The data indicate that many cities are facing similar demographic changes or soon will be. Seattle may be leading the way forward with its Race and Social Justice Initiative to rid the city of institutional racism.

Seattle's RSJI contains many of the elements that would make any citywide initiative successful, as noted in the work of Siegel, Haugland, and Chambers (2003). The elements, shown here, are a useful set of guidelines to follow:

1. Recognize that a problem exists.
2. Commit to developing solutions by the mayor, city council, and managers.
3. Develop a strategic plan.
4. Increase the capacity of city staff.
5. Provide extensive training on the nature of the problem and skills-based training.
6. Increase the diversity of the workforce: Workforce equity.
7. Improve access to city contracts by people of color: Economic equity.
8. Improve delivery of services to immigrant and refugee communities.
9. Provide better access and influence for communities of color: Public engagement.

The RSJI is a work in progress with many successes, but it still has obstacles to overcome. Seattle found that recruiting employees of color was easier for entry-level positions with low barriers to entry. This situation may be very similar to what other organizations, public or private, are experiencing. The increasing diversity of society has been a recent phenomenon. Thus it may not be unusual to have organizations where the employees of color are clustered in the entry- and lower-level positions. The impending retirement of the baby boomers may alter these dynamics.

Seattle is developing policies to help employees with upward mobility and to create professional development opportunities for employees. This is an area where the lessons from the private and public sector initiatives merge. The private sector initiative demonstrated that cultural characteristics can be misunderstood by managers and slow the career mobility for employees of color. The private sector programs showed that programs to increase the cultural competence of employees had a real return to the organizational bottom line. Once employees of color understood the requirements for career mobility and had culturally competent managers, they were more innovative and provided better solutions.

UVM shows that a commitment and plan are not enough. There has to be an organization-wide effort and, where appropriate, additional resources. Otherwise, the efforts can falter.

5.6 Summary and Conclusion

There have been many private and public multicultural programs. The number of programs is increasing as the demographic changes create new immigrant communities and a more multicultural workforce. The focus in the multicultural programs has varied from working with managers and employees to reducing institutional racism. Managers and employees can learn much from these programs.

The supervisor–employee relationship is central to developing culturally competent organizations. Improving supervisor–employee relationships depends on understanding the cultural context of leader–follower relationships. Feedback from the multicultural executives and employees indicated that they did not feel part of the organizational culture. They had good relationships with their supervisors, but many supervisors did not provide critical feedback or include them in their social networks. Managers and employees were aware of the negative societal stereotypes of multicultural people. African Americans were sensitive about not contributing to being viewed as stereotypical angry blacks. Individual employees sometimes contribute to negative social perceptions.

Immigrants are changing the cultural landscape of many communities. The City of Seattle initiated its Race and Social Justice Initiative to rid the city of institutionalized racism. The city's leaders made efforts to foster workforce equity by improving the diversity of the city workforce. They are working toward better relationships with the immigrant communities. Seattle is being forward-thinking in developing solutions for the demographic changes many communities will be facing. Other communities can learn from their effort.

Likewise, UVM initiated diversity efforts. The lesson here is that to be successful includes following through at all levels and that top-executive support needs to be supplemented with organizational support.

The overall finding, especially from the private sector initiatives, showed that culturally competent programs could contribute to the organization's success. Multicultural and diverse employees involved in such programs were more energized and took on additional assignments and training. They made better business decisions and were better ambassadors for their companies. The employees now understood how to navigate the organizational culture. They could see for themselves a clear pathway to a bright organizational future. The managers applied the cultural competencies they learned to all their employees. Cultural competence is the gift that keeps on giving.

Chapter 6

Cultural Competencies for Executives

> Difference is of the essence of humanity. Difference is an accident of birth and it should therefore never be the source of hatred or conflict. The answer to difference is to respect it. Therein lies a most fundamental principle of peace, respect for diversity.
>
> **John Hume**
> *Nobel Peace Prize lecture, 2008*

6.1 Introduction

The foundation cultural competencies are for cross-cultural individual interactions with other employees. The research on cultural competence also shows the importance of creating culturally competent organizations. The lessons from the research on federally mandated culturally competent delivery of services to immigrant and minority communities reveal the importance of structuring the organization to be culturally competent (Betancourt et al. 2003; Brach and Fraser 2000; Cross et al. 1989; Davis and Donald 1997).

Siegel, Haugland, and Chambers (2003) created an organizational framework for cultural competence. Their framework requires cultural competence to be included in any mission statement and strategic plan that includes management accountability and a budget. The management structure should also have a position responsible for cultural competence. In other words, the organizational framework for cultural competence includes managerial cultural competencies. Whereas the foundation cultural competencies are the basis for individual interactions, the managerial cultural competencies relate to the organizational roles and responsibilities of the various management levels in an organization. The top executives, managers, supervisors, and employees will each have their own specific duties in creating a culturally competent organization.

The managerial cultural competencies should also incorporate the U.S. Office of Personnel Management (OPM) leadership competencies for managing diversity. According to OPM's "Guide to Senior Executive Service Qualifications" (OPM 2010a) these competencies show managers and employees how to leverage diversity by "fostering an inclusive workplace where diversity and individual differences are valued and leveraged to achieve the vision and mission of the organization" (p. 33). The managerial communication competencies discussed in Chapter 4 in this book show managers and employees how to treat others with courtesy, sensitivity, and respect and how to consider and respond appropriately to the needs and feelings of different people in different situations. Knowing the managerial cultural competencies and having performance measures in place make it easier for employees interested in joining the Senior Executive Service to document and describe how they meet these requirements for managing diversity.

One additional aspect is also necessary for the executive cultural competencies. Many top executives are political appointees who serve for a limited time. The relationship between the political appointees and the senior civil service executives is particularly crucial in developing culturally competent organizations. How that relationship is forged can determine the success or failure of any cultural competence initiative, as well as any other initiative. It is at this boundary that political philosophy meets formal organizational requirements. Interesting dynamics can develop across this management boundary. The foundation cultural competencies can be used to create a good working relationship for the successful implementation of organizational initiatives.

6.2 Cultural Competencies for Executives

In their book *The Leadership Pipeline,* Charan, Drotter, and Noel (2001b) provide a useful framework for developing the managerial cultural competencies. They describe the six passages through which employees transition on their journey from an entry-level employee to, in the case of the public sector, secretary of a department and president. There are equivalents for state and local governments. The importance of the passages is that new skills are required in the new position that cannot be gained in the previous and lower positions. These are the managerial skills that can be adapted to create managerial cultural competencies for each management level. Charan et al.'s (2001b) description of the six passages is adapted to the public sector:

1. From assistant secretary to secretary of a department.
2. From senior civil service executive (Senior Executive Service [SES] in the federal government) to assistant secretary heading a large agency within the department.
   2.1. It is at this level that the political appointees and the senior civil service executives work together the most closely.
3. From manager of a large subunit to Senior Executive Service.
4. From managing other managers to manager of a large subunit within an agency.
5. From supervisor to managing other managers.
6. From employee to supervisor.

Each management level has its own skills, timeframes, and work values; the transition from one level into a higher-level position requires learning new skills, timeframes, and work values. Table 6.1 identifies the six stages and the skills required for each management level. The management skills for each level are the traditional and generic management skills. The descriptors have been adapted to make them appropriate for public sector managers and employees and then extended to incorporate cultural competence into an organization. The cultural competencies are adapted to be appropriate for the functions at each management level.

These competencies are also useful for managers and employees who are interested in career mobility and successful long-term careers. Real-life examples from the experiences of many managers are presented in this chapter to give additional insight and to show how the managerial competencies may be used in an organization.

In federal government, the top executives are the department secretary, deputy secretary, undersecretary, assistant secretaries, and some SES personnel who may be either political appointees or career civil servants. Most of the top executives are more than likely political appointees. Political appointees can be appointed at almost any federal government general schedule (GS) rating. For those who are interested, the Plum Book lists all political appointments. This book lists more than 7,000 federal civil service positions in the legislative and executive branches that may be appointed noncompetitively. The Plum Book is published alternately by the Senate Committee on Homeland Security and Governmental Affairs and the House Committee on Governmental Reform after every presidential election.

The boundary between the top political appointees and the top career civil servants is a particularly sensitive boundary. Political appointees, especially when transitioning from one political party to the other, bring different philosophies and cultures into an organization. States and local governments, depending on the size of the organization, will have comparable organizational cultures. Titles may differ, but general responsibilities will be roughly similar. In smaller states and local

Table 6.1 Cultural Competencies for Executives

Organizational Level	Roles, Responsibilities, and Duties	Managerial Cultural Competencies
In the federal government: secretaries of departments In state governments: governor and secretaries In large cities: mayors and department heads	1. Executes the president's vision and agenda 2. Shapes the organizational culture 3. Serves as motivational leader (cross-cultural motivation) 4. Spends significant time developing relationships with legislative bodies, other governments, and community groups	1. Strategically leveraging diversity from executive departments, external constituencies, legislators 2. Developing relationships with legislators, interest groups, national community groups, state governments (many will be multicultural) 3. Communicating (cross-culturally) to inspire diverse and multicultural external constituencies and employee groups
In the federal government: deputy secretary, undersecretary, assistant secretary In state governments and large cities: department heads within large departments In small cities: mayor or city manager	1. Acts as organizational strategist 2. Balances present and future goals 3. Has political savvy to implement political agenda 4. Develops relationships with external constituencies and internal constituencies	1. Strategically leveraging diversity to develop more effective organization 2. Preparing organization to be culturally competent 3. Developing relationships with legislators, interest groups, community groups, organizational unions (where employees are unionized)
In the federal government: Senior Executive Service and GS-15s	1. Manages multiple departments 2. Understands how to implement the organization's strategic plan	1. Leveraging diversity to implement strategic plan 2. Developing culturally competent middle managers

Table 6.1 Cultural Competencies for Executives (Continued)

Organizational Level	Roles, Responsibilities, and Duties	Managerial Cultural Competencies
In state governments and large cities: subdepartment heads In smaller cities: department heads	3. Is organizationally savvy	

governments, the responsibilities may be more compressed, with individuals having more responsibilities. The foundation cultural competencies can be helpful in bridging the political-career divide in public organizations.

Executives shape the organizational culture and develop the long-term strategy for their organizations. In times of stability, their focus tends to be on management and effectiveness. Management uses rational and technical tools to improve effectiveness. When the environment is changing and the organization needs to change, executives need to be inspirational communicators, because change can create ambiguity and anxiety in employees. Inspirational communication focuses on the emotional aspects of assuring employees that the organization will effectively respond to the changes. Organizations composed of very diverse employees require language that is inspiring in several cultures. Executives develop relationships with legislative bodies, interest groups, and community organizations. It is in this interconnected web of relationships that programs are developed and defended.

The major agency heads are the bridge from the political appointees to the rest of the organization. Depending on the organization, some heads may be political appointees or career employees. They help refine the organization's political vision and strategic plan. Whereas the top executives develop the broad strategic vision and goals, the agency heads focus on the narrower mandate of their individual agencies. The agency heads work with the senior civil service executives to implement the strategic vision and develop performance measures.

6.3 The Political Appointee and Career Civil Servants

The relationship between political appointees and the senior career officials is a fascinating and interesting one. Understanding the dynamics between political appointees and career civil service employees is important to the successful implementation of organizational initiatives. Political appointees and career civil service employees can bring different perspectives to the organization. The world of political appointees and the world of career civil service employees can be seen as two different cultures. The political appointee may have more organizational authority than the senior career officials who report to that position. That authority is counterbalanced by the organizational knowledge the senior career officials have that the political appointees normally lack. All career employees know that political appointees will be there for only a limited amount of time.

There are two aspects of cultural competence that are useful for bridging the political and civil service boundary. The first aspect acknowledges that the foundation cultural competencies can help in forging effective working relationships. When a political appointee and a career employee meet, they are coming from different cultures—a political culture and an organizational culture, each with its own cultural characteristics. These cultures are considerably different, but the foundation cultural competencies were developed for this purpose.

The second aspect is that although for the most part policies come from the political appointees, it is the career civil servants who implement them. The senior civil servants have typically been in the organization for a long time and know how to "get things done." An effective merging of the two cultures ensures success for cultural competence and diversity initiatives.

The second-level executives may be either political appointees or career employees. In the federal government the assistant secretaries need to be confirmed by the senate. Other levels of government may have different requirements for a second level. The strength that political appointees may bring to these positions is a more finely tuned ear to political constituents and congressional members. Political appointees frequently bring with them fervor for implementing a new agenda. Yet many are not familiar with the bureaucratic world they are now tasked with managing.

Campaigning and managing are two very different endeavors. It is easy for some political appointees to see the career staff as being linked too closely to the previous administration and for the appointees to be dismissive of the senior government employees. In the federal government, the assistant secretaries frequently have to rely on career SES employees, many of whom may have spent extensive time in federal government. They can be helpful in assisting political appointees navigate unfamiliar bureaucratic terrain. While it is unlikely that career SES employees will overtly hinder any new appointee's agenda, it is highly possible they may not be as helpful as they can be. One of the author's mentors revealed that as a young career federal employee, he saw people in the organization who knew where the quicksand was and pulled out the signs. If they liked you, they would tell you where the quicksand was before you stepped into it, he said. This is good advice for anyone entering government service.

Career employees bring with them a long association and often a better understanding of the inner workings of the department and the other career employees than do political employees. Many of the career SES employees have their own relationships with members of Congress and their staff and may also have long relationships with members of congressional committees. Many of the career employees also know their careers depend on how they are viewed by the career SES, and when the political winds change, the career SES will more than likely still be there. Memories can be long.

Career employees need good working relationships with the political appointees, however. They may have to work together for a long time. It is worthwhile for both to develop a good working relationship. The cultural competence model and the foundation cultural competencies are a good starting point to develop these relationships. Both the political appointee and the career employee are facing individuals coming from different cultures. The cultural competence model can be helpful in bridging the cultural differences between the worlds of the political appointees and career civil service employees.

Political appointees bring their enthusiasm to implement the president's agenda. If they have never worked in government, they may be unaware of the procedural nature of the bureaucracy. Political appointees generally come from a campaign that had its own set of rules and was geared to quick and more free-flowing action than found in government administration. Campaigns tend to have a high emotional and partisan intensity. It is not uncommon for appointees to carry this intensity into government positions without realizing that that they are not in campaign mode anymore. Some appointees will carry that intensity with them and believe that they have a mandate to change government, and they may be impatient to accomplish those changes.

The relationship can be more sensitive when there is a transition from the administration of one party into the administration of another political party. If one party has been in power for eight years, the career employees may have incorporated the political philosophy of that party. Those career employees who demonstrated the most enthusiasm for an incumbent political party's agenda may have done very well and been promoted. When a transition in political parties happens and the political appointees arrive with their enthusiasm and desire for quick changes, and they meet the career employees who thrived in the previous administration, there is a possibility for a clash of wills. Distrust can easily arise and create a tense relationship with negative results for both. Many a political appointee of both parties has stumbled badly over a lack of knowledge of the inner workings of the bureaucracy. It is possible to move career SES, after a period of time, into other, less desirable positions.

6.3.1 Political Transitions and Their Effects on Managers

There is a fascinating and interesting dance of power that occurs when political appointees and senior career staff work together. The power can shift to either the political appointee or the career employees. The next two examples show the sides of that dance. Understanding the dynamics can be useful to creating a more effective relationship.

Example 6.1: The Changing of the Guard

Early in his career as a federal career employee, one of the authors was fortunate to see a political change from one political party to another with a very different political philosophy. The senior career employees responded with the behaviors that had made them successful in the previous administration, only the behaviors were no longer effective. Somehow the realization that a new political philosophy was now being implemented had not dawned on them. In the old administration when the top officials wanted a program cut out by the Office of Management and Budget (OMB), the senior career employees went to the president and got their program back in the budget. In the first budget cycle under the new presidency, however, when one of the agency's programs was cut out of the budget and the senior career employees tried going to the president, they never got to see him. Instead, they heard from OMB, in no uncertain terms, how this behavior was unacceptable and not to be repeated. There was much frustration among many of the senior career employees. Many, being long-time government employees, retired. The smarter ones went to the library to read the books on which the current administration based its political philosophy. They thrived and were successful in the new administration.

Example 6.2: Dogs Will Hunt

The reverse also happens. In the same administration, a senior political appointee was meeting with his staff. He was new in his position. He had a mandate to cut costs. The career employees were advocating an expensive testing program critical to the success of a much larger program. The political appointee, being from Texas, responded, "Nope, that dog won't hunt." The career employees looked at each other for several minutes; then the senior career employee looked at the political appointee and said, "Sir, we understand your position. But we want you to understand that if the major program fails, you will be the one responsible for that failure." The political appointee looked at the ceiling for a few moments and then said, "Include the testing program."

6.3.2 Using the Foundation Cultural Competencies to Bridge the Political and Civil Service Boundaries

The foundation cultural competencies can be effective in creating working relationships to successfully manage diversity. Although the focus is on race, ethnicity, gender, sexual orientation, and social class, the cultural competence model and the foundation cultural competencies are also successful at bridging other differences. The first step for the political appointee and the career employee is an understanding that two different cultures and perspectives are merging. There will, more than likely, be cultural differences. We will assume that both employees are competent at what they do. The political appointee brings in the direction for the organization, and the career employee brings in the bureaucratic expertise. Political language can differ from bureaucratic language. Appointees without government experience may want to do things in the most expedient manner without understanding the bureaucratic requirements. In contrast, career employees may be so entrenched in the bureaucratic requirements that they may respond by saying, "It cannot be done." Understanding and acknowledging that cultural differences can exist becomes the first step. Doing so becomes more complex, however, when there are racial, ethnic, gender, sexual orientation, or social class differences as well. While it is helpful if both the career employee and the appointee are culturally competent, bridging the organizational culture can begin with only one of the participants. Respecting the other's culture is the first pillar in the bridge.

The boundary where the political and career employees meet is important to the success of any initiative of the new administration. Once a culturally competent relationship is established across this boundary, the top executive's vision for managing diversity and creating a culturally competent organization can be implemented and translated into managerial performance measurements and standards. The top department executive, typically a secretary assisted by a deputy secretary for federal and state governments, establishes the strategic direction of the initiative for managing diversity. For counties and municipalities, the top executive may be the county commissioner and city manager.

6.4 Major Department Heads

The major department heads are the bridge from the political appointees to the rest of the organization. Depending on the organization, some heads may be political appointees or career employees. They help refine the political vision and strategic plan. The top executives develop the broad strategic vision and goals, whereas the department managers focus on the narrower mandate of their individual departments. The department managers work with the next, lower-level managers to implement the strategic vision and develop performance measures.

Participants of a multicultural leadership program identified the department heads as being the least supportive of managing diversity. The department heads become central to the success of managing diversity in an organization. Department managers translate the top executive's strategic communications into management goals and objectives. Their efforts are pivotal to the success of managing diversity or any other organizational endeavors.

6.5 Leveraging Diversity

In many public organizations, the top executives are generally political appointees with a layer of career officials just below the appointees. The elected president, governor, county commissioners, or city councils appoint the executives. Tasked with implementing the political agenda of the elected officials, they develop the strategy to implement their organizations. The top-executive levels work with legislators who are interested in the mission of their departments. The top executives also work with constituency and community groups. Creating culturally competent organizations can be part of the strategic plan.

Leveraging diversity is preparing the organization for cultural changes driven by demographics. The organization will be in a better position to recruit from the increasingly multicultural applicants pool as the baby boomers retire. Creating a culturally competent organization is also leveraging diversity. Because there may be an increase in the number and size of immigrant and minority communities, the organizational leadership will be communicating with the culturally diverse communities.

The president, governor, mayor, or county head, in conjunction with his or her appointed top executives, is responsible for developing global and domestic strategy. Managing diversity is an organizational responsibility that includes establishing a representative bureaucracy and developing an effective, highly performing, and culturally diverse workforce. The executives of the major departments manage diversity by articulating its importance. The traditional method is to issue a policy detailing the department's diversity policy. If there is an existing diversity policy, updating the policy can serve to refocus attention on diversity.

The cultural competence or diversity initiative shows the executive's commitment to diversity. The initiative is a concrete statement the executive can use in discussions with community leaders and elected officials as evidence of a commitment to diversity. The commitment helps solidify the relationship with community leaders and legislators, a relationship that then serves to develop support for other administration initiatives. Executives, community leaders, and elected officials are working as a team on the diversity directive and as part of the team on other initiatives.

Communication for executives should inspire and motivate employees, and it should be cross-cultural. Inspirational communication resonates emotionally. The executive presents a persuasive message in which employees see themselves as instrumental to the organization's success. An inclusive message where all employees see themselves as active partners in the solution can generate enthusiasm.

There may be those individuals who question whether cultural competence and diversity initiatives are worthwhile. Although it may be clear that not every employee will enthusiastically embrace diversity initiatives, a critical mass of employees can be reached. Diversity can divide and create much discomfort. Some employees may believe that diversity initiatives will give certain advantages to some employees at the expense of other employees. Others may believe that their lives have been fine without diversity, which will just complicate their work lives. There are those who may believe that because of their diversity, they will be at a disadvantage. There will be those employees who would like to find a way to bridge differences but are afraid they may be labeled racist, sexist, or antigay if they are misunderstood. As with many issues that are uncomfortable, creating a culture where diversity is not an issue but an organizational strength can inspire employees.

The demographics of the United States and many European countries show an aging and predominately white population who are retiring and being replaced by multicultural employees. In one company, 95% of the supervisors of multicultural employees were white. The supervisors were included in a multicultural leadership training program. In informal conversations with the trainers, many of the white supervisors said that they did not know why they were there, but they really appreciated being included. Assessments of the multicultural leadership training program showed that more than three-quarters of the supervisors applied what they learned at the training program and applied it to other employees. Inclusiveness means including everyone. Thus cultural competence is not just for white managers, but for all employees. The range of diversity is so great that no matter what group an employee is part of, there will be many other employees who will be different. Cultural competence will be necessary for all employees. Inclusiveness of all employees will bridge the cultural divide.

The importance of establishing a diversity initiative is that it communicates to employees that each individual is important. It signals to employees an inclusive message that their diversity strengthens and contributes to organizational success. It is a signal to employees that diversity is important and that their efforts contribute to the organization's success. It is also a message to the legislature, city councils, and constituent groups that are beginning to reflect the demographic changes of the country that they are being taken seriously. That message can be reinforced in subsequent meetings with this group.

The department or agency heads and functional managers transform the strategic vision into implementable plans and performance measurements. Leveraging diversity as part of the department's strategy requires the same efforts as any other departmental initiatives, but in a more culturally competent manner.

6.6 Creating the Future by Leveraging Diversity as a Strategic Goal

Getting the right people and keeping them in the organization is always a leadership goal and also a challenge. Creating an organization that people want to work for is the first step. Multicultural and diverse applicants need to see an inclusive and welcoming organization where they will have the opportunity to achieve their individual successes. Word-of-mouth is a powerful marketing tool. When employees are happy with their work situation, they pass the word along to other people they know. Diversity management can lead to positive levels of job satisfaction and can be particularly important to employees of color (Pitts & Jarry 2005).

Executives can shape the organizational culture to leverage diversity. The first step is identifying the cultural changes caused by the changing demographics. The various racial and ethnic groups are not evenly spread around the country. States may have a more limited number of different racial and ethnic groups. The federal government, which hires employees from throughout the country, will see a larger number of different racial and ethnic groups from which to select its employees. Tolerance for gay, lesbian, bisexual, and transgender individuals varies from state to state. Some states are conservative, whereas other states are more accepting of gay, lesbian, bisexual, and transgender people. Women will be the majority of the workforce, and the gains women have made will continue.

Inclusiveness is a key component of leveraging diversity. Everyone, including white males, should feel they have a place and long-term future in the organization. If a diversity initiative is already in place, the top executive should reenergize the initiative. The importance of the diversity initiative should be articulated in terms of the importance to the effectiveness of the organization and not just for social equity. The importance of hiring the best employees from a diverse pool of applicants should be a key part of the diversity initiative. All employees should feel they have the opportunity to achieve their career goals. It is not enough to have a diversity initiative; the top executive should also take symbolic steps by actively championing diversity to the employees and the public. Experience from multicultural leadership in the private sector showed that whereas top executives understood and championed diversity initiatives, members of the management layer beneath the top executives were not as supportive. Diversity should be part of the performance standards for all managers, not just top executives. The diversity initiative should also include training for all employees. This is a role that human resources can fill.

The top executives develop relationships with their legislative bodies. At the federal level, secretaries, undersecretaries, and assistant secretaries develop relationships with their respective authorization and appropriation committees. They work with representatives and senators on these committees as well as committee staff, usually in conjunction with their offices of legislative affairs. Some of the political appointees already have relationships with individual legislators and their personal staffs. States have similar dynamics. Counties and cities also have legislative bodies. Elected legislators are beginning to reflect the diversity in the country. They can be helpful in supporting diversity initiatives. This support for diversity can also translate into support for the agency's programs as well.

Multicultural groups with significant populations usually have community groups that provide services or represent these communities. There are many women's groups that represent their interests. There are also several groups that represent the interests of the gay, lesbian, bisexual, and transgender community. Top executives can reach out to these groups to establish relationships to support diversity initiatives. These groups are also helpful in recruiting talented employees. They can likewise help in supporting other programs and initiatives, because they usually have relationships with elected representatives who can support the department's programs.

By reaching out to external constituencies, the top executives can create a favorable image of the organization such that applicants for employment consider it their first choice. Attracting the top applicants gives managers better employees. Jim Collins, in his book *Good to Great* (2001), said that getting the right people on the bus was the first step in transforming an organization from good to great. Attracting the top talent helps accomplish this goal.

Attracting the top talent is the first step. Retaining top talent becomes the second step. Lessons from the private sector indicate that employees are more productive when they see a long-term future for themselves in the organization. Human resources can develop the training programs for managers to teach them to be culturally competent.

The supervisor–employee relationship is key to the effectiveness of the organization and the future of the employee. Employee problems usually manifest themselves in the employees' relationships with their supervisors. Many careers are derailed when employees have problems with their supervisors that cannot be resolved. Even when this problem may be performance related, cultural characteristics may get in the way of resolving the issues. First-generation employees or people whose parents are not professionals may not know how to resolve problems in professional work settings. Their experience in resolving problems is limited to the way family problems were resolved. In some cases, these methods may translate into professional settings. In many other cases, the patterns of resolving problems in their families may prove dysfunctional in professional work settings. In other cases, there may be a great social distance between the employee and the supervisor. The employee may feel uncomfortable and intimidated in any interactions with supervisors and may not know how to resolve problems in a professional manner.

Example 6.3: How to Leverage Diversity for Organizational Effectiveness

Mary Lou, who is white, had recently been appointed assistant secretary of a major department in a large federal agency. Mark, one of her career SESs, walked into her office accompanied by one of his clerical employees, Donna, who wanted to talk with her. Donna is an African American in her thirties. Her parents were working class and did not have high school diplomas. Donna had a high school degree, but she did not have any college education. As happens when a new manager is appointed to head an agency, Mary Lou had heard many stories about the employees who worked in her immediate office. She had heard that one of Donna's previous supervisors, who had a reputation as being vindictive, had tried to fire Donna. Donna took the department to court and acted as her own attorney. She won her case and defeated the department's lawyers. Mary Lou recognized that in Donna she had a very smart individual. After all, with just her high school degree and her intelligence she had beaten the law school–educated lawyers. Mary Lou was fascinated and made a point of making frequent stops at Donna's workstation and chatting with her. One of the first things Mary Lou noticed was that Donna would not look at her and was very brusque and almost disrespectful in her responses. Mary Lou's first reaction was to feel upset at being treated this way, but she decided to set this reaction aside and continue the conversation. After a few conversations, some social and some work related, Mary Lou realized that Donna was a very good employee and a great performer. She also noticed that when Donna talked with other African Americans in the agency, her tone of conversation was quite different and more sociable. When Donna communicated with any of her white colleagues, however, her tone and demeanor changed.

Mary Lou invited Mark and Donna to sit at her conference table. She knew both well by now and asked, "What's going on?"

"Donna wants to talk with you," Mark said.

Mary Lou turned to Donna and asked her, "Donna, what's going on?"

Turning to Mary Lou with tears in her eyes and sobbing softly, Donna replied, "Mary Lou, they are trying to fire me and I don't want to lose my job."

Mary Lou already knew that Donna's problems were not performance related but came from cross-cultural miscommunications and that Donna was an employee worth keeping and developing. Mary Lou looked Donna directly in the eye, paused, and with all the seriousness she could muster said, "Donna, no one is going to fire you as long as I am here. I can't promise you anything after I'm gone, but while I'm here, no one will fire you. I'll stop by often and see how you're doing."

Mary Lou continued to stop by to check in with Donna and ask what she was working on or how her projects were working out. She noticed that over time, Donna's communication was less brusque and friendlier, the same way she related to her African American friends. At the next town hall meeting Mary Lou had with her office staff, she awarded Donna a plaque of recognition and letter of commendation specifying in detail exactly why Donna merited the recognition. The letter of recognition was placed in Donna's personnel file and a copy was sent to the secretary of the department. Donna was the first African American employee ever recognized for her contributions, and there are many African American employees in that agency. Interestingly enough, many of the employees, not just the African Americans, started improving their performance. Mary Lou continued to recognize at her town hall meetings all the employees with exceptional performance.

Several months later, during Black History Month, a few employees in Mary Lou's office approached her to let her know they were on the committee selecting speakers for the Black History Month events at the department. The African American employee group had invited a well-known husband and wife, who were both actors, to be speakers. Representatives of the African American employee group asked Mary Lou if she would introduce the actors at the department event where they would be speaking. The representatives of the African American employee group let Mary Lou know that they had copies of the book. Mary Lou gave the employees the money to buy the book. Several hours before the event, the employees brought the book to Mary Lou and asked her if she wanted to meet the couple to have them autograph the book. They then took her to meet them; the couple autographed Mary Lou's copy of their book and wrote a complimentary message. At the event, the secretary of the department recognized Mary Lou and invited her to introduce the very special guests. Mary Lou was the only non–African American on the stage. She still has and treasures the autographed book, which she has read several times. She still continues to be inspired by their message. Donna is still with the agency, and her career has gone very well.

Multicultural employees have informal networks in which they share information. It is common for multicultural employees to share information, for example, about how they are treated by their various managers. Executives can use such multicultural informal networks to leverage diversity.

The discussion has thus far focused on leveraging diversity for organizational effectiveness. Yet leveraging diversity has benefits for managers beyond the organizational unit for which they are responsible. Employees have work and social relationships beyond the organizational unit in which they work. Whereas managers have working relationships with affinity groups and community groups, they have access to other resources and support that can help them be more effective at their current positions. This extensive multicultural network also provides them with an informal and powerful channel of communication about the effectiveness of the culturally competent manager. Such information can easily reach the ears of higher-level managers, who can be helpful to the career advancement aspirations of lower-level managers. Doors will open for them.

It is easy to notice and focus on one aspect of diversity and to forget that many people have characteristics that include many areas of diversity. Race, ethnicity, biracial status, gender, social class, sexual orientation, religion, and disabilities are some areas that create diversity. These characteristics can create many different combinations in one person. Some of the aspects of diversity may be more noticeable than others. People may be more sensitive about one aspect than another, and this sensitive area can vary from person to person. Such variety creates many opportunities for any two individuals to find areas of commonality between themselves.

While some of the aspects may serve to create social distance between two people, there may be mutually shared aspects that can serve to bring two people closer to create common ground. Common ground and a shared culture provide a more solid launching pad to bridge differences. Common ground can provide a comfort to explore the differences more easily than just by focusing on the differences. Common ground can create more resilient work relationships that overcome minor misunderstandings.

6.7 Preparing the Organization to Be Culturally Competent: Shaping the Organizational Culture

One of the leadership skills for top executives is shaping the organizational culture. Shaping the organizational culture is one of those concepts that is good in principle but can be difficult in practice. In government organizations where political transitions are common, for example, the career employees know that they will be subject to the "flavor of the day," that is, to the particular desires of the party in power. They know that this too will pass, and so they can be very patient. Employees can be quite good at articulating what managers want to hear while maintaining the same behaviors they used successfully in the past.

There is an old management saying, "What gets measured gets done." A large part of shaping the organizational culture is putting in a performance measurement system to track the success of the cultural change. The top executives must articulate the importance of the mission of the organization to the people it serves. They must also stress that it is the employees of the organization who, working together, serve those citizens.

Employees are usually aware of the societal discussions about the importance of managing diversity. The top executives can reinforce their commitment to managing diversity by their actions. Where there are employee groups organized around the various diversities or affinity groups, the top executives can meet with such groups on a fairly regular basis to hear their concerns and applaud their successes. For top executives, listening is more important than talking at these meetings.

Example 6.4: Creating Common Ground with External Groups to Develop Better Relationships

Angela, who served on a presidential transition team, was talking with the president of a constituency group important to the department for which she was preparing the transition. Angela asked the constituency group's president what the secretary of the department could do to develop a good relationship with the group. The constituency group's president responded:

> It would be great if the secretary would meet with us, and it would be even better if the secretary knew who we are and what we do. We would appreciate it very much if the secretary would listen to our concerns and us and not just do all the talking. We could have a great relationship if the secretary would get back to us on what her department is doing about our concerns. We know that all our concerns may not get dealt with, but we would like to hear that this was more than a courtesy visit. We can make a great difference in people's lives if we work together.

This response provides good advice for top executives and department and agency heads, as well as functional managers. Doing what the constituency group's president suggested is particularly important when managing diversity and meeting with affinity groups. Before meeting with an affinity group, meet with the group's leaders to set the agenda for the meeting. Ask what the group's leadership and members would like from the top executives and what their concerns are. Work out a common ground and shared culture where both parties can contribute to the goals of the department. It may not be possible for the top executives to meet or address all the needs or concerns of the group, but efforts can be made in the right direction. This effort should be a partnership where both parties come together to support the goals of the department. This approach creates a team with a good working relationship.

For top executives, symbolic communication can be very effective in shaping the organizational culture. Can the top executives point to examples where members of the affinity group have done exceptionally well? These employees should be recognized at the meeting. Attention should be paid to other symbolic actions such as photo opportunities. These photo opportunities should be planned in advance; advance planning can help prevent awkward moments.

Where the top executives are actively shaping the organizational culture, the process is easier for department heads and middle managers. Many employees understand the importance of diversity, and so the task for department or agency heads is more a managerial and technical process. Department heads and middle managers have powerful roles in managing diversity and any other initiative. They understand the organization's culture and dynamics. They have organizational savvy, which is how they attained their current positions. Organizational savvy can be defined as the emotional intelligence of an organization. One of the foremost examples of organizational savvy at work is the ability to develop a give-and-take approach with others. The basics of this approach go back to the kindergarten playground, where share and share alike is a daily rule. But this also means that you should expect to give back if someone in the organization helps you out.

Many department heads also develop relationships with members of their legislative bodies and community and constituency groups. In some ways, this is similar to what the secretary of the department and other top executives must do. For many department heads, however, the relationships with legislators and community groups are more focused on the particular mission and mandate of their particular agency. Department heads may give speeches to conferences of their constituency and community groups. Typically, department heads may want to have their speech detail what their department is doing for the groups. The speech may contain many statistics about how well the department is helping the groups. The relationship created is that the department head is always talking and the members of the group are listening. A politically savvy department head may make this approach work. Others may find that creating this kind of relationship may not be very effective.

The cultural competence model starts by having the particular community, constituency, or affinity group guide you. The leaders of the constituency or community group know the needs of their members very well. Many of the group's posts are elected positions. To be elected, the leaders have to know the needs of their members. Listening to the leadership is the first step.

Working with culturally diverse community and constituency groups is a symbolic communication that the department's leaders are serious about managing diversity. Good relationships with culturally diverse community groups help shape the organizational culture. The message the leadership sends to the employees is one of inclusiveness. If the organization's leaders are inclusive of external culturally diverse groups, they are also inclusive of culturally diverse employees.

A solid common ground or shared culture makes it more likely that misunderstandings will not lead to conflict. The working relationship that results from the respect, inclusiveness, and common ground makes it easier to overcome any misunderstandings. There is enough depth to the working relationship that misunderstandings become learning opportunities, not gateways to conflict. What led to the misunderstanding can then be explored in the comfort of the common ground, and both parties can learn and move on.

Leadership–follower dynamics are important to demonstrating respect. The manager is the figure of authority and will be treated with respect and deference. When a manager sees employees who come from family-oriented cultures where great deference is shown to figures of authority, they may see employees who are polite and very nice, who do what they are told and work very hard. These family-oriented cultures may span more than one racial or ethnic group, and each group will have its own cultural variations. Looking at employees from such a culture, what the manager may not see is that when they feel they are not respected, they may still be very nice and polite. On the surface, then, everything may seem fine. The multicultural employees may be polite and may do what is required but can become passive-aggressive. They can pretend to know much less than they really know. They may do the routine work but then respond that something new cannot be done or they do not know how and have never been taught. They will say so politely and nicely. This situation is dysfunctional for both the employees and the manager and can create a dysfunctional work environment.

As noted, employees who come from cultures where figures of authority are given deference and not questioned tend to be very polite and deferential. Politeness can be a way of life and reciprocity is part of the culture. Thus the employee expects to be treated with respect and politeness as well. Organizations can be bottom-line oriented, where business is conducted brusquely. In such environments, there is little time for niceties in communication. Many organizations experience periods of quick turnaround or have to complete projects under great pressure. High-stress environments tend to bring out the best and the worst in employees. Tempers may flare as deadlines loom. Managers under intense pressure can become terse and demanding. A tense environment is created that provides fertile ground for misunderstandings and conflict. The aftermath may linger for months.

In these cultures, maintaining good relationships can be paramount. More emphasis is placed on maintaining relationships than on accomplishing tasks. In contrast, organizations can be more task oriented. When managers and employees are emphasizing different aspects of a situation, they can be working at cross-purposes. Each is emphasizing what each sees as important, but the other person is not responding in the expected way. Intense frustration can build across this divide that can erupt into conflict. Each person is working very hard to make the situation better, but the result is that the situation gets worse. It is a small step to making the other person the one at fault. Cultural competence can sidestep these problems.

In many relationship cultures, it is common to give gifts, especially when one is requesting a favor from another person. The giving of gifts is embedded in the social fabric of the society and is a common way of life. Employees from such gift-giving cultures may be from the Middle East, Latin America, and Central America, as well as some parts of Asia. Public organizations have ethical guidelines that preclude managers and employees from receiving gifts over a certain monetary value when conducting public business. The easy solution is to refuse the gift outright, but doing so can create an awkward cultural moment. The employee may see this rejection of the gift as a personal rejection. There are better ways to handle such a situation in a culturally competent manner. A manager can use this as a learning opportunity to explain the ethical organizational culture and what is allowable. For example, if they have coffee together, do the ethics regulations allow the employee to buy the coffee? Some organizations have a specific dollar limit for the amount of gifts. The manager can explain how to handle requests like this in a manner that meets the ethical requirements of the organization. This can be the beginning of the manager being a mentor to the employee.

A manager may have employees who come from cultures that are more competitive, where negotiating for everything is a way of life. These cultures may also span more than one racial or ethnic group and sometimes even social class. Many work interactions thereby become negotiations. The employee may ask for resources or rewards that may be impractical. The problem for the manager is the reverse of the situation with polite and deferential employees. Instead of politeness and sometimes passivity, the manager faces an employee with abundant energy who can sometimes be too aggressive. In this case, the manager must resist the temptation to respond with the same energy and assertiveness. Two intense human energies can create quite a tempest. The manager communicates respect by demonstrating an understanding that the employee sees this highly energetic approach as a path to success. The manager can explain that while high energy is good, it has to be channeled into creating collaborative working relationships. Good working relationships are created by having people move toward you, not away from you. An energy that is too intense can push people away. Respect for others also means letting them know what they are doing that is getting in the way of their success. The manager can explain the cultural requirements of the organization. Usually employees are appreciative of feedback that is beneficial to their careers. Giving critical feedback can be a sensitive process. By communicating respect and inclusiveness, the manager creates the common ground for providing critical feedback. Common ground has already been established, and common ground means the employees know that the manager has their best interest at heart.

Part of respecting an employee's culture is the responsibility for explaining the requirements of the organizational culture. In a private sector organization for which one of the authors helped develop a multicultural leadership training program and executive coaching, the organization would forgive much in employees, but keeping quiet and not actively participating in meetings was the kiss of death for the employees. Once common ground has been created, a manager can explain the organizational cultural requirements. Mutual respect is a two-way relationship.

A manager shows respect for the abilities of the employee by explaining the requirements the employee is expected to perform.

Part of managing diversity is the manager–employee relationship. At this organizational level, the employees are also managers of organizational subunits. The other aspect of managing diversity is seeing that diverse employees are developing good working relationships among themselves. In some ways, this may be more difficult. A quick and easy test for the cultural competence of the employees is noticing with whom they spend their informal time. Do they spend their coffee breaks or lunches with employees like themselves or with other diverse employees? People tend to be more comfortable with others like themselves, perhaps because social interactions seem easier. Where members of one cultural group are few in number, they may perceive themselves as different and want to socialize together for a sense of belonging and comfort. Although individually comforting, this may serve to isolate them and create social distance with others. When a new employee joins an organizational unit where employees have been there a long time, it is not unusual for the long-time employees to comment on any differences they perceive in the newcomer. It is also common for the new employee to become aware of the comments. Focusing on differences can create social distance between the new employees and the long-time employees.

Helping employees become culturally competent can depend on how diverse the organization is. In an organizational culture where diversity is a recent phenomenon and one cultural group is dominant, the dominant cultural group may not see a need to be culturally competent. The group members' experience is that they did not need to be culturally competent before, so why would they need to be culturally competent now? There may be confusion. Does cultural competence really mean affirmative action? What are employees really being asked to do, and why is it important? Why can't the new employees just assimilate?

Two aspects of being a culturally competent manager are respect for all cultures and inclusiveness of all cultures, including the dominant culture. The manager communicates respect for the views of the dominant culture and ensures that its members feel included. Where there is an organizational diversity initiative, the manager explains how employees will support and implement the initiative. The manager reinforces the message that the bottom line is how to best maintain organizational effectiveness. The reality is that diversity is now much greater than at any earlier time. The communities that organizations serve are more diverse and so are the employees. To deal with this diversity, managers must turn to cultural competence as one of the newly emerging leadership and management skills. Cultural competence is expected of all employees, not just managers. Long-time employees can help by welcoming new employees, including them in their informal network, and explaining the organizational culture. They can show the new employees "how things are done here." Organizational effectiveness relies on team effectiveness. This is another tool for creating effective work teams.

6.8 Communicating to Inspire Diverse and Multicultural Employees

At the executive level, communication should inspire the employees to put forth their best efforts. Inspirational communication becomes more important during times of change and anxiety. Inspiration comes from connecting on an emotional and symbolic level with employees. Connecting on an emotional level with employees who are culturally diverse can be difficult. Once executives have made managing and leveraging diversity a priority, affinity groups can be used to tailor the message to particular groups. Affinity groups are groups of employees with a common background. Affinity groups include racial and ethnic groups such as African Americans, Asians, and Hispanics. There are also affinity groups that are gay, lesbian, bisexual, and transgender. Affinity groups have meetings and may, in large organizations, have their own conferences. Executives can meet with each of these groups with messages focused for each group. The focused and tailored messages are developed in conjunction with the leaders of each group. Developing a working relationship with the leaders benefits both the executives and the affinity groups. The working relationship, which can help to prevent problems and also aids in developing support for leadership initiatives, arises from inclusion and working as a team for the betterment of both. The foundational cultural competencies set the framework for working with affinity groups, which together with the executives are teams working to make the organization more productive and to solve any problems.

The affinity groups work with the executives to create messages and symbolic actions that are culturally correct and effective. The leaders of the affinity group can help the executives fashion a message about what is important to their members and what message will resonate with them. Photo opportunities will also arise from these meetings. Top executives meeting with and listening to affinity groups provides a powerful symbolic message that the executives are serious about diversity initiatives. Affinity groups, as members of the team, can let their members know what their responsibilities are and what they can do to make the organization more productive and provide more opportunities for group members.

6.9 Developing and Mentoring Managers to Be Culturally Competent

Top-level managers are as critical to the success of any cultural competence initiatives as the top executives. Top-level managers who are usually civil servants and not political appointees are the individuals who implement the executive agenda. The participants of the private sector multicultural programs discussed in Chapter 5 identified this level of managers as not being as supportive of managing diversity as were the top executives. There may be parallels in the public sector. Top-level managers have usually spent many years in the organization. They have probably been involved in organizational affirmative action programs and may see cultural competence as a variation of affirmative action. Top-level managers may be more internally focused and less aware of the changing demographics. The managers who report to them may be long-time employees and not as diverse a group as the newer employees. They may also be unaware of the organizational demographic changes.

Executives can help by emphasizing the importance of cultural competence and managing diversity in today's organizations. As the baby boomers retire, the organization should be positioned to attract the best new employees. Their replacements will be more diverse and multicultural. Executives can model cultural competence and be supportive of the top-level managers' training. Performance standards and measures ensure the top executives' seriousness about managing diversity. Culturally competent top-level managers will then be well positioned to develop and mentor the managers who report to them.

Managers, who report to the top-level managers, need an understanding of what cultural competence is and what it is not. They also need an understanding of how cultural competence will help them be successful. The changing demographics in today's organization require managing an increasing number of multicultural and diverse employees. Culturally competent managers are equipped to bring out the best performance in their employees, so that working together they can create a high-functioning organization. Cultural competence is not just for white managers; cultural competence is necessary for all employees. Top-level managers should emphasize the support offered by the top executives. The importance of cultural competence to careers can be addressed, as well as how cultural competence will be part of the performance measurements. It is in the managers' best interests to be on board the cultural competence train.

6.10 Summary and Conclusion

The various management levels have different responsibilities, and cultural competencies can be developed for each management level. In most public organizations, the top executives are political appointees. They bring into the organization a political, strategic, and more externally focused vision. They are responsible for implementing the political agenda of the elected officials, whether they include the president of the United States, the state governor, county commissioners, or the local mayor and city council. The cultural competencies for executives enable them to leverage diversity to support the political agenda and develop relationships with legislators, interest groups, and other governments. The executives will be communicating to inspire diverse and multicultural constituencies and employee groups.

The top-level managers are the management layer beneath the appointed executives. Many top-level managers are major agency heads. They are usually career and civil servants with long tenures in their respective departments. They have most likely seen several political transitions. In some ways, these managers may be the more resistant management group. Although they may be aware of societal demographic trends from news reports, they may be less aware of the demographic changes further down in the organization. Some individuals may see managing diversity as a passing trend, the "flavor of the month," and not be as diligent in implementing diversity initiatives. For these managers, it will be helpful for the executives to communicate the importance of the diversity initiatives and their willingness to track the implementation of these initiatives through performance standards and measurements.

The primary cultural competency for the top-level managers will be to develop and mentor the managers who report to them. Having several layers of managers who are culturally competent leverages diversity and ensures the implementation of diversity initiatives.

Chapter 7

Cultural Competencies for Middle Managers and Supervisors

For those who have seen the earth from space, and for the hundreds and perhaps thousands more who will, the experience most certainly changes your perspective. The things that we share in our world are far more valuable than those which divide us.

Donald Williams
Wisdom Quotes, n.d.

7.1 Introduction

Middle managers and supervisors are the level between the top managers and the employees who are individual contributors. Their management duties may vary from managing large organizational units to overseeing a handful of employees. Individual contributors do not have anyone reporting to them and do not normally have supervisory duties and responsibilities. For the purposes of this book, middle managers oversee other managers, whereas supervisors are responsible for employees or individual contributors. Middle managers can be seen as the employees who translate and implement the organizational vision, initiatives, and strategy developed by the top executives. The success of organizational initiatives often rests on the shoulders of the middle managers.

In Appendix 4 of his book *Working with Emotional Intelligence*, Daniel Goleman (2000) includes a section on managing diversity based on the work of Stanford psychologist Claude Steele. Steele's approach comes from his understanding of the emotional dynamics that undermine performance in minority groups. Several of the points made are in agreement with the work of other writers. Valuing multiple perspectives can be seen as respecting cultural differences. Affirming the sense of belongingness is being inclusive. An emphasis on learning and understanding shows that competence can be gained through on-the-job training.

In the same book, Goleman (2000) mentions five social skills that are essential for handling another person's emotions. These social skills can be seen as essential for the middle managers and supervisory levels of management, which serve as the bridge between the top executives and the employees. The five competencies are:

1. Influence
2. Communication
3. Conflict management
4. Leadership
5. Change catalyst

These five competencies are core leadership competencies as well and are contained within the guidelines that the U.S. Office of Personnel Management (OPM) uses to evaluate candidates hoping to advance their careers into the ranks of the Senior Executive Service (SES).

Another indicator of the importance of the core leadership competencies described above is the Hay Group (2004a), who have developed an assessment and evaluation method that uses emotional intelligence for leadership training as well as other organizational training requiring emotional competencies. The Hay Group has developed surveys to measure emotional competence and has validated the level that corresponds to effective leadership.

The five social skills can also be placed in a cross-cultural context, where they can be used in combination with one cross-cultural skill supporting another. Emotional competence is easier when working in a monocultural environment. Reading social and emotional cues across cultures can be difficult. Social and emotional cues can vary tremendously across cultures. Quiet and respectful employees who do not look managers in the eye and who do not contradict the manager may be seen as lacking emotional intelligence and the potential for leadership. Employees of color may have difficulty interpreting social and emotional cues of other employees and vice versa. Having employees act as guides to their cultural characteristics provides understanding of how they interpret social and emotional cues.

Managers can have tremendous influence on the employees. Employees are frequently more familiar with the managers than they are with the top executives, whose priorities the managers interpret. In many cases this arrangement can work well; in some cases, though, the managers may provide their own priorities that may differ from those of the top executives. Many top executives assume, however, that their priorities are always followed. It is worthwhile for top executives to see if their priorities have been properly transferred to the rest of the employees.

Typically, middle managers focus more on internal organization and less on working with community groups. The exceptions are those organizational units that provide services to community groups or individuals outside of government. Middle managers may not be as sensitive to or aware of the societal changes in their environment. They may be long-time employees who have become set in their ways and may be reluctant to change. Ensuring that these managers have the cultural competence training and executive support can make cultural competence initiatives successful. Good performance standards and measurements help executives determine the progress of their organization's initiatives.

Middle managers are responsible for the results of major organizational units. Many will have been with the same agency or departments for many years, and they will have great institutional memories. As middle managers rise through the organizational career ladder, they may do less hands-on work, but they still need to be technically current to be successful. Keeping up with the state of the art is important. They still need to communicate with the technical experts, and having a common language helps in maintaining good communications. The managerial cultural competencies work quite well for managing any differences besides cultural differences.

Some organizations may have second-level managers, who are responsible for overseeing supervisors, who are happy staying at that level. Many come from the more technically focused areas of the organization. They are excellent at what they do, but for their own reasons they have decided they do not want to get involved in the politics of the organization. Other managers reach a certain level of management and for their own personal reasons decide that they do not want to rise any higher in the organization. These employees can be a great organizational resource, or they can retire on the job. The challenge for their managers is keeping them engaged.

Supervisors manage employees who are in entry-level positions. They should be technically competent in the same skills as the employees they manage. They are responsible for their organization's team efforts. As managers, they should also be responsible for developing their employees. The supervisors will probably be the first to experience the changing demographics and an increase in employees with multicultural backgrounds. In 2010, it is projected (Yen 2010) minority births will overtake white births. The multicultural population is younger and beginning to influence the K–12 school system. The U.S. Census Bureau projects that at some time in the 2020s minorities will outnumber whites in the K–12 school system. Women are projected to become more than half the workforce in 2010 (Cauchon 2009). These timeframes show the tipping point where minorities and women cross the 50% threshold. These demographic changes are already happening; and as these individuals join the workforce, the supervisor will usually be the first to manage the increasing diversity in the workforce. Cultural competence will be required from the supervisor and the employees the supervisor manages if they are both to enjoy successful experiences.

Team leader is a position that has been gaining in importance in many organizations that use teams to work on special problems or to solve organizational problems. A team leader is appointed to head the team. Frequently, the team leader does not have the direct-line authority that supervisors usually have. Persuasion and developing good team relationships becomes the mechanism for effective team results. With the increasing diversity in the workplace, persuasion and developing work relationships will have a cultural context.

7.2 Cultural Competencies for Managers and Supervisors

The managerial cultural competencies are designed to be appropriate for middle managers and supervisors. Table 7.1 describes the skill sets and cultural competencies required of middle managers and supervisors.

The managerial cultural competencies focus on being responsible for fairly large organizational units and being a manager over several layers of management. Success in managing several units depends on the effectiveness of the work teams that compose these units. In the evolving multicultural work world, these will be multicultural teams composed of many employees of varied diversity. Blending all the employees with different perspectives into effective teams becomes a priority for managers.

Besides being responsible for the results of their organizational units, managers can play a pivotal role in developing managers and supervisors who report to them. Managers may have entered government service 10 or 15 years earlier, when there was less employee diversity, as well as less emphasis placed on managing diversity and being culturally competent. They may not see the importance of being culturally competent in today's changing world. As new and more multicultural employees join the organization, these managers may welcome the increased diversity, or they may not see a need to be culturally competent. The higher-level managers may also have lower-level managers reporting to them who have also been with the organization for many years and may have a similar perspective. These individuals may have organizational distance from the more multicultural employees who are recent entrants to government service.

The cultural competence model of culture, communication, misunderstandings and conflict, and leader–employee relationships is still applicable for these managers. Cultural competence is good management and helps the organization be more effective. When employees feel included as an integral part of the organizational

Table 7.1 Managerial Cultural Competencies for Middle Managers and Supervisors

Public Organizational Level	Roles, Responsibilities, and Duties	Managerial Cultural Competencies
Middle managers	1. Manage large organizational units 2. Be a superb manager 3. Develop other managers 4. Be technically current 5. Develop relationships with upper-level managers	1. Developing culturally competent middle managers 2. Creating effective diverse and multicultural teams 3. Mentoring diverse and multicultural middle managers
Supervisors	1. Deliver team results 2. Be technically competent 3. Develop employees 4. Develop relationships with middle managers and functional managers	1. Developing culturally competent employees 2. Mentoring diverse and multicultural managers 3. Developing cross-cultural manager–employee relationships

culture, they will more likely be effective employees. Not letting cultural differences lead to misunderstandings and conflicts creates a collaborative work environment. Managers can ensure that all levels of the manager–employee relationship are culturally competent.

7.3 Developing Culturally Competent Managers

Communicating the importance of cultural competence and what it means—and just as important, what it does not mean—helps managers understand cultural competence. Cultural competence does not mean that certain employees get special or preferential treatment. It does mean that employees may bring with them various cultural characteristics and patterns of communication that may be different from the norms in the organization. These employees may not fully understand the organizational culture and what is expected of them. It also may be difficult to use appearances to understand the cultural characteristics that employees bring with them into organizations.

Managers should know the importance of:

1. Managing diversity
2. Understanding how cultural differences can hinder organizational effectiveness
3. Understanding the informal organization and its effects on cultural competence

They should also develop specific skills to become culturally competent managers. They should know how to:

1. Communicate in a culturally competent way
2. Be an effective cross-cultural mentor
3. Establish cultural competence performance standards
4. Measure cultural competence performance

7.4 Mentoring Multicultural Managers

Effective mentoring can help all employees and especially diverse employees. Some organizations initiate official mentoring programs. Barak and Levin (2002) recommend mentoring as a way of including diverse employees into the inner circles of the organization and of helping them design successful careers. The Korn/Ferry International study (1998) showed the benefits of employees who had mentors. Many multicultural employees do not fully understand the organizational culture. Managers and supervisors can mentor these employees on the requirements of the organizational culture. Many multicultural employees do not know how to handle problems at work and may, at times, express their issues in less than appropriate ways. Mentors can show them how to express their problems in a more acceptable fashion.

Mentors can benefit as well. Managers who are good mentors benefit by the increased performance of their employees. Managers enjoy the benefits of having fewer employee problems. Managers can mentor employees on solving problems with other managers and employees. Employee problems with each other can be thorny issues and can create dysfunctional workplaces.

Managers and supervisors can mentor employees on effective conflict resolution. In many cases, managers can intervene before simple misunderstandings can escalate into bigger problems. Managers are frequently in a better position to handle problems in a more effective manner than the employees themselves. Mentoring other managers and employees allows a manager to get a better sense of what is happening in the informal and social aspect of the organization. The insight is helpful in preventing problems.

The downside to official mentoring programs happens when managers sign up to be mentors just to enhance their own careers. These managers will benefit their career by showing they are official mentors. Informal mentors can be as effective as official mentors, however, and can in many situations be more effective. Informal mentors help employees for the sake of the employees' development and not just their own careers.

There are many benefits to being an informal mentor. A manager will:

1. Have a better understanding of the informal social organization
2. Know when there are misunderstandings and conflicts among the employees
3. Be able to defuse misunderstandings before they degenerate into conflict

By mentoring employees, culturally competent managers help employees:

1. Become more effective
2. Feel they are an integral part of the organization
3. Be more willing to undertake additional assignments

Furthermore, employees who are successful and are promoted into other positions can become a managerial resource for the mentor.

7.5 Becoming a Culturally Competent Mentor

A manager first needs a solid understanding of the managerial cultural competencies (explained in Chapter 3):

1. Respect for and understanding of other cultures or diversities
2. Communication in a multicultural and diverse world
3. Creation of a common ground or a shared culture
4. Adaptability or flexibility
5. Inclusiveness as a way to create effective teams and collaboration

The manager then learns the important aspects of mentoring in cross-cultural settings:

1. Showing respect for cultural differences
2. Having the adaptability and flexibility to respond to diverse employees and managers
3. Knowing how to communicate in a culturally competent manner
4. Including everyone in the opportunity to be mentored
5. Getting an employee's permission to be mentored
6. Knowing on which important aspects to mentor an employee
7. Being able to communicate constructive criticism effectively

Mentoring employees should be a voluntary activity that is inclusive of everyone. One reason mentoring should be voluntary and inclusive is so that no one feels left out; thus there is less likely to be a sense of this opportunity being yet another benefit for minorities. A second reason is that employees who volunteer are letting the manager know they are actually interested in improving their performance. Investing extra energy on these employees can have a better payoff than just mentoring everyone. This approach is a good way to identify potentially high-performing employees. If the employees who did not volunteer complain that they are left out, the manager can explain that they did not volunteer but are welcome to do so at any time.

To ensure that the mentoring relationship is successful, there should be a written contract that lays out the responsibilities of the mentor and the employee being mentored. Both parties to the mentoring relationship can now clearly see what is expected of each. (See DVD for a sample mentoring and coaching template.) The contract should include the following details:

1. The responsibilities of each party
2. The differences between validation and feedback
3. The employee's list of career aspirations
4. The career skills that are being mentored:
    a. Performance
    b. Reputation
    c. Relationships
    d. Visibility
    e. Conflict resolution
5. The understanding that being mentored may mean accepting additional assignments and learning about the organizational culture
6. The agreement that the mentor will quit the mentoring relationship only when the employee has learned as much as desired or when he or she stops doing the assignments (i.e., an understanding that the mentor ends the relationship only when the employee being mentored ends the relationship first)

The first agreement is required because the mentoring relationship provides feedback on an employee's strengths and weaknesses; this should be a confidential relationship where discretion is the rule. Confidentiality allows an employee to raise issues with the assurance that they will not be revealed to other managers and employees. The confidentiality agreement is part of establishing common ground and a common culture. The relationship begins with trust. The employee being mentored also agrees to being given validation and feedback and agrees to accept the assignments given by the mentor. The employee also agrees to the confidential nature of the mentoring relationship and to being discreet in discussing the mentoring relationship with anyone else.

It is crucial that both the mentor and the employee being mentored understand the difference between validation and feedback. Validation is acknowledging the excellent performance an employee is doing. It is a "good boy" or "good girl" response. Feedback is letting the employee know what he or she is doing well and also what needs to be improved. Validation can make one feel good and says, in effect, "Continue what you are doing." Feedback is more valuable, though it may not feel as good. It lets one know what needs to be done to improve one's performance.

Example 7.1: Validation versus Feedback

John had been working very hard on an assignment, When he finished, he walked over to his boss's office and handed it to his supervisor, Sally, and said, "I finished this and I want to know what you think." Sally told John, "I have some work to finish today, but I will read it tonight and give you my thoughts on it tomorrow." The next morning John walked into Sally's office to ask, "What do you think about it?" Sally pulled his work from her briefcase and said, "There are some good parts, but there are other parts that still need a lot of work. I've marked the parts that still need work." She looked up from John's work and saw from the look on John's face that he had been asking for validation, not feedback.

It is important that both parties clearly understand whether validation or feedback is being given by the mentor. Validation feels very good to both. It is fulfilling to receive validation that one is doing well, and it is gratifying for managers to acknowledge when an employee is doing great. Validation or positive feedback usually conveys the message that the employee should continue doing what he or she is doing. But it is feedback or constructive criticism that allows an employee to develop career-enhancing skills and to make changes to avoid derailing his or her career.

The mentor includes in the contract that the employee agrees to be mentored on the skills and competencies that are necessary to the career aspirations the employee wants to achieve. The mentor will let the employee know what the organizational culture requires of upwardly mobile employees for them to achieve their individual career aspirations. This step is crucial in being a culturally competent manager. In this step, the employee accepts his or her *willingness* to become an effective member of the current organizational culture.

7.6 Mentoring Career Skills

Knowing how to have a successful career is important to many employees. It is especially important to multicultural employees. The experience from the multicultural leadership programs showed that many of the multicultural employees did not know how to have successful careers. Part of the training was showing them how to develop successful careers. Working with their supervisors, they developed long-term career plans. The employees were provided constructive feedback. They learned how to correct their shortcomings. Knowing they had a long-term future with the organization increased their motivation and productivity. The managers gained from having more motivated and productive employees.

The manager mentors employees in five areas:

1. Performance
2. Reputation and credibility
3. Relationships
4. Visibility
5. Conflict resolution

The five areas are work related. The importance of mentoring in work-related areas lies in this not becoming a discussion of the relative merits of one culture versus another. The discussions should revolve around what skills an employee needs to develop to match his or her career aspirations to the requirements of the organizational culture.

Cultural characteristics may become part of the discussion. People from cultures with high deference for figures of authority may use a formal title or Mr. and Miss or Ms. when addressing their mentors. After the relationship has been in place for a while, the mentor may feel more comfortable with a less formal address but may find that the employee being mentored has a difficult time using less formal titles. Other employees may be more informal in their relationships with other managers and employees, even when organizational protocol may require more formal titles. The mentor may discuss when organizational protocols require more formal addresses and when it is proper to be less informal. In some situations, formal titles and more formal behavior denote respect. Being less formal, in the proper circumstances, implies a good working relationship and also can convey respect.

As the manager mentors employees from different cultures, he or she can learn about the cultural characteristics of those cultures. The manager knows what to expect when he or she meets other employees and managers from those cultures. As a manager mentors more diverse employees, he or she learns more about the different diversities that employees bring into an organization. Thereby the manager's understanding of the different cultures and diversities increases. Understanding the cultural and diversity characteristics of employees helps to prepare the manager to understand the immigrant and minority communities and to reach out to gay, lesbian, bisexual, and transgender groups. Reaching out to these communities is a cultural competency for top executives. Mentoring is a good preparation to be considered for the top executive positions.

Employees need to know how they are performing. A manager does a disservice to employees when he or she does not let them know that their work is not meeting the required standards. John, for example, was a dean at an Alaskan university. Joyce was a secretary who reported to his executive assistant. Originally from the backwoods of Idaho, Joyce was a wonderful and well-liked person who could not do enough for anyone. Everyone liked her; she really was a wonderful person. She spoke with a backwoods, rural accent and in her speech used many colorful and quaint rural expressions. Her speech was fine for informal conversations, and sometimes her expressions were charming. She wrote letters in the same way she spoke, however. Consequently, her writing did not meet the requirements for formal professional correspondence. She was so nice that no one would tell her that her English needed improvement. Colleagues would just quietly rewrite her correspondence. Joyce thought she was doing great.

When a clerical position opened in the dean's office, Joyce applied for it and thought she would be given the promotion. But because of her backwoods English and lack of knowledge of the more formal English required for written communications, she was not given the position. Joyce went to see the dean to find out what happened. After the dean explained why she was denied the promotion, Joyce started crying. She asked the dean why she had not been told before. The dean told her that she was so nice that no one wanted to hurt her feelings. Joyce said that had she known, she would have taken classes to learn proper English. The look on her face let the dean know just how grave a mistake he had made, and it is a mistake he never made again. He also made sure that Joyce got the proper training to improve her English, and he became her mentor.

Claude Steele (Goleman 2000) makes the point that providing challenging work conveys respect for a person's potential. This is an important consideration in mentoring employees, especially employees who are considered to be minority or who are women. It is likely they will hear from other employees that they got the position only because of their status. Challenging assignments convey to all employees that these are talented employees who merit respect for their abilities. They are not being treated in any special manner; they face the same, if not more, challenging work assignments as other employees. Giving employees challenging assignments is letting them know that they are really respected as employees and that they really are valued team members. That respect can easily turn into confident and competent employees.

7.6.1 Mentoring on Reputation and Credibility

Reputation is how others view a manager or employee and can be considered a measure of a manager's or employee's credibility. Mentors can provide employees with invaluable feedback about how others perceive them. The feedback is work and performance related. Mentoring an employee is an area that may involve feedback about cultural characteristics as well as gender, sexual orientation, or social class.

Example 7.2: Mentoring Strategies

Jerry is a director. Kim, who is Asian, has recently been hired. Jerry knows that she is very knowledgeable and capable. She is also reserved and extremely polite. He has also noticed that at staff meetings, she tends to be very quiet. Paul, a former college football player, is physically large and has a lot of energy. He tends to dominate the staff meetings. Assistant Secretary Katy has asked Jerry to mentor both Kim and Paul.

Jerry invited Kim to see him to let her know that Assistant Secretary Katy wanted him to mentor her. He explained to Kim what would be involved and what was expected from both of them. Between them they worked out a mentoring agreement, which both signed. They made an appointment to meet for mentoring.

When they met for the mentoring meeting, Jerry told Kim:

> Kim, I have now worked with you long enough to know how good you are [validation], and I really appreciate having you as a valued member of the team [inclusiveness]. Our team is really critical to the mission of the department, and the secretary really counts on us to deliver. I think I know you better than the other members of the team do because I work closer with you than they do. I want you to know that they perceive you as being too quiet and not contributing when we have meetings [reputation—how others see her]. We need everyone on the team to contribute, and you do, but just in meetings with me. How do you see it [asking for her perceptions]?

Kim replied:

> I know that I should say more, but I still don't feel very comfortable here yet. Paul intimidates me. He is a big man and has so much energy; I don't know how to stop him long enough for me to say anything. In my family, if I interrupt someone, my parents would let me know that it isn't proper for me to interrupt people when they are talking. I come from a quiet family; we don't fight for who is going to talk [cultural characteristics]. It's easier for me to just let you know what I'm thinking in our meetings.

Jerry thought about what Kim said for a few minutes. Jerry looked at her and said:

> Kim, I understand. Once Paul gets started and on a roll, he is hard to slow down or stop. But you told me that you wanted to rise higher in the organization. To be seen as having the leadership to rise to the levels you want, you will have to demonstrate that you can manage team meetings [teaching about the requirements of the organizational culture]. I now understand you better knowing about your family background [common ground and a shared culture—you have a safe environment to talk about your background]. I had to learn many new behaviors to get to where I am, and I will still need to learn more to get to where I want to go [empathy]. I know that I'm asking you to do something that is difficult for you; and yet, it is something you will need to succeed in your career aspirations. Let me make this suggestion: In meetings where Paul is on a roll, raise your hand and wave it until you get Paul's attention. When Paul looks at you, look him in the eye and tell him, "Paul, I like what you have to say, and I like the energy you bring to the meetings. I would like to respond to some of what you said, and I would like to know if anyone else has anything they would like to contribute." Because we are a team [you are part of this team], if for some reason Paul does not stop, I will intercede and tell Paul, "You know Kim. I like what Kim said, and I would like to hear what others have to say [you are part of the team and you have my support]." What do you think?

Kim looked at Jerry and said, "I'm willing to do it if you support me."

Jerry responded, "You have my support, and this will go a long way to having you develop the leadership skills for the next level. I'm proud of you for your willingness to try [validation]. I like having you as part of this team [we are a team and inclusiveness]. And, by the way, I would like to know more about your family, if it's okay with you [letting Kim determine her comfort level in what she discloses about her family]."

Kim laughed and said, "Sure, if you really want to know. Thanks for your help."

7.6.2 Mentoring on Relationships as a Way of Creating Effective Multicultural Teams

The quality of the relationships with others is important to career success. Successful relationships with others allow employees to bring additional resources to their jobs. The first set of relationships to develop is the working relationships with other members of the organizational unit. There are benefits for the supervisor-mentor. Having a work group where employee relationships are good and employee problems with other employees are minimized helps a supervisor have more time to focus on work-related problems. The manager will spend less time solving thorny employee problems. The organizational unit will become a better functioning team. Mentoring employees on having good relationships with each other makes it easier for the supervisor to discover employee problems when they are small and relatively easy to solve. Small problems left unattended can become difficult personnel issues.

Example 7.3: How to Build Cross-Cultural Relationships

Tom, who is white, had just come to work for a new organizational unit. Lynn, an African American, was the director's secretary and had been part of this organizational unit for a long time. Her director was also African American. Lynn was very good at her duties and was extremely protective of her supervisor. After a few days, Tom noticed that Lynn was gruff with him and that whenever she could find a reason, she was very critical. Tom did not know Lynn that well and did not know why she was treating him so badly. So, Tom made a point of stopping by her office a few times a day, sitting down in a chair by her desk, and telling her, "Hi, I just stopped by to see how you were doing." The first few times Lynn would say, "Fine" and then not say anything. Tom would wait a few minutes and then ask her a work-related question: "Lynn, I need your help. I'm going to be traveling in another week. What do I need to do to make it easier for you to do the travel?" Lynn would explain to him what he needed to do.

Over the next few days, Tom noticed that Lynn would mention her church activities. On his visits over the following days, Tom would ask her about her church activities. Over time, Lynn opened up about her work and life experiences. She mentioned that her boyfriend had a motorcycle. Tom mentioned that he had a similar bike. Lynn introduced him to her boyfriend when he visited, and Tom and her boyfriend talked about motorcycles. Within a few months, Lynn became as protective of Tom as she was of her director.

> One Friday, Lynn told Tom, "I'm having some of the church members over for dinner on Sunday and I would like to invite you to meet them. Would you come?"
>
> Tom looked at Lynn and said, "Of course I would; what time and where do you live? What can I bring?"
>
> "Your appetite," said Lynn, and then she gave him the time and directions.
>
> When Tom showed up at Lynn's house, he was the only white person there. Lynn introduced him to the church members. Tom had great food and good conversations with the church members. Other employees, including the African American employees, noticed the way Lynn was treating Tom and would comment to Tom, "How did you get her to treat you so well? I wish she would treat me the same."

After an employee has developed good relationships with all his or her co-workers, the next step is to develop good relationships with employees in other organizational units. Having good relationships with employees in other units can bring additional support and resources to a work team. Employees in other organizational units can facilitate the effectiveness of work teams. The supervisor-mentor can work with an employee to determine which relationships with employees in other organizational units he or she will develop. The relationships should be with employees who can help the supervisor's work unit. As a senior vice president told the multicultural employees who were participants in a multicultural leadership training program: "We expect you to effectively manage the resources under your control. It is helpful to your career advancement if you bring resources to the table that are not under your control. The more you bring, the better you will do."

Managers can use their employees to establish strategic relationships with other organizational units. The manager can then use these relationships to increase support and resources for his or her own organizational unit. As a mentor from long ago once told one of the authors, "It is very helpful if when you go to ask someone for help or for something you need, it is not the first time you meet him or her" (G. Allison, pers. comm.) This comment is sound advice.

7.6.3 Visibility

Once an employee has been mentored on performance, reputation and credibility, and relationships, it is time to give that employee greater visibility within the organization. Explain to the employee that he or she will be representing you at meetings. The employee should understand that he or she is now representing your office and you. How others perceive this employee is how they will see your office and you. Visibility here is not about the employee's performance but about how you and that person's co-workers are viewed as a result of that performance. The employee is, in short, the representative of the office and you. It shows great respect to an individual when you give him or her a great challenge. Doing so validates the person's capabilities. One of the central tenets of cultural competence is showing respect to others regardless of their cultural background. Such respect also includes showing that employee how that respect is earned and once earned, how that respect is validated through more challenging assignments.

Once an employee has agreed to be given greater visibility within the organization, let your supervisor know what you will be doing for your employee. After your supervisor has agreed, contact your colleagues and let them know what you are doing and why. Ask them to help train and educate your employee, and let them know you are willing to do the same for them. Be specific in what you would like them to do.

At the first meeting to which you take the employee for an introduction to your colleagues, make sure there is a chair available for him or her. That chair should not be at the table, but behind you. Ask the employee to take notes during the meeting, and then make time to compare notes after the meeting. Ask the employee to notice who is receptive and who has questions about whatever topic is on the table. Also ask the employee to read the social cues your colleagues are giving, and then discuss the observations. The multicultural leadership training assessments of the participants showed that many could not read cross-cultural social cues. This part of the training is about learning to read cross-cultural social cues. You know your colleagues and their personalities and quirks very well from your previous meetings. You are now training your employee in reading their social cues.

Once the employee has learned to read the social cues, it is time to let him or her represent you at the meeting without you there. Before sending the employee to represent you, ask your colleagues to let you know how your employee did. You need to know what the employee did well and what he or she needs to improve. Understanding what needs improvement will be of the most value to the employee. Let your employee know that you will be getting feedback from your colleagues and that you will be sharing that feedback with him or her. Also let your employee know that there is always the possibility that one of your colleagues may try to be manipulative; your employee should be prepared for that possibility. People being human sometimes cannot resist that temptation. One of your colleagues may, for example, try to get your employee to commit you and your office to something you may not really want to do. Tell your employee to say under such circumstances, "I'm just representing my supervisor, and I would like to get her [or his] opinion before I give you that commitment. I will check with her [or him] as soon as I get back, and I will make sure that she [or he] or I will let you know. Now let me be sure that I understand what you are want from her [or him]. Please tell me again while I write it down." Let the employee know that if someone asks something he or she does not know, the employee should say, "I don't know the answer to that, but as soon as the meeting is over, I will find out and check with my supervisor. I will try to get back to you today, but no later than tomorrow." Tell the employee to tell the group at the end of the meeting, "Thank you for helping me today. Knowing how to effectively represent my supervisor is important to my being a better employee and understanding how you have meetings will make me a better employee. Thank you so much."

The employee who represents you and your office needs to know what his or her words in the meeting communicated to the group. Tell the employee that the messages communicated are these:

1. I know that you outrank me, and I will be very respectful of who you are.
2. I will not commit my supervisor without her [or his] knowledge.
3. I will not pretend I know something when I do not; I will find the information you need, and then and only then will I give you that information.
4. I am willing to learn what will make me a more effective employee.

It is also important for the manager to understand that once others in the organization see what a great employee the person you are mentoring is, it is only a matter of time before someone offers him or her a job that will usually be a promotion and hard to refuse. Let the employee know that an offer of promotion may occur as part of the mentoring process and that you are very comfortable with that possibility. Let the employee know that when that happens, you expect him or her to help mentor other of your employees in their career development and that part of the mentoring relationship is the mentee's mentoring others.

Although it may seem odd to encourage valued and valuable employees to leave your organizational unit to take other positions just as you have helped them to be really valuable employees, doing so does have very real benefits for your career as well. When employees move to other positions, they will be well situated to help you with support and sometimes with resources. A position has now become open in your organization that will be a promotion for someone who is ready for that next level or for someone new to the organization who has skills you need but none of your employees possess. For that position, the job description will have to be redone. Having a great relationship with the human resource (HR) office will facilitate that process. It is career-helpful to establish great relationships with several offices: human resources, the budget office, public affairs, and the inspector general if your organization has one. If you have the reputation of developing and mentoring employees, you will have an effective office and many employees wanting to work for you. Higher-level managers will also be eager to have you work for them.

7.6.4 Conflict Resolution

Conflict resolution is added to the list of competencies for all employees. Organizations are rife with current conflicts and conflicts waiting to happen. Some of the conflict will come from the formal organization and the battles for turf and resources. Other sources of conflict will come from the informal and social organization. Employees will bring their own complete personalities into the workplace. The complete personalities will include aspects that are not always conducive to good organizational relationships. Many times an employee's social and family conflicts will be brought into the workplace, thereby creating human drama that can create turmoil in the workplace.

The first step in mentoring employees on conflict resolution is letting them know that they have a choice to make. They can be effective or they can be right, but they cannot be both. For career mobility, being effective will be more helpful than being right. Choosing to be effective does not mean that an employee is choosing to be wrong, just that being effective is the organizational measure for career success. When an employee chooses to be right rather than being effective, that employee is communicating selfishness, that "I am more important than the organization."

What the manager brings to the mentoring relationship is good judgment: knowing when the employee should solve the problem and when to step in, knowing when the problem is personal, requiring a resolution by the employee, and when it is serious enough to need an organizational intervention. If the situation is one where the employee conflict violates the conduct for employees as established by the employee handbook, the manager should intervene and effectively resolve the problem. Having a good working relationship with the HR office is helpful in stopping problems while they are still small.

Example 7.4: How to Resolve Conflicts

Alisha, who is African American, is a director in a state agency where there was a small amount of tension between the African American employees and the white employees. Three of her employees who are smokers were outside having their smoke breaks. The three employees are good friends with each other. All three are white, and one, Vanessa, is female. All three work for one of Alisha's supervisors. Vanessa is a special assistant to her supervisor and with her supervisor's help has rapidly risen through the ranks. Janie, another of Alisha's employees, was walking by the group when she heard one of the men say to Vanessa, "The only reason that you have done well is that of the special assistants, Bob sits on his left and Kyle sits on his right and you sit on his lap." All three started laughing. While the three were comfortable with the remark, Janie found the comments very offensive and reported them to Alisha.

Alisha knew she had to resolve the situation effectively without adding to any of the tensions. She called their supervisor, knowing that he would not deal with the situation. She explained to him what she was planning to do and why it was important. She reached out to her contact in the HR office, Randy, who is white. Alisha explained the situation to him and asked for his help. He agreed, and together they met with the three employees. Alisha explained the reason they were meeting with them and the situation that had to be resolved. Randy then explained why they had to be more careful about their conversations at work and that it did not matter that they were comfortable with the conversation. Another employee was offended by the comments. Randy explained that whereas outside the workplace they could say anything they wanted, they had an organizational responsibility not to contribute to a hostile work environment. Alisha ended the meeting by letting the men know what great employees they were, that she knew that they now knew what they had to do, and that she was very comfortable that there would not be a repeat of the situation. The three employees apologized. Alisha shook their hands, smiled, and said, "We are a little wiser now, and thank you for helping us resolve this." Looking a little sheepish, they left her office. Alisha thanked Randy for his help, saying, "With your help, it became an organizational issue that had to be resolved and did not become a personal issue between me and them. Thank you."

Before sending an employee to resolve a conflict with another employee, work with the individual to ensure that he or she is aware of any cultural characteristics that each of them may have that would exacerbate the problem. Also ask the individual to determine what commonalities they both share that could become common ground and a shared culture for them to build a good working relationship. Because good working relationships develop over time, this goal will require continuing effort and cannot be accomplished as a one-time task. Ask for progress reports and monitor the developing relationship. Validate any progress for both employees. In terms of the other party to the conflict, stop by the employee's office to mention that you were told about his or her willingness and effort in resolving the conflict. Thank the employee, acknowledging how grateful and appreciative you are and how the effort to resolve the problem has helped your organization. Mention that you will let the employee's supervisor know how helpful the effort has been to you.

Initially, it will take more of a manager's time to mentor employees. The payoff will be fewer employee problems. Unattended small problems fester and grow worse. Then when least expected they flare up and usually consume more of a manager's time to resolve than the manager spends in the mentoring process. Even when the problem is resolved, there may remain a lingering negative residue.

Not all employees are willing to be mentored or to do what is required. There will be enough volunteers, however, for the manager to create an effective work team. Employees who want to be mentored let their managers know that it is worth their effort to invest in them. Managers then know in whom it is worth investing their time, efforts, and influence. As the mentored employees become better and more productive employees, they will advance in their careers. The mentoring manager's influence and effectiveness increases with more managers willing to help and now being in better positions to provide resources and support.

7.7 Supervisors

There are three cultural competencies for supervisors:

1. Developing culturally competent employees
2. Mentoring diverse and multicultural managers
3. Developing cross-cultural manager–employee relationships

Supervisors are in a position to see the demographic changes before higher-level managers see the changes. The demographic changes show an aging white population having fewer children than the multicultural population. Many of the younger multicultural population will be entry-level employees as they leave universities and high schools for employment.

Supervisors may also be younger and less experienced than higher-level managers. They may not be as knowledgeable about the organizational culture. It is worthwhile for supervisors actively to seek mentoring before they mentor their own employees. Supervisors will also need the same mentoring skills as those necessary for higher-level managers. Their managers can help them acquire these cultural competencies.

Performance is the cornerstone and the first building block. It is not worthwhile proceeding until good performance is achieved. An employee must perform well before any other mentoring can take place. For supervisors, a common skill set is required:

1. Delivering team results
2. Being technically competent
3. Developing employees
4. Developing relationships with middle managers and functional managers

Supervisors are presumed to be technically competent. They are usually promoted because of the technical expertise they demonstrated when they were individual contributors. The first and third elements of the skill set are closely related. Team results depend on effective and productive employees working well with each other.

In today's world of rapidly changing demographics and greater visibility of the various diversities, it is the supervisor who may be the first level of management to encounter the changes. Immigrants and children of immigrants are entering the workforce in large numbers. For many, their first job may be an entry-level position. Thus, it may be the supervisor who first encounters the wave of diversity and the myriad cultures that are beginning to enter the work world. The ability of the supervisor to mentor employees from different cultures and employees who bring other diversities into an organization will prove to be particularly valuable. Supervisors introduce new employees into the organizational culture. This makes cultural competence valuable in understanding how cultural characteristics influence the organizational behavior of employees.

Immigrants and children of immigrants may be unfamiliar with organizational cultures and not know how their own cultural characteristics are perceived in the organization. University students rarely learn about real, working organizational cultures and what skills are expected of them when they become employees. In addition, university students, especially multicultural students, may have unrealistic expectations about careers and what is required of them in work situations. The early task for supervisors is ensuring that new employees, whether immigrants or children of immigrants, educated or not, understand what is expected of them.

An early introduction into the requirements of the workplace will have long-lasting benefits. Explaining the technical requirements of employees' positions and what is expected in terms of job performance can prevent misunderstandings that create tension in the workplace. The explanation of the workplace requirements should include the supervisor–employee relationship. Cultural characteristics can complicate the supervisor–employee relationship. Even when both the supervisor and the employee have monochronic cultural characteristics, an employee may have unrealistic expectations about how quickly he or she may be promoted or just how hard he or she has to work to be effective. If the supervisor has monochronic cultural characteristics and the employee has polychronic cultural characteristics, the potential for misunderstandings can increase. The employee may do the job quietly yet effectively and not let the supervisor know what has been accomplished, assuming that the supervisor already knows. The employee may finish an assignment and wait to be given another assignment. From the employee's perspective, working in this manner means being a good employee, and so he or she expects to be rewarded. The supervisor may not see it the same way. He or she may see the employee as unmotivated and consequently give assignments to other employees, those with monochronic cultural characteristics. The supervisor is more familiar with this type of relationship. The potential for misunderstandings and conflict is now in place. "Why am I not being treated the same way as the other employees," the polychronic employee may wonder, without understanding that he or she is contributing to the misunderstanding. He or she may not be aware that there is a problem.

Feedback from the participants of the multicultural leadership training programs showed that employees wanted to understand what was required for them to be successful. Supervisors wanted to be effective as well. Understanding the cultural characteristics that were creating dysfunctional and less-effective relationships gave them the tools to be better supervisors. All their employees now shared a common understanding of what was required for their success. The unwritten rules were now explicit, and everyone was aware. Individual employees could now make their own choices about their career advancements.

The participants of the multicultural leadership programs had also become more culturally competent. They now understood the effect of their cultural characteristics and how these characteristics could affect their relationships with their supervisors and other employees. They were aware that it was their responsibility to reach out to their supervisors and other employees in a culturally competent manner. They now were aware that respecting cultural differences is a two-way relationship. They had to respect and understand other cultures as well.

7.7.1 Creating Effective Diverse and Multicultural Teams

As the supervisor develops culturally and organizationally competent employees, he has employees who can lead work teams and who can successfully be assigned to cross-functional teams. He knows that the employees can now represent him effectively and can enhance his reputation and credibility as an effective supervisor. His employees are now capable of leading teams composed of diverse employees comfortably and effectively. Through the mentoring process, he knows when employee problems are developing and can take the steps to resolve the problems before they become critical.

7.7.2 Working through Touchy Issues

There are many touchy issues that can arise among employees in the day-to-day operations of any organization. The issues that can arise may be categorized as performance issues and people issues where employees do not get along.

7.7.2.1 Performance Issues

Performance issues can be further divided into capability, willingness, and cross-cultural misunderstandings. A capability issue is one where the employee does not have the training or skills necessary to do the required performance. Having employees who have been in their present positions is not a guarantee or assurance that they have the required skills.

New employees can be hired with the expectation that they have the skills. In some cases, that may not happen. Although this issue can be handled as part of the probationary period, it may be more beneficial to see if the employee is willing to learn. New employees create the opportunity for supervisors to initiate mentoring. The expectations that new employees bring into an organization can amaze even seasoned and experienced supervisors. The different perceptions that new employees bring into organization can be viewed as a form of diversity. In this sense, an employee's expectations can be treated in the same way as cross-cultural and gender diversity even when the supervisor and employee are from the same racial or ethnic group or the same gender. The earlier that common ground and a shared culture are established and a good working relationship is developed, the more likely there will be fewer problems.

7.7.2.2 Cross-Cultural Issues

Resolving cross-cultural issues can be sensitive and tricky. The HR office can be a very helpful partner in resolving cross-cultural issues. Cross-cultural issues can be very difficult, because the issues can cross the line into creating a hostile environment. The HR office can determine on what side of the hostile workplace environment the issue falls. Working with the HR office also protects the supervisor.

Many cross-cultural issues arise from the social and informal aspects of organizations. Employees usually cluster with other employees with similar characteristics. It is fairly common for employees to discuss issues they have seen on television at work. The discussions that generate the most intensity arise from issues relating to race and ethnicity, same-sex marriage and benefits to gays, men versus women, religion, and politics. These conversations can happen in the cafeteria and employee offices or cubicles. When people are discussing issues, they may become absorbed in the conversations and be unaware of other employees who may be nearby. The employees who are discussing the issues may be comfortable with the views they are each expressing, yet other employees within earshot may find the views offensive and may complain to their supervisors. The problem is now the supervisor's to solve.

Mentoring provides an early warning system to supervisors and managers. Issues may arise as part of regular mentoring sessions. Because developing good working relationships is part of the mentoring process, cross-cultural issues become teachable moments. It is a learning opportunity for the employee to resolve a cross-cultural issue while creating or deepening a cross-cultural relationship. It strengthens an employee's cultural competence and creates a model for other employees. Any problem or issue that can be handled informally prevents a future large and messy problem for a manager or supervisor. Problems and issues remain small, and the workplace environment becomes more conducive for employees to be effective team members.

Example 7.5: What the Real Issue Is

Roel is an employee in a northeastern city government. He had reached out for mentoring to Joy, a white manager, who is not in his own organizational unit. One day as part of his regular mentoring sessions, he mentioned to Joy that he thought that he was being discriminated against for his thick Spanish accent. Roel did have a thick Spanish accent, so his claim of being discriminated against for his accent got her attention. She asked Roel to explain what he meant. Roel explained that employees and other managers would treat him badly, and the tone in their voices was condescending. Joy told Roel that she would check with others to see if she could determine what was going on and that they would talk about her findings at their next session. Roel agreed.

When Joy checked with others in Roel's department, she was told that Roel's former supervisor was in charge of the budget office and frequently had to deny budget requests that other managers had made. Roel was the employee who delivered the message to the managers who were higher in the organizational hierarchy than he was. Apparently, Roel delivered the denials with great glee and an evident sense of superiority. Roel's supervisor had left for another position, and the managers were just getting even for the way Roel treated them when his former supervisor protected him. Roel's treatment had nothing to do with his thick accent. At their next mentoring meeting, Joy told Roel that she had found out the way he was being treated was payback for the way he treated the managers when his supervisor protected him. After further conversation, Roel owned up to his behavior, and they mapped out a strategy for him to improve his working relationship with the managers. The strategy began with Roel reaching out to the managers and apologizing to them for his behavior; he let them know that he knew better now and would like to have a better working relationship with them.

In organizational units where there is not much mentoring, it is best to handle cross-cultural issues with assistance from the HR office. The supervisor is protected from making mistakes because he is working collaboratively with human resources in solving sensitive employee issues. Having human resources involved places the sensitive issue in the context of the larger organization and not just a supervisor overreacting to an employee issue. Outside assistance also assigns greater gravity to the issue and lets the employees know the problem could rapidly become a more serious issue.

Any time there is a cross-cultural or other sensitive issue that has to be resolved, supervisors have a good opportunity to reinforce the professional standards that employees are expected to meet. Employees benefit from occasional reminders. These are also opportunities for managers to shape the organizational culture by emphasizing organizational values.

7.8 Summary and Conclusion

Managers provide a crucial link in the success of organizational initiatives. They convey the priorities of the top executives, and they develop other managers. In the public sector, higher-level managers frequently have been government employees for many years. They have seen top executives come and go. Some may not be as enthusiastic in embracing new initiatives, especially initiatives they do not personally consider important. Effective top executives will not assume that their managers are fully committed to their initiatives. Spending time ensuring that their managers are committed and know they have the top executives' support can go a long way in bringing about the success of the initiatives.

Developing other managers occurs by two methods: social modeling and mentoring. The manager is the role model for other managers. In the absence of mentoring, other managers learn from the behavior of their supervisor. Employees do not always choose the managerial characteristics their managers would like them to embrace.

Mentoring other managers develops managers with the cultural competence skills to create effective diverse and multicultural teams. Mentoring also allows managers to have their finger on the pulse of the formal and informal aspects of the organization. Emerging issues and problems can thus be resolved before they become large problems that create a tense work environment. Mentoring is also an informal performance measurement. An employee's performance is monitored and improved by the mentoring process. In this sense, mentoring may become a more powerful performance measurement system than the organizational performance measurement system. As in most efforts, there is more work in initiating mentoring efforts in the initial development. After a short time, the mentoring becomes an integral part of the organizational culture and becomes less time consuming.

Supervisors may be the first to experience the changing demographics. Immigrants and children of immigrants tend to be younger than the white population. The proportion of employees of color is growing in many organizations. Many will be new entrants into the labor force. Many will also be first-generation college students whose families may be unfamiliar with organizational cultures. These new employees may be unaware of the professional requirements of the organizational culture or may have inaccurate perceptions of what is expected of them. Given that these individuals are new to an organization, it is the supervisor who may first experience the rising wave of multicultural employees who may exhibit many different cultural characteristics. Culturally competent supervisors become the key to unlocking the career potential of these new employees.

Chapter 8

Cultural Competencies for Employees

> What we have to do … is to find a way to celebrate our diversity and
> debate our differences without fracturing our communities.

U.S. Secretary of State Hillary Clinton
BrainyQuote, n.d.

8.1 Introduction

Developing cultural competencies for employees is interwoven with the organizational skills required of any employee. Understanding and developing the foundation cultural competencies becomes a career currency for an employee. These are skills that are necessary at all levels. The organizational culture in the United States can be considered to be monochronic. Employees who come from polychronic backgrounds and from a social background that is not familiar with the organizational cultural requirements will find this chapter useful. This chapter focuses on the organizational requirements for long-term career success. Many organizations have monochronic cultures. Employees with polychronic cultural characteristics may be unaware of all the monochronic cultural characteristics. This chapter should help managers with monochronic cultural characteristics mentor polychronic employees. It is also helpful for polychronic employees in developing long-term career plans.

New employees usually focus on the immediate requirements of their new positions. Seeing the first position as the first step of an organizational ladder has long-term payoffs for employees. The first step is the springboard to a successful career. Examining the elements of successful management training programs such as the Presidential Management Fellows (PMF) and the Executive Core Requirements (ECQ) for the Senior Executive Service (SES) can enlighten an employee to the requirements for career success. Entry-level employees who understand the long-term requirements for career success can start planning for successful careers.

Such training as provided by the U.S. Office of Personnel Management's (OPM) PMF program offers valuable lessons for employees who hope to develop and attain their career aspirations. After a competitive selection process, PMF graduates negotiate directly with federal agencies to see who will hire them. Included in most PMF offers are several elements that are useful for all employees:

1. High-level agency mentors
2. Extensive training
3. Rotations to other organizational units of the agency or to other appropriate agencies or congressional committees
4. Visibility to the top executives of the agency
5. Challenging assignments

Employees who are not in the PMF program can duplicate the elements of the program to develop their long-term career success. The authors would recommend that graduate students consider applying to the PMF program, which used to be the Presidential Management Intern (PMI) program before it became the PMF program. The program has been very successful in advancing the careers of many civil servants, and there are many successful alumni of the PMI program in and out of government. (Information on the PMF program can be accessed at http://opm.gov by putting PMF in the OPM search function.)

The technical skill sets for employees are typical skill sets required of individual contributors or employees who do not supervise other employees or for new entrants into organizational positions. The cultural competencies allow employees to integrate cross-cultural skills into their relationships with their supervisors and with other employees.

8.2 Cultural Competencies for Employees

Cultural competence is a required skill for all employees regardless of race, ethnicity, gender, sexual orientation, and social class. The demographics show an increased diversity among all employees. Regardless of the racial or ethnic classification an employee may identify with, there will be many employees who come from different groups. So the elements of the cultural competence model—namely, culture, communication, misunderstandings and conflict, and leader-follower dynamics—will be helpful in establishing good working relationships with the supervisor and co-workers, especially given that the employee may be working with other employees and reporting to a supervisor who may be culturally different.

Employees must also learn about the organizational culture and its professional and work requirements. Immigrants and children of immigrants may not be as familiar with organizational work cultures and they may have inaccurate perceptions of what is required at work. Employees should reach out to their supervisors to let them know that they are willing to learn what is required of them to be productive members of the organization and that they are willing to be part of the work team. Whereas employees with monochronic cultural characteristics may find the work culture more familiar, employees with polychronic cultural characteristics will have to make a determined effort to know what is required of them. Being aware of one's cultural characteristics makes it easier to make the adjustments necessary to be an effective team member. As the saying goes, employees should be comfortable in their own skin. Everyone has his or her own cultural characteristics that may differ from those of others. Understanding that different cultural characteristics affect employee relationships is the important point.

Example 8.1: The Polychronic Culturally Competent Employee

Laila is a new employee who has been hired to work for a city department. The city has been undergoing a demographic shift with its growing immigrant community. Laila comes from a culture with polychronic cultural characteristics. After being in the department a week, she is still learning her new job. She walks into Wendy's office. Wendy is her supervisor and a white female. She tells Wendy:

> I've been here a week, and I'm still learning what I need to do. I like it here, and I want to make sure we have a good working relationship. I come from a culture where we give great respect to those who are in authority. We do not question what we are told, and we value relationships a lot. I tend to be quiet and do what I'm told to do in the way I'm told to do it. I would be glad to tell you anything you want to know about my culture. If you want me to behave differently, please let me know. I would appreciate your working with me on this. I really want to do well in this job.

Example 8.2: The Monochronic Culturally Competent Employee

Violet, who comes from a monochronic culture, may say this to Wendy:

> I've been here a week, and I'm still learning what I need to do. My parents have taught me that for me to be a leader, I have to show initiative and make suggestions on changing the system. I believe in asking questions to make sure that what you tell me is the best way to accomplish my work. At the university, we were taught that we would not be successful unless we got promotions every year. If you see it differently, let me know. My parents expect me to be successful, and I would appreciate your help in making me successful.

The intent of these conversations is to develop a good working relationship with your supervisor by letting the supervisor know how you see the organizational culture. The supervisor will let you know what is expected for good performance from employees. Laying out the work expectations creates common ground and a shared culture. Asking the supervisor to help you learn what is needed to be a good employee creates common ground for creating a good working relationship. It also creates a team of your supervisor and you working to make you successful. By letting your supervisor know that you are comfortable talking about your cultural characteristics, you also create a comfortable environment for achieving the critical success needed to improve work performance. In essence, you are laying the groundwork to have your supervisor mentor you without asking him or her to be your official mentor.

Establishing good working relationships with co-workers is also of paramount importance. Understanding that organizations have cultures and that you are entering a new culture is helpful in forming good working relationships. Showing respect to other cultures is a central concept of cultural competence. Respect should be demonstrated to employees who have been working in the organization for a long time. They will know how the system works, and they can be invaluable in helping you be a valued employee.

Example 8.3: Creating Common Ground and a Shared Culture with Your Supervisor

An introductory conversation can be simple:

> Hi, you can call me, Tom. My parents are from Korea, and I'm the new guy here. I would be glad to let you know anything you would like to know about me. I know that I have much to learn and that with your experience you can help me a lot. May I check with you when I have a question? I would like you to feel comfortable giving me critical feedback. I really would like to have a good relationship with you. If there is anything I can do to help you, I would be more than delighted to be helpful.

These beginning conversations serve to keep the employee and the supervisor working as a team. Being open to discussing one's own cultural characteristics creates a safety zone that allows supervisors to feel more comfortable offering critical feedback. One of the main reasons employees suffer career setbacks is their having a bad relationship with their supervisor. These conversations create a common ground and a shared organizational culture, thereby allowing a reporting relationship that is collaborative. It is also the beginning of a mentoring relationship that research has shown is beneficial to employees of color and women.

Establishing mentoring relationships is helpful to an employee's career success. The emphasis is on having many mentors. Having mentors who are different in terms of racial, ethnic, gender, sexual orientation, and social class will prove to be the most helpful to employees. Having mentors who are racially or ethnically different or are of another diversity will foster cultural competence. Mentors who are culturally different can sometimes benefit an employee in ways that mentors who are similar cannot.

Example 8.4: The Importance of Informal Mentors

Theresa is an African American assistant secretary in a federal department. One of her friends in the same department is Ellen, a white assistant secretary. One day on the walk back to their offices after their meeting with the deputy secretary, Theresa told Ellen, "Ellen, I need a favor. I am supporting Patty for this position. Patty is African American, and I think it may be perceived as self-serving if the recommendation came from me. Would you recommend her and advocate for her selection?" Ellen turned toward Theresa and replied, "Of course I would. I know Patty well. She has asked me for advice several times."

Having mentors has become so popular that many managers are inundated with requests to be mentors. In programs similar to the PMF program, it is easier to designate official mentors. When developing informal mentors, however, it is generally better to not ask for a formal mentoring relationship. The first thought many managers have when asked to be official mentors is, "How much work is this going to be?" They may respond that they are too busy to officially mentor at this point.

A more successful approach is to establish a mentoring relationship first by introducing yourself. This conversation can be similar to the conversation that an employee has with his or her supervisor when first hired into a position. As a mentor once told one of the authors, "When you go to someone to ask for a favor or ask him to do something for you, try as hard as you can to not let this be the first time you meet this person." Informal mentoring situations can occur as part of developing working relationships with other employees. Although establishing relationships with others who are culturally similar may be more comfortable, a better strategy is to reach out to employees who differ culturally. Each group has its own informal social network and can open up a source of organizational information. Once the relationships are in place, an employee can start asking for information about navigating the organizational system. An employee can then assess the value of the information that is given, and a mentoring relationship grows over time.

8.3 Establishing Leadership Cultural Competencies for Employees

A good starting point for employees to understand the leadership qualifications is OPM's ECQs, the core qualifications for executives. (The ECQ information can be accessed at http://opm.gov by using the search function for ECQ.) Usually, SES training programs are limited to GS-14s and GS-15s. Nevertheless, these programs teach executive participants competencies that new employees or employees who wish to have long-term career mobility can begin to learn. Many requirements can be demonstrated at entry-level positions for university graduates; these positions tend to be at the GS-5, GS-7, and GS-9 pay grades. There are equivalent pay grades at the state and local government agencies.

8.3.1 Managerial Cultural Competencies and Executive Core Qualifications

The foundation cultural competencies, described in Chapter 4, are key to developing the executive core qualifications. As foundation cultural competencies, they are cultural competencies for all employees. The foundation cultural competencies are:

1. Respecting and understanding employees from other cultures
2. Communication in a multicultural and diverse workplace
3. Creating common ground
4. Having adaptability or flexibility
5. Encouraging inclusiveness to create effective teams and collaboration

Some of these competencies are also included in the executive core qualifications. The ECQ for leading people is providing an inclusive workplace. Inclusiveness is also one of the foundation cultural competencies. The leveraging diversity competency for leading people is valuing or respecting diversity and individual differences. Respecting and understanding diverse employees is also one of the foundation cultural competencies. The flexibility competency is part of the ECQ leading change. Adaptability and flexibility are also one of the foundation cultural competencies. These foundation cultural competencies become the doorway for developing other core qualifications for executives. The following section discusses these ECQ and how cultural competence enables acquiring these competencies.

8.3.2 Leading Change

OPM (2010a) defines leading change as "the ability to bring about strategic change, both within and outside the organization, to meet organizational goals" (p. 9). OPM lists and defines six competencies under leading change:

1. Creativity and innovation—develops new insights into situations; questions conventional approaches; encourages new ideas and innovations; designs and implements new or cutting-edge programs/processes.
2. External awareness—understands and keeps up-to-date on local, national, and international policies and trends that affect the organization and shape stakeholders' views; is aware of the organization's impact on the external environment.

3. Flexibility—is open to change and new information; rapidly adapts to new information, changing conditions, or unexpected obstacles.
4. Resilience—deals effectively with pressure; remains optimistic and persistent, even under adversity. Recovers quickly from setbacks.
5. Strategic thinking—formulates objectives and priorities, and implements plans consistent with the long-term interests of the organization in a global environment. Capitalizes on opportunities and manages risks.
6. Vision—takes the long-term view and builds a shared vision with others; acts as a catalyst for organizational change. Influences others to translate vision into action.

In developing the multicultural leadership program for an organization, the consultants asked the CEO what skills he wanted to see in his employees. The skills he was looking for in his employees, he answered, were strategic thinking and business acumen. Strategic thinking is planning for the long term and being aware of changes in the organization's environment and how those changes will affect the organization.

Many refer to this competency as the marshmallow test. Do you want one marshmallow now or two marshmallows in an hour? *The New Yorker* (Lehrer 2009) reported on the work of Walter Mischel and his colleagues on delayed gratification. Dr. Mischel would take young children into a room and tell them that they could have one marshmallow now or they could have two when he returned to the room. Some of the children were studied into their late thirties. The researchers discovered that the children who waited for the larger reward had better lives and relationships. The children who waited also scored higher on their SATs by an average of 210 points than the children who could not wait. The competency revealed in this study, strategic thinking, is related to seeing today's work in the context of the long-term success of the organization in a changing environment.

For an employee, being strategic can be as simple as determining what to do with your spare time at work. After learning the requirements of a position, many employees find that they can do the work in less than eight hours. How do you handle the spare time? Do you relax and enjoy the rewards of your efficiency? Do you use the spare time to acquire new skills or to take on an additional project? For employees, the answer can be an organizational version of one marshmallow now or two marshmallows later.

The second defined competency, external awareness, is being current on world and societal trends and their effect on organizations. Although when the current recession will end remains unclear, public organizations will be undergoing many changes in the near future. Recessions tend to increase expenditures for social programs such as unemployment and Medicaid as people are laid off. Revenues are reduced as income tax revenues and sales taxes drop. As housing and property values fall in many parts of the country, property tax revenues drop accordingly. Many states and local governments face large deficits and struggle to find ways to cut government spending. The federal government has very large deficits that are likely to continue for some years. At some point, in the very near future, reducing the very large deficits will become a political necessity. The demographic changes are generating acrimonious debate. The societal debate will find its way into the workplace as employees discuss their views of the demographic changes. Change will happen fairly rapidly.

The questions for an employee are several: How will these societal changes affect the work I do and the work my organizational unit does? What new skills and competencies will I have to acquire? Preparation can begin now, rather than under pressure when changes are mandated. Being knowledgeable and prepared, an employee can offer appropriate changes instead of having changes mandated by someone else.

Employees who have polychronic cultural characteristics and who have respect for figures of authority may find this task challenging. As a student with polychronic cultural characteristics said during a focus group, "I will work really hard; and when I'm finished, I'll ask for more work, but I won't do anything to change the system." Systemic changes are required when the environment changes and previous ways of doing work are not as effective. A good mentoring relationship will help in overcoming the challenges these cultural characteristics can create in the workplace. In contrast, employees with monochronic cultural characteristics may find it easier to espouse systemic changes. The caution here is in how to advocate systemic changes in a way that is harmonious with the organizational culture. Having a supervisor who is a good mentor can help pave the way for proposing any systemic changes.

The third defined competency, resilience, is one that can have a cultural component. Some cultural groups may be risk averse; that is, they may avoid any type of risk taking. In executive coaching sessions employees of color and some women commented that they felt they could not make even one mistake in the workplace. They also reported that they felt as if they did not quite belong and they would be found out. Many employees said they would be hesitant to take a major risk if they thought they might not be successful. Such risk aversion is not resilience.

A president of one of the organizations where the multicultural leadership program was conducted said that he had crucible roles for any employees he was considering for top-executive positions. Crucibles are containers used to melt metal or glass, and can withstand great temperatures. Crucible is used to describe organizational assignments that are difficult and that put the employee under great pressure. The crucible roles were assignments so difficult that whether an individual could successfully complete the project remained unclear. Part of the assessment was how the employee would handle failure.

A common saying is that to be successful, one has to take risks. There is truth in that adage, but not the whole truth. Successful managers and employees take risks, but the smart managers and employees take risks while using a safety net. The safety net is the network of mentors, including the supervisor. Mentors invest time and energy in an employee. Good mentors want their investment of time and energy to have a payoff. They will use their organizational resources to help the persons they are mentoring to be successful. An employee who has good mentors is undertaking not an individual assignment but a team assignment, with the other members of the team being the mentors. An employee who has mentors from different ethnic or racial groups or of a different gender, sexual orientation, or social class also has access to the informal network of these groups. That access comes from the mentors.

8.3.3 Leading People

OPM defines the concept of leading people as the ability to lead people toward meeting the organization's vision, mission, and goals and the ability to provide an inclusive workplace that fosters the development of others, facilitates cooperation and teamwork, and supports constructive resolution of conflicts.

There are four competencies that define leading people:

1. Conflict management—encourages creative tension and differences of opinions; anticipates and takes steps to prevent counterproductive confrontations; manages and resolves conflicts and disagreements in a constructive manner
2. Leveraging diversity—fosters an inclusive workplace where diversity and individual differences are valued and leveraged to achieve the vision and mission of the organization
3. Developing others—aims to increase the ability of others to perform and contribute to the organization by providing ongoing feedback and by providing opportunities to learn through formal and informal methods
4. Team building—inspires and fosters team commitment, spirit, pride, and trust; facilitates cooperation; motivates team members to accomplish group goals

Although leadership is usually described as a management skill, it can also be demonstrated at any organizational level. Leadership can be considered as part of the employee skill set of delivering team results. Being an effective team leader or effective member of a team begins with having good working relationships with all the team members. Diverse teams have members with different cultural characteristics, and thus an employee who understands the individual cultural characteristics and how they can help or hinder teamwork is in a position to facilitate communication across diversity boundaries and to motivate team members. Inviting employees from other cultures into your informal social group and being invited by other employees into their informal social groups is a way to demonstrate inclusiveness. By recognizing the cultural characteristics that may hinder team cohesion and commitment, an employee can communicate organizational objectives in a way that all team members will understand regardless of their cultural characteristics. That ability is otherwise known as leveraging diversity by fostering an inclusive workplace.

Conflict management is defined as encouraging creative tensions and differences of opinions, but not letting them degenerate into counterproductive confrontations. On the surface, conflict management appears to be an attempt to achieve contradictory and mutually exclusive goals. On the one hand, differences, and their accompanying tensions, are to be encouraged. On the other hand, confrontations are to be prevented.

8.3.4 Results-Driven Goals

OPM defines the concept of being results driven as the ability to meet organizational goals and customer expectations, as well as the ability to make decisions that produce high-quality results by applying technical knowledge, analyzing problems, and calculating risks.

There are six competencies that relate to being results driven:

1. Accountability—holds self and others accountable for measureable high-quality, timely, and cost-effective results; determines objectives, sets priorities, and delegates work; accepts responsibility for mistakes; complies with established control systems and rules
2. Customer service—anticipates and meets the needs of both internal and external customers; delivers high-quality products and services; is committed to continuous improvement
3. Decisiveness—makes well-informed, effective, and timely decisions, even when data are limited or solutions produce unpleasant consequences; perceives the impact and implications of decisions
4. Entrepreneurship—positions the organization for future success by identifying new opportunities; builds the organization by developing or improving products or services; takes calculated risks to accomplish organizational objectives
5. Problem solving—identifies and analyzes problems; weighs relevance and accuracy of information; generates and evaluates alternative solutions; makes recommendations
6. Technical credibility—understands and appropriately applies principles, procedures, requirements, regulations, and policies related to specialized expertise

Working with cross-cultural mentors can develop accountability, decisiveness, and problem solving. A good mentoring relationship is a two-way relationship. The employee checks in regularly with the mentor. These regular mentoring sessions include status reviews of projects and discussion of any questions the employee may have. The status reviews of ongoing projects keep the supervisor up-to-date, so there are no surprises. The employee can also use the mentoring sessions to ask questions about the projects. To communicate willingness and initiative, the smart employee begins the discussion with an opener such as, "This is the work I have already done on this project. Do you know if I have missed anything or if there is someone I should check with?" Here, the employee is revealing the extensive work he or she has completed and is not depending on the supervisor to provide all the answers. If the supervisor makes suggestions, then the supervisor is part of the decision-making process (the safety net). The employee knows that the supervisor is comfortable with the work being done. Keeping a record of the mentoring meetings creates a record for any performance appraisals.

It is during these mentoring sessions that cultural characteristics may become evident. If an employee is risk-averse, a good supervisor and mentor will point this out. If an employee is respectful of figures of authority and therefore waits to be told what to do, a good supervisor and mentor will also point this out. It is such critical feedback that contributes to career advancement. These moments are learning and teaching opportunities. A culturally competent employee will explain the cultural reasons for his or her own behavior. The employee can then ask for help in learning more about the organization's cultural requirements. In two-way cultural competency mentoring, the mentor teaches the employee about the organizational cultural requirements, and the employee teaches the supervisor and mentor about his cultural characteristics. Both persons are learning about their own and the other's individual cultural characteristics while creating common ground or a shared organizational culture.

At the other end of the spectrum of cultural characteristics, someone with more aggressive monochronic cultural behaviors may be asked to tone things down—to take a step back, to move a bit slower and take more time. This is also a learning and teaching moment for both the employee and the mentor.

In today's unsettled economy and uncertain future, there are many changes that will have to be made. Uncertainty creates an opportunity for employees to undertake new assignments to explore new ways of conducting business. Such reassignments should happen only after employees have established a good track record of their regular duties. These calculated risks are taken using the safety net of the mentoring relationship with the supervisor and in frequent consultation with other mentors.

Many new and young employees feel that their accomplishments should be based on their individual knowledge and efforts. Accomplishments based on one's knowledge and effort are ego satisfying, but are very limiting when it comes to career advancement.

8.3.5 Business Acumen

Business acumen, according to OPM (2010a), is the ability to manage human, financial, and information resources strategically. Technical credibility comes from an employee having well-developed business acumen.

There are three competencies that compose business acumen:

1. Financial management—understands the organization's financial processes; prepares, justifies, and administers the program budget; oversees procurement and contracting to achieve desired results; monitors expenditures and uses cost-benefit thinking to set priorities
2. Human capital management—builds and manages the workforce based on organizational goals, budget considerations, and staffing needs; ensures that employees are appropriately recruited, selected, appraised, and rewarded; takes action to address performance problems; manages a multisector workforce and a variety of work situations
3. Technology management—keeps up-to-date on technological developments; makes effective use of technology to achieve results; ensures access to security of technology systems

Business acumen, or the knowledge of the organizational infrastructure, is one of the top two skills one CEO said that he wanted to see in his employees. Organizations have an organizational culture that is defined by the policies and procedures that dictate the way the organization operates. In a way, this relationship is analogous to what can be observed in human societies, where knowledge and social practices define cultures. In the case of the formal organization, the knowledge and practices are written down in myriad policies and procedures. Written policies and procedures make it easier to understand the formal culture. Decisions are usually made within the policies of an organization. It is therefore wise to know the organizational policies before voicing solutions to organizational problems.

Example 8.5: How Not to Show Business Acumen

Arnold is a new employee of a county office. During the period of time that gasoline was approaching $4 a gallon, Arnold's supervisor, Veronica, was conducting a staff meeting. The topic was ways to reduce the rising costs of gasoline to county employees. After a few minutes of discussion, Arnold proposed his solution: "Why don't we put everyone on a four-day work week. This will save the employees the fifth day of driving." Veronica quickly responded, "We have a union contract, and any work over an eight-hour day is paid overtime. We're not ready to do that."

By venturing an opinion without understanding how the county's personnel policies and union contract would affect the operations, Arnold communicated that he is the type of employee who would shoot off an opinion off the top of his head, rather than proposing a workable solution within the policies of the organization. It is easier to prevent a bad impression than to correct a bad impression once it is made.

The formal organizational culture is tempered by the informal and social culture that develops from the interactions of managers and employees. It is the cultural characteristics that employees bring into an organization that gives each organization its social adaptation of the formal organizational culture.

The formal organization can be the common ground to create a new and shared culture that blends in all the different cultural characteristics. The formal organizational structure frames and creates the boundaries within which organizational operations are conducted. Some of the boundaries are sharply delineated. Other boundaries are more diffuse and require interpretation. The formal organizational structure is a neutral structure and is not infused with social and cultural characteristics that can create misunderstandings and conflict. Employees who come from cultures where they are expected to be quiet and not to question figures of authority can use the formal organizational structure to create a shared culture. Learning about the organizational requirements allows an employee to engage his supervisor in a relatively neutral discussion about how the policies are implemented. The employee indicates his willingness to learn what is required to be a better employee. The employee is also demonstrating initiative by learning the formal organizational culture. Willingness to learn and to be a better employee and demonstrating initiative are qualities most supervisors would love to have in any employee.

Understanding the budgeting process and having a good working relationship with the human resource (HR) office is always beneficial to employees. Understanding the budget process is critical to developing new programs. For example, in the federal budgeting process, in the spring of 2010, federal agencies were spending the current year's budget. Budget hearings were being held in the congressional authorization committees for the federal budget that was to begin in October 2010. (Hearings before the appropriations committees are usually held in the summer.) The federal agencies were holding meetings on what to submit to the Office of Management and Budget in September 2010 for the federal budget beginning in October 2011. That means that any program that has not been well developed will probably not be considered until the budget that begins in October 2012. This process reflects strategic thinking and planning.

Employees are well served by having a good relationship with the HR office. All personnel actions are taken with the concurrence of the HR office, which can help to ensure its organization is culturally competent. Employees who are culturally different can have a mutually beneficial relationship with the HR office.

Employees establish common ground with their supervisors in creating a working relationship within the organizational culture. Asking questions about the implementation of organizational initiatives can be the beginning of an informal mentoring relationship. As supervisors and employees together create a shared organizational culture, they are developing a working relationship. A safe environment for discussing social and cultural issues develops as they develop a good working relationship and establish mutual comfort with each other. This sense of safety is particularly useful for employees who are introverts or who do not feel culturally comfortable in the work situation. They are creating a culture that now includes them, and they do not have to feel like outsiders trying to be accepted by an unfamiliar culture.

As with anyone entering any foreign culture, an individual willing to learn and understand the new culture is more likely to be accepted. In many cases, people are willing to tolerate cultural miscues when they know the individual is trying to learn the cultural mores. They will usually try to be as helpful as they can be. The same tolerance can develop in organizational cultures, where cultural errors may become learning opportunities instead of mistakes.

A supervisor's informal mentoring of an employee learning the organizational requirements also creates a team. As mentors invest time and energy in employees, they have a vested interest in helping them become successful. An employee's success is now supported by a team of people, not just by the individual efforts of the employee.

Business acumen is an excellent way of showing your supervisor that you are mastering the skill sets required of employees. Mastering functional assignments, being an excellent contributor, and building supervisor and team relationships all demonstrate business acumen.

8.3.6 Building Coalitions

OPM defines building coalitions as the ability to work together to achieve common goals internally and with other federal agencies, state and local governments, nonprofit and private sector organizations, foreign governments, or international organizations.

There are three competencies that constitute coalition building:

1. Partnering—develops networks and builds alliances; collaborates across boundaries to build strategic relationships and achieve common goals
2. Political savvy—identifies the internal and external politics that impact the work of the organization; perceives organizational and political reality and acts accordingly
3. Influencing and negotiating—persuades others; builds consensus through give and take; gains cooperation from others to obtain information and accomplish goals

For an employee, building coalitions is an internal activity usually limited to the organization or agency for which the employee works, though some employees may work together with state and local agencies or with nonprofit or private sector governments. Furthermore, some federal departments, as well as some state offices, have agencies that work in other countries, and so coalitions may extend abroad to those locations.

Building relationships with other midlevel managers is part of the technical skill sets for employees. Because the foundation cultural competencies facilitate building coalitions, any good supervisor would depend on an employee who is culturally competent to partner with other agencies and organizational units. Partnering with others and influencing and negotiating flows from the cross-cultural relationships that have been created by using the foundation cultural competencies. The sense of teamwork has already been created, and an employee can draw from the team to build consensus and gain cooperation from other employees.

8.3.7 OPM Executive Core Qualifications, Technical Competence, and Cultural Competence

OPM executive core qualifications, developed for the SES, are also well-suited competencies for executives in state and local governments, nonprofit organizations, and many other organizations. Although the core qualifications were designed specifically for executives, many of the competencies can be learned and demonstrated by nonsupervisory employees as well as by managers. The advantage to understanding the requirements as a nonsupervisory employee is that an employee can begin to demonstrate the competencies and to create a record of accomplishments. This record creates a strong resume that facilitates promotions into the management records. As the employee continues to demonstrate the competencies, continuing promotions are easier to achieve. If the employee wishes to become an SES member, he or she has already developed a managerial track record that shows the employee's qualifications for the SES.

8.4 Developing a Long-Term Career Plan

Developing a long-term career plan helps employees at all levels in the organization. The participants of color and many women in the multicultural leadership programs revealed that though they were familiar with the concept of career plans, they did not have any such plans. A career plan, which is an informal or formal agreement with an employee's supervisor about the performance and progress the employee hopes to make, should be about learning the skills necessary for the employee to be able to contribute, productively and effectively, to the organization for the long term.

Having a long-term career plan signals to the managers of the organization that the employee is considering a long-term career with the organization. Managers who invest in the employee can see a long-term payoff in helping train a more productive employee. Another advantage of developing a long-term career plan is that the employee who does so is letting managers know that he or she is capable of strategic thinking (i.e., planning for the long term or future). Strategic thinking is one of the critical leadership skills that managers look for.

Although doing so may sound counterintuitive, it is best not to emphasize promotions in the long-term career plans. Overly emphasizing promotions communicates that ambition is the foremost motivation for learning. It is better to develop a career plan that emphasizes the skills the organization needs. Over time, as the employee learns new skills and competencies, the promotions will come. Good managers are always on the lookout for talented employees, and a capable and competent employee will always be in demand. Doors will open for these employees, though many times the employee may not even be aware that these doors exist.

Long-term career plans are an excellent way to develop cultural competencies, especially for employees who possess more polychronic skills than monochronic ones. Employees from polychronic cultures may have cultural characteristics that are not compatible with the behaviors expected of employees in organizations. Because managers do not see the behaviors they expect, the contributions of polychronic employees may be less well recognized than the behaviors of monochronic employees.

Programs such as the Presidential Management Fellows (PMF), which has been in existence for many years, are designed to develop future leaders. As noted earlier, there are several important elements of the PMF program:

1. High-level and cross-cultural agency mentors
2. Extensive training
3. Rotations to other organizational units of the agency or to other appropriate agencies or congressional committees
4. Visibility to the top executives of the agency
5. Challenging assignments

Although getting high-level mentors is difficult for new employees who are not receiving PMF training or involved in a similar leadership program, it is possible to develop mentoring relationships with other managers. Mentors are critical to career success. (Because mentoring is so critical, a following section will be devoted to initiating and developing mentoring relationships.) Training is available to many employees and, when job related, is paid for by the organization. Training is also an investment in career success. An employee willing to pay for his or her own training related to a long-term career plan is communicating willingness to invest personal resources to become a better employee. That willingness makes it easier for a manager to send an employee to organization-sponsored training classes.

Managers may have difficulty giving a new employee a rotation to another unit. It is possible for employees to volunteer for cross-functional assignments, where they work on projects with employees from other organizational units. This cross-assignment allows the employee to learn about other organizational units and to develop contacts in other units. Such an assignment will benefit an employee almost as much as a rotational assignment.

Visibility to senior executives may not be possible, but visibility to other managers can easily be arranged. The majority of the employees of color in the multicultural leadership program, for example, were not well known outside their own organizational units. Visibility to other managers is very doable for any employee. It is an opportunity to showcase an employee's capabilities and competencies. Managers who are mentoring employees can be very supportive of these efforts.

Once an employee has mastered the day-to-day operations of a particular job, he or she can volunteer for challenging assignments. Someone who is an excellent employee at his or her job is communicating that he or she belongs in that position. Many managers expect excellent performance at the level of their employees' assigned duties. It is the challenging assignments that give employees an opportunity to develop capabilities that prepare them for career advancement.

Similar to OPM's SES Executive Core Qualifications, the elements of the PMF program are career strategies that can be emulated by employees at any level in the organizational hierarchy. Developing these qualifications, at any level, gives an employee a documented and demonstrated record of accomplishments. This facilitates an employee's ability to become a top executive if that is the employee's choice.

8.5 Creating a Long-Term Career in Diverse and Multicultural Organizations

There are four parts to a long-term career plan: performance, relationships, reputation or credibility, and visibility (see Figure 8.1). All four factors are required for long-term success. The usual focus is only on the first factor, performance or the technical requirements of the position. Good job performance is necessary but not enough for long-term success, however. Good relationships, the second factor, especially cross-functional and cross-cultural relationships, make it easier to bring more resources to one's job performance. Relationships allow one to draw upon resources controlled by other employees. This ability can make one more effective. The third

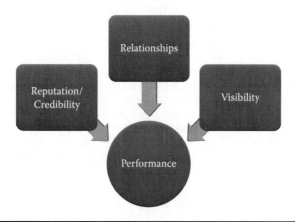

Figure 8.1 **The culturally competent career plan.**

factor, reputation, reflects how others see you and the professional credibility you have as an employee. Many employees do not have an accurate perception of how others see them. Reputation precedes you and shapes the way others will see you. What this means is that reputation is the credibility you have established with others. It is fairly common when someone new comes into an organization for colleagues to call that individual's network of people to see what kind of reputation the newcomer has established elsewhere. One's reputation and credibility can be managed and relate to visibility, the fourth factor, which means being visible to the higher levels of the organization. Visibility is easier if an employee is seen as a good performer and has a good reputation.

The first step in developing a culturally competent career plan is letting your supervisor know that you would like help in developing such a long-term plan. Let your supervisor know that you want critical feedback, not just validation, and that you truly want to prepare yourself for a long-term career with the organization. Make clear that you are willing to take additional assignments and training if they will help you develop new skills. Describe the four elements of the career plan: performance, reputation and credibility, relationships, and visibility.

8.5.1 Performance

The first step is ensuring that your performance is excellent and that you want feedback on how to improve your performance. This is the time to be comfortable in mentioning any of your own cultural characteristics that you are aware of and to ensure your supervisor that you are comfortable discussing any of the cultural characteristics that may be holding you back. Having both the supervisor and employee comfortable with discussing the cultural characteristics is cultural competence. It is the beginning of establishing the organization as common ground and a shared culture to which both belong.

Example 8.6: How to Create a Culturally Competent Career Plan

Sylvia comes from a culture that respects figures of authority and where it is disrespectful to ask a lot of questions. Ann is her supervisor. As part of the coaching, Ann can say, "Sylvia I have noticed that during meetings you are quiet and don't ask questions. From our conversations, I know that you have questions, but I don't see you asking them. I am beginning to hear people say that you are not interested and are too passive in the meetings and that you are not contributing to the discussion. I know how good you are, but others are not seeing how good you are. How can I help you participate more? During the meeting, I can ask you, 'What do you think?' Would that be helpful?"

Using the long-term career development plan with both parties agreeing to provide feedback creates common ground or a shared culture. The feedback sessions are on work- and performance-related requirements. Using work-related feedback keeps the sessions from moving into an uncomfortable racial, ethnic, or other diversity area in a way that may be uncomfortable to the employee.

Ann is communicating several important messages:

1. We (working as a team) are preparing you for long-term career success.
2. I am willing to help you acquire the skills you need.
3. I am culturally sensitive by creating common ground in how we deal with cultural characteristics.

If a supervisor does not offer an employee the opportunity to develop a long-term career plan, the employee, Sylvia, in this case, can ask the supervisor, Ann, "Ann, I have been here awhile and I really like working here. I would like you to help me develop the skills I need to be successful in the long term. I would like your advice on how to make my performance better and help me develop relationships that would make us more effective. I'm new and don't know the people in the organization that well. I would like to have a good reputation with others. Would you check to see how others see me? I also know that part of the advice may be critical, but if it helps me do better, I'm ready to hear it." Working on visibility can wait until the mentoring relationship has been there for a while.

By making such comments, Sylvia is communicating a number of important messages:

1. I like working here and want to be successful, and I am willing to do my part.
2. You and I are working as a team.
3. I am willing to accept critical feedback. [Some supervisors may not want to give critical advice unless they are sure it will be received well.]
4. I want to develop relationships that will make us both more successful.
5. I understand that once you have invested time and energy in me, you will be more willing to support my success. It will be part of your success as well.

When a supervisor agrees to an employee's long-term career plan, coaching or mentoring should be made an explicit part of the agreement. It is this agreement for mentoring that provides the rationale for discussing the differences that may impede an employee's progress. Part of this agreement is providing feedback on areas that need to be improved. Thus the employee should agree to receiving feedback as part of the long-term career plan. A manager can then coach an employee on what is required to be successful. Where there are cultural differences that may affect an employee's progress, coaching becomes the way to describe the necessary changes. Cultural differences are discussed in a way that improves an employee's success. For example, if part of the individual's culture is being aggressive and that employee is viewed as being too pushy at work, the coaching would center on that employee's reputation and the required behaviors. If an employee from another culture has relationships exclusively with other members of that employee's cultural group, then coaching addresses the need to develop other relationships and how to do that. Here, coaching may also involve introducing the employee to the manager's network of diverse relationships.

8.5.2 Reputation and Credibility

Reputation and credibility are others' perceptions of an employee. It is almost impossible to determine one's own reputation and credibility, since most employees will not answer honestly if the reputation is negative or if an employee is not considered credible. Feedback on reputation and credibility from a supervisor is not enough, because many employees treat their supervisors differently than they treat other employees. Give your supervisor the permission to check with your co-workers and other managers you may work with for their impressions of you. Giving explicit permission to have your supervisor check with others serves two purposes: One is that you are aware that you are a representative of your office and are sensitive to how you and the office are perceived by others. The second is that if you do have a problem with another employee or manager, you are willing to correct the situation. Both aspects are likely to enhance the supervisor's impression of you.

Employees can benefit from being the expert or go-to person for some aspect of the organization's business. Any of the competencies in the ECQ business acumen are very good expertise to possess. Financial management, human capital management, and technology management are excellent areas of expertise to have. To reach the top-executive levels, some knowledge in all three areas is critical. If reaching the upper levels is part of your career plan, you can acquire the expertise through a combination of classes and conversations with the appropriate office in the organization. In some ways, technology can be considered another culture, with the cultural competencies coming into play. Technology has its own language and worldview. Meeting with others in the organization who manage these areas also allows you to develop working relationships with employees who are in a position to help you. As mentioned earlier, if you need to ask someone for a favor, do so of someone you already know, not of a colleague you have just met.

Credibility is of the utmost importance for an employee. It determines the confidence your supervisor and others have in your work. Establishing credibility can be as simple as letting your supervisor and others know where you got the information you are using and then asking if they have any additional information or know of any other sources you can use. This approach is an informal version of the method of citations that university students and faculty use when writing papers. This approach establishes the credibility of the work. It is important to let others see how you present their views and provide feedback. Doing so lets everyone know that you are diligent in your work and that you want it to be accurate.

Using the cultural competence model, the coaching will include developing good relationships with other employees. Being culturally competent creates better relationships. Knowing how to create good relationships with others makes it easier to provide opportunities for that employee to gain visibility with other parts of the organization as well as the higher echelons of the organization. (A checklist for this type of coaching is provided on the DVD.)

Example 8.7: How to Build Reputation and Credibility

Abel was the first intern in the Presidential Management Intern (PMI) program, the precursor of the PMF program, in the comptroller's office at NASA. Bill, the comptroller was one of Abel's mentors. Several months after joining the comptroller's office, Abel was given the responsibility of being the program analyst for the Hubble Space Telescope, known internally as the space telescope. Because of problems, the space telescope's budget had just been increased from over $700 million to over a billion dollars. Abel had to brief Bill regularly on the status of the space telescope. The administration and Congress showed great interest in the progress of the project.

When briefing Bill, Abel would pick up his briefing package, which he would leave with Bill's secretary, Bonnie, the evening before. Abel would present the briefing package to Bill and sit down. Bill would quickly look at the report and then say, "Where are we on the space telescope?" Abel would begin his briefing. It was common for Bill to stop Abel and gruffly ask, "Where did you get that information?" Abel would then give Bill the name of the engineer or scientist with whom he had consulted, and Bill would holler out to Bonnie, "Bonnie, get this person on the phone for me." Bonnie would call the engineer or scientist whom Bill wanted to talk with, and Bill would put him on the speakerphone. "I have Abel with me," Bill would say, "and he is telling me that you told him this." The engineer or scientist who had given the information to Abel would answer, "Yes, that's exactly what I told him." Bill would then hang up the phone and repeat the process during the briefing. Bill would continue asking questions until Abel was out of information. Then Bill would say, "Okay, get that information and see me in a couple of days."

One day Abel was in his office when Bill walked in and said, "Abel, get your telescope briefing book. We are going to see the administrator." As they walked to the administrator's office, Bill asked, "What are the current issues on the telescope, and how are we going to solve them?" Abel quickly briefed Bill on the issues and solutions. By the time he finished, they had reached the administrator's office. After a few minutes of social conversation, the administrator asked Bill, "Tell me what's happening with the space telescope?" Bill told the administrator the exact same words that Abel had just told him. After a moment of elation at hearing his own words come out of Bill's mouth, the enormity of the responsibility of his briefings hit Abel. Now Abel understood why Bill had put him through such a difficult process. After this, Bill never checked with Abel's sources. By this time, Bill had confidence in the work Abel was doing.

Treasure any mentor who puts you through a challenging process. That mentor will make you a better employee.

8.5.3 Developing Relationships

Developing relationships with the supervisor and other employees also requires using the foundation cultural competencies. It is becoming increasingly likely that the relationships will be cross-cultural relationships as well as relationships that cross gender, sexual orientation, and social class. Building relationships with your supervisor and team as well as other managers requires both technical skill and cultural competency.

When developing cross-cultural relationships with others, it is important to consider the organizational culture as if it were a different culture. Employees and other co-workers may have been with the organization for many years. They have an established place in the organizational culture that must be respected if you are to develop good working relationships. They are the employees who can guide you into the organizational culture and help with your integration into the day-to-day life of the organization. The employees are the keepers of the informal or social organization, and they exercise choice when deciding with whom they share that knowledge. Giving these employees their due respect for their knowledge of the organization is also a cultural competency. Validate their expertise, and let your supervisor and the employees know how they have helped you. Doing this shows the employees that you are establishing a two-way relationship of mutual respect. Your co-workers will know that their helping you will be acknowledged and rewarded.

When interacting with other managers, it is wise to let your supervisor know of the interactions. No supervisor or manager likes to be surprised. When another manager tells your supervisor of the conversation you had, the supervisor is in a position to say, "I know, he [or she] told me about the conversation. Thank you for helping him [or her] and me." Such openness lets both managers know that you are not playing one against the other, and consequently both will have greater confidence in you, which will bode well for your career.

8.5.4 Visibility

The fourth part of the career plan is understanding that others will perceive you as a representative of your organizational unit. Mentoring how to develop cross-functional relationship is important to the success of your unit. Other managers can support your unit and help your supervisor and co-workers become more successful. This step is the beginning of learning how to establish strategic relationships with other agencies and departments.

Supervisors can mentor and coach employees to help them develop these relationships. As your expertise in representing your unit increases, the supervisor may introduce you to other managers from whom he or she wants support. Your organizational visibility increases through this step. Your ability to develop cross-cultural and cross-functional relationships makes it more likely that your supervisor will rely on you to represent your organizational unit more and more.

As your organizational visibility increases and your reputation and credibility increase, it becomes more likely that you will receive a phone call from another manager asking you to apply for a position that is now open. It is then time to talk with your supervisor, as mentor and coach, to guide you through your response. If your supervisor is supportive, then it is time to develop the continuation of your relationship with your supervisor after you move. Your relationships should last for your entire career, because you never know when you will need help from someone you once worked for or with. Your successful career has begun.

8.6 Acquiring Diverse and Multicultural Mentors

The value that mentors provide to the career success of employees has been well documented. The Korn/Ferry International study (1998) of multicultural employees showed the importance of mentors to the career success of women and employees of color. Programs such as the Presidential Management Fellows build in formal mentors as part of their program. How does an employee manage to acquire mentors who will be helpful to their career success?

Having formal mentors sounds beneficial, and it can be. The Korn/Ferry International study, however, pointed out that informal mentors could be even more helpful. Being a formal mentor, in concept, sounds simple enough. In practice, what being a formal mentor entails is unclear. Asking someone to be a formal mentor is asking a busy manager to take on unspecified responsibilities. Many managers may decline, since they do not know what will be required of them.

A much easier method and possibly more productive approach is having many informal mentors. Informal mentors are any individuals who can help an employee; they do not necessarily have to be high-level managers. The focus for an employee is assembling a team of other employees who can help him or her be successful. The first mentoring relationship should be the employee's supervisor. The supervisor–employee relationship is always a critical relationship for the success of an employee.

Developing diverse and multicultural mentors is the next step. It is easier to establish work relationships with others who share our own cultural characteristics, yet it is more beneficial to have a diverse set of mentors. Reaching out to mentors who are culturally different may be more difficult, but doing so opens up new networks for an employee. The foundation cultural competencies will be particularly useful in establishing cross-cultural relationships. It is likely that employees will have well-developed relationships at work with others who share similar cultural characteristics. Having diverse mentors opens up these networks to an employee.

Establishing mentoring relationships with diverse mentors happens after first developing a personal working relationship. In this process, you should introduce yourself to the prospective mentors. Then stop by to say hello with enough frequency to establish a comfortable personal working relationship. Once the comfortable working relationship has developed, you can ask work-related questions or ask the prospective mentor his or her opinion about a project you are working on. Let the mentor know how the advice has helped you. It is this feedback loop that maintains the mentoring relationship. If an informal mentor has been particularly helpful, it is appropriate to send an informal thank-you note expressing how the advice was helpful. As you reach out to colleagues, some will be more responsive than others. The responsive colleagues are the individuals who will become your informal mentors.

8.7 Creating Relationships with Diverse and Multicultural Employees

In today's increasingly diverse organizations, it is likely that most workplaces will include many employees with diverse backgrounds. Since these employees are co-workers, a working relationship will develop. The relationships can be shaped in a way that enhances and further develops cultural competencies. Realize that organizations have a culture as well as an ethnic background. Employees have established an organizational identity that melds their personal backgrounds with the organizational requirements. Their organizational identity should be as well respected as their own racial or ethnic background.

The initial conversations between employees may be work related, but they will invariably venture toward more personal and social topics. Employees are curious about fellow employees, and volunteering information about your background can ease a cultural conversation. It is as simple as saying, for example, "My parents emigrated from Ghana, in Africa. If you have any questions about me or what I know about Africa, please, feel free to ask me. I like sharing information about my background." This introduction opens the door to discussing cultural differences in a more positive and comfortable atmosphere. Such a conversation happens more easily over coffee or lunch. Over time, these conversations establish culturally competent relationships with co-workers and other employees.

8.8 Executive Protocols and Manners

Executive protocols and manners are not explicitly included in the cultural competencies. Learning executive protocols and manners can help accelerate career advancement, however. In today's informal world of text messaging, Facebook, and Twitter, common executive courtesies seem to have been ignored and forgotten by many employees. There is an increasing informality in both personal and business affairs. Someone well versed in executive protocols and manners will easily stand out as one who can be trusted to communicate with officials at all levels.

There are several guides to executive protocols and manners. A particularly worthwhile guide is Letitia Baldrige's *New Complete Guide to Executive Manners*

(1993). Baldridge served in several U.S. embassies and was the chief of staff to Jacqueline Kennedy in the White House, and so she understands the executive protocols and manners that guide the every relationship of top executives. By learning such protocols and manners as Baldridge discusses, an employee communicates an understanding of the workings of the top executives.

The basis of executive protocols and manners is respect for others. In some ways, this respect is a form of cultural competence, with the added emphasis of organizational culture. Some topics addressed in these guides include the following:

1. Comfortably relating with others
2. Conducting business lunches and dinners
3. Receiving people from outside your organizational unit
4. Having cultural competence
5. Engaging in executive communications
6. Knowing appropriate dress

In addition to these areas, it is also important to know where to be formal and where to be informal. Within the organizational unit, informality may be the rule. Being formal in interacting with co-workers, for instance, may be viewed as being pretentious. It is always good form, however, to be more formal when meeting people who are higher in the organization. Some executives may express a desire to be addressed by their first name or nickname. The danger in this invitation is that it implies the executives want an informal relationship. This is rarely the case. It is usually better to err on the side of formality.

The emphasis here has been on verbal communications. Yet written and telephone communications are just as important as verbal communications, if not more so. In verbal communications, the involved parties can see each other. If a communication or gesture is not well received, one can immediately see the reaction and adjust one's communication style. Written and telephone conversations prove more problematic. Especially in written communications, the writer is not present when the letter or memo is read. The writer has no ability to immediately correct a miscommunication. Any negative impression that is left is usually lasting and detracts from one's reputation.

Finally, a protocol issue that touches all employees aspiring to be culturally competent has to do with how we classify each other. Which is the proper racial or ethnic classification, for example, *Hispanic* or *Latino*? Does one describe an employee who is an immigrant from Africa as African American? It is always better to check with the recipient of the written communication before using a term. Checking for the recipient's preference is also a form of respect.

In today's diverse and informal world of work, the employee who knows how and when to use executive protocols and manners will surely stand out as the knowledgeable employee.

8.9 Summary and Conclusion

Cultural competencies for employees are interwoven with technical work requirements. Programs such as the Presidential Management Fellows Program and the core qualifications for applicants to the Senior Executive Service (SES) provide guides for employees. Employees can initiate learning the skills necessary for the SES at any point in their career. The SES executive core qualifications include cultural competencies. The earlier in the career process that learning begins, the easier to acquire the skills.

Work in an organization is accomplished through an interconnected web of organizational relationships. The cultural competencies for employees facilitate developing a network of supportive mentors, managers, and co-workers. This network of supportive mentors, managers, and co-workers can accelerate career success for any employee. Employees may discover career options that they may never have realized existed.

BUILDING THE CULTURALLY COMPETENT ORGANIZATION

Chapter 9

Establishing the Organizational Cultural Competence Framework

9.1 Introduction

Many organizations are now more multicultural than in the 1990s. The increased diversity has brought new cultural characteristics into what were once essentially monocultural organizations. Not all the new cultural characteristics are closely attuned to the predominantly monochronic requirements of the organizational culture. Managing diversity is moving from recruitment of protected groups to establishing cultural competence, that is, integrating the diverse cultural characteristics in high-performing organizations. A cultural competence framework facilitates the integration of the various cultural characteristics.

In public organizations, the cultural competence framework will be developed in a political and politicized environment. The demographic forces that are driving the need for cultural competence are also fueling a societal debate on the identity of the United States. There are similar discussions in Europe. The United States, more than Europe, is facing a tipping point. There have been many newspaper articles and television news stories about the United States becoming a no-majority country. Minority births were projected to outnumber white births by 2010 (Yen 2010), and that tipping point has been reached. Europe has smaller numbers of immigrants, but their cultural and religious differences seem to be starker. People are seeing the cultural effects of the demographic changes, and the public debate on immigration has been controversial. It is in this social and political milieu that cultural competence will have to be implemented.

Affirmative action opened up organizations to minorities and women, who had been denied many opportunities. Women and minorities have made many gains since the beginning of affirmative action. Many saw affirmative action as an effort to achieve social equity and fairness for all citizens, Currently 1 out of every 12 people in the United States was born in another country. Estimates are that 10% of the population are the children of immigrants, and almost 1 in 4 people are first- or second-generation Americans. In 1970, six years after the passage of the Civil Rights Act, 88% of the population was white and 11% black. Hispanics, who can be of any race, accounted for 5% of the population (Waters and Vang 2006). There are still many people who see race relations in terms of black and white, but in the intervening years since affirmative action initiatives were implemented, our racial and ethnic reality has become much more complex than just black and white.

Cultural competence is different than affirmative action, and the necessity for it is also different. The need for cultural competence is being driven by demographic changes. The retiring baby boomers will, by their sheer numerical size, leave a considerable gap in the workforce. The recession may delay some retirements, but the trend is inevitable. The baby boomers will eventually retire. The Campaign for Youth (2010) forecasts that by 2030, 76 million people will enter retirement and only 41 million new workers will enter the workforce. The Pew Hispanic Center (Passel and Cohn 2008), whose list of racial and ethnic classifications of the working-age population (18–64) is shown in Table 9.1, sees births as playing a greater part in the rise of the Hispanic and Asian populations.

The classifications and projections in the table show that in 2005, two-thirds of the working-age population was white and that nonwhites were about one-third of the working-age population. The numbers show the effects of the retiring baby boomers being replaced by a more multicultural workforce. While the actual 2050 percentages may vary depending on future immigration rates, the long-term trend will not. The U.S. workforce is experiencing unprecedented numbers of non-white employees.

Table 9.1 Working-Age Population by Race and Ethnicity

Year	2005	2050
White	68%	45%
Hispanic	14%	31%
Black	12%	14%
Asian	5%	10%

Source: Data from Passel, J. S., and D. Cohn, *U.S. Population Projections: 2005–2050*, Pew Research Center, Washington, DC, 2008.

For organizations, the increasing multicultural workforce is becoming the applicant pool. Recruitment from this pool will grow more competitive. The private sector, federal government, and local and state governments will all be competing for employees from this applicant pool. Experiments done by Williams and Bauer (1994) showed that students rated the organization that had a policy for a managing diversity policy as more attractive than the control organization, which did not have such a policy.

Successfully recruiting from multicultural applicants, many of whom may be first- or second-generation Americans, is only the first step. Managing this vastly diverse workforce is the second step. When the demand for labor is greater than the supply, workforce mobility becomes easier. Retention of employees will depend on effective managers who can manage a diverse workforce.

The findings reported in *Best Practices in Achieving Workforce Diversity*, a report issued by the U.S. Department of Commerce and Vice President Al Gore's National Partnership for Reinventing Government Benchmarking Study (1999), still have relevance today. The executive summary states, "Organizations that can develop and employ the necessary policies and procedures to do this [being able to attract and retain the best and most qualified workers] will maintain a competitive advantage among their counterparts and increase their effectiveness" (p. 1). The executive summary further states, "Yet, Federal organizations must compete to recruit and retain the best talent if they hope to achieve their bottom line, their statutory missions" (p. 1).

Managing diversity is not just a U.S. initiative; the European Commission on Employment, Social Affairs and Equal Opportunities has a Web site: For Diversity–Against Discrimination (http://www.stop-discrimination.info; European Commission, Employment, Social Affairs and Equal Opportunities n.d.). In the commission's pamphlet titled *Managing Diversity at Work Can Be Challenging*, demographic change is seen as creating challenges for business. The pamphlet describes some of the benefits of a diverse workforce as enhancing creativity and innovation, reducing staff turnover, and increasing employee satisfaction. The For Diversity—Against Discrimination Web site lists the following benefits of managing diversity effectively:

1. Attracting, recruiting, and retaining people from a wide pool of talent
2. Reducing the costs of labor turnover and absenteeism
3. Contributing to employee flexibility and responsiveness
4. Building employee commitment and morale
5. Managing better the impact of globalization and technological change
6. Enhancing creativity and innovation
7. Improving knowledge of how to operate in different cultures
8. Improving the understanding of the needs of current customers and clients
9. Assisting in the development of new products, services, and marketing strategies (European Commission, Employment, Social Affairs and Equal Opportunities n.d.)

10. Enhancing the organization's reputation and image with external stakeholders
11. Creating opportunities for disadvantaged groups and building social cohesion

The reasons for developing diversity initiatives need to be defined in a way that differentiates the effort from affirmative action and establishes the importance of diversity to the organization. Affirmative action provided some measure of fairness and equity for several groups, but cultural competence is an imperative, as stated in the EU Initiative, because the workforce is now diverse in a way that it has never been before.

9.2 The High-Performance Organization

As of this writing, the United States is facing many difficult problems: a troublesome recession, high unemployment, high deficits, and two wars. Societal problems are growing more difficult and require better solutions from all our government agencies. Complex and difficult societal problems require high-performance government organizations.

The high-performance organization is the organization that consistently performs better than its competitors. In the U.S. Office of Personnel Management's (OPM) 2010–2015 strategic plan, titled *A New Day for Federal Service* (2010b), one of the strategic goals is to make the federal government a high-performance organization. Some of the strategies are on succession planning, leadership development, training, and partnering the human resource office with agencies on strategic and operational issues. Cultural competence and managing diversity can contribute to turning an agency into a high-performance organization. Much of *Cultural Competence for Public Managers* complements the OPM strategies by using cultural competence in ways that help an organization become highly performing. (For those readers who would like more information on high-performance organizations, the American Management Organization published the results of a 2007 study the organization commissioned, *How to Build a High-Performance Organization: A Global Study of Current Trends and Future Possibilities, 2007–2017.* Although the study is of organizations in the private sector, there is much information that is useful for public managers.)

Some common elements of high-performance organizations are leadership, strategy, culture, and talent. In some ways the private sector may be ahead of many government agencies in creating high-performance organizations. Private sector companies have to strive in a more competitive environment than do government agencies. Many of these companies are aware of the demographic changes in the country and the increased buying power of the growing multicultural groups. So managing diversity has become an integral part of their long-term strategy. Support comes from the companies' top leaders, who are attempting to create a more inclusive culture for employees and want to have the employee base that can make them excel. These elements are also useful and productive in the public sector.

Assessments of the multicultural training programs mentioned in Chapter 5 showed that cultural competence training resulted in a hard bottom-line return to the companies. Their diverse employees provided more and better business solutions. Diversity can enhance creativity and innovation, which are qualities that are particularly useful when facing global challenges. Participating managers used their newly acquired skills on all their employees. Inclusiveness of all racial and ethnic groups, including whites, created a more supportive environment for the multicultural programs.

Cultural competence becomes the strategic tool to manage diversity. Culturally competent policies can help create a culture of inclusiveness where diverse individuals can achieve their career aspirations. An organization will then find it easier to attract recruits, as well as retain valued employees, from a much wider talent pool.

9.3 How Current and Future Situations Set the Stage for Culturally Competent Practices

Legislative requirements have been the main drivers of affirmative action and diversity. Recognizing the current demographic reality and the implications of the cultural change that is currently underway provides a way to add another dimension to the discussion on diversity. Cultural competence is a management necessity.

Many successful management techniques and practices were developed when organizations were less culturally diverse. The emerging organizational workplace contains employees with many diverse cultural characteristics that create a new cultural context for managers. Managers must now see management practices in a cultural context.

Even concepts such as equity theory, in which employees make comparisons of their inputs and outputs, have to be seen in a cultural context. (Equity theory as a way of resolving difficult issues is discussed in Chapter 14.) In forming perceptions of equitable treatment of employees, organizations composed of employees who come from several different cultural groups will use culture in addition to the concepts of inputs and outputs in equity theory. The comparison shifts from individual employees to individuals from the various cultural groups.

An individual who became a manager when the organization was less diverse has had a long time to develop working relationships with employees who are the most culturally similar to him or her. As diversity increases, that manager may still spend more time with, give more recognition to, and assign the most important assignments to culturally similar employees. From the manager's perspective, doing so makes sense. These are the employees who have been dependable in the past, who are the most familiar, and with whom the manager already has long-established relationships.

Employees may see that the manager spends more time with and rewards culturally similar individuals more so than individuals from their different cultural group. They may see themselves as effective but recognize that they are not getting the same rewards. Undercurrents of cultural tensions begin to build. To avoid this dynamic, having all the employees understand the changing culture can provide a rationale for cultural competence policies and practices.

9.4 Reasons for Culturally Competent Policies

Many organizations have diversity initiatives. The diversity initiatives and the increasingly diverse applicant pool have increased diversity in most organizations. Cultural competence helps to integrate the diverse workforce into high-performing employees. The emphasis should begin with the supervisor–employee relationship, a key relationship in creating a high-performance organization. Employee relationships with each other are also important in creating a high-performance organization. The leadership should establish the organization as being inclusive of all employees and recognize that diversity contributes to better and more innovative solutions.

Cultural competence is a strategic tool and becomes an integral aspect of the strategic plan for human capital development. It is helpful to have an assessment of human resource needs of the organization for the next 10 years. During this period, many baby boomers will retire. Having an assessment of the recruiting needs of the organization for this period of time and the demographics of the applicant pool creates the business case for requiring cultural competence. Cultural competence is required for more than social equity and fairness; it is also a business necessity. Diversity, by its very nature, brings with it many different cultural characteristics that can affect workplace dynamics. Cultural competence and managing diversity can contribute to an organization's becoming highly performing by increasing innovation and having more motivated employees.

A cultural competence framework begins with a rationale that frames the context for managing diversity:

1. Establishing reasons for cultural competence policies
2. Being a high-performance organization
3. Having the ability to fuse all the diverse elements in today's workforce into a high-performing organization with culturally competent employees
4. Recognizing and valuing diversity as a means to becoming a high-performing organization
5. Fostering inclusiveness of all employees
6. Recruiting, developing, and retaining the best employees from diverse applicant pools

The rationale explains the transformative role that cultural competence plays in the performance and effectiveness of the organization. The framework rationale also establishes the connection between cultural diversity and performance. Cultural competence is inclusive such that all groups are valued members of the organization. The last part of the message is that the future of the organization lies with diverse employees.

9.5 The Culturally Competent Organization

Siegel, Haugland, and Chambers (2003) published an article titled "Performance Measures and Their Benchmarks for Assessing Organizational Cultural Competency in Behavioral Health Care Service Delivery." The researchers developed a set of performance measures and then had an expert panel and consumer focus groups review the measures. The expert panels contained experts from all the major racial and ethnic groups. The results provide an excellent framework for instituting culturally competent policies. The approach used by Siegel, Haugland, and Chambers (2003), the National Association of Social Workers,w and the Georgetown University Center for Cultural Competence is adapted in Table 9.2 to make it easier for public managers to use.

9.6 Defining Diversity

One of the more important points in *Best Practices in Achieving Workforce Diversity* (1999) is the differentiation of the meaning of diversity beyond the more traditional categories of race, ethnicity, and gender. The report adds age, religion, and disability as prime dimensions. As secondary dimensions, the report adds "communication style, work style, organizational role/level, economic status, and geographic origin (e.g. East, Midwest, South)" (p. 3).

Cultural competence is moving beyond the emphasis on groups of employees who are designated as protected groups, that is, those groups whose members may have experienced some forms of discrimination because of their group characteristics. The *Best Practices* report extends the definition of diversity to include organizational cultural characteristics, such as work style, organizational role or level, and communication. Work style and communication are influenced by monochronic or polychronic cultural characteristics, as well as by social status. The classifications of biracial, multiracial, and bicultural, as well as the proliferation of people from many different countries with their own distinctive cultures that are grouped in one racial or ethnic classification—as are Hispanics—makes it more difficult to know the cultural characteristics by identifying racial or ethnic classification alone.

The definition of diversity is being broadened to include differences that go beyond the more traditional race, ethnicity, and gender categories. Cultural

Table 9.2 Components of a Culturally Competent Organization

Organizational Component	Yes	No
1. Cultural competence is part of the organization's mission statement.		
2. Being a culturally competent employee is part of the strategic plan.		
3. The strategic plan contains an implementation plan for cultural competence.		
4. There is an Office of Cultural Competence.		
5. The director of the Office of Cultural Competence is part of the management structure.		
6. The Office of Cultural Competence has its own budget.		
7. Cultural competence training is provided to managers and employees.		

Source: Adapted from Georgetown University Center for Child and Human Development, National Center for Cultural Competence, *Foundations of Cultural & Linguistic Competence*, http://www11.georgetown.edu/research/gucchd/nccc/foundations, 2009; National Association of Social Workers (NASW), *Indicators for the Achievement of the NASW Standards for Cultural Competence in Social Work Practice*, NASW, Washington, DC, 2007; Siegel, C., G. Haugland, and E. Chambers, Performance measures and their benchmarks for assessing organizational cultural competency in behavioral health care service delivery, *Administration and Policy in Mental Health*, 31 (2), 141–170, 2003.

competence is becoming a requirement of the organizational infrastructure. Many management tools, including policies and management practices, are evolving as they adapt to the cultural changes happening in today's organization.

9.7 Creating Culturally Competent Practices

Policies are, after all, just written statements. It is the practices that give life to the policies, and it is the practices that are the management aspect of policies. Without the accompanying practices, policies are easy to ignore.

As early as 2000, OPM recognized that diversity is more than numbers and that it means different cultural perspectives. *Building and Maintaining a Diverse and High Quality Workforce* (OPM 2000) states, "Another important aspect of diversity derives from different cultural perspectives. As an employer, the Federal Government has made great strides in achieving representational diversity. There is, however, still work to do. Misconceptions and misinformation should be replaced by facts, and stereotypes replaced by awareness" (p. 5). There is a broader cultural diversity in government agencies since 2000. Much of it has been driven by immigration from many different countries in the world.

The same report describes some of the challenges to communication: "A diverse workplace may present other challenges in the area of communication across cultures. For instance, the Federal workplace culture sometimes assigns a specific significance to the workplace behavior of employees (e.g. assuming that sustaining eye contact is a sign of directness and honesty) that may be different from the values in an individual employee's culture (e.g. considering it disrespectful and hostile to sustain eye contact)" (p. 6). The report alludes to the cultural requirements of the organizational culture and how various cultural characteristics can create miscommunication and misunderstandings.

Example 9.1: Language Miscommunication

An assistant secretary, Peter, had become friends with a political appointee, Ed, in the department of legislative affairs. Ed is Irish and from Boston. Peter, the assistant secretary was taking three days off and wanted to visit Boston, so he called Ed to ask him where to stay. Ed told Peter that the Lon Waff Hotel was a very nice hotel and to stay there. Peter asked his wife if she would make the reservations. She agreed, and Peter told her, "Ed said to stay at the Lon Waff Hotel. I don't know who Lon Waff is, but he must be important, since he has an hotel named after him." His wife made the reservations. As the taxicab approached the hotel, his wife poked Peter in the ribs and said, "Look at the name of the hotel." The name of the hotel is the Long Wharf. Peter just shook his head and smiled.

As the example illustrates, even regional differences in dialect can create miscommunications. Imagine the cultural language miscommunications that can occur, then, when first-generation immigrants with close ties to their parents' culture bring their cultural perspectives into the workplace.

OPM's report *Building and Maintaining a Diverse and High Quality Workforce* (2000) points out that many minority employees do not feel they are treated fairly, with substantial numbers of minorities reporting that they were subjected to blatant as well as subtle discriminatory practices in the workplace. In contrast, employees who are not minorities believed that discrimination is minimal. These figures are similar to those reported for multicultural experiences in the Korn/Ferry International study (1998). The same OPM report cited a 1996 U.S. Merit Protection Board (MSPB) study that found that minorities have lower average grade levels than white male employees, even after controlling for differences. Minorities received lower performance ratings and fewer cash awards than did whites in professional and administrative positions. Also, fewer minority employees received developmental opportunities to serve as acting supervisors in the absence of their managers. Several years have elapsed since the study, so one hopes that progress has been made. But even with progress, the practices may leave a residue of similar circumstances.

A New Day for Federal Service (2010b), OPM's 2010–2015 strategic plan, has as OPM's vision the notion that the federal government will become the country's model employer. Accordingly, in valuing diversity, the plan states, "We honor our employees and customers through inclusiveness and respect for the various perspectives and backgrounds that each brings to the workforce" (p. 5). This value is intended to bring out the best in diverse employees. The value is the public face of diversity for the federal government. However, the government's guide for federal agencies, *Building and Maintaining a Diverse and High Quality Workforce,* also reports a darker undercurrent, where day-to-day practices do not reflect published policies.

Whereas the cultural competence policies are the public face and the intent of the organization, it is the practices that determine the difference between a high-performance organization and just another government agency here to help you. It is in this cultural milieu that the cultural competent practices will make the difference between a highly performing organization or just another government agency. Furthermore, establishing the practices starts from the executives articulating and communicating why the employees are there. As John Berry, the director of OPM, states in his introduction to the 2010–2015 strategic plan:

> The Civil Service of today carries forward that proud American tradition. Whether it is defending our homeland, restoring confidence in our financial system and administering an historic economic recovery, ensuring adequate health care for our veterans and fellow citizens or searching for the cure to the most vexing diseases—we are fortunate to have our best and our brightest to rely upon. Our people are our most important tool in facing any challenge, and we forget that at our peril. They are not merely part of the equation, like capital or technology. They ARE the equation. (OPM 2010b, 1)

The executives create culturally competent practices in the way they communicate. As John Berry has done in OPM's strategic plan, other executives can articulate how important each employee is to solving the challenges facing the country, or state, or county, or city, or municipality. Having the performance and diversity of employees embedded in the strategic plan paves the way for performance standards and measurements. The value and importance of each employee should be reiterated at any public speaking opportunity. The public and the employees should be able to see the value of the contributions of public employees.

The second part of culturally competent communication is to address the cultural changes the country is experiencing. Yes, the country is on the way to losing its white majority, and diversity and cultural change are here. Even if all immigration were to stop today, the birthrates are such that we will still be a country without a racial or ethnic majority. The United States is now composed of many different cultures, each with its own cultural characteristics and languages. In addition, women have become the majority of the workforce. Gays, lesbians, bisexuals, and transgenders will continue to gain rights similar to those enjoyed by all other citizens. The United States is no longer a country built on manufacturing, and so many blue-collar employees will be seeking government employment. That is the reality, and our job is to focus on diversity to help in solving today's problems and not to let it divide us. Giving voice to reality can help relieve whatever anxieties exist. The world is undergoing many changes, and the future is uncertain. Ambiguity is difficult for many people to deal with, and free-floating anxiety can crystallize around and build on any small event. Approaching the cultural changes head-on can relieve the free-floating anxiety.

Addressing the reality does raise a key question for each employee: "What does it mean for me?" Inclusiveness of all employees acknowledges the current reality. Unfortunately, affirmative action, while well intentioned, has not always been applied in a proper manner. There are anecdotal incidents of managers telling white applicants, "You really deserved the promotion [or job], but we had to give it to a minority candidate [or a woman] so we could meet our quotas." This response to affirmative action requirements may have led whites to feel resentful in having missed opportunities reserved for minority candidates.

Inclusiveness of all employees has to be a resonating message. White supervisors who participated in the private sector multicultural leadership programs would comment at the beginning of the program that they did not know why they were there, but they appreciated being invited. After the end of the sessions, the white supervisors said they had learned much about the different cultures and that they were now able to communicate better with their multicultural employees. Follow-up surveys showed they were using culturally competent communications with all their employees.

The top leadership communicates that the road to becoming a high-performance organization leads to effective teams composed of strong supervisor–employee and employee–employee relationships. While diversity is valued and makes an important contribution, it can also make communicating across those differences difficult. Executives should emphasize the importance of all employees learning to communicate across cultural differences. The managerial cultural competencies for executives, middle managers, and supervisors (discussed in Chapters 6 and 7) are a way of creating culturally competent practices for managers.

9.8 Creating a Supportive Organizational Climate

The OPM 2010–2015 strategic plan provides guidance in creating a supportive organizational climate. The process begins with two values expressed in the strategic plan: respect and diversity. Regarding the value of respect, the OPM (2010b) plan description explains, "We extend consideration and appreciation to employees, customers and stakeholders fostering a fair, open and honest workplace environment. We listen to the ideas and opinions expressed by others" (p. 5). Regarding the value of diversity, it states, "We honor our employees and customers through inclusiveness and respect for the various perspectives and backgrounds that each brings to the workforce" (p. 5). Both values are also integral to cultural competence. Respect for others is almost always expressed first in definitions of cultural competence. Inclusiveness and respecting the contributions that diversity brings to the organization are part of cultural competency also. Respect and diversity are two of the values that drive the strategic plan.

One of OPM's strategic goals is to "help agencies recruit and hire the most talented and diverse Federal workforce possible to serve the American people" (2010b, 10). One of the strategies for creating a diverse workplace is creating an environment where diversity is valued and can be leveraged for organizational productivity. Leveraging diversity is also one of the SES core qualifications for executives. Including this requirement as an SES leadership qualification to be demonstrated by employees makes managing diversity a structural requirement for career success.

Two additional strategies focus on providing opportunities for advancement and career training. First, policies and practices must ensure all segments of society an opportunity to be hired and to advance. The participants of the multicultural leadership program discussed in Chapter 5 described their lack of career development as being their greatest source of dissatisfaction. Their motivation increased tremendously, however, when they had long-term career development plans, which had their manager's agreement and support. We must remember that many employees who are the children of immigrants and employees of color may not be familiar with the requirements of career success. Second, the organization or agency must provide education and training where employees can learn to value diversity. The assessment of the multicultural leadership program showed the value of cultural competence training for all the diverse employees and their managers. The participants and their managers continued to be culturally competent in their workplace. They also became role models for the other employees. OPM further supports these efforts in another of its strategic goals with an emphasis on providing training for federal employees. The strategies encourage training programs that prepare employees for promotion and position them for developing successful careers. Leadership training programs are also emphasized.

The OPM strategic plan also contains indicators that measure the progress being made in meeting the strategic goals. One of the indicators or performance measures for determining progress on valuing diversity is the use of employee surveys to measure employee and manager satisfaction. Indicators for training are the increase in leadership development and other training opportunities for employees.

Organizations can create a supportive climate for cultural competence by including in their strategic plans the strategies to leverage diversity. Performance measures or indicators of progress show the progress or lack of progress that an organization is making.

9.9 Summary and Conclusion

Cultural competence is evolving with societal cultural changes. Globalization may be seen as making the world more complex. Countries and their economies are more interdependent. Problems are becoming more complex and more challenging to solve. There remains disagreement on how to get the economies of the United States and Europe back on track. In the United States, many state and local governments are struggling to balance their budgets, and many are facing employee layoffs and cuts to social services. More is being asked of governments. Responding to the complex challenges will require the best efforts of government employees. As shown in the OPM strategic plan for 2010–2015, there is now a greater emphasis on government organizations being high-performance organizations.

Best Practices in Achieving Workforce Diversity, issued by the U.S. Department of Commerce and Vice President Al Gore's Benchmarking Study (1999), began expanding the definition of diversity to include other aspects such as communication style, work style, organizational role or level, economic status, and geographic origin. Leveraging diversity is increasingly being seen as a way to contribute to high-performing organizations. Leveraging diversity is also an OPM SES leadership requirement.

Developing cultural competence and managing diversity seem to be transitioning from an emphasis on having a diverse and representative workforce to a focus on managing the cultural diversities that now exist in many organizations. This change of direction does not mean that organizations are representative of the communities they serve nor that there is no longer a need for recruiting diverse employees. Even the OPM 2010–2015 strategic plan has the goal of recruiting and hiring the most talented and diverse federal workforce possible. Some employees may, however, see the continuing efforts to recruit a talented and diverse workforce as yet another version of affirmative action, rather than an attempt to foster cultural diversity and competence. What it does mean is being very clear that cultural competence values the contributions that diversity can make to a high-performing organization.

It is important to be explicit in defining diversity in a broader context. Diversity includes many different cultural characteristics; and where there are different cultural characteristics, there is the potential for misunderstandings and problems. The assessment of the multicultural leadership training programs discussed in Chapter 5 showed that once managers and employees understood how the cultural differences were affecting workplace interactions, both managers and employees used the cultural competence they had learned to the benefit of the organization.

Training programs should include a description and discussion of the different cultural characteristics.

The work of Siegel, Haugland, and Chambers (2003), in association with the National Association of Social Workers and the Georgetown University Center for Cultural Competence, and OPM's 2010–2015 strategic plan, as well as many others, show a convergence when it comes to cultural competence and organizational structure and diversity policies. There should be support for cultural competence from the top executives. The multicultural leadership programs also demonstrated the value of having the top executives attend symposiums, cultural competence training, and problem-solving workshops. The attendance of the top executives communicated how truly supportive they were and how important cultural competence is to their organization.

Cultural competence policies need an organizational structure for managing diversity to help implement the policies. An office of diversity or an office of cultural competence provides such an organizational structure to oversee the implementation. A budget and staffing will be needed. Depending on the resources of an organization, this structure can be done through reorganization or the creation of a new office. The rest of the organizational effort can be accomplished in collaboration with the human resource office. These efforts are aimed at developing and conducting cultural competence training. Cultural competence can become part of an employee's and manager's performance appraisals. Surveys can be developed and administered to determine the progress of the cultural competence initiatives and the organizational support for leveraging diversity.

The traditional management tools of policies and practices are being adapted to a more culturally diverse organizational environment. Managers and employees are in the process of becoming more culturally sensitive or intelligent.

Chapter 10

Human Resource Management and Cultural Competence

10.1 Introduction

One could argue that the department of human resource management (HRM) was not originally a partner in helping employers become the best they could be. This fact is observable in the early days of Taylorism and later with the Ford assembly line. Taylorism refers to the efforts of Frederick Taylor to make factory work more efficient. Taylor would conduct time and motion studies to make employees more like machines. Employees were seen as a way to keep production moving. Issues of safety and ethical responsibility were seen as obstacles to getting the work done. Employees had little, if any, rights despite the fact that trade unions were coming of age. This chapter addresses the current formation of HRM and examines its role in helping to shape an appreciation of cultural competencies in the workplace.

10.2 The Evolving Field and Its Inattention to Diversity

Students always want to know why the term *human resource management* is used in graduate courses, but yet the university's Web site continues to use the term *personnel management* in describing its courses. A flip response is that individuals working in the registrar's office are not informed of the changes in the field. This is actually not far from the truth. Almost every field evolves and goes through a metamorphosis. This is not surprising or seemingly that unusual. For example, given its contemporary purpose, psychology has seen a great deal of change since its inception; and its always changing diagnosis of what is considered perverse is something that has helped many people living within various societal walls. For example, many practitioners in the psychology field prior to the 1970s considered being gay abnormal. Now, many practitioners consider being gay just another form of human sexuality.

This is the case with HRM, once considered only an office to police employees, to hire them and fire them. Today, HRM has a much different role and should be seen as a partner in achieving an organization's mission. Rudiger Klimecki and Stefan Litz (2004) argue that HRM is in fact evolutionary. The authors point out that HRM has the ability to hinder or help individuals grow and develop within their organization. Indeed, public personnel did act to hinder the growth of individuals and the organization that employed them. However, given a new understanding of what human resources and human development means, HRM has created a new sense of being and purpose for the field.

A critique of the HRM field cannot begin without a review of Fredrick Taylor's scientific management theory. Over the years, many scholars have torn apart the theory; none have viewed the theory on the basis of social equity and social justice limitations. In its most basic form, scientific management was supposed to be the way in which personnel managers and employees worked together with an understanding of what the other needed to accomplish. A main criticism leveled at this theory was, however, that employees felt tied to the same work functions every day they worked. Employees were denied room for creativity or new ideas in carrying out their work functions. Employees resented this restriction, as they felt like cogs on an assembly line (Fisher, Schoenfeldt, and Shaw 2003).

This result was not necessarily the intent of Taylor's theory. Growing up as a Quaker, he did value people. However, he did not value work inconsistencies and mismanagement. Still, parts of scientific management were useful, such as employees knowing about each other's functions and job responsibilities. This idea can still be found in the contemporary HRM system whereby employees are trained in areas other than their own. This approach makes sense from a workload perspective as well.

10.3 Managing Diversity

Given the complexities and challenges associated with having a diverse workforce, managing diversity has become a major concern for human resource (HR) managers. Indeed, only the most skilled and astute manager will be able to address the challenges that managing diversity will bring now and in the future (Earnest and Shawnta 2003; Seyed-Mahmoud 2004). In fact, in his 1995 book *Managing*

Diversity in Organizations, Robert Golembiewski argues that in the past, issues of diversity were easily forgotten, with the exception of race. But even if racial diversity was ignored in the past, it cannot be ignored in the future. By 2020, the percentage of Americans of European decent will decrease from 75.1% reported in 2000 to just 53%. The number of Hispanic and Asian Americans is expected to triple, while African Americans are expected to double (Ruth-Sahd 2003).

Organizations must strive to become more responsive to employees (Golembiewski 1995, 3). In fact, managing diversity should not be seen as an issue at all. All employees should be valued and celebrated for the unique talents and strengths they bring to the organization. But with such a notion comes conflicts, and mangers will need to use these conflicts as a vehicle for positive change (Tshikwatamba 2003).

Riccucci (2001, 1) postulates that the U.S. workforce will look vastly different in the 21st century than the workforce looked in the last century. According to Riccucci, white women, people of color, gays, lesbians, and people from different generations will populate the workforce of the future and in fact are doing so now. Therefore, both public and private sector organizations will need to develop strategies for ensuring that such a workforce remains vibrant and respectful of all employees (2001, 3). Such strategies as affirmative action programs employed by many organizations no longer guarantee diversity management (though they did not in the first place). Therefore, organizations will need to change their culture to embrace the different groups of employees who will populate their workforce (Shin and Mesch 1996).

As a way to manage diversity, Hays, Bartle, and Major (2002) created a model named *climate theory*. The model seeks to create a supportive work environment for opportunity. The core of the model addresses such factors as experiences, culture, and cognitions. Together these experiences create perceptions about fair treatment in the workplace.

10.4 Obstacles in Diversifying HRM Curricula: A Lack of Teacher Preparation and Coverage

The curriculum of any HRM program can be life changing or in fact transformative for graduate students. But programs cannot expect students to graduate with cultural competencies without proper instruction from faculty who have these competencies and the commitment to the subject themselves. Nor can programs expect students to have experiences through coursework if, in fact, the courses are not in the curriculum in the first place.

The starting point for any curriculum reform is first with the faculty members themselves. There is a strong correlation between what faculty are teaching and what students are learning. According to Omiunota Nelly Ukpokodu (2003), faculty should have a deep grounding in diversity areas. This is rarely the case, however. Although some K–12 faculty receive diversity training while in graduate school, the same faculty will often opt for teaching K–12 education usually in the better schools, that is, in schools with better-than-average pay and smarter students. These schools are often in the suburbs, are homogeneous, and are often taught by middle-class suburbanites (Curtis 1998). Ukpokodu (2003) argues that the traditional curriculum has failed to educate future students and future faculty. The traditional curriculum has historically not taught about issues addressing identity, different cultures, and different perspectives (Le-Doux and Montalvo 1999).

Nonetheless, some teachers coming out of teacher preparation programs (K–12 education) are at least aware of issues of diversity, although many of them wonder about the value of learning about differences as they relate to such fields as math and science (Milner 2005). In fact, when the word *diversity* is mentioned, we have often seen white Americans roll their eyes dismissively. Such a reaction only under-scores the disconnect between students of diverse backgrounds and a majority of the teachers (Chase 2002).

Obviously, most HRM faculty do not come out of teacher preparation pro-grams and thus are not necessarily grounded in the latest trends in diversity chal-lenges or new pedagogical tools. Still, according to the diversity literature, faculty preparation in teaching diversity issues remains a challenge across the board and regardless of field. It must also be noted here that the literature addresses diversity in a way that implies only white faculty must learn and acknowledge concerns of diversity. However, the truth is that diversity involves everyone. For example, students studying HRM and public administration at Jackson State University, a historically black university in Mississippi, must know that not all employees in the workforce are heterosexual or Christian.

Indeed, one of the largest issues looming over faculty preparation is faculty mem-bers' acknowledgment of their own biases and stereotypes of differences (Sanchez 1996). Interesting enough, such biases must also be examined by faculty who teach at institutions in rural environments without much diversity. Students studying in these locations need faculty who can teach diversity issues even more, regardless of discipline (Nelson 2004). For example, Middlebury College, in Middlebury, Vermont, claims to be a progressive college embracing diversity, but Middlebury will need to demonstrate its claim through action and not merely rhetoric. It will be imperative for Middlebury faculty members to infuse diversity into the curriculum on a more than fundamental level.

"Our teachers are poorly equipped to deal with the new America," according to Mona Vijaykar (2001, 12). There is a basic unwillingness to shed old notions and stereotypes about certain groups. Despite the fact that there are evaluative measures associated with curriculum standards, Vijaykar argues that it is still very simple for faculty members to become frustrated with implementing a multicultural cur-riculum and abandon its merits. Therefore, faculty and senior administrators must ask themselves, "What is my level of commitment, level of preparation to teach a diverse curriculum, and commitment to changing my own values and antiquated notions of what diversity is not?"

Still, most faculty members have little motivation in diversifying the curriculum and have even less knowledge of pressing modern-day issues. This leaves the burden for diversity teaching to women and faculty of color (Trower and Chait 2002). Educating HRM students on diverse issues cannot be merely left to those faculty coming to the programs with diverse backgrounds. Curriculum reform must also be achieved among the majority faculty as well.

10.5 Why Is HRM Curricular Reform Needed?

In 2002, Martha Dede wrote about the important functions of an HRM system. Dede researched several HR agencies and found that there were commonalities they all shared. Dede found that six functional areas or clusters constitute the HRM field. Briefly stated, these are:

1. Position classification and compensation
2. Recruitment and examination
3. Employee training and development
4. Performance appraisal, promotion, and discipline
5. Labor relations and collective bargaining
6. Equal employment opportunity and diversity

The value of Dede's research is that it created a vehicle for graduate students to systematically learn about the key functions of a HRM system. Prior to her research, there had never been much consideration given to the fact that graduate students were graduating from public affairs programs without a solid foundation in or understanding of how HRM systems worked.

The criticism of Dede's work (2002) is that it did not provide serious consideration for how students may create a dialogue about social justice issues such as race, gender, sexual orientation, social class, and cultural competencies. This is particularly important because public affairs students will go into public service–related careers that deal with the public. A lack of knowledge in these areas will mean an inability for students to relate to their contingent staff or even supervisor.

A further examination of the HRM programs indicates an absence on diversity topics.

Table 10.1 indicates that 100% of the accredited programs surveyed had such core requirements as budgeting and management, versus 95% of unaccredited programs having a core requirement. Interestingly, only 39% of accredited programs had a diversity course despite the fact that the National Association of Schools of Public Affairs and Administration (NASPAA) has strongly recommended that diversity be included in curricula offerings. Unaccredited programs had nearly the

Table 10.1   Public Affairs Program

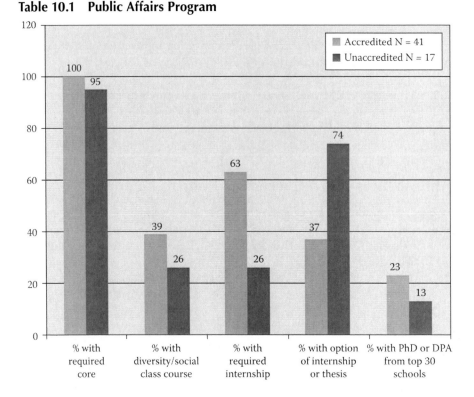

same amount of diversity course offerings despite not having NASPAA guidelines to encourage them. This comparison raises the questions as to what employers can expect from graduates of accredited public affairs programs. Whereas 63% of accredited programs had a required internship or field placement experience, some 74% of unaccredited programs had an internship or thesis option. Again, is the expectation of NASPAA programs that there will be a more rigorous academic standard? Table 10.1 does not bear out this notion.

Finally, the table clearly indicates that a sizable number of both unaccredited and accredited programs have faculty from the top 30 doctorate-granting programs in the United States. Attracting a well-qualified faculty should be the goal of any public administration program. However, there are also well-qualified potential faculty members who may be at lesser-known programs or institution. The University of Baltimore's DPA program, for example, is relatively new to doctorate education, but it has produced some highly qualified graduates over the last few years. Having a broad range of faculty from different institutions will assist a program to reform its curriculum and prepare a more diverse graduate. Programs that hire faculty from the same institutions or same two or three institutions greatly hinder their students' ability to learn from a broad array of people with different interpretations.

10.6 Elements of Diversity

Table 10.1 indicates a need for the inclusion of cultural competencies in HRM curricula. The chart's limitation is that it does not specify what types of competencies should be in place. This section argues that attention to women's issues ought to be part of the reform. The section goes further, however, by suggesting that women of color should also be a key part of the reform as well, specifically as it relates to issues of leadership and discrimination. It is not the intention here to pit one oppressed group against another oppressed group. However, research continues to demonstrate that women of color are still greatly marginalized. Consider the examples in Tables 10.2 and 10.3.

Concentrating on the position of dean in higher education is important because it is the first major step up the administration ladder. It is the testing ground for higher-level administrative positions. In a Web content analysis of the position of dean at Golden Gate University (GGU, a private institution) and the University of Vermont (UVM, a public institution), it is obvious that women of color continue to lag behind white female and white male deans. Of a total 16 deans' positions between the two institutions, only one is held by a woman of color as compared to seven white women and six white men. This contrast is particularly jarring with GGU, a well-established urban university situated in the business district of San Francisco, California. There is seemingly no reason why more women of color and, indeed, even men of color do not occupy a dean's position at the university. Even if GGU did not want to do a national search for an unfilled dean's position (which is unlikely), there is a large enough qualified population of women of color and professionals of color living in the Bay Area to fill the position. Indeed, GGU is in conflict with its own mission statement, because neither the deanery, nor the president, nor many of its students are diverse.

GGU's mission statement is clear:

> Golden Gate University prepares individuals to lead and serve by providing high-quality, practice-based educational programs in law, taxation,

Table 10.2   Golden Gate University Sitting Deans' Positions

GGU	Dean of Color	Women	Men
School of Law		X	
Ageno School of Business			X
School of Taxation		X	
School of Undergraduate Studies		X	

Source: Data from Golden Gate University, http://www.ggu.edu, 2010.

Table 10.3 The University of Vermont's Sitting Deans' Positions

UVM	Dean of Color	Women	Men
College of Agriculture and Life Sciences			X
College of Arts and Sciences		X	
College of Education and Social Services	X (female)		
College of Engineering and Mathematics			X
College of Medicine			X
College of Nursing and Health Sciences		X	
Continuing Education		X	
Graduate College			X
Honors College	X (male)		
Rubenstein School of Environment Natural Resources		X	
School of Business Administration			X

Source: Data from University of Vermont, http://www.uvm.edu, 2010.

business and related professions—as a nonprofit institution—in an innovative and challenging learning environment that embraces professional ethics and diversity. (GGU 2010)

At UVM, the only dean of color is Dr. Fayneese Miller, who came to the university as a dean and professor, having had a successful academic career at Brown University for 20 years. To date, she is the only female dean of color that the institution has had since it was chartered in 1791. This situation is particularly alarming, because UVM prides itself on having a social justice mind-set. Indeed, on its Web site the university touts its past accomplishments regarding this fact. For example, the university admitted the first women students to Phi Beta Kappa in 1875, and the first African American was admitted in 1877. Over the years, the university has tried to increase the diverse representation of its students and, to a lesser extent, the faculty.

Search committees at UVM have made the following comments about not attracting women of color:

1. People of color do not like Vermont because it is a rural state.
2. There are no qualified people of color to teach or work at UVM.

3. The weather is too cold for people of color.
4. People of color will not be happy in Vermont because there are too few other people of color to have a community.

Research conducted by UVM's own affirmative action office and independent sources suggest that these points are invalid and serve as excuses for search committees not to work really hard in seeking candidates of color for senior administrative positions such as deans.

If women were seen as nonessential elements of the workforce during the turn of the 20th century, then women of color were seen as even less. As part of many graduate programs in public administration, education, and leadership studies, we find that women and women of color specifically continue to be absent from HRM studies, thus not having a voice. In Taylor's scientific management work (1967), he could not possibly have included women of color whose roles were clearly that of servant and/or secret object of sexual desire for white men. Indeed, if women were considered worth less than half of what a white male was worth, and still less than men of color, it can be argued that women of color were at the bottom of the social chain.

In *Women of Color in Leadership: Taking Their Rightful Place* (Johnson and Harris 2010), it is argued that studies in the field of public administration, leadership studies, and education have left women out of consideration. Some might argue that this omission was unintentional, but others will claim that women of color were never on the radar of individuals such as Taylor. In 2010, using program Web sites that offered campus-based doctoral programs, Johnson and Harris created a graduate program table based on variables such as courses offered about women and women of color. Each program in the sample offered the EdD (doctor of education), DPA (doctor of public administration), or PhD (doctor of philosophy) as well as degree in public administration, leadership studies, or education.

Table 10.4 demonstrates a number of interesting findings. First, none of the programs offer a core requirement involving women's courses directly, though several sample programs do offer one or more courses in diversity as part of their core requirements. This is definitely a step in the right direction, because many diversity courses address gender, sexual orientation, social class, and race (Johnson 2009a; Oldfield and Johnson 2008). The challenge with many diversity courses is, however, that there is no guarantee that specific topics will make it into the class content, specifically issues related to women of color or other related gender issues, each time the courses are taught.

Second, whether issues about women of color, leadership, and social justice are taught in any of the sample programs' core course requirement on women is not evident. This is not necessarily to suggest that individual faculty may not alter course descriptions from year to year. However, the data from the content analysis may suggest that little, if any, attention is paid to issues pertaining to women of color. This lack is perhaps alarming at best, given that Web materials are often used

Table 10.4 Women's Programs, Spring 2011

University /College Name	Course Name(s)	Total Number of Core Courses	Term Requirements	Number of Diversity Courses
1. Gonzaga Doctoral Program Leadership Studies[a]	Leadership and Feminist Ethics	Elective	Four Courses/12 Hours	0
2. University of Maryland Eastern Shore/ Organizational Doctoral Program[b]	0	0	N/A	0
3. University of Vermont/Doctoral Program in Leadership and Policy Studies[c]	Women and Leadership	Elective	Four Courses/12 Hours	1
4. University of San Diego/Leadership Studies[d]	Leadership for Development of Women	Elective	Six Courses/18 Hours	3
5. Bowling Green State University/ Leadership Studies[e]	0	0	26 Hours	2
6. James Madison University/PhD in Strategic Leadership[f]	0	0	Four Courses/12 Hours	0
7. Hamline University/ DPA Program[g]	0	0	Five Course/20 Hours	0
8. St. John Fisher College/EdD Program in Executive Leadership[h]	0	N/A	Twenty Courses/60 Hours	3
9. NC A&T University/ PhD in Leadership Studies[i]	0	0	24 Hours	1

Table 10.4   Women's Programs, Spring 2011   (Continued)

University /College Name	Course Name(s)	Total Number of Core Courses	Term Requirements	Number of Diversity Courses
10. University of San Francisco/Doctorate in Organization and Leadership[j]	0	0	9 Units	0

[a] Gonzaga University. n.d. Leadership Studies Doctoral Program (Ph.D.). http://www.gonzaga.edu/Academics/Colleges-and-Schools/School-of-Professional-Studies/Degrees-Programs/PhD-Studies/default.asp

[b] University of Maryland Eastern Shore. n.d. Organizational Leadership Doctoral Program. http://www.umes.edu/ORLD/Default.aspx?id=12404

[c] University of Vermont. n.d. Educational Leadership and Policy Studies (Doctor of Education). http://www.uvm.edu/academics/catalogue2010-11/?Page=read.php&p=/Colleges_and_Schools/College_of_Education_and_Social_Services/Academic_Offerings/Educational_Leadership_and_Policy_Studies_(Ed.D.)&SM=collegemenu.html

[d] University of San Diego. n.d. Leadership Studies Doctorate. http://www.sandiego.edu/soles/programs/leadership_studies/academic_programs/doctoral_program/index.php

[e] Bowling Green State University. n.d. Leadership Studies. http://www.bgsu.edu/colleges/edhd/eflp/leadership/

[f] James Madison University. n.d. PhD in Strategic Leadership. http://www.jmu.edu/leadership/curriculum.shtml

[g] Hamline University. n.d. Doctorate in Public Administration (DPA). http://bulletin.hamline.edu/preview_program.php?catoid=8&poid=499&returnto=178

[h] St. John Fisher College. n.d. EdD in Executive Leadership. http://www.sjfc.edu/academics/education/departments/edd/

[i] NC A&T University. n.d. The Department of Leadership Studies. http://www.ncat.edu/~lstudies/

[j] University of San Francisco. n.d. Doctorate in Organization and Leadership. http://www.usfca.edu/soe/programs/leadership/ol_dr/

for recruitment and retention. One must argue that a graduate program's Web site reflects the values and commitment of its faculty and students.

Certainly, another group that Taylor was not thinking about and a group that has been historically overlooked in HR research is made up of individuals that identify as lesbian, gay, bisexual, or transgender. In 2008, Oldfield and Johnson published a first-of-its-kind book that addressed social class and sexual orientation. There have been books published on sexual orientation and, to a limited degree, social class. However, no other book has as specifically addressed the challenges that individuals from working-class and poor backgrounds and who are lesbian, gay, bisexual, or transgender face in the workplace.

Many consider the work of Oldfield and Johnson to be a seminal piece because it illuminates the shared experiences of people who have not traditionally been included in the progressiveness of the workplace.

Example 10.1: Sexual Orientation and Social Class

A colleague one of us had met at a national conference recently come out as both a lesbian and a working-class academic. To her surprise, she said, she encountered perhaps more prejudice from colleagues because of her socioeconomic origins than because of her sexual orientation. Although she faced considerable homophobia, she spoke of her ongoing battle against classist comments from professors and students of higher socioeconomic origins. She said these insults were leveled against her and the working class in general. She explained that coming out as a lesbian and a working-class academic forced her to reflect more on how both her sexual orientation and her socioeconomic origins affect the way she approaches life inside and outside the academy. (Oldfield and Johnson 2008, 3)

If the field of HRM is to continue to evolve from a rudimentary personnel system office, there must be a concerted effort to have HRM viewed seriously as a partnership. The partnership must first be with graduate programs that offer HRM courses and/or programs. This is our first line of defense for a reform that is long overdue. We cannot expect graduates to learn about cultural competencies after graduation. Issues of gender, sexual orientation, race, and social class must be embedded in every HRM course offering. This requirement includes the budgeting classes and classes on state and local government as well.

The second partnership must be with organizations that have HRM units, which must be in a position that reports to the top person in charge of the organization. Only then can the unit really accomplish its work, which is to broaden and embrace the development of each employee working for the organization. Indeed, it has been almost 100 years since Taylor's manifesto, a manifesto that was lacking in many respects. What HRM knows today is that the worth of individuals and their contributions to the organization must be celebrated. It would be interesting to discover what Taylor would say today about cultural competencies were he alive.

10.7 Creating Culturally Competent Orientation Programs

Orientation programs introduce new employees into the organizational culture, and new employees form their impression of the organization through the orientation. Many orientation programs just inform new employees of their benefits and review the employee handbook and code of conduct. Other orientation programs include the organizational vision and what is expected of employees to implement that vision. It is the rare HRM book that provides thorough coverage of orientation programs. Yet, it is the orientation program (or lack of orientation program) that forms the initial view of the organization and the way it views employees. Well-done orientation programs can convey to new employees the message that they are valued. Conversely, the lack of well-structured orientation programs can communicate that new employee are on their own.

Including cultural competence and diversity in an orientation program begins with defining diversity and its value to a highly performing organization. The OPM strategic plan for 2010–2015 illustrates the value of diversity through its goal to "help agencies recruit and hire the most talented and diverse Federal workforce possible to serve the American people" (2010b, 11). OPM proposes promoting diversity and inclusion in the federal workforce by:

1. Helping agencies create an environment that values workforce diversity and leverages diverse talent to achieve results.
2. Promoting policies and practices to ensure all segments of society, including people with disabilities, have an opportunity for employment and advancement.
3. Providing Federal employees and managers with educational and training opportunities aimed at creating and maintaining a culture where diversity is valued and promoted.
4 Pursuing recruitment and retention efforts focused on attracting diverse talent. (OPM 2010b, 11)

The orientation program lays the foundation for diversity by explaining that diversity is valued and that leveraging diversity creates a highly performing organization. Employees are supported in their efforts to leverage diversity through education and training.

Once the value of diversity and leveraging diversity for results have been explained, the orientation can define and explain what diversity is for the organization. Much of the writing on cultural competence and managing diversity still focuses on the inclusion of diverse groups into an organization. That focus has recently been shifting to managing the wide range of diversities now found in the modern organization.

10.7.1 Defining Diversity and Cultural Diversity

Entrants into today's workforce and current employees are individuals who bring into the organizational culture myriad cultural characteristics. It is the diversity of backgrounds and perspectives that when properly focused can lead to innovation and better solutions. Diversity can also create misunderstandings and conflict. Tapping into the richness of diversity starts with respecting other employees as individuals, taking into account their diverse perspectives. Employees and managers thereby harness diversity into a productive organizational culture.

Defining diversity can have two components: one is the traditional definition of diverse groups, and the second is a discussion of diverse cultural characteristics. Classification of diverse groups can include race, ethnicity, gender, social class, sexual orientation, disability, age or generational definitions—baby boomers, generations X and Y, or millennials, for example—and organizational role. The classification for the groups is broader than the traditional notion of diversity, which refers to protected groups. The intent is to focus employees on the cultural characteristics more than the classification. No individual fits exclusively into just one of the classifications. Individuals are instead combinations of the various classifications. Each individual has cultural characteristics that are a blend of the cultural characteristics of the various classifications. The cultural characteristics are the qualities that add richness to diversity.

For the purposes of an orientation program on cultural competence, a few cultural characteristics are listed in Table 10.5. In reality, a description of diverse cultural characteristics can shift the discussion from comparing the merits of belonging to one group versus another to identifying the cultural characteristics that all employees bring into an organization and the effect of those cultural characteristics on organizational productivity and effectiveness. This discussion of individual characteristics evident in most cultures also serves to create common ground or a shared culture that is the organizational culture.

Any individual, regardless of the combination of groups to which he or she belongs, can possess any of the groups' diverse cultural characteristics to varying degrees. The cultural characteristics the individual brings to the organization can affect employee–supervisor relationships as well as employee–employee relationships. They also can be either helpful or detrimental to career advancement.

The individual-versus-group orientation determines how individuals view their work. Employees with an individual work orientation see themselves as having the primary role in their job. Employees with this orientation tend to say, "I did ..." and "I accomplished ..." as they describe their contributions. There is some advantage to being able to describe your role in this way, and the ability to do so is sometimes

Table 10.5 Cultural Characteristics

Monochronic Characteristics	Polychronic Characteristics
Individual as starting point	Group as starting point
The job comes first	People and relationships come first
Power distance: Equality	Power distance: Deference to authority
Accepts uncertainty	Avoids uncertainty
Long-term orientation: Organizational context	Short-term orientation: Immediate task

seen as leadership. This approach can help supervisors to show excellence in performance. Individual excellence is an unwritten expectation for many people in the United States. The individual orientation can be detrimental, however, if the other employees begin to see the individually oriented employee as just being out for himself.

Example 10.2: Individually Oriented Employee

A secretary of a federal department held a retreat that involved numerous members of the department, including the deputy secretary, undersecretary, assistant secretaries, and members of the secretary's personal staff. The assistant secretaries were assigned to groups and given a departmental problem to brainstorm and to develop solutions for. During the presentations, Tim, the spokesperson for one of the groups, gave his presentation. Tim focused his entire attention on the secretary as he spoke about how central he was to determining the solution. All his sentences began with "I." He never mentioned the contributions of the other team members.

Tim had been well liked before his presentation. During the presentation, however, the assistant secretaries just kept looking at each other and with slight movements of their heads would point to Tim. Later, Tim was not invited to relaxation sessions held at the bar. His behavior was the topic of conversation. After that, all the other assistant secretaries withheld their support for any initiative Tim wanted.

Employees who are group oriented tend to come from family-oriented cultures where there is much deference given to figures of authority. There is greater tendency to be quiet and ask no questions. The positive side of being group oriented is that these employees are easier to work with in terms of relationships because they will work harder to maintain good relationships. Being group oriented, such individuals will be more inclusive of their co-workers and fellow team members. What may become detrimental, in their case, is that their individual contributions and leadership may not be as evident as when co-workers or team members are more individually oriented. In the latter case, the employee's contributions will be highlighted twice, once by the group-oriented fellow employees and then by the employee in question voicing his or her own contributions.

Example 10.3: Group-Oriented Employee

Nina, a director in a state agency, is highly group oriented. She is very effusive of the contributions and abilities of her co-workers and team members. Everybody likes working with her. Over time, she has noticed that many of her co-workers have been promoted. Nina receives good performance evaluations, but the promotions are not there. She is beginning to become bitter about her work experience.

Employees who are job oriented place the work first and often see the worth of others through the way they do their work. Although placing the job first can make an employee more effective in the short term, in the long term the employee's relationships with others may suffer and become detrimental to establishing a long-term career.

Employees who are relationship oriented focus on creating good relationships with other employees. Establishing good relationships with other employees can be helpful in the long term by fostering supportive co-workers. An employee's effectiveness can suffer, however, when he or she may be unwilling to make decisions or delegate appropriately if doing so would hurt a relationship. Employees who value relationships may also be unwilling to voice their opinions if doing so would contradict a co-worker, even if the employee's opinion would be more helpful.

Example 10.4: Job-Oriented and Relationship-Oriented Employees

Eliud, a director of an agency in a large city, is very job oriented. He is known for being directive and exacting of his employees when there is deadline looming. He is extremely hands-on on all agency projects. After a project is completed successfully, Eliud goes to each employee involved and apologizes for being so directive and exacting. He takes the employees to lunch or brings them flowers or a small gift. Eliud has become the go-to person for any special project the city manager wants done quickly. On the other hand, Eliud's staff members look outside their doorways before leaving their offices to see if Eliud is coming. When he talks with any employee about the immediate project that needs to be done, the word quickly spreads, and his employees find convenient excuses to be meeting with other agency employees in their offices. They look for and find other positions as quickly as they can.

Jessalyn is a director in the same city government as Eliud. A relationship-oriented employee, she works assiduously to cultivate good relationships with her staff and co-workers. Her staff and co-workers think the world of her as person. She would rather take on work herself than assign it to one of her employees if it would create a difficulty for them. She is very considerate of her colleagues and does not contradict them at staff meetings. Everyone really likes her, but she is not considered as effective as Eliud. Employees really enjoy working for her, and she has no trouble filling any vacancies in her agency.

Employees can also vary in their tolerance for ambiguity. Some employees may be quite comfortable with ambiguous assignments and be willing to create their own structure. They may be quite familiar with the entire organizational structure. Such tolerance for ambiguity is seen as a leadership skill by many organizations. The downside to having high levels of tolerance for ambiguity is that an employee may, in providing his or her own structure, supersede the supervisor—or as is expressed by some managers, "get ahead of the parade." Other employees may, in contrast, be more ambiguity averse. These employees want explicit instructions on what to do and how to it. These instructions can ensure that the employee completes an assignment in the exact manner that is required by the supervisor, but this need for explicit directions can also create an impression that the employee is not very competent.

Time perceptions are another area in which employees can vary. Employees who are short-term-oriented, for example, focus on the immediate task. They may accomplish the task exceptionally well. Once having accomplished the task, however, they are more likely to wait for the next assignment. In contrast, employees with a long-term orientation to the job will be more likely to see their current task as part of the long-term strategy of the organization. The short-term-oriented employee will likely relax after a task has been completed, whereas the long-term-oriented individual will be preparing for the next assignment, which he or she will see in the context of the organization's long-term strategy. Having a long-term perspective and being familiar with the organization's long-term strategy is a prerequisite for career advancement into the executive levels.

There may be other cultural characteristics that a particular organization may want to highlight as important. Discussion of individual cultural characteristics shifts the conversation from the relative merits of a particular group to the organizational characteristics necessary to create and maintain a high-performance organization. Discussing individual cultural characteristics can help the conversation from becoming racialized. Different individuals, even if they belong to similar groups, may have diverse cultural characteristics that may be very difficult to ascertain from an individual's physical appearance.

Discussing the various individual cultural characteristics and how they play out in the organizational culture also serves to socialize employee to the organizational characteristics that are required for career success. The experience from the assessments of the multicultural leadership programs discussed in Chapter 5 was that many employees, especially employees of color and women, had not really understood the organizational requirements for career success in their organizations. Understanding the career path to organizational success liberated the extra energy and motivation for employees to excel. Building the pathway to career success can be very helpful to getting new employees socialized into the organization culture of high performance.

10.8 Cultural Competence Organizational Measures

The HR office can be a helpful partner in creating a culturally competent organization. Typically, the HR office is responsible for developing employee policies and practices. The HR office can also be central in extending the HRM information system to include cultural competence. Much of the effort in diversity for human resources has been ensuring that organizations are recruiting, retaining, and promoting employees from protected groups. Human resources can now be a helpful partner in developing culturally competent policies and practices.

To be helpful, the employees of HR offices should be well versed in cultural competence. These employees should see cultural competence as melding the various cultural characteristics that employees bring into an organization to create a high-performance organization. They should be the first to take and understand the cultural competence orientation program. That perspective guides the approach to the organizational measures.

The cultural competence measures shown in Table 10.6 are derived and adapted from Siegel, Haugland, and Chambers (2003) and from the work of the National Association of Social Workers (NASW, 2007) and the Georgetown University National Center for Cultural Competence (2009). The organizational measures can

Table 10.6   Organizational Cultural Competence Measures

Measure	Yes	No
1. Is cultural competence mentioned in the mission statement?		
2. Are cultural competence initiatives included in the strategic plan?		
3. Does the strategic plan mention that cultural competence can leverage diversity to create a high-performance organization?		
4. Is there an Office for Cultural Competence?		
5. Is there a Cultural Competence Advisory Committee?		
6. Is the Human Resource Office involved in cultural competence?		
7. Does the Human Resource Office provide cultural competence training?		
8. Does the Human Resource Office have employees who understand the cultural and linguistic requirements of the community groups for whom the organization provides services?		

Source: Adapted from Georgetown University Center for Child and Human Development, National Center for Cultural Competence, *Foundations of Cultural & Linguistic Competence*, http://www11.georgetown.edu/research/gucchd/nccc/foundations, 2009; National Association of Social Workers (NASW), *Indicators for the Achievement of the NASW Standards for Cultural Competence in Social Work Practice*, NASW, Washington, DC, 2007; Siegel, C., G. Haugland, and E. Chambers, Performance measures and their benchmarks for assessing organizational cultural competency in behavioral health care service delivery, *Administration and Policy in Mental Health*, 31 (2), 141–170, 2003.

be divided into three areas: policies, organizational structure, and practices. The development of policies mirrors the development of any major organizational initiative.

As shown in Table 10.6, using questions is the best approach to developing cultural competence. Organizations are in various stages of development, and the answers to the questions create a profile of the cultural competence of the organization. Depending on the answers, the organization can refine the profile to emphasize the measures that are most important to the top executives.

10.9 Human Resources as the Feedback Loop for Policy Development

It is fairly common for HR offices to have some variation of a management information system. The system is used to track job analysis and classifications, compensation and benefits, recruitment, applicant pools, affirmative action, selection, performance appraisals, and participation in training and development. Human resources can also conduct workplace and employee surveys to measure the implementation and progress of cultural competence initiatives.

If feasible, expanding employee classifications of diversity can provide specific information on the diversity of the employees. The rationale for expanding the classification is to determine how diverse the organization truly is. This task is more easily accomplished through anonymous employee surveys that also include workplace dynamics and satisfaction. On such surveys, racial and ethnic classifications for Hispanic, Asian, and Pacific Islander can include countries of origins, with blank lines to accommodate any country left out of the classifications. African American can include countries from Africa and the Caribbean, with blanks for employees with origins in other countries. The classification for white can include European countries as well as leave blanks for other countries such as South Africa. There can be a classification that includes the length of time the respondent's family has been in the country (e.g., third generation or later, second generation, first generation, and immigrant). Gender and sexual orientation should also be part of the demographic information. Also important is social class. In addition, information about length of tenure in the organization allows an analysis of employee diversity over time and can be an indicator of the changing demographic composition of the organization. Organizations whose diversity hires are more recent may need greater emphasis on cultural competence and managing diversity.

Information on the distribution of diversity in the organization can provide valuable feedback on the best approach to sustaining cultural competence efforts. If multicultural employees are relatively evenly distributed in the organizational hierarchy, diversity efforts are working. When multicultural employees are located predominately in the lower levels of the organization, it is worth examining the reasons. For instance, multicultural employees may have less tenure and have had less time to advance through the organizational ranks. If, however, the multicultural employees average long tenures, there may be structural impediments to their career advancements. Their cultural characteristics may not be perceived as being leadership characteristics. Building cultural competence into the performance measurements of managers, as well as into employee surveys of how culturally competent employees perceive their managers and fellow employees to be, can provide feedback for fine-tuning cultural competence efforts.

An analysis of employee grievances and disciplines can reveal which employees are experiencing problems. If the distribution of employee problems mirrors the diversity of the organization, there is less likelihood that the problems are being driven by the diversity. If members of diverse groups are overrepresented, however, there may be issues of cultural competence that merit further analysis. In these and other cases, HR offices can provide policy makers with critical feedback to help them develop and sustain cultural competence initiatives. Continued monitoring of the progress allows for fine-tuning the initiative.

10.10 Summary and Conclusion

As an academic field, human resource management is still evolving. Many HRM or public personnel management books cover the federal affirmative action and equal employment opportunity laws and the associated compliance agencies; yet there remains a dearth of coverage of cultural competence requirements and the need to manage diversity. Classes about managing diversity are still lacking in many public administration programs, even though the National Association of Schools of Public Affairs and Administration recommends their inclusion. Many issues relevant to women of color and the lesbian, gay, transgender, and bisexual community, for example, have not received adequate attention in HRM curricula.

Cultural competence orientation programs can educate employees to help them become culturally competent. The orientation program can begin by explaining the value of diversity to innovation and productivity that can help create a high-performance organization. Diversity can be explained as both membership in diverse groups and the cultural characteristics an employee brings into an organization. The definition of groups includes not only all protected classes but also such additional classifications as social class. Monochronic and polychronic cultural characteristics provide an understanding of how cultural characteristics can be helpful or detrimental in the workplace. Employees may have cultural characteristic from one or both orientations, or they may have some other combination. Which cultural characteristics an employee has is difficult to judge from an individual's appearance.

The cultural competence orientation program explains how the cultural competence model of culture, communication, misunderstandings and conflict, and leader–follower relationship is important in the workplace, and this book provides many examples in each area. Participants of such programs may also provide their own examples to further educate fellow participants about facets of culture. As an addition, mentoring can provide common ground and a shared culture between supervisors and their direct reports as well as create a shared culture with other employees. Thus the organizational culture can become a shared culture for all employees.

Organizational measures for cultural competence are described as questions, the answers to which provide the current state of the cultural competence of an organization. The questions allow each organization to create its own profile and to customize which measures to emphasize.

Employee workplace surveys serve to provide the employee's perspective. The surveys, along with data on employee grievances and problems, can guide the fine-tuning of cultural competence efforts. The HR office can be the feedback loop that provides the current progress on cultural competence.

Chapter 11

Using Cultural Competence to Develop International Collaborations

11.1 Introduction: Cultural Competence in Context

Cultural competence is good not only for the United States but for the global community as well. This fact has been observed by the business community for some years now. Although concerned with the bottom line, businesses have long since understood the need for cultural competence as a way of conducting business on the world stage. Therefore, attending to the specific needs of how business is carried out is important to the sustainability of any multinational corporation. Attention to racial and gender differences is not new to many companies. Some practices in these areas have, however, not been the most enlightened.

McDonald's, for example, now operating in India, knows that selling beef burgers violates the cultural and religious norms of that country, so selling lamb burgers would be a more prudent way to go. By the same token, Pepsi experimented with selling different flavors of its product in France several years ago and found that the Pepsi Cola popular in the United States was not popular in France. To force certain flavors of Pepsi Cola on the French because Americans enjoyed them would have been suicide from a business perspective.

To have a more complete understanding of cultural competence, it is helpful to understand race theory and gender politics, as well a sexual identity politics. This chapter first turns its attention specifically to race theory and how it affects people living in the United States, though the same theories are applicable abroad. The second part of this chapter addresses how public managers can obtain international experiences and maintain relationships.

11.2 Race Theory

The public sector does not have the mandate of concerning itself with the bottom line the way business does. What the public sector does have, however, is a responsibility to maintain the public good and provide equitable public service. Some 30 or 40 years ago, managers hired employees who were very much like them. Indeed, before the creation of the Equal Employment Opportunity Commission (EEOC) and, to a degree, post-EEOC, many public sector managers could be observed most often hiring other white males, not infrequently from privileged backgrounds and with strong family connections. Many of these past hiring practices have now ended. Hiring corruption still occurs, albeit in a more covert manner. In an effort to understand racial identity and racial politics, we turn to two key contemporary psychology scholars who have written extensively on racial identity: Beverly Tatum and William Cross Jr.

Although seeming to apply only within a country, race theory is also helpful in understanding cultural dynamics that may come into play in international collaborations. In this context, the National Association of Social Workers (NASW 2007, 14) identifies two requirements where race theory can be helpful for cultural competence and social diversity:

1. Social workers should understand culture and its functions in human behavior and society.
2. Social workers should obtain education about and seek to understand the nature of social diversity and oppression with respect to race, ethnicity, national origin, color, sex, sexual orientation, marital status, political belief, religion, and mental or physical disability.

According to NASW, social workers are required "to examine their own cultural backgrounds and identities to increase their awareness of personal assumptions, values and biases" (NASW 2007, 19). Of further importance, "cultural competence includes identifying how absence of knowledge, fears, ignorance, and the 'isms' (racism, sexism, ethnocentrism, heterosexism, ageism, classism) have influenced their attitudes, beliefs, and feelings" (NASW 2007, 21). Seeing international collaborations through the lens of race theory can also help managers and employees engaged in international joint ventures. One must keep in mind that because the Internet has created worldwide access to news anywhere at any time, people from elsewhere around the globe are aware of the cultural struggles taking place in the United States.

According to Beverly Tatum (2003), covert racism is a much more insidious issue because it is difficult to trace, but its effects are nonetheless penetrating. According to Tatum, many individuals in America's dominant group have found ways to hide their unwillingness to change their beliefs and approaches to racial matters. These people are perhaps the most difficult to address because many of their actions go undetected. Covert racism can still be seen not only in the ranks of people in the United States but in other countries as well. Take, for example, Great Britain. In a country where multiple racial and ethnic groups reside, there has yet to be a nonwhite prime minister, the highest office in the country. When in 2010 David Cameron became the new prime minister, his election to office continued a legacy of white men from privilege leading the country, as was forecasted some years before (Taylor 2006).

Whether such a legacy can be considered covert racism is unclear. What we do know, however, is that a person of color has yet to occupy the prime minister's position. It would be interesting to field the opinions of residents living in Great Britain about electing a person of color to the highest post in the land. Many of these individuals would probably indicate that they have no problem with electing a black or Indian to this position. Those same people may very well vote against such candidates on Election Day, however. This hypocrisy is what makes covert racism all the more dangerous.

In 1971, William Cross Jr. developed Nigrescence theory, which became one of the most seminal pieces of research on racial identity, especially as it relates to African Americans. According to Cross, there are five stages of racial development. First is the *pre-encounter* stage; this stage is when a person is aware of racial implications. Then comes the *second encounter*, which refers to the first time that a person is aware of his or her racial identity. A first-grade student, for example, is asked to trace his or her hand and color in the outline. Most young students would draw the correct racial color, though others may not. A teacher or classmate may tell the student that the hand is colored incorrectly. This scenario represents the pre-encounter stage, according to Cross.

Third is *immersion*, when individuals take on all of the attributes of their race. They may elect to eat only the food of their race and to wear only the dress of their race. According to Cross, this stage is problematic because it excludes others races from being involved in their lives. An extreme example of the immersion stage is seen in such groups as the KKK or skinheads. Cross argues that this stage is occupied by the dominant culture. Evidence also suggests that groups such as the Black Panthers of the 1960s and 1970s could be seen as fanatical. Still, there are less extremist views of immersion. Tatum offers the following example from her own life:

> When I was in high school, I did not sit at the Black table in the cafeteria because there were not enough Black kids in my high school to

fill one. Though I was naïve about many things, I knew enough about the social isolation to know that I needed to get out of town. As the child of college-educated parents and an honor student myself, it was expected that I would go on to college. My mother suggested Howard University, my parents' alma mater, but although it was a good suggestion, I had my own ideas. I picked Wesleyan University in Middletown, Connecticut. It was two hours from home, an excellent school, and of particular interest to me was that it had a critical mass of Black and Latino students, most of whom were male. Wesleyan had just gone co-ed, and the ratio of Black male students to Black female students was seven-to-one. I thought it would improve my social life and it did.

I thrived socially and academically. Since I had decided in high school to be a psychologist, I was a psychology major, but I took a lot of African American studies courses—history, literature, religion, and even black child development. I studied Swahili in hopes of traveling to Tanzania; although, I never went. I stopped straightening my hair and had a large Afro à la Angela Davis circa 1970. I happily sat at the Black table in the dining hall every day. I look back on my days at Wesleyan with great pleasure. I maintain many of the friendships I formed there, and can't remember the name of one White classmate. (Tatum 2003, 75)

Emersion is the fourth stage; and according to Cross, this is a problematic stage because it is the complete opposite to Stage 3. In Stage 4, the individual has completely shunned any traits of his or her race in support of another race. The terms *Uncle Tom* and perhaps *Oreo* are dated (and derogatory) terms the black community coined to describe other blacks who did not ascribe to their ways of behaving, dating, dressing, speaking, and voting. Indeed, one might argue that emersion is a form of internalized racism. An example of this stage may be African American heterosexual men who partner with or date only white women. The same can be suggested about African American gay men who find pleasure only in partnering with white men. This characterization is particularly important to note because many African American men will fall into the stereotypical trap that suggests that the only good partner is a white one.

The emersion stage also can be applied to other races as well. For example, a white teenager from the suburbs may elect to listen only to rap music and interacts only with teenagers of color and speaks in what may be considered black vernacular. This emersion is not a bad thing to do; however, if it is at the exclusion of friendships with other white teenagers, then that is a problem.

The final stage of Cross's racial development theory is *internalization*. This stage is when a person accepts his or her race and embraces the positives and the limitations. This is a stage of maturity because the individual recognizes the values in other races as well. Both theorists, Tatum and Cross, make invaluable contributions to society with their concepts of race, racism, and the formation of race. What limits both theories, however, is the exclusion of international issues and practices.

Although Tatum and Cross did not directly address international issues and practices, there is much in their work that is applicable to international relations (that is why race theory is included in this chapter and not earlier chapters.) Collaborating with professionals from other countries is working with professionals who are likely to be from another race or ethnicity. They will definitely come from a different culture. The same dynamics of race theory can come into play in international collaborations. Even when a professional has overcome the immersion stage and progressed to internalization when working with professionals within his or her own country, interacting with people from another culture can cause even an enlightened person to regress to the immersion stage. One's pride in one's country and one's perceived superiority can shape the conversations in subtle and not so subtle ways.

It can be fairly common for someone from the United States to see international collaborations as an opportunity to show someone from a foreign country how advanced we are. That sense of superiority can affect the tone of voice and the way we converse. Professionals will quickly pick up on such subtleties. In reality, professionals from other countries may be better educated and have better experience than their counterparts in the United States. They may also have more international experience than their U.S. counterparts. It is therefore best to approach international collaboration from the internalization stage. This relationship is to be a collaboration of professionals, and the best way to engender respect for oneself and for one's country is to communicate respect for the other's professional expertise, country, and culture.

11.3 What's Up with Xenophobia?

The preceding section has created a context for the nature of this chapter, which addresses the importance of international awareness for public managers. But first we should come to grips with something that is paralyzing a great deal of the United States, and that is xenophobia. In its purest definition, xenophobia refers to distrust of individuals or groups from other countries. Such a fear engenders deep-seated hostility and hatred that leads to physical and mental distress inflicted on others because they are not U.S. citizens. Fear may, for example, stem from a misunderstanding that good U.S. jobs will go to foreigners, a situation that will, in turn, lead to the destruction of our economy.

The irony of this myth about foreigners taking our jobs is that the United States was founded on the backs and sweat of people from other countries. First, of course, in a long line of infractions committed by landowners in this country was slavery, in which millions of Africans were brought to the United States against their will to work without pay for decades. To date, the effects of slavery can still be felt with a deep-seated racism that is ever prevalent in many parts of the country.

It is interesting that well-intentioned liberal people forget that many of their relatives were newcomers to the United States at one point as well. Certainly, this fact is observable from the late 1800s until about the 1920s, when millions of immigrants arrived in the United States primarily from western and eastern Europe. The treatment they were afforded was neither welcoming nor friendly. Through hard work and determination, these individuals and their families, without many resources, were thrown into a situation where they had to learn, work hard to earn money, and thrive. Now, almost 100 years later, many ancestors of these immigrants have turned their backs on the newest immigrants trying to secure a better life in the United States.

President Barack Obama's 2008 victory was not without comments about his race. Despite being of mixed heritage, Obama is considered to be African American, a false characterization. His background was not called into question as such, even though his father was from Africa. However, Obama is actually no different than the immigrants who arrived on our shores from European countries. He is the son of a father (Barack Obama Sr., Phi Beta Kappa) who came from Kenya to study at the University of Hawaii at Manoa and to make a better life for himself. This history indeed demonstrates the American dream.

11.4 The Recent Passage of Arizona's Controversial Bills

Although it is not the intent of this chapter to single out one U.S. state from another to point out the state's lack of civil rights for people of color and people from other countries, a comment must be made about Arizona, a state that has had many issues pertaining to race. Many other states are considering legislation similar to that passed in Arizona. The state of California made international headlines with its passages of Proposition 8, which denies marriage to same-sex couples (Johnson 2009a). Still, Arizona has had a contemporary history of making missteps, intentionally or unintentionally, on issues of race. Arizona was one of the last holdouts to officially recognize as a national holiday the birthday of Dr. Martin Luther King Jr. The fact is that the holiday was passed into national law in 1986, but it took the state of Arizona until 1992 to recognize the holiday. If living, King would have been impressed with the economic boycotts that eventually led Arizona to change its policy to adopt Martin Luther King Day, among them the largest boycott of the state, when Super Bowl XXVII was relocated to California (Galloway 2010; Kareem 2009).

In 2010, the governor of Arizona signed into law SB 1070, which would make it legal for police officers of that state to check passports and other documents of individuals appearing suspicious (Archibold 2010). This law is one of the most stringent and divisive anti-immigration measures passed in generations. In fact, it is so much so that President Obama publicly weighed in on the matter, calling the policy destructive and asking for a careful review of the bill. Obama's involvement with the bill is significant because most U.S. presidents do not make judgment on state law. The bill was legally challenged as being unconstitutional and there is an injunction against its implementation.

The issue here is one of profiling the state's large Hispanic population. Profiling is an insidious practice in which certain racial and ethnic groups are targeted for overt scrutiny by law enforcement. This strategy was observable immediately following the September 11 attack on the World Trade Center in New York City. Following this attack came a huge backlash against anyone who looked Middle Eastern or stereotypically Muslim.

On May 11, 2010, Arizona's governor signed into law a second bill, which is a policy that prohibits the instruction of ethnic studies in Arizona public schools K–12 and also in charter schools (Cooper 2010; Fernandez 2010). This bill came on the heels of the first. The concern expressed about this bill is that it assumes that instruction about ethnic studies will promote violence against a race of people, namely, white Americans. Yet, an understanding of one's cultural background leads to a better understanding of other cultures as well. The bill also assumes that ethnic studies is exclusionary, limiting which races can take classes such as Mexican Literature or The History of Jim Crow. The reverse is true. These courses are open to any student who wants to engage in critical dialogue about the topic. The area of ethnic studies is extremely important to ensure that American history is taught without partiality and with respect for diversity. It is in ethnic studies that students can receive this information.

As of this writing, the news media is reporting that Sen. Russell Pearce is planning to push a legislative bill that would allow Arizona to refuse to accept or issue a birth certificate—as such a recognition of U.S citizenship—for any child born in Arizona whose parents are undocumented immigrants. Because the right to U.S. citizenship is guaranteed by the Fourteenth Amendment, it is unclear whether if passed, Senator Pearce's bill would pass constitutional muster. As of April 2011, the Arizona legislature had not passed the bill.

The discussion of SB 1070 focuses on illegal immigration and its effect on Arizona. The television media usually shows televised footage of immigrants crossing the U.S.–Mexican border, and the implication is that all immigrants are Mexican. While many of the undocumented immigrants are from Mexico, many others are from other countries. Undocumented immigrants who overstay their visas make up as much as 45% of all the undocumented immigrants in the United States, yet there has been relatively little mention of these undocumented immigrants, who may be of other races or ethnicities. Passage of the Arizona law that outlaws ethnic studies and possible passage of a bill to deny U.S. citizenship to any baby born of undocumented parents imply that the fears may be about more than undocumented immigration.

The passage of the bills in Arizona and discussions to pass similar legislation in other states coincides with the televised and print media coverage of the demographic changes the country is undergoing. Many print articles and televised media reports on the U.S. Census projections indicate that at some time in the 2040s the United States will no longer have a racial or ethnic majority. Four states—Hawaii, New Mexico, California, and Texas—and the District of Columbia, as well as 300 counties in the United States, no longer have a racial or ethnic majority. Currently, there have been reports on television that 2010 is the year in which minority births will outnumber white births. Hispanics are mentioned as the ethnic group that will have the largest increases; this group is projected to increase from being one in six to almost one in three people in the United States. Underlying the numbers is a tremendous cultural shift and change for the United States.

The demographic changes with the accompanying cultural shift will continue. Hispanic and Asian birthrates are much higher than the birthrates for the white population. It is likely that over the next few years, the public debate on the cultural shifts will continue. As with any major change, positions in the debate can range from the extreme and acrimonious to the more moderate and accepting. Cultural competence will evolve and happen in the midst of these discussions, which will affect attitudes about cultural competence in both domestic and international relations. One can imagine the more acrimonious debates on immigration affecting collaborations with government officials in Mexico or officials from other countries with émigrés to the United States.

11.5 International Collaborations for Public Managers

Race theory can be informative in developing international collaborations. Many people in the United States and other Western countries are in the immersion stage. It is appropriate and expected for citizens to feel pride in their own country. There are some people who take a further step, not only having pride in their country but also feeling superior to citizens of other countries. The underlying attitudes serve as backdrop to any international collaboration. In various venues, President Obama has spoken of a new world order, with the United States working collaboratively in a global community. Some critics in the United States see this notion of collaboration as the United States giving up its supremacy on the world stage. It is not the intent here to discuss the merits of either position but to illustrate how such perspectives of one's own country relative to other countries and how such internal dialogues as those about immigration create a backdrop that can color interactions with government officials from other countries.

There may be some government officials who believe international collaboration means providing U.S. expertise to other, less-developed countries. The reality is that many foreign government officials may have received their education from universities in their own country as well as in the United States or Europe. Thus some foreign officials may have educational and world experience that greatly exceeds that of many U.S. government officials.

Approaching international collaborations from the internalization stage, rather than the immersion stage, can create more successful international collaborations. Successful international collaborations result from the cooperative efforts of professionals who happen to be from different countries. All the participants have much to contribute to the successful effort. Cooperation comes from all participants communicating respect for each other and establishing common ground.

If the international collaboration results in a continuing relationship that includes social aspects such as having lunch or dinner together, then current controversial issues can be discussed in the cultural context in which the issues develop and are resolved. The ability to discuss controversial issues yet disagree while maintaining a good working relationship shows how truly professional the participants are.

11.5.1 Domestic Considerations

It will be important for public managers to have a firm understanding of cultural differences as the world evolves and the dominant population shrinks. As evident with Arizona's policy on immigration and ban on ethnic studies, the field of public affairs will need to produce individuals who can make a difference in their organization by promoting cultural competency as a way to make all employees feel celebrated.

The question is, Where do we start? These lessons should begin with the way we educate and prepare our public affairs graduates and our future and current managers for a world that includes an understanding of global or international competency. As recent as 2004, Johnson criticized the field of public affairs for not creating the types of opportunities that would allow graduate students an opportunity to work in marginalized communities (2004, 509–510). Here, Johnson suggests that MPA programs and the like should be willing to create spaces where their students can receive the types of training that will empower and enlighten them as managers. Many of these marginalized communities include individuals who hail from other countries and need special services. However, these types of internships are not easily found in many of the U.S. public affairs graduate programs.

Rice (2008, 22) notes that as communities of Spanish speakers increase, they will need additional services. Managers will need to know the cultural differences between Spanish speakers from Spain, Spanish speakers from Mexico, and Spanish speakers from Argentina, for example. Rice cites as examples Web site translations and incentives for employees to learn other languages—solid examples of what individuals can do to address portions of the international population. However, more must be done. Public affairs graduate programs must be willing to include issues of race and international affairs in course offerings and internship practices. Today it is more likely than ever that given the dynamics of a globalized society, government employees may be asked to participate in international collaborations.

11.5.2 Developing International Relationships

A key way to foster international interest for public managers is for them to develop international relationships. A heightened awareness of others often happens as a result of connections made with people outside the United States. This approach is another practice that public affairs programs have generally not engaged in. Many university business programs have internships where their students have to study abroad for a semester or two. The philosophy driving semester-abroad programs has yet to impact public affairs programs, a situation that presents an interesting challenge for public affairs professionals. However, it is one that can be handled with great benefits.

There are many ways that a public manager can compensate for not having had international experiences during undergraduate or graduate school to create international relationships. Observe the following examples:

1. Involvement with an international professional organization or professional organization with an international focus can be extremely helpful. Such organizations include the American Society for Public Administration, which fosters ways for managers to meet colleagues from other countries and engage in meaningful workshops and best practices. The Sixth International Conference on Public Administration (ICPA 2010) is an example of a key opportunity to develop relationships on a global and meaningful level.

2. The myth of the American family is that they would pack up each summer and head off to Europe for a vacation. This may be true for some families but certainly not every family. Because of financial constraints, tight schedules, fear of flying, or an assortment of other reasons, families may not travel abroad. The question remains, How does one acquire a sense of the importance of international affairs, travel, relationships, collaborations and the like without having an actual international experience?

Example 11.1: International Engagement

Ted Allen James grew up in an upper-middle-class African American family in Washington, DC. Both his parents, graduates of Johnson C. Smith University (Charlotte, North Carolina), also hold doctoral degrees, Phi Beta Kappa, in political science from Georgetown University. They worked hard to provide Ted with the essentials of life such as love, food, shelter, and education. As an only child, Ted had always been impressed with television shows such as *The Brady Brunch* and *The Cosby Show*. The families in each of these shows appeared to live exciting lives that involved a fair amount of children and lots of traveling.

Ted's mother is a highly respected school superintendent, and his father is an executive director of a nonprofit organization based in Washington. Therefore, there was never a great deal of time for family vacations such as those depicted on Ted's favorite television shows. Certainly, international travel was out of the question as well. Ted had longed to go aboard for many years, maybe even attending a boarding school in Montreal, Canada. His family did manage occasional trips to North Carolina in order to visit relatives or visit the campus of Johnson C. Smith University, where Ted was expected to attend college. In Washington, Ted attended the Duke Ellington High School for Performing Arts, where he majored in dance. This is where he also developed connections with students coming from the Sudan, the Congo, and Costa Rica to attend the prestigious high school. On graduation, Ted entered and graduated from the Julliard School (New York City). Because of the demanding schedule of his dance major, Ted did not have an opportunity to study aboard the way some of his classmates did. However, his appreciation for international affairs never left him because of the international aspects present at Julliard.

Instead of entering dance as a profession, upon graduation from Julliard Ted entered a Masters of Public Administration (MPA) program at DePaul University. There, influenced by his father, Ted focused on nonprofit organizations, and he had an opportunity to study different polices at a number of performing arts agencies throughout the United States and Great Britain.

Ted graduated with an MPA from DePaul in May 2007 and secured grants and other donations to start his own nonprofit, public organization located in Buenos Aires, Argentina. The purpose of Ted's organization is to engage artist of all types to explore international opportunities in exposing their craft on a global stage. As executive director of Eucentro de Artes, Ted is committed to combining into one practice his love of the arts, international relationships, and nonprofits.

3. A final way to establish and maintain international contacts and relationships is technology. Over the past few decades, we have seen the advent of computers change the way in which we live. Indeed, once thought to handle only business transactions, computers are now viewed as a must-have in almost every facet of contemporary life. Such applications as Skype and different Web seminars make it possible to connect with people abroad with leaving one's home or office. This is also where many public affairs programs are excelling by offering degree programs online or abroad.

11.6 Creating International Opportunities

International opportunities for international collaborations can be planned, or they can arise unexpectedly and serendipitously. Being culturally competent creates a sense of having possibilities and competencies that make international collaborations not only possible but also probable. Today's globalized society almost requires global collaborations. There are many states that send delegations to other countries. Some cities create sister-city agreements with cities in other countries. Many universities sign cooperative agreements with universities in other countries. Furthermore, many federal departments have agencies with international responsibilities. The U.S. Departments of Agriculture, Commerce, and Labor, respectively, have agencies with international responsibilities. States and local governments send international delegations for economic development and to solve cross-border problems; the nature of their work may involve employees who normally do not do international work.

Example 11.2: They Are Sending Me to Bosnia. What Do I Do Now?

Leo was an assistant secretary in the mid-1990s. One day he got a call from the secretary's office explaining that she wanted to meet with him. He walked into her office and was invited to sit down. Looking at the secretary, he said, "Madame Secretary, you wanted to talk with me?" She answered:

> Yes, Leo. I know that you are a Vietnam veteran and that you are familiar with veterans and the issues they face when they return from war. The president has just concluded the Dayton Peace Agreement on Bosnia-Herzegovina. There is concern that the veterans will be returning but the economy may not have jobs for them. Many will still have their weapons, and we don't want them to be a destabilizing force. The World Bank is funding a program for veterans and their families. The competitors are the French, the Irish, and the International Labor Organization. I want you to go there to talk with the ministers and put a program together. I want us to be awarded that funding.

> Leo responded, "Madame Secretary, if you want me to go, I am willing; but I must tell you that I don't know anything about Bosnia-Herzegovina, and I don't have any international experience." She replied, "Michael from our international office will help you and travel with you. Just remember, we want to win that funding." "Yes, Madame Secretary. I'll talk with Michael, and I'll be on my way there," said Leo. As Leo walked out of the secretary's office, he kept thinking, "How am I going to do this?"

> Leo has a degree in public administration but no training in international relations. However, in the past he had traveled to several countries, where he enjoyed meeting the locals and learning about their cultures. They frequently invited him into their homes for dinner. Leo's wife worked for a nonprofit agency that was doing work in Bosnia-Herzegovina. He met with the agency's president, who briefed him on what she knew of the situation. She also gave him the names of two psychologists familiar with the needs of the veterans and their families. She would call them and let them know that Leo would be meeting with them.

> Michael from the international office met with Leo to brief him on what was happening in Bosnia-Herzegovina and let him know that he would be handling all the protocols for the meetings. He wanted Leo to develop the program for the veterans and their families. When they arrived in Sarajevo, they went to the U.S. embassy to let them know what they would be doing there. The economics attaché, Bill, who knew the language, volunteered to drive them to the meetings and to interpret. There was not much of an economy in the country, and the largest bill that could be exchanged was the equivalent of $20. Anything larger than a $20, and no one had the money to exchange it. Leo and Bill called their contacts, the two psychologists, and took them to dinner. They were given a good briefing of the situation and the veterans' needs. There were still many buildings

with the windows shot out and bearing the marks of war. Leo thought, "I'm not in Washington, DC, anymore."

Before scheduling the meetings, Leo had asked Michael who made the decisions. Leo said the Bosnian government would decide whose proposal to accept. Leo knew the key would be the meetings with the ministers, for these would be critical to their success. At the first meeting, Leo, Michael, and Bill were led into a conference room. When Leo looked around, he noticed that the windows were still broken and there were bullet holes in the walls. Leo knew that he was way out of his comfort zone. Bill provided the introductions and the purpose of Leo and Michael's visit. A secretary came in with a pot of Turkish coffee and served everyone. The small cups were half sugar and half coffee.

Bill had instructed Leo to continue to face the minister and not him, because he would be translating, and he had told Leo to use short sentences so that he could translate accurately. Michael was to take notes so that no one would forget what was said. Then Bill had told Leo to remember that he was representing the United States, and that how the ministers and others there saw him would influence their perceptions of the United States. Leo had smiled and said, "Bill, that is just what I need, more pressure." They had all laughed.

After a short time of social conversation, Leo told the minister what he had learned about the situation from the psychologists. He asked the minister to please further educate him on the needs of his agency. Leo would ask clarifying questions. Then he began working with the minister on putting together a plan that would fulfill some of the needs of that particular agency. The meetings with the other ministers were similar. The meeting with union officials was different, however. The union members, who were all drinking, offered Leo, Michael, and Bill a drink. This was a 10:00 a.m. meeting. They declined and said that coffee would be just fine. The union insisted that they wanted to restart the automobile plant that had employed their members. The cars were not selling that well, though. Leo told the union representatives that restarting the plant would not be feasible but that he was willing to explore other alternatives. After an hour of intense discussions, with the union members continuing to drink and insisting that they wanted the automobile plant reopened, Leo looked at them and said that he did not know how to make that happen, but that he did not want to leave without finding a way to help their members. To do that, he said, he needed their help. This way, they could get help for their members while they continued to make requests to have the plant reopen. They agreed.

After meeting with all the ministers and the union representatives, Leo and Michael put together a proposal and briefed Bill. Bill was comfortable with the proposal, so they then scheduled short meetings with all the ministers and the union to fine-tune the proposal. When everyone was happy with the proposal Leo, Michael, and Bill thanked everyone. The United States was granted the funding, and the secretary was happy with the results. The program was very successful and was later replicated in at least two African countries.

Leo reflected on his experience and realized that he had learned a number of things:

1. When you are meeting anyone from another country, you will be perceived as representing your country and organization.
2. Respect for others, their country, organization, and culture, is paramount in being successful.

3. Organizational protocol and understanding the role of their organization is also part of cultural competence.
4. The way to treat others is the way they are treated in their country and organization and not the way we treat others in our own country.
5. You can be formal and gracious at the same time.
6. You can listen to a translator while looking at the person you are meeting. It is important to be sensitive to any reactions the person may be experiencing.
7. To be successful, participants should work as if they are part of the same team, for in reality they are.
8. Work with others as if you trying to develop a long-term relationship.
9. Understand that different countries have different customs and accept the differences.
10. And last, three cups of Turkish coffee may be one too many. That much caffeine can make one talk too much and too fast.

Opportunities can happen quickly. Being culturally competent prepares an employee to be successful. Employees should not assume, however, that just because their parents have come from a particular country and they themselves know the language, they are culturally competent when it comes to international collaborations. International collaborations are between participants who are members of organizations as well as countries. The participants represent their respective organizations as well as their respective countries. Because their organizational roles are significant, it is important to treat others as they are treated in their organizations and not necessarily as you would treat someone in a similar position in your own organization, which may be more informal.

Example 11.3: Knowing the Culture Does Not Mean Knowing International Protocols

Mario, a diplomat from the Mexican consulate, approached Janie, a faculty member at a southwestern university. Mario was concerned because several local government officials had invited Mexican government officials to discuss possible joint projects. The local government officials are Hispanic, and many had family members who lived in Mexico. They visited their family members living in Mexico frequently. They knew the culture, the customs, and the language. However, they did not know international protocols. The result was that in their interactions with the local officials, the Mexican government officials felt they were not treated with the proper respect. The local officials did not know the Mexicans' official titles and sometimes confused lower-ranking officials as being the leaders.

Mario and Janie put together a presentation that included role playing how to meet and greet international delegations. The participants were told to prepare for visits by learning titles and how to address dignitaries. The local government officials learned to ask how the dignitaries were to be seated. They also learned how to end meetings and what to do as a follow-through after the meetings.

The workshop was very successful. An initial understanding of international protocols can be learned from books, but it is best to prepare for meetings by working with staff members from the foreign delegation to ensure that they are comfortable. Most high-level foreign officials have staff members who are responsible for arranging meetings. Some of the areas that should be agreed to before the meeting are:

1. Who are the members of the delegation, what are their titles, and how do they want to be addressed?
   a. Will biographical narratives of the members be provided to everyone?
2. What is the organizational ranking of the members?
3. Where will the initial meeting be?
4. How will the greetings be conducted, and what are the protocols?
   a. Is a handshake enough?
   b. Will there be hugs or embraces, and if so, what is the protocol for the hugs?
5. What is the agenda for the meetings?
6. Will there be a lunch or dinner, and if so, what are the protocols for the seating arrangements?
   a. If the lunch or dinner is being catered, is there agreement on what is being served?
   b. Will alcohol be served?
7. What would be a proper follow-through after the conclusion of the meetings?
8. Are there going to be any media representatives, and has there been agreement by all members that it is okay for the media to be there?
   a. Will members of the media speak the language, or is a translator required?
9. Will there be any photo opportunities, and if so, what is the protocol for the photo, who will sit where?
10. Will there be an exchange of gifts?
    a. What are appropriate gifts?
    b. Have ethics requirements for receiving gifts been met?
11. What follow-through actions are appropriate after the conclusion of the meetings?
12. Is there anything else we should know?

Although books on international protocols and executive manners are helpful, it is always better to find a staff member from the visiting delegation to work with in making the arrangements. Working with a staff member to ensure the proper protocols communicates respect and the importance given to the meetings. Members of the visiting delegation, knowing that one of their staff members has helped with the agenda, will be more receptive and will understand that they are meeting fellow professionals. Also, just as important, working with a staff member of a high-ranking official and establishing a professional relationship means that one has someone in another country who will usually take one's call or answer an e-mail. That professional relationship developed with the staff members opens the door to future collaborations and projects with the high-ranking official.

Janie, from our earlier example, learned one more important point, particularly significant for anyone from the United States who is collaborating with another professional from a country in this hemisphere—namely, that whatever the country, we are all from the Americas, and we are all Americans. People from the United States have grown accustomed to referring to themselves as Americans and seeing the term *American* as reflecting only U.S. values and meanings. In reality, however, all people from a country in this hemisphere, whether from North, Central, or South America, can consider themselves Americans. This inclusive notion is why this chapter begins with the topic of race theory.

In the same way that different people progress through the various stages in terms of the racial or ethnic diversity within their own countries, the same dynamics come into play in international collaborations. Even when individuals are in the internalization stage in their personal and professional relationships within their own countries, they may be in the later immersion stage in their international relationships. It is easily understood why many people would take pride in their own country and even see their own country and culture as superior. It may take some reflection and thought, however, to fully understand that respecting others and their country and culture in no way diminishes one's own country. In fact, communicating respect for another's country and culture will reflect an enlightened perspective and foster greater respect for one's own country. Sometimes such culturally competent communication is as simple as saying one is from the United States, rather than saying one is from America.

11.7 Developing International Relationships

Creating international collaborations is much easier than ever before in today's globalized society. The ease in developing international collaborations should not, however, mask the increased importance of cultural competence and the added requirements of international protocols. One of the most important tasks is finding a staff member of the foreign delegation to work with in initiating and developing collaborative projects. The staff member becomes the linchpin in ensuring the success of any visits or meetings and in continuing the relationship.

Having a clear reason for an international collaboration can facilitate the process. Many officials only see the benefits that will accrue to their organizations. Little thought may go into understanding what the benefits will be for the organization in the other country. Finding a staff person with whom to collaborate can lead to a collaborative effort that benefits all parties to the agreement.

Example 11.4: Reaching across the Border

Jerry, a faculty member at a university in Alaska, was asked by the American Society for Public Administration (ASPA) conference chair to put together a panel on the Alaska National Wildlife Refuge (ANWR). Whether to drill for oil has been a controversial topic of discussion. The conference chair wanted representatives from Canada, who oppose drilling in ANWR, to be on the panel. Jerry called the central phone number for the Yukon Territorial Government. He explained what he wanted and was transferred to Stan, an employee with the Yukon Territorial Government.

Jerry explained to Stan what he wanted. Stan said that his government opposed drilling. Jerry explained that the good news was that Stan could explain his government's position to government employees, university faculty and administrators, and students. The bad news was that he would have to pay his own way. Stan said he would check before responding to the offer. Later, Stan called Jerry back to say he would go. Stan took his place on the panel on ANWR, which included presenters from the Alaska Department of Natural Resources, the Coast Guard, the oil industry, and the environmental community as well as the Yukon Territorial Government, and had an intense and informative discussion on the merits of drilling for oil in ANWR.

The initial phone call to the Yukon Territorial Government led to a long-term relationship between Jerry and Stan. That relationship included Jerry and his colleagues creating a one-time MPA degree taught in Whitehorse, Yukon Territory, Canada, for their government officials. It is amazing how often a simple phone call can lead to productive international collaborations.

11.7.1 Universities and International Collaborations

For university administrators and faculty to travel to other countries is fairly common. Universities sign a variety of agreements with universities abroad. Faculty members travel to other countries to collaborate on research and on programs such as Fulbright scholarships. It is important to keep in mind that when traveling to other countries, administrators, faculty, and students are representing their own country and university. Reviewing the checklists presented earlier in this chapter can contribute to a more productive trip and the development of long-term relationships.

Universities have a different management structure than government organizations. The differences are worth exploring in the context of international relationships. Universities have faculty governance, and it is not easy for university administrators to assign responsibilities to faculty members outside their agreed-to workloads. One of the authors was talking to a provost of a university about international agreements. The provost said that signing international agreements was the easy part. Finding people to implement the agreements was the difficult part, and that is why many agreements just ended with the photo opportunity.

Example 11.5: Asking for an Agreement Is Not Enough

Deborah (Debby) is a faculty member in a university in Alaska at a time when there is much interest in working with other countries in the Pacific Rim. Debby has a student, Stephanie, who studied in China. Stephanie was going to a language institute in China to refresh her Chinese language skills. Debby and Stephanie thought it would be a good idea to send a letter of introduction and an invitation to develop a collaborative agreement signed by the university's chancellor. Debby approached the chancellor, who agreed to sign the document. Debby and Stephanie then crafted letters including the proper protocols. The letters were both in English and Chinese. Once the chancellor signed the letters, Stephanie took them to China with her. When Stephanie returned, she brought with her a translated letter from the president of the language institute. The letter proposed many activities, including faculty and student exchanges, visits of administrators to both institutions, and joint projects. Debby and Stephanie were both excited at the response. Debby took the letter to the chancellor and waited for his response. The chancellor never responded to the letter.

Disappointed and angry with the chancellor for not acknowledging or responding to the letter, Debby stayed away from him for two months. One day, however, while she was thinking about the letter, she realized that the reason that the chancellor had not responded was that she had not prepared for the response. Instead of giving her chancellor a wonderful opportunity, she had handed him a problem—how to respond to the requests in the letter. Debby made an appointment with the chancellor. At their meeting, she told him that she had been angry with him for not responding. He said that he was aware of her anger. She then told him that she realized that she had focused only on the letter and not on the response, which put him in a rather awkward position. He smiled and said, "Yeah, you did."

Later, Debby worked with Jerry to develop an MPA program for the Yukon Territorial Government employees. Stan, a government employee with whom Jerry had established a relationship, had asked Jerry to see if the university could provide an MPA program for their government employees. The Canadian universities would not provide local classes but instead wanted the employees sent to their universities, which was simply not feasible. Debby and Jerry worked out an agreement for classes to be taught at the community college in Whitehorse, the capital of the Yukon Territory. Faculty from both institutions would teach classes. Having learned a difficult lesson from the China experience, Debby made sure that all the pieces of the implementation were in place. Because the Yukon Territorial Government was paying for all the expenses, she even made sure there was a reserve to account for any changes in the value of the two currencies. When all the planning was complete, Debby and Jerry took the agreement to the chancellor and explained it in detail. Debby looked at the chancellor and told him, "Everyone who is participating is in agreement. Everyone is onboard. It is now ready for your signature." He looked at her, smiling, and said, "I'll sign it."

University international collaborations are worthwhile and are needed now more than ever. As illustrated, they do take considerable planning. In fact, they require considerably more planning for long-term workable projects than for comparable projects undertaken by government agencies.

11.8 Working through Difficult Issues

Invariably when developing international collaborations, difficult issues will intrude to create what may seem insolvable dilemmas. Institutions in different countries operate under different rules, and what may be allowable for an organization in one country may violate laws or ethics requirements in the other country. Officials may be used to different protocols. A request by a principal from one country may be seen as outrageous and unacceptable under the policies and procedures of the other principal. A juncture appears at this time. The collaborative work and end or the problems can be overcome.

The best approach to overcoming problems is having culturally competent and knowledgeable staff work out the problems. Using staff to work out the details for the principals has two advantages. The principals are spared from having to work out difficult issues and can maintain friendly and respectful relationships. The staff members can use the opportunity to create an international team that has overcome difficult issues. Professional relationships are strengthened when the participants know that the other official will work with them in a productive manner and accomplish their mission. Both have been battle tested and survived. Overcoming difficult problems creates strong professional bonds and trust.

Example 11.6: There Has to Be a Way

While Debby, Jerry, and Stan (from the previous example) were working to create an MPA program for the employees of the Yukon Territorial Government, they encountered one of those insurmountable problems. Some of the employees chosen to take the MPA did not have bachelor's degrees. Because of accreditation regulations, if someone does not have a bachelor's degree, he or she cannot receive a master's degree. To further complicate the problem, many of the employees who did not have bachelor's degrees were First Nations (the indigenous people of Canada). For them to complete the same coursework and not receive a master's degree would create difficult political problems for the government.

Looking at Debby and Jerry, Stan said, "This is a deal breaker. They have to receive a master's degree."

"That's impossible," Jerry responded. "There is no way we can do that." The three just looked at each other in silence.

Then Debby interjected, "Stan, we can end it here and we all lose something. We work well together, and we can find a way to do this if we don't give up. What do you think?"

Jerry jumped in and asked Stan, "Why is it important for the employees to enroll in the MPA and to get a degree?"

"We want our employees to be better trained and educated," Stan answered. "The degree will show they have the education, and it can help with their promotions. That's why the degree is important."

Debby inquired, "What if we give certificates of completion to everyone who successfully completes the program? Only the students who have bachelor's degrees will get a master's, but everyone gets a certificate of completion."

Jerry added, "Would you check with the president of your college and we will check with our chancellor to see if they are willing to give each student a letter of congratulations for completing a rigorous course of study in public administration. Also check to see if your personnel people will accept the certificate as certification of completing a course of study for all the students."

At their next meeting, Debby, Jerry, and Stan had everyone's agreement on the course of action, and the MPA program could proceed.

In organizing their international collaboration to establish the MPA program, Debby, Jerry, and Stan learned a number of lessons:

1. Approach difficult and seemingly insurmountable problems with the intent of maintaining a good working relationship.
   a. This approach makes it easier to find innovative solutions that work with everyone.
   b. Even if a solution cannot be found, the working relationship and sense of being team members remains and keeps the door open for future relationships.
2. Always check to see that the solutions fit within each member's organizational framework, policies, and procedures.
   a. Get concurrence from all involved principals.
3. Remember that the sense of professionalism under fire creates a professional bond that makes it easier to develop future collaborations.
   a. The trust that has developed in the approach creates a sense of confidence that makes it easier to undertake difficult projects.
4. Understand that the same approach works just as well intraorganizationally as it does internationally.
5. Foster personal friendships, for they can enrich the lives of all the participants.

Refusing to let the seemingly unsolvable problems stop them and not letting difficult problems destroy the working relationships created a deeper professional relationship and allowed a now-personal relationship to emerge for all three.

11.9 Maintaining International Relationships

The strong bonds that develop from solving the many problems that always show up in the course of creating international collaborations forge strong professional relationships. Many of these relationships will continue on a personal and social level. Communications across borders are easily facilitated by electronic mail and technology such as Skype. It is easier than ever before to keep in touch and maintain the relationship.

These ongoing relationships benefit the principals and not just the staff. The staff members are now points of contact who are in a position to help each other when the principals need information or assistance on other projects in their respective countries. They can draw on their own professional network as well as the professional network of their principals. One initial phone call can create a lifetime of professional international collaborations.

11.10 Summary and Conclusion

The purpose of this chapter has been to demonstrate first how racial formation occurs by two contemporary theorists, Beverly Tatum and William Cross Jr. Both of these theorists have done groundbreaking work in identifying the importance of race development, a topic that few scholars have tackled. Second, the aim of this chapter has been to connect racial development and identity with the importance of understanding the significance of international relationships and experiences. Ted James has served as a scenario for how individuals can engage in a life that is committed to international activities.

Adding international protocols to cultural competence helps ensure that international collaborations are successful. Different countries have different cultures with different requirements for organizations. When collaborating with officials from other countries, use the checklists included in this chapter. The checklists help to ensure that all the appropriate bases are covered. The more planning that goes into a visit or meeting, the less likelihood that there will be any surprises. It is the rare surprise that creates a good outcome. Stay within the agreed-to format and do not improvise. Make sure that everyone who is involved agrees to any proposed changes.

International relationships can begin with a phone call expressing the willingness for a collaborative relationship. Follow the protocols and determine what the benefit would be to the other parties from their perspective. Staff people for the principals are worth their weight in gold, even in today's prices for gold. Developing a professional working relationship with the staff professionals can have the payoff of a successful international collaboration.

The staff member becomes the conduit for maintaining long-term international relationships. Today's technology makes it easy and convenient to maintain regular contact. The staff member has access to his or her own professional network as well as his or her principal. This can open up new vistas for anyone wanting to continue international relationships.

Difficult problems always seem to accompany developing international relationships and joint projects. The approach to solving the problems is more important than forcing a solution. Approach problem solving with the attitude that it is an opportunity to create a long-term relationship, for in the long run the long-term relationship is more important than insisting on one's own solution as the answer. Being a professional means being able to work through the tough issues. When people are working with each other for the first time, there is no better way to show one's professionalism than being able to work through the tough times while keeping a good working relationship.

Trust is shown by the approach used in working through tough and contentious issues. Once the issues have been resolved and dealt with, the strong relationships remain. Resolving difficult issues professionally and deepening the long-term working relationship together create a confidence and willingness to undertake more difficult projects and collaborations, and that can lead to future career successes for all parties.

CASES IN CULTURAL COMPETENCE

Chapter 12

Cultural Competence in Health Care

To be without health insurance in this country means to be without access to medical care. But health is not a luxury, nor should it be the sole possession of a privileged few. We are all created b'tzelem elohim—in the image of God—and this makes each human life as precious as the next. By "pricing out" a portion of this country's population from health care coverage, we mock the image of God and destroy the vessels of God's work.

Rabbi Alexander Schindler
Past President, Union of American Hebrew Congregations
North Carolina Council of Churches, n.d.

The health of a society is truly measured by the quality of its concern and care for the health of its members.... The right of every individual to adequate health care flows from the sanctity of human life and that dignity belongs to all human beings.... We believe that health is a fundamental human right which has as its prerequisites social justice and equality and that it should be equally available and accessible to all.

Imam Sa'dullah Khan
Islamic Center of Southern California
North Carolina Council of Churches, n.d.

12.1 Introduction

Chapter 1 briefly discussed how the health care industry, especially in the delivery of services to immigrant and minority communities, has published the majority of the academic study and case studies on implementing cultural competence organizationally. A majority of the academic research, organizational assessment of culturally competent workplaces, and development of standards and best practices has come from the health care industry, including the social services and mental health services to immigrant and minority communities. Many of the standards and guidelines about cultural competence have been developed by members of the health care industry, including the social services.

This chapter describes how cultural competency has been put into action in the delivery of services and in health administration: through the delivery of health care services, including a holistic approach, in health administration, hospital administration, and human services administration, which includes mental health services. The role that the federal government has played in the evolution of cultural competence in health care is discussed along with a description of additional resources available to the public manager.

Nowhere has the need been so great to incorporate principles and best practices in cultural competence than in how health care is delivered. This is just one need that must be addressed. The differences in costs, issues of cost containment, an aging international population with greater-than-ever expectations of the health care industry, critical labor shortages in trained medical personnel at every level from the certified nurse assistant (CNA) through surgical specialists, these are just a few of the major issues facing the health care industry.

Cultural competence in the health field began as simply providing linguistic services to an increasingly mixed and diverse population so that critical communication can take place in the consumer's native language. These basic language translation services have evolved into the exploration of differences in how disease and illness is viewed and treated in diverse communities, how public health issues such as the treatment of HIV/AIDS is delivered, and how mental health services are provided to widely divergent communities of consumers.

Cultural competency is one the main ingredients in closing the disparities gap in health care. It is the way patients and doctors can come together to talk about health concerns without cultural differences hindering the conversation, but enhancing it. Quite simply, health care services that are respectful of and responsive to the health beliefs, practices, and cultural needs of diverse patients can help bring about positive health outcomes. Remember that the definition of cultural competence is the ability to manage diversity—in all the forms that means in our increasingly diverse world—in the public workplace or, as is the focus in this chapter, in a variety of health care organizations or delivery systems.

Differences in culture may influence the entire health care system in a number of ways. Some of these are the very definition of what health is, that is, the healing process and wellness belief systems. The very perception of how illness, disease, and their causes are perceived is affected by culture. These perceptions include both those held by the patient (consumer) and the behaviors of patients (consumers) who are seeking health care and their attitudes toward health care providers. Culture will influence the delivery of services by providers who look at the world through their own limited set of values, which can compromise access for patients from other cultures. As described in Chapter 3, culture is defined as the knowledge, values, beliefs, attitudes, religion, perception of time, spatial relations, concepts of the universe, and symbolic communication that are shared by a group of people. Coming to terms with cultural characteristics in the health care system alone contains challenges to the practitioner, academic researcher, and most certainly the public manager who is responsible for his or her agency's response to the pressure to become culturally competent.

The increasing population growth of racial and ethnic communities and linguistic groups, each with its own cultural traits and health profiles, presents a challenge to the health care delivery service industry. The provider and the patient each bring to the health care experience individual learned patterns of language and culture, which must be transcended to achieve equal access and quality health care.

The reality is that the changing worldwide demographics means that countries look like very different places than they once were (see Chapter 2, which describes how globalization and immigration are changing the world). In the United States alone, currently one in eight people was born in another country. The increase in diverse communities challenges basic assumptions and definitions of what a nuclear family looks like, for example. Organizations are a reflection of what is occurring in the larger society. The fact that there are no clear majority groups—a trend that will only strengthen in the years to come—removes much of the pressure on new immigrants to assimilate in order to get along and get ahead in their careers in their host country. With no clear majority, what would these newly arrived groups assimilate to?

Nowhere does the need for cultural competence become more important than in the health care system and delivery of services to widely divergent communities. The health care industry has acknowledged this for some time and has taken the lead in developing guidelines, standards, principals, assessment tools, and the like in order that health care service providers continuously improve the safety and quality of health care that is being delivered.

> Cultural competence is not a panacea that will single-handedly improve health outcomes and eliminate disparities, but a necessary set of skills for physicians who wish to deliver high-quality care to all patients.
>
> **J. R. Betancourt**
> *(2004, 954)*

Research and interest in cultural competency in health care, especially in defining it, developing principles and standards, and designing conceptual models and theories, has been increasing exponentially since the start of the 1990s. Goode, Dunne, and Bronheim (2006) of the National Center for Cultural Competence completed a research study for The Commonwealth Fund that showed an increase of a single article in 1990 to 303 articles from 1990 to 2005 published on cultural competency in health care. The study attributes this rising interest to the increasing diversity in the United States along with the publication of standards of practice in cultural competency and a public policy agenda that focuses on the elimination of health and mental health disparities. What has not been studied as much has been results of how theory is translated into best practices and action in the health care industry.

12.2 The Federal Government's Role in Developing Cultural Competence in Health Care

The federal government has played a major role in promoting cultural competence through legislative change or executive orders. The health care and education fields have especially been required to make institutional changes to incorporate culturally competent principals and culturally competent practices. For over 60 years, beginning with the 1946 Hospital Survey and Construction Act, the federal government has encouraged institutional change toward cultural competence.

Major legislation in the form of the Civil Rights Act of 1964 and the Social Security Act in 1965 moved people and agencies receiving federal funds to address issues creating obstacles and barriers that were cultural. This focus has been encouraged through requirements placed on any organizations that receive federal funding and through shaping the public bureaucracy (Rice 2010).

A special note needs to be made on the enormous impact the Civil Rights Act of 1964 had on changing the very fabric of U.S. society. The 1960s challenged society to come to terms with racial and gender discrimination and discrimination against immigrants. As Embrick and Rice (2010) noted, before the societal changes of the 1960s, the American melting pot was really an exclusive club made up of white males. Asians, Latinos, and many of the dark-skinned Europeans were excluded from the melting pot, as were women, who were being encouraged to go back to their kitchens at home to make way for the thousands of men who had fought in World War II.

The U.S. federal government's responsibility in health care is administered through the Department of Health and Human Services (DHHS), which is made up of the office of the secretary and eleven agencies whose mission is "protecting the health of all Americans and providing essential human services, especially for those who are least able to help themselves" (http://www.hhs.gov/about/whatwedo .html).

The DHHS's Health Resources and Services Administration (HRSA) is the major repository of information about cultural competency in health. HRSA is the major source for funding for culturally competent programs in health, mostly through the competitive grant process. The HRSA Web site has links to several topics developed using a Web-based delivery platform. The HRSA Web site currently divides its cultural competency resources into the following categories:

■ Assessment tools
■ Culture/language specific
■ American Indian/Alaska Native/Native Hawaiian
■ Asian American/Pacific Islander
■ Hispanic/Latino/Spanish
■ Disease/condition specific
■ Health professions education
■ Research
■ Rural
■ Special populations
■ Technical assistance
■ Training curricula
■ Web-based training

Example 12.1: Changing Directions: Strengthening the Shield of Knowledge (Trainer's Manual)

The HRSA Web site contains many of the trainer's tools, including PowerPoint slide shows and manuals for both participants and trainers. *Changing Directions: Strengthening the Shield of Knowledge* is a train-the-trainers project used in Native American communities in educating groups on the disease HIV/AIDS. It is a very helpful example in that it deals with a culturally sensitive topic by using cultural practices familiar to the participants. The following list shows the organization by topic area. Note that all information may be downloaded and used.

• Cover page, author's page, acknowledgments, cover interpretation
• Training agenda
• Opening ceremony and ice-breaker
• Cultural influences, values, and identities
• Traditional teachings: sacred hoop, four directions, seven grandfathers, and animal totems
• Sacred expressions: gender, sexuality, and sex
• Communication pitfalls, tips and strategies
• Cross-cultural healing elements
• Integrative approaches
• Closing talking circle

The manual for participants in the training program contains more detail than found in the trainer's manual and provides reference material. Among the many topics included are these:

- Native American culture: a historical perspective
- Sphere of influence and overlapping identities
- Introduction and relevance to HIV work
- Pitfalls and tips for building cross-cultural competence
- Smudging ceremony and sacred smokes
- Sweat lodge ceremony
- Apache tears
- Storytelling
- Talking circles
- Drumming and dancing
- Herbs
- Native healers and medicine people

Changing Directions: Strengthening the Shield of Knowledge is a comprehensive train-the-trainers program developed for the Catawba Indian Nation HIV Training Initiative. This program is an excellent example of cultural competence in the delivery of health care. The white Western model addresses the biomedical explanation of illness (the how), whereas Native American healers, or medicine people, address spiritual explanatory dimensions (the why) and use healing practices. Healing practices are used to release negative, hurtful, or painful thoughts and feelings and create processes to help deal with the depression that accompanies the diagnosis of a major disease such as HIV/AIDS.

In the exercise Apache Tears, it is explained that obsidian stones can be used to collect a person's sorrow and depression, which can then be released as the person lets go of the stones. The application to HIV work is in using the Apache Tears in a ritualistic manner to support healing and deal with death, grief, and loss. The project uses other cultural practices as ways to strengthen and support medical treatment that is being given to a patient. Smudging and sacred smoke is used to cleanse and purify both the physical and spiritual body. Sacred herbs are discussed as a way to relieve some of the side effects of HIV treatment, including nausea.

HRSA provides a wealth of information on cultural competency, describes projects funded by the agency, and makes resources available to the public on a wide range of topics. The topics appear as health literacy resources that include assessment tools, culture- and language-specific clinician guides, information on reaching special needs population groups on public health issues, and a wide variety of technical assistance projects and training curricula.

The DHHS Office of Minority Health has published national standards on culturally and linguistically appropriate services, summarized on its Web site. The 14 standards described are directed at health care organizations and are grouped by themes. Referred to as CLAS (culturally and linguistically appropriate services) national standards, the distinction is made between those standards that are federal mandates, or requirements for all recipients of federal funds, and those that are just guidelines and recommendations. Standards 6 and 7 are the two that are federally mandated:

- Standard 6: Health care organizations must assure the competence of language assistance provided to limited English proficient patients/consumers by interpreters and bilingual staff. Family and friends should not be used to provide interpretation services (except on request by the patient/consumer).
- Standard 7: Health care organizations must make available easily understood patient-related materials and post signage in the languages of the commonly encountered groups and/or groups represented in the service area.

The remaining 12 standards are grouped by themes:

- Culturally competent care
- Language access services
- Organizational supports for cultural competence

These national standards on culturally and linguistically appropriate services (CLAS) have been further studied and reported on. The DHHS Office of Minority Health's Web site (http://minorityhealth.hhs.gov) provides a wealth of information on both national standards and final reports that list case studies and profiles of sites that have effectively implemented the CLAS standards. The Web site has a section on cultural competency complete with training modules and information that can be downloaded and used by anyone. Topics covered in the section on cultural competence are definitions of cultural competency; guides and resources; training tools for physicians and others; policies, initiatives, and law; the 14 CLAS standards, and organizational information about the DHHS Office of Minority Health.

> Of all forms of inequality, injustice in health care is the most shocking and inhumane.
>
> **Reverend Dr. Martin Luther King Jr.**
> *North Carolina Council of Churches, n.d.*

The cultural competence model encompasses the dimensions of culture, communication, misunderstandings and conflicts, and leader–follower relationships. At one time, there may have been the implied expectation that newly arrived immigrant populations abandon most cultural practices and viewpoints of their country of origin or their orientation in favor of the predominant views and practices of the host country. This notion may further be described as assimilation, or "Be like me: follow my rules, do it my way, treat me in the same way that I expect to be treated."

Assimilating into the host country's culture, values, beliefs, and practices is no longer possible because there will be no clear ethnic majority in the years to come. Currently, one in eight people in the United States was born in another country. The demographic changes to come and increasing pressure to have public organizations reflect the diverse society they are part of will continue. The health care industry in the United States has known, even if only conceptually, that major change is required in order to provide quality health care to an increasingly diverse population. A worst-case scenario is that health care service providers at the very least want to avoid expensive litigation resulting from medical errors and misunderstandings. If the business case is taken into consideration, the health care industry recognizes that in order to capture greater market share in the increasingly diverse communities of this country, providers must respond in culturally competent ways.

In Chapter 5, the authors described the standards for cultural competence in social work practice developed by the National Association of Social Workers (NASW). Significant work was undertaken in describing how members of the social work profession could incorporate these standards into their daily practice of providing one-on-one services to an increasingly diverse population in ways that remained true to their code of ethics and dedication to and respect for the individual in need. Rather than reiterating these standards here, the authors refer the reader to Chapter 4 and to the NASW publication *Indicators for the Achievement of the NASW Standards for Cultural Competence* (2007).

12.3 Delivery of Services

There are numerous limitations, however, in how the health care industry has approached the study and practice of cultural competency. Among those limitations are:

- Overemphasizing definitions for cultural competence and terms associated with it rather than taking a practitioner viewpoint that is more concerned with what works
- Applying a linear or monochronic perspective on how the medical and social services establishments show evidence of being culturally competent, with an emphasis on principals, guidelines, and standards rather than a willingness to learn the methods other cultures have successfully practiced
- Failing to acknowledge limitations with the Western rational medical model in dealing with illness and specific diseases or conditions

- Given the traditional Western rational practice of medicine, knowing very little about the mind-body-spirit connection in how healing takes place and how treatment is given
- Lacking understanding of (or failing to acknowledge) the importance of prayer and meditation, religious and spiritual practices, and the role of the healer or shaman in some cultures
- Not acknowledging that the health care system using primarily the Western medical model can be alienating, especially to people without experience or understanding to help them sort out what they are going through

Modern medicine has experienced successes that could only have been dreamed about even a few years ago. We put enormous faith in the medical establishment to keep us healthy and to continue to advance in finding ways to alleviate pain and suffering and to make progress in curing us of the numerous diseases and conditions that have plagued us. Yet we are beginning to understand the limitations in relying solely on a medical model that separates body from mind or psyche. Integrating cultural competence into modern medical practices may provide new and innovative ways to treat the whole person: body, mind, and spirit. This integrated approach may be especially useful when dealing with chronic conditions and conditions linked to such societal factors as environmental conditions, poverty, toxic environments, and stressful workplaces.

Example 12.2: From Cultural Collision to Cooperation

An integrated approach to the delivery of health care services has been in operation for a number of years in the southwestern regions of the United States. Community health workers, or *promotoras*, have recently been given formal recognition through a certification process arranged through the Texas Department of State Services. *Promotoras* reach out to people who tend to be underserved, especially in rural communities and *colonias*. They are equipped with information about health and social services available to low-income families and others unable to afford basic health screening and examinations. *Promotoras* can be paid, or they can be volunteers.

In Chapter 2, an example was given of the life-and-death repercussion of cultural misunderstanding. The example shows how ignorance of values and beliefs regarding the treatment of illness other than by methods that predominate in the current Western medical model can cause tragedy. The book *The Spirit Catches You and You Fall Down* describes this cultural collision and resulting tragedy in a very real way. As you may recall, the book describes what happened when Lia Lee entered the U.S. medical system diagnosed as an epileptic. Her story became a tragic case history of cultural miscommunication. Parents and doctors both wanted the best for Lia, but their ideas about the causes of her illness and its treatment could hardly have been more different. Lia's doctors attributed her seizures to the misfiring of her cerebral neurons; her parents called her illness *qaug dab peg*, "the spirit catches you and you fall down," and ascribed it to the wandering of her soul. These distinct interpretations are a dramatic example of cultural miscommunication that results in conflict and distress.

Merced County, California, hospital health care providers have taken the lessons learned from this example of miscommunication and conflict and established a number of programs that facilitates understanding between the established medical professionals and Hmong shamans. Funded by the California Endowment Foundation, one example is a seven-week certificate program in which shamans and physicians from the local hospitals exchange health care experience and information. Shamans serving the large Hmong population in the region take tours of hospital facilities and participate in Western-style medical education sessions conducted by hospital physicians. Additional exchanges are conducted in which physicians are invited to view ceremonies conducted in the shamans' homes. Shamans tour all hospital facilities, including operating and emergency rooms and other units. On completion of the seven-week programs, shamans are presented with embroidered jackets to wear while making hospital visits. The teams of shamans and physicians who have completed this program have traveled abroad to several Laotian and Thai communities and have thus been able to compare different lifestyles, living conditions, and medical facilities. They have also visited settlement camps and refugee living quarters on Buddhist temple sites in Laos and Thailand.

12.4 Culturally Competent Health Administration

Health administration is a professional field relating to the leadership, management, and administration of hospitals, hospital networks, and health care systems. Nonprofit agencies and community-based organizations are considered health administration, and the field of health administration may include other configurations, such as public–private partnerships, health advocacy and legislative groups, institutes, coalitions, and the like. Health administration academic programs are also included in this definition.

An example of cultural competency in hospital administration is Growing Our Own, the project undertaken by a nonprofit agency that acted as the broker and manager of a complex multimillion-dollar, three-year endeavor. The project successfully trained over 200 people from a high-poverty region to fill critical labor shortages in nursing and the allied health professions.

12.4.1 Growing Our Own: The Rio Grande Valley's Strategy for Coping with the Nursing and Allied Health Shortage

12.4.1.1 Case Study Summary

The goal of Growing Our Own was simply to enable area hospitals to meet their need for nurses and allied health practitioners with local residents. The project also meant providing youth with sufficient information to plan a career in health care. Health care is the fastest-growing industry in the Rio Grande Valley, with the area ranking among the most distressed areas in the country in terms of the shortage of health care professionals. Hospitals in the Rio Grande Valley need culturally competent, bilingual professional staff and spend upward of $50,000 to recruit abroad to fill their immediate labor needs. In recruiting foreign nurses, hospitals employ staff that are not well versed in cultural sensitivity in dealing with a predominately Hispanic population. In order to address the critical labor shortage in the nursing and allied health professions in South Texas, the Valley Initiative for Development and Advancement (VIDA) formed the Rio Grande Valley Allied Health Training Alliance comprising 11 hospitals, five educational institutions, two workforce development boards, and several faith-based community organizations. The Alliance designed a strategic plan that had several objectives, with the major goal of enabling area hospitals to use local residents to meet their need for nurses and allied health practitioners.

12.4.1.2 Case Study Solution

The Alliance designed and implemented an innovative model program that successfully met the organization's ambitious objectives in addressing the obstacles and barriers to filling job vacancies in the regional hospitals with people from local communities. This success was a major achievement on many fronts, especially given the highly specialized health training and certification required of health professionals.

The model was innovative in that an entirely new and temporary organizational structure had to be constructed in order to achieve the level of collaboration and cooperation the project needed to be successful. In the Rio Grande Valley region in the borderlands, not only were the 11 hospitals in competition with each other but the five educational institutions drew from some of the same population as well. Approximately 150,000 "Winter Texans" escape the snow everywhere from Canada on down to make the region their homes, many in the numerous mobile home communities. About half of the primarily Hispanic population receives either Medicaid, Medicare, or other government assistance for health care.

12.4.1.3 Case Study Results

Growing Our Own met, or exceeded its major project objectives (Rio Grande Valley Health Training Alliance 2006). There were more than 250 new nursing or allied health professionals that the region did not have prior to the implementation of this project. Since the start of this demonstration project, a remarkable 94.7% retention and graduation rate was achieved. A proprietary clinical scheduling system and database were created through the efforts of the Alliance. In addition, 79 youth scholars enrolled and graduated from dual-enrollment courses, in which high school students completed college courses while still attending high school in order to gain specialized training and experience in the health care field as well as tuition assistance (Rio Grande Valley Health Training Alliance 2006).

Postspecialty occupational training modules were created and offered as a result of this demonstration project. Through project funding, sophisticated computer-driven neonatal and obstetric simulation models were purchased and shared among the educational institutions, resulting in cost-savings to the campuses, which would have either been forced to purchase their own or do without. The hospitals were able to hire locally from among bilingual, culturally competent applicants, rather than having to recruit abroad in such places as the Philippines.

12.5 Culturally Competent Hospital Administration

As is self-evident, hospital administration is concerned with hospitals, hospital networks, health care systems, health maintenance organizations, and the like. An example of cultural competency in hospital administration is the LEAD case study that took place over a three-year period.

12.5.1 LEADing Organizational Change: Advancing Quality through Culturally Responsive Care (LEAD)

12.5.1.1 Case Study Summary

The California Endowment funded a three-year initiative to improve the delivery of culturally appropriate care in California's public hospitals. Advancing Quality through Culturally Responsive Care (LEAD) objectives were achieved through four components: leadership, education, accountability, and dissemination. The project was developed through a partnership between the Center for the Health Professions and the California Health Care Safety Net Institute. The Institute is the research and education component of the California Association of Public Hospitals and Health Systems. Nineteen public and nonprofit hospitals, academic medical centers, and comprehensive health care systems make up the California Association of Public Hospitals and Health Systems. They serve more than 2.5 million Californians annually. Of all their patients, 69% are on MediCal or among the uninsured. Of their patient population, 48% are Hispanic/Latino, 29% white, 12.5% black, 6.5% Asian, and 3.9% reported as other (California Association of Public Hospitals and Health Systems n.d.). Hospitals within the system self-selected and applied for one-year grants and technical assistance in order to improve the quality of services and the cultural competency of their hospital.

12.5.1.2 Case Study Solution

The biggest success LEAD achieved was in providing language services throughout the California public hospitals. Project staff reported that it was essential that the CEOs committed to the goals and objectives through written letters. The most successful hospitals realized that making small, incremental changes yielded higher results than taking too much on at one time with their grant awards. Most of the hospitals had realized that they must make changes in order to adapt to the increasingly diverse patient population, yet they needed a little push to begin the process. The grants became a motivator to make those changes to become more culturally competent as a hospital, academic medical center, or comprehensive health care system.

12.5.1.3 Case Study Results

An important feature of the program was that the CEO of the hospital applying for these grants had to sign a letter of commitment to the program. LEAD was founded on the principle that cultural competency was not simply another management initiative that becomes forgotten after the final report is produced. The Institute emphasized cultural competence as a quality-of-care issue. It was found that the hospitals that took on large-scale changes were the least successful. The program evaluation cautioned against doing too much too soon in making changes leading to the culturally competent hospital. The participating hospitals had difficulty quantifying and documenting their successes with LEAD. This problem was unfortunate and made project evaluation, even using anecdotal information, very difficult. The successful hospitals had internal project "champions" who were not necessarily the CEO. Support from the top leadership and the CEO was essential. Many hospitals used advocacy organizations to assist them in becoming more responsive to the community the hospitals served. Some hospitals found it challenging to become more responsive to community feedback, and using advocacy groups helped them overcome this challenge. Other hospitals felt that patient surveys alone could indicate progress toward becoming more community centered.

12.6 Culturally Competent Human Services Administration

Human services administration incorporates cradle-to-grave programs and mental health service providers. Many, but not all, of the social or human services programs serve low-income or the most in-need members of our society. Medicaid, child care, children and families, supplemental nutrition programs, temporary assistance for needy families, the homeless, mental health services, people with disabilities, substance abuse and addiction, domestic violence shelters, and senior citizen programs would all be considered human services administration. The national initiative to develop cultural competency, discussed next, works in the area of human services.

12.6.1 The Cultural Competency Initiative, National Consumer Supporter Technical Assistance Center (NCSTAC), Mental Health America

12.6.1.1 Case Study Summary

The National Consumer Supporter Technical Assistance Center (NCSTAC) is funded by a grant from the Center for Mental Health Services and the Substance Abuse and Mental Health Services Administration. The mission of NCSTAC is to strengthen consumer organizations through research, informational materials, training, and financial aid. The Cultural Competency Initiative began in 2000 with a mission to increase understanding of ethnic and racial disparities in mental health treatment and to support projects that address barriers to adequate treatment. The shift in the U.S. population with more diverse communities to serve is having a significant impact on the mental health services system. The NCSTAC used a competitive selection process to award 10 grants of $5,000 each to conduct an annual project to address issues of cultural competency in the recipients' communities.

To that end, the Cultural Competency Initiative produced "A Cultural Competency Toolkit" (available at http://www.ncstac.org), which summarized the 10 grant sites that participated in the Initiative. The 10 sites described the lessons grantees learned from conducting these projects. Most of the grantees were state affiliates of mental health associations.

12.6.1.2 Case Study Solutions

There was wide variation in the results obtained from the grants, all addressing issues of cultural competency of mental health service providers. The solutions were all aimed at increasing a process of transformation in the mental health services communities and meeting the challenges created by an increasingly larger and much more diverse client population. The purpose of the cultural competency "toolkit" was to strengthen consumer organizations, whether in the form of leadership training, recruiting more members from diverse communities, producing educational materials, participating more actively in the public policy process relating to the provision of mental health services, or transforming organizations to meet future challenges. ("A Cultural Competency Toolkit" on the NCSTAC Web site has a chapter describing each of these projects in detail.) The 10 grants developed various solutions, as shown in the following list.

- Alaska's Mentor Project: Leadership training for five Native Alaskans through a three-day legislative "fly-in" (Native Alaskans flown into Juneau, the state capital, from remote villages in order to learn the state public policy process, meet with representatives, and receive mentoring from community activists)

- Allegheny County, Pennsylvania: produced a guidebook on how to replicate a highly successful multicultural outreach and education project they had conducted
- Georgia: increasing awareness of symptoms and treatment of depression among the African American community by replicating a project that had accomplished the same
- Hawaii: Involved members of the Native Hawaiian and Asian American communities in strengthening their existing speaker's bureau
- New Mexico: provided technical assistance to groups wanting to create their own projects at state locations that had not previously been involved
- Philadelphia: trained elder advocates on the mental health needs of older members of their communities, building upon an already existing project
- South Carolina: given the state's growing retiree population, founded an elder's taskforce
- Texas: outside the Houston area, used brown-bag lunches at a counseling center as the vehicle for learning more about Asian American mental health care needs and concerns
- Utah: used cultural competency monies to conduct a two-day conference for 200 mental health professionals on the needs of minority communities, including a section on the deaf culture
- Washington: created a call-in service with a real person answering calls so more members of minority communities could learn about mental health services available in their area

12.6.1.3 Case Study Results

The 10 sites participating in the NCSTAC Cultural Competency Initiative produced a variety of products and leadership training experiences (accessed at http://www.ncstac.org). The NCSTAC Web site includes a number of publications and fact sheets that can be used by any individuals who are interested in moving their organization toward becoming more culturally competent in meeting the mental health service needs of a growing, diverse population. Most of the topics have been developed for nonprofit agencies and include technical assistance involving key areas, among them:

- Arranging fund-raising, managing finances, obtaining computer donations
- Conducting community needs assessments, assessing the need for systems transformation
- Writing grants
- Working with the media, volunteers, other community groups
- Establishing advisory boards
- Engaging in advocacy: voter drives, candidate forums, coalition building

12.7 Additional Resources on Cultural Competency in Health Care

A wealth of information is available on promoting cultural competence in the health care field along with reducing the disparities in service delivery to minority and diverse communities. At last, doubt has been removed that access to health care in the United States is uneven at best and perhaps even nonexistent for the growing numbers of potential consumers among immigrant, minority, and diverse population groups. There is also very little debate that this situation is unacceptable in an industrialized country like the United States. Without question, the issues about access to health care are at the forefront for a number of reasons, including President Obama's push for health care reform and the reality of loss of access to health care for millions of Americans in this weak economy.

There are numerous Internet sources for information about cultural competence in health care. Of these, a few Web sites contain important links and information and deserve notice:

■ California Health Care Safety Net Institute, http://safetynetinstitute.org
■ Cross Cultural Health Care Program, http://xculture.org
■ National Center for Cultural Competence, http://www.nccc.georgetown.edu

12.7.1 California Health Care Safety Net Institute

The California Health Care Safety Net Institute (SNI) is dedicated to enhancing the quality of care; promoting efficient, coordinated care; and eliminating health care disparities for the California network of public hospitals. On the SNI Web site (http://safetynetinstitute.org) is a section on publications and resources that provides Web addresses for a number of sources, including several on health education. An example of the information provided is CultureMed, which maintains an extensive catalog of sources, including those in languages other than English, on health education and cultural competency.

12.7.2 Cross Cultural Health Care Program

The Cross Cultural Health Care Program, as described on the group's Web site, acts as a bridge between communities and the health care industry and is dedicated to providing culturally competent and linguistically appropriate training and consulting. Based in the state of Washington, the Cross Cultural Health Care Program articulates its vision as "healthcare in every community and every community in healthcare" (http://xculture.org). Founded in 1992 as a nonprofit agency, the organization is especially known as a leading trainer of professionals in medical interpreter training programs. It is also known as an information clearinghouse on cultural competence and the CLAS standards. The resource guide on the group's Web site lists resources by the following areas:

- Nonprofit and university-based organizations
- Government agencies and regulations
- Articles on cultural competence
- Other related resources, including online courses, conference proceedings, and guides
- Listservs and "current awareness"
- Medical subject headings

The Cross Cultural Health Care Program Web site also contains summaries of events held on cultural competence and posts announcements about upcoming conferences and training events.

12.7.3 National Center for Cultural Competence, Georgetown University Center for Child and Human Development

The National Center for Cultural Competence (NCCC), a department within Georgetown's University Center for Child and Human Development, is especially known for self-assessment and organizational assessment tools, as well as for the work its researchers have done in defining what is meant by cultural competence and in developing the various conceptual models and the framework that further defines terms. The NCCC has developed a number of values and principles for cultural competence that are further described on its Web site (http://www.nccc.georgetown.edu). The descriptive information and one-page fact sheets on cultural competence case studies and projects are extremely valuable.

12.8 Medical Tourism

Medical tourism is an emerging aspect of cultural competence in health care. Simply stated, medical tourism involves patients going to a different country for medical procedures or products, including urgent or elective care. Patients may experience cost savings that reflect charges 90% lower than the cost of comparable care in the United States. Some estimates suggest that the industry is large, with an almost limitless growth potential (Borrego et al. 2009). In 2004, an estimated 150,000 foreigners sought health care in India alone, a growth rate of 15%. In 2005, one hospital in Thailand served more than 50,000 patients from the United States, a 30% increase from the previous year. An estimated 100,000 U.S. citizens are health tourists for cosmetic procedures. Many retired people from the United States move to the U.S.–Mexico border every winter as "snowbirds," attempting to escape the cold north of the border. Many of these snowbirds use the pharmacies and dental offices in Mexico.

Numerous countries are encouraging medical tourism industries, including some of the more prominent countries with established medical tourism industries, among them Costa Rica, India, Thailand, and Singapore. More than 120 hospitals are accredited by Joint Commission International (JCI), an arm of the organization that accredits American hospitals participating in Medicare. Many physicians in these hospitals are U.S. board certified. The American Medical Association (AMA) has issued guidelines on medical tourism.

U.S. companies are beginning to incorporate medical tourism in their employee health plans. Maine-based supermarket chain Hannaford Bros. Co., for example, under its self-funded insurance plan administered by Aetna, allows its insured employees and their dependents to go to Singapore for surgical hip and knee replacements. Another U.S company, Wisconsin-based Serigraph, allows employees to go to India for such elective procedures as joint replacements or back surgery. The company pays the full cost of the medical care, travel, and lodging. The employees pay no deductibles, and the company estimates savings of 50% to 60%.

Blue Cross Blue Shield of South Carolina is exploring medical tourism as part of its insurance coverage. Currently it provides coverage for its members for medical procedures performed in Thailand. Companion Global Healthcare is a subsidiary of Blue Cross Blue Shield of South Carolina and has a managed-care network of foreign hospitals its members can use.

The health care legislation signed into law by President Obama has three aspects that may affect medical tourism:

1. Most people are expected to be covered by health insurance.
2. Private insurance companies will get many new customers.
3. There is little in the health care bill that lowers health care costs.

Currently, the news media is reporting that employer-based health insurance companies are estimating cost increases of about 9% (Reuters 2010). The increases for individuals who buy their health insurance on the open market are projected to be as high as 20% (Theim 2010). Out-of-pocket expenses for patients is an important consideration. High deductibles and copayments can create an incentive for private health insurance companies to increase their use of medical tourism with savings for both the patient and the companies.

Meanwhile, the countries that will be the most successful in developing medical tourism industries will be those whose hospitals are culturally competent in their relationships with foreign patients. Medical tourism is becoming more competitive as health care costs rise.

12.9 Summary and Conclusion

This chapter has described how cultural competency has been put into action in a variety of health care settings: through the delivery of holistic health care services in health administration, hospital administration, and human services administration, which includes mental health services. The role the federal government has played in the evolution of cultural competence in health care has been discussed, and additional resources available to the public manager have been pointed out.

Nowhere has the need been so great to incorporate principles and best practices in cultural competence than in how health care is delivered. This is just one need that must be addressed. The issues of disparities in cost, cost containment, an aging international population with greater-than-ever expectations of the health care industry, and critical labor shortages in trained medical personnel at every level are just a few of the major issues facing the health care industry.

This chapter has given examples of cultural competency put into practice in the delivery of services, health administration, hospital administration, and social services organizations. Additional resources have been provided to the reader, who can delve into numerous projects and examples of cultural competency in the health care industry.

Chapter 13

Cultural Competence in Higher Education

13.1 Introduction

The way in which higher education is approached today has changed significantly from how it was approached in the 20th century. Many more U.S. colleges and universities have become student centered and rely less on rigid norms of accessing achievement and the like. Schools of higher education such as Reed College, for example, pride themselves on allowing students to find their own academic path. As the oldest and most notable academic society, Phi Beta Kappa has maintained an over-200-year tradition of supporting a lifelong curiosity in the liberal arts and sciences. The landscape of modern universities has shifted from authoritarian leadership to a student-centered environment. Attention has only recently been made to the area of cultural competency. Indeed, if our population is changing, we then need our institutions to change as well. Higher education is in many ways the place where public managers are receiving their knowledge of the world. We cannot expect this population to have an understanding of governing different people or being governed by different people if higher educational institutions do not provide those skills and that information.

In 2010, the Pew Research Center reported on a growing trend, namely, the increasing numbers of students of color now making up America's first-year college and university classes (Fry 2010). Details of the trend are shown in Table 13.1.

As shown in Table 13.1, in 2008 there was an overall 6% college enrollment of all racial and ethnic groups. Hispanics represented the largest increase with 15%, followed by blacks with 8%. Whites represented a 3% increase, which is a dramatic shift from even 20 years ago.

Table 13.1 Total First-Time, Full-Time First-Year Enrollment in Colleges, Universities, and Trade Schools

	2008	2007	First-Year Enrollment Increase
Total	2,588,675	2,445,015	6%
Race or Ethnicity			
White	1,520,507	1,481,925	3%
Hispanic	300,584	260,315	15%
Black	367,432	339,175	8%
Asian or Pacific Islander	146,802	137,996	6%
American Indian or Alaskan Native	25,163	24,703	2%
Nonresident Alien	55,160	49,591	11%
Race or Ethnicity Unknown	169,603	151,310	12%
Two or More Races	3,424		
Total	2,588,675	2,445,015	

Source: Data from Fry, R., *Minorities and the Recession-Era College Enrollment Boom*, Pew Research Center, http:// pewresearch.org/pubs/1629/recession-era-increase-post-secondaryminority-enrollment, 2010.

In 1992, Karen Dewitt of *The New York Times* reported that there was an unprecedented growth of students of color in higher education. This growth in fact outpaced that of white students of the same age group, 18–23 years old. Dewitt speculated in her report that the increased number of students of color could be explained by aggressive recruitment strategies by colleges and universities. Better financial aid packages could also lead to increased enrollment for students of color, though this fact alone would also lead to more white student enrollments as well. Ironically, Dewitt warned that the increased numbers of students of color could indeed drop or reverse if the country were to enter a recession. This notion is actually counterintuitive as educators and economists have known for years that more people enroll in school during times of a recession. This fact was also observed in the 2010 Pew Research Center report (Fry 2010), which puts Dewitt's warning at bay by suggesting that whether in or out of a recession, students of color are enrolling in higher education in numbers never before seen in the United States.

The Pew Research Center Report (Fry 2010) also suggests that the increase in students of color is widespread among all categories of U.S. colleges and universities. Earlier speculation suggested that higher education enrollments among students of color were concentrated primarily at the community college or less-than-two-year tier of schools. While there are large numbers of students of color in these levels, it must be noted that white students are also found at this level as well. The implicitly biased views continue to suggest that lower-tier schools are the ones that students of color can generally afford or gain admission into. This finding has not been demonstrated, according to the Pew report.

13.2 Reasons for Higher Education Cultural Competency Models

It is clear that previous models of cultural competencies are not going to work in the 21st century. Despite attempts at improvements, higher education remains, for the most part, a microcosm of the dominant culture and its value system (Shin 2008). The current and future college population is and will continue to be the most diverse in the history of the United States. Therefore, it is important here to discuss four of the many populations that will occupy higher education in even greater numbers than now. The populations include:

1. Students from the working class
2. Students of color and from the working class
3. Students of color from the middle class
4. Faculty who are gay and from working-class backgrounds

All these populations have a place in our society, but they receive little attention from higher education. One of the only models used for assisting working-class students is TRIO, a set of programs that offers students additional support to stay in college, involving them in tutoring and graduate school essay assistance, for example.

Students from working-class or poor backgrounds continue to experience isolation and feelings of self-doubt when they enter a four-year college or university. Some of these students may even flunk out or drop out of college for an assortment of reasons, including a lack of money. Many institutions rely on services from the TRIO programs to address social-class issues for first-generation students and working-class students. Many of these students are also of color, though many are white as well. This population of students, regardless of race or ethnicity, continues to be at risk for dropping out of college or not entering in the first place.

The limitation with TRIO is that it is a federally funded program and is not located in every college or university where its services are needed. In fact, very few institutions host the program when compared with those that need it.

On the other end of the social-class spectrum are those students of color attending predominantly white institutions, or so-called PWIs, who come from solid middle-class backgrounds with college-trained parents. These students have not grown up in the Robert Taylor housing projects in Chicago or the Tenderloin area of San Francisco, for example, but nonetheless need to be valued and supported in college as well. Indeed, as the United States departs further and further from the ugly history of slavery, the country is now witnessing generations of college students who are the third- and fourth-generation college graduates in their families, especially African American families. A testament to this fact comes from historically African American college fraternities (Johnson 2009a, 165) such as Alpha Phi Alpha (founded in 1906) and Omega Psi Phi (founded in 1911), which were established at the turn of the 20th century. These organizations have had as members multiple generations of the same families. This is certainly the same with such historically African American sororities as Alpha Kappa Alpha (founded in 1908) and Delta Sigma Theta (founded in 1913). These organizations and other historically African American societies demonstrate that we are now seeing multiple generations of college-trained black families living in the United States. Some observers may argue that these graduates come from privileged backgrounds and should not be seen as part of the new paradigm shift. However, students of color still face discrimination and isolation at PWIs despite their class and social backgrounds. Still, if we want an inclusive and well-trained citizenry, we must put away the antiquated notion that all students of color are poor and all white students are privileged. Certainly we need to rid ourselves of the notion that working-class students can make it through college without assistance.

Students who identify as lesbian, gay, bisexual, or transgender, often collectively referred to as LGBT, often feel left out of the landscape of social justice. Research demonstrates that LGBT college students feel marginalized because of their sexual orientation or gender identity. Many colleges and universities around the country now have an LGBT office, which provides services for students in the LGBT community. We are also seeing an increase of LGBT college presidents, among them Raynard Kington (Grinnell College), Ralph J. Hexter (Hampshire College), and Charles Middleton (Roosevelt University), to name but a few of the approximately 21 to date (Fain 2010).

However, LGBT senior administrators and executives often move from one university to another institution, and so for them a hellish campus environment may be short lived. On the other hand, tenured and tenure-track faculty do not move from one institution to another nearly as much. Given this fact, very few colleges and universities offer a campus environment where LGBT faculty still feel comfortable being themselves. An antiquated notion of a faculty member is that he or she is heterosexual and from a privileged background. Ironically, this notion still holds true for many institutions and such academic fields as history and engineering. Being LGBT for some faculty may not be as much of an issue because they may already have a partner or may live in an urban area where the dating pool is large and has many outlets, among them gay dance clubs or such movie theaters as the Castro in San Francisco.

But gay culture for faculty teaching in such rural states as Vermont, Maine, and Wyoming may be nonexistent. Additionally, LGBT faculty often continue to teach at institutions where they are expected to function in the heterosexual norm. Take, for example, an LGBT faculty member who attends a faculty dinner alone. A well-intentioned colleague may say to this person, "When are you having a kid?" The assumption here is that the LGBT faculty will adopt a hetero-normative approach to life that includes at minimum adopting a child or two and essentially appearing as straight acting as possible. The complexity of being both working-class and LGBT may create even more barriers than those faced by heterosexual faculty peers.

In 2008, Oldfield and Johnson published a first-of-its-kind book about LGBT and working-class faculty from different universities in the United States and Europe. The book, which has received a great deal of attention, especially in higher education, speaks to the paradigm shift that needs to happen as cultural competency takes center stage. One reviewer had this to say about Oldfield and Johnson's book:

> What I did not expect was to be glued to the pages and have my assumptions contradicted. The 13 personal and professional stories of young people journeying towards professorship were all different, riveting, and well edited. Oldfield and Johnson have done the field of current and prospective faculty, as well as scholars and researchers in the field of higher education, gender studies, and sexuality study, great service by selecting compelling life accounts to illuminate varied aspects of this profound, hitherto invisible, and silenced journey. The editors have brought this experience out into the open for public examination and have made sure each chapter includes extensive detail and reflection. The result is that the reader walks through the experiences of academics who have struggled with not just one, but *two* major subordinate society issues in reaching into an upper middle class profession (Wishik & Pierce, 1991): sexual identity and class.
>
> One of the great surprises for me is the more significant role that *class*, not sexual identity, has to play in these stories. While youthful years might be dominated by sexual identity struggles, violence, and oppression; the difficulty of the journey to academia is overshadowed by class more so than sexual identity. As I will relate this does not mean that the sexual identity issues are minor in this journey; instead it means that class is so much more dominant, all pervasive, and hard wired into the autobiographers' beings, families, and senses that it was the major issue chasing at their heals throughout, and often still. (King 2009, 94)

The value and significance of Oldfield and Johnson's work (2008) is that it speaks to what happens when institutions of higher education do not have a system in place to affirm and celebrate its LGBT and working-class faculty. Often these individuals feel damaged, which can lead to lifelong negative consequences. As suggested by Oldfield and Johnson, sexual orientation and social class are identities that receive little attention regarding faculty life. The authors believe that such a combination of identities creates a well-informed professor as well as a compassionate instructor in the classroom, as the following example illustrates.

Example 13.1: I Can't Get Away from My Working-Class Roots

Although I attempted, like Wylie, to "get away from my background" by pursuing education, teaching at a regional university led me back to my working-class beginnings. Like Hooks, I have experienced contradictions along the way. Nonetheless, through all the contradictions, I have come to understand my place in academe and how to effectively educate students in the culture classroom. Working with college students will always present me with intellectual challenges and remind me to reexamine my place in academe in light of such challenges. This continues to be true as I have discovered in my recent move to a new academic position at the University of Maryland, Baltimore County (UMBC), a research intensive and "honors" institution in the University of Maryland System. Indeed, this new position will require me to "reexamine where I stand" by confronting a new series of contradictions, as I move more in the direction of privilege as a professor with more research opportunities and less teaching responsibilities. Still, it will allow me to continue to come into close physical, intellectual and social proximity with students from a variety of backgrounds, including many transfer students who come from the local community colleges. Hakin Hasan argues that many academics who teach at the best colleges and who conduct research on the urban poor have little or no contact with their own research subjects. For this reason, he stresses the importance of academics and community to "give lectures and share ideas with low-income students who are on the front lines of social problems." Over time, my commitment to events like "Night of Compassion" that engage my queer and working-class identities in meaningful ways can only grow. This essay is a testament to this allegiance. (Provencher 2008, 79)

Yet another example as to why an understanding of LGBT working-class faculty is important is the following biography, also from Oldfield and Johnson (2008).

Example 13.2: Where Are Our Higher Education Models?

When I was graduated from The Ohio State University in 1962, my class background and lesbian identity, especially since I wasn't out, were much less important in regard to my finding an academic position than the simple fact of my gender. Few women were being hired for college and university positions. I still have a copy of a letter from a prestigious Midwestern university saying, "while [your] record [is] very good [they] had decided to hire a <u>man</u> (their underline) instead."

My major advisor had been consulting on developing a clinical psychology program at a prestigious private university in Atlanta and recommended me for a position there. I was delighted to return south, finally home again, where the weather was pleasant and I spoke the same language as the natives. Like my mother, I immediately bought my own home at age 25.

Living in Atlanta, I crossed several communities and classes. Weekdays I dressed up and went into the genteel halls of the university. Late afternoon I would return to my suburban home, and evenings and weekends I would dress down and join lesbian friends in softball and basketball games. One boundary, however, was impermeable. My gay and lesbian friends never met my straight colleagues and vice versa. I was either trying to pass as straight or living openly in the gay world. And, my straight friends were matchmaking at every turn, never knowing I would rather *have* a wife than *be* one.

Being a graduate student is a class by itself. Becoming a faculty member at a university brings one into a social class of some prestige and stature. As I walked the academic halls, I was as far from family, the steel mills of Birmingham and the Florida swamps as one can imagine. My life was no longer one of waiting tables in the college dining room or binding books in a dusty office, nor would I face the prospect of making a living through physical labor. I had also escaped the early marriage and children that were the fate of so many of my high school peers. I was single, made a good living, and worked at a job I loved.

Life within academe was pleasant but sometimes embarrassing as well. I learned to quit saying <u>De</u>troit and <u>po</u>lice but I remember my humiliation at mispronouncing <u>A</u>rab in front of my class one day. I began to think I would never speak the English of my students. I was also one of the first of the very few women faculty in my college. As had been true in graduate school, all my mentors were male. Looking back, I am not surprised they had a difficult time relating to a young, working class lesbian from an entirely different culture.

Then one afternoon, I was at home reading a psychology journal. I vividly remember the telephone call from the Dean of Students asking if I would consider becoming the Dean of Women. This was my second year at the University and the administration had few women to turn to when the current Dean of Women abruptly resigned. I took the position and was quickly caught up in a round of social activities where I was expected to host gatherings and model manners for college coeds. Perhaps the most jarring responsibilities were supervising the strong sorority system that was deeply entrenched in the campus culture. Not only did I deal with the sorority sisters but with their parents and national representatives of each group. I appreciated the opportunities for the young women to gather in small groups and expand leadership roles for themselves, but I abhorred those moments with a crying parent whose daughter had been "cut" from her preferred sorority. First the group "rushed" you and encouraged you to come to think of them as "sisters." Then one's sisterhood was abruptly denied and the poor girl was rejected via some unknown criteria that brought her very being into question. Being an outsider myself, I could appreciate the pain of being excluded. I could do little to change the sorority system although we tried a number of approaches to open doors to everyone who wanted to belong. I never mentioned my sexual orientation but was somewhat attuned to class differences. I had never attended a "Tea" before and now I had to pour it. I admired the elegantly dressed parents and sorority representatives and had no clue where they shopped or how they had attained a taste for fashion. I wore pearls but preferred blue jeans. (Strickland 2008, 109)

Both of the foregoing examples speak to the need of models that are inclusive of higher education, but especially those individuals who have historically not had a voice or representation in the academy.

13.3 The Tilford Group Cultural Competence Model

There have been many institutions of higher education that have given thought and consideration to cultural competency in one respect or another. However, few have had the success demonstrated by Kansas State University. During the mid-1990s the Tilford Group at Kansas State University embarked upon an ambitious way to approach the issue of cultural competency at their institution. Assembled around a common goal that includes the respect of all students, their culture and their personhood, the Tilford Group designed a process for accomplishing the aims of the group, which would be implemented across the university (Johnson and Rivera 2007).

The model includes nine different components that are all connected (see Figure 13.1). Such areas include attention to curriculum, faculty, and assessment and evaluation. The evaluation component of any model is extremely important, as this is the measure by which objectives are judged to be effective. Unfortunately, this is the weakest area of most models, especially regarding programs related to diversity. For example, the University of Vermont has a mandatory six-credit diversity requirement for all undergraduate students. The requirement was implemented in 2008; however, it was an unfunded mandate. This means that deans and other program managers must implement the new mandate without any additional resources. The weakest part of the UVM cultural competency model is a lack of quantitative and qualitative evidence that measures students' perceptions of cultural differences before and after taking the six-credits of diversity education.

An outgrowth of the Kansas State University model became the Pittsburg State University (PSU) Tilford Group (http://faculty.pittstate.edu/~ananda/Tilford .html). Founded on the same principles, the Pittsburg group has the same functions as the Kansas State University group and uses the same process for infusing the concept of cultural competency throughout the curriculum, faculty, and administrators. Created in 2007, the PSU group acts as a model for the Kansas system of colleges and universities. The goals of the PSU group are to:

1. Be the umbrella organization of all the diversity and multiculturalism activities on campus
2. Bring diversity and multiculturalism to the classroom and curriculum

Figure 13.1 The Tilford Group's multicultural development process. (From the Tilford Group Web site, http://www.tilford.ksu.edu, 2010.)

3. Participate in the Performance Agreement activities
4. Act in partnership with student government to achieve diversity and multi-culturalism goals

The late Dr. Michael Tilford, graduate dean at Wichita State University, started both the Kansas State University and Pittsburg State University groups. Tilford's belief in cultural competency is a testament to how important senior administrators are in establishing such a system on campus. Faculty and student involvement is also important. Many changes occur on campus because students and faculty push their agendas. Senior administrators have a responsibility to support these initiatives and provide the resources to make them happen. Many presidents and provosts "charge" taskforces and other consulting bodies to gain important information on campus climate and various other matters. However, the important information gathered by these committees often remains unused by the very individuals who have charged the committees.

13.3.1 The Tilford Group's Process Model

Through a series of focus-group meetings with faculty, students, and other constituents in 2000 to 2001, the Tilford Group came up with the following attributes that each citizen of Kansas State University should process. Initially, the group focused on the needs of the students attending the university. However, concerns about the faculty's lack of knowledge about cultural competency also surfaced, for many faculty were not attuned to the differences students brought with them to the campus.

13.3.2 Diversity Competencies

I. **Knowledge:** Awareness and understanding needed to live and work in a diverse world
   - **Cultural Self:** Ability to understand one's ethnic identity and how it influences identity development
   - **Diverse Ethnic Groups:** Knowledge of diverse ethnic groups and their cultures
   - **Social, Political, Economic, and Historical Frameworks:** Awareness of how social, political, economic, and historical issues impact race and ethnic relations in the world
   - **Changing Demographics:** Understanding of population dynamics related to ethnic minority and majority citizens
   - **Diversity Implications for Career:** Understanding of how diversity impacts the academic discipline, career, and professional development

II. **Personal Attributes:** Traits needed by those who live and work in a diverse world
   - **Flexibility:** The ability to respond and adapt to new and changing situations
   - **Respect:** An appreciation for those who are different from one's self
   - **Empathy:** The ability to understand another person's culture by listening to and understanding his or her perspective

III. **Skills:** Behaviors and performance tasks needed to live and work in a diverse world
   - **Cross-Cultural Communication:** Verbal and nonverbal communication skills in interaction with those who are culturally different from one's self

- **Teamwork**: The ability to work in culturally diverse groups toward a common goal
- **Listening**: The intention and ability to attend to what others are saying
- **Conflict Resolution**: The ability to resolve cultural conflicts that occur between individuals and groups
- **Critical Thinking**: The ability to use inductive and deductive reasoning to understand diverse perspectives
- **Language Development**: The ability to speak and write more than one language
- **Leadership Development**: The ability to provide multicultural leadership

13.4 Challenges in Building a Cultural Competency Curriculum

There are two key challenges that must be addressed before a college curriculum can be transformed using cultural competency as a sustainable model. The first is acquiring knowledgeable faculty. In other words, who will teach the courses, and what skill set and level of education will they have?

The myth is that anyone can teach cultural competency courses or diversity-related courses. It should not be the case that the same training required to teach engineering should be used to teach cultural competency. Some institutions are more concerned about implementing cultural competency courses than about who will teach them. Moreover, many institutions aim to offer just a class or two in order to meet state or national accreditation standards. However, to put individuals in a classroom without proper training in cultural competence does a disservice to the students as well as the institution. The former Race and Culture program housed at the University Vermont, for example, gave way to the six-credit diversity course requirement in 2008. During the 15-year run of the Race and Culture program, faculty interested in teaching in the program needed to have a doctorate, an ongoing faculty appointment at the university, and both coursework and experience in the areas of race, gender, sexual orientation, and social class.

Another challenge that academic programs may need to address is whether to have a few courses focusing on cultural competency or have the topic covered in all the classes within the academic program. It would be ideal to believe that the topic could be covered in all courses of any given program, but the truth is that most programs will not opt for this approach. This is primarily because many Caucasian faculty and some faculty of color believe that they do not possess the skills to address cultural competency in their classes. Although this situation is understandable, it puts an extra burden and stress on faculty of color to teach primarily diversity-related courses regardless of what the courses are named. Doing so may not appear to be an overwhelming problem. However, during promotion and tenure reviews faculty of color often hear that all the "their" courses are about diversity and thus lack academic rigor. Most of the committees on diversity are also left to faculty of color to populate.

13.5 Overcoming Obstacles to Culturally Competent Faculty

A primary strategy to addressing the first challenge—namely, acquiring knowledgeable faculty—is to hire faculty who possess these skills and have the required knowledge already embedded in their work. To be sure, a few universities do offer doctoral programs in social justice, though some only offer concentrations in the area, as do Georgetown University and American University. Other universities may offer a master's degree in social justice, as does DePaul University. Academic hiring officials must go beyond asking candidates if they believe in concepts of diversity. Most applicants will typically reply yes. A savvy manager will, of course, request demonstrated and documented evidence of such beliefs. For example, research and teaching are key areas in which faculty members demonstrate their commitment to a particular focus. Even in perhaps such a seemingly unlikely field as business, potential faculty may have written about or taught classes about socially conscious business practices such as those followed by Ben & Jerry's Ice Cream. Evidence of such commitment can also be discovered in an applicant's transcript by noting specific classes and concentrations.

It is a given that not all existing faculty will want to teach classes about or with cultural competency content, however; nor should they. This hesitancy may characterize faculty of color as well as Caucasian faculty. In other words, one of the greatest mistakes a department chair or dean can make is to mandate that a faculty member teach in the area of diversity if the person has not been hired to do so originally, though a department chair or dean can inspire faculty to teach these courses (with the appropriate skill set) and offer a course release or other compensation. For example, a faculty member who teaches a five-course workload may have to teach only four courses if his or her cultural competency course has more than 50 students. Another form of compensation may be extra salary or research funds if the faculty person takes on an extra course that addresses cultural competency.

Another approach to acquiring skilled faculty to teach courses related to cultural competency is to make opportunities available to faculty who do not have the skills but do have a desire to teach such courses. Indeed, no social movement was achieved with only one segment of a population. The women's rights movement, for example, was not limited to heterosexual white women. There were lesbians and men and also women of color on the fighting lines as well. It is with this notion that we must assist faculty (and administrators) who want to be involved with curriculum change, but who feel unprepared. One of the key ways to accomplish this goal is through collaborative learning. Dodd et al. (2000, 180–181) suggest that there are five important points to keep in mind when using collaborative learning to fight ignorance and provide education to faculty and administrators:

1. Cultures have pride in their traditions and customs.
2. Educators may not have experience in working with certain students.
3. Collaboration must occur on all levels in a school environment.
4. Cultural competency in education is essential for all educators.
5. Collaboration among cultures means empowerment for all cultures.

In the following scenario, Dodd and his colleagues (2000) very clearly illustrate the five parts of collaborative learning. The limitation of the scenario is that it addresses a K–12 school setting. However, the scenario is still applicable for higher education faculty and administrators because collaborative learning cuts across all educational boundaries.

Example 13.3: Collaborative Learning

Joe Marx called Terry into his office and related his conversation with Dr. Jacobs. Terry apologized profusely to Astor's mother, saying that his intentions were not to insult but to promote the opportunity for learning among all of the students in his class. Principal, teacher, and parent agreed that the following actions would help to correct the problem.

Terry would enroll in graduate work at a university in a program of study designed to help individuals learn more about different cultures. The principal, a graduate of Yellowstone University, suggested he attend summer school at YU for several reasons. Being located in the West, it was far from small-town Iowa where he grew up, and even farther from urban Chicago where he was teaching. Because YU is near several American Indian reservations, it had a strong Native American Studies program. Also, the Latino population in the urban area where Yellowstone is located had grown considerably during the last decade. Attending classes at Yellowstone would expand Terry's worldview in at least three ways:

1. Immersion in a new and different environment
2. Course work in Native American Studies
3. Rooming and studying with people from different ethnicities who would also be in the program

Terry would co-teach two classes each day with Ms. Ramos, a veteran teacher of 25 years. Working with Ms. Ramos would help him to better understand the St. Washington student backgrounds and the community.

Terry would provide the same opportunities for his African American students to participate in class activities as those afforded all other students. This would help him to see that full participation in class would increase all students' motivation, improve their self-esteem, and sustain their cultural pride. (Dodd et al. 2000, 171)

The value of the preceding scenario is that it provides an opportunity for both administrators and faculty to work together in creating an environment for all students. There are some individuals who really want to understand more about different cultures and alternative life lifestyles. Therefore, "a pointing finger" is not going to accomplish this goal. Instead, strategies for working together are important. Out of this process will evolve a better curriculum and culturally responsive students, faculty, and administrators.

13.6 Cultural Competence for University Administrators

Universities are experiencing the same cultural dynamics as other organizations in society. Baby boomers are members of the faculty and administrators, and some are already beginning to retire. As they do, administrators and faculty will become more diverse. The changing demographics can create cultural misunderstandings.

The numbers of administrators of color are increasing. Some forward-thinking university presidents and provosts hire deans of color. In some situations, a new dean joins a college where most of the faculty are white and have been working together for many years. The faculty members have developed a strong faculty governance system. In today's changing higher education environment, deans may be asked to make changes in their college. In this case, you have a new dean of color from outside the institution and an entrenched white faculty. Management issues and cross-cultural issues can easily become intertwined under such circumstances. A tense environment is the result.

A female dean of color was recounting her experiences in such a situation. She said that when she invited faculty colleagues to her home for dinner, only about half the white faculty would come. They would eat and then leave. The few faculty of color would come and stay for the evening, however. She was never invited to any of the white faculty social gatherings, although the faculty of color did invite her. She also mentioned that her proposals were met with a solid bloc of resistance. After two years, she left for a dean's position at a more multicultural university.

Faculty are becoming more diverse. There are many students from other countries in PhD programs and when they obtain their PhDs, they apply for faculty positions in the United States. In many instances, this means using H1-B visas to allow them to accept faculty positions. Universities need to be well versed in the H1-B process to successfully hire these applicants. Following the correct procedures and timelines is critical to the successful hiring of these applicants. Having employees in the human resource office who understand the requirements can ease the process. Failure to correctly follow procedures and timelines can jeopardize the legal status of the applicants. Special attention needs to be given to faculty on H1-B visas who move to another university, because the new university may need information from the faculty's previous university. The previous university may not be as timely in providing the information because the individual is no longer the university's employee and human resources may not see the urgency.

Issues with human resources not following correct procedures and timelines can create much stress to the faculty members who are also facing the stresses of being on tenure track and having to publish. One faculty member was describing the horrors of accepting a position at a university where the staff were not familiar with the requirements of the H1-B process. Her former university was not being responsive to her current university's enquiry for information. If her current university's H1-B process was not completed in time, she would lose her current H1-B visa and would be facing deportation. She had difficulty getting information from her current university's administrative and human resource staff. In the end, it all worked out well and she got her H1-B visa. She is still recovering from the emotional toll from her experience.

As more faculty of color, including faculty on H1-B visas, join departments in colleges, the same cross-cultural issues that have been explored in previous chapters come into play. There may be similar dynamics for LGBT faculty. The transition from being a doctoral student to a becoming a faculty member at another university is not always easy, and even less so for diverse and minority faculty. For example, an Asian female professor was discussing her experience when she accepted a faculty position at a university where her friend, a white female, was also a faculty member. They had been doctoral students together and had developed a friendship. The Asian professor described the relationship as their being like sisters. She said their relationship now was okay as long as she deferred to her friend. When the Asian professor exerted herself, the relationship got tense. The relationship had changed now that they were faculty members of the same department.

Like the faculty population, the student population is changing. The demographics point to an increase of Hispanics and many first-generation college students. There may also be an increase in students who may formerly have entered blue-collar occupations now entering universities as they seek new opportunities. Faculty who understand the changing culture may be more successful with such students. Many of the students may have polychronic cultural characteristics. These students will be very polite and deferential and may not ask questions in class. The faculty may assume that they know what is required to be successful university students, but often these students do not. For example, an instructor who had just taken a faculty position at a university where the students possess these characteristics commented on what he had discovered. He said that when the students turned in their first written assignment, he noticed that although they could write, they were unable to structure their writing. He told the students that he wasn't seeing the structure necessary for a successful paper. He told them, "There can only be two reasons for this. One is you haven't been shown how to structure a paper, or two, you are messing with me because I'm new. I really would like to hear that you are messing with me because I'm new." The students explained that had not been shown how to structure a paper. Understanding the problem, the new faculty member now starts a class with the structural requirements for any assignments.

The relationship between the faculty and students can be affected by cross-cultural interactions in the classroom. A white faculty member moved from a university in the Midwest, where the students were predominately white, to a university in the Southwest, where the students were Latino and most were first-generation university students. The students were polite, deferential, and asked few questions. The teacher's response to the cultural characteristics was to assume a superior attitude and talk down to the students. The students responded by dropping the class and not taking his classes even when they were required. They would look for any alternative, even taking the class at another university or online at other institutions and then trying to substitute that class for the required class taught by that faculty member. The faculty member is still having trouble attracting enough students to meet his minimum class-size requirements.

Such societal and cultural changes are not just a U.S. phenomenon. Countries in Europe are beginning to experience similar issues. Erlanger (2010) reported in his article in *The New York Times* that France is trying to diversify its elite universities, which are overwhelmingly white. The responses to this effort sound quite similar to the same arguments used in the United States: Entrance to the universities should be based on merit, not on race, ethnicity, or religion. The fear is that to do otherwise would diminish the quality of education at the universities.

In some ways, the cultural changes in society are mirrored in the changes occurring in the school and university systems and the workplace. As has been previously mentioned, globalization is creating cultural changes in many places in the world. University administrators who recognize the changes can minimize cross-cultural misunderstandings and problems. Forward-thinking administrators will also see the opportunities this change creates for their institutions, which may be more attractive to multicultural students than are their competitors.

13.7 Summary and Conclusion

The changing demographics and cultural changes are also evident in higher education. The usual categories of race or ethnicity, gender, sexual orientation, and social class are becoming more complex and intertwined. Students can belong to all four groups, with each student having a unique set of cultural characteristics depending on the combination of characteristics gained from each category. A student who is black, gay, and the son of very successful professional parents may exhibit different cultural characteristics than, say, a student who is black, gay, and from a single-parent and poor household. Visual cues may not be good indicators of cultural characteristics.

The Tilford Group, as discussed earlier in the chapter, has developed one of the better cultural competence models for universities. Their diversity competencies are similar to those in other cultural competence models, but they are adapted for university settings. Among cultural diversities are respect for and understanding of other cultures, cross-cultural communications, conflict resolution, teamwork, flexibility, and empathy.

Wherever people with different cultural characteristics interact, there is a potential for cross-cultural misunderstandings and problems. In the university, cross-cultural interactions can occur in the classroom, among faculty, and between faculty and administrators. With minority births becoming the majority in 2010, there will continue to be an increasingly multicultural student body in the future. The universities that best understand the implications of that changing demographics will be in a better position than others to attract students. Furthermore, faculty who understand the cultural characteristics of their students are in a better position to prepare their students for the challenges ahead. Universities can indeed become culturally competent institutions, and culturally competent public managers will note that many topics discussed in previous chapters apply to universities as well as to other public and private organizations.

Chapter 14

Resolving Difficult Employee Issues

> If you wait for people to come to you, you'll only get the small problems. You must go and find them. The big problems are where people don't realize they have one in the first place.
>
> **W. Edwards Deming**
> *(Coyner 2008)*

14.1 Introduction

A colleague who was writing her thesis on organizational stress titled a chapter "Organizations Are Perfect Except for the People in Them" (Borrego 1980). Anyone who has been a manager for any length of time can attest to the ever-present challenge in resolving employee problems. Employee problems can be placed into two categories: problems between supervisors and employees, and problems between employees.

The bifurcation of employee problems into management problems with employees and employee problems with supervisors can mask the importance of the supervisor–direct-report relationship and its contributions to employee problems. Many of the books that discuss solutions make either the employee or the supervisor the problem. In fact, many workplace problems arise from misunderstandings between the supervisor and the employee.

As organizations continue to become more diverse, the informal organization will continue to include groups of employees who are culturally similar. In large organizations that are very diverse, however, there will be enough diversity that individuals will form affinity groups. These different cultural groups may interpret managerial actions differently. Perceptions of who a manager spends time with, whether he or she treats all the employees the same or instead rewards employees who are culturally similar more than employees who are culturally different, will be perceived from the cultural perspectives of the employees. (This topic will be discussed later in the chapter.)

Employees having problems with other employees are usually handled through supervisory intervention. Where there are union contracts, employee problems will be dealt with in accordance with the contract requirements.

Any bookstore will contain shelves of books on resolving employee problems. The approach to solving employee problems will vary from taking a legal perspective to documenting employee problems. Human resource and personnel management textbooks, for example, will detail acceptable employee behavior and the process for documenting employee problems. The textbooks will usually have a section on employee assistance programs (EAP) that can help resolve employee problems. Other books focus on developing employee successes as well.

Given the abundant resources already covering these aspects of supervisor and employee problems, this chapter will focus on cross-cultural (in the broadest sense) problems and how cultural competence, emotional intelligence, and resiliency can prevent and resolve these employee issues. Cross-cultural employee problems can be very sensitive to resolve because they can easily cross into allegations of discrimination and hostile work environment.

14.2 Defining the Types of Employee Problems

For the purposes of this chapter, cross-cultural employee problems can be classified into two organizational relationships: the relationships of employees with other employees and the supervisor–employee relationship. The problems may arise from the same cause, but they will manifest themselves differently because of the authority relationship inherent in the supervisor–employee relationship.

14.2.1 Irresolvable Employee-to-Employee Problems

At the outset, it is worthwhile to dispense with one type of employee problem, one that exists in many organizations and most managers have experienced some variation. Most problems can be rationally traced to an incident or attitude that precipitated the problem. Some problems arise almost spontaneously; and while there may be many actions that can be pointed to as precipitating or continuing the problem, the situation defies most logic. There is almost a Zen quality to such employee problems. The simplest explanation is that employees will mistreat each other just because they can. As a senior manager once said, "I don't understand why employees go around poking each other in the eye just because they can." This type of problem tends to arise and disappear in ways that seem to defy managerial logic and training.

For such problems, the only managerial solution is to make explicit to the employees the expected behavior and the consequences of not correcting the inappropriate behavior. If the behavior continues, the manager should realize the problem is going to get worse and be prepared to follow through with organizationally approved sanctions. There will almost certainly be a small subset of problems that fit this category. Fortunately, most problems can be dealt with effectively and in a way that improves working relationships.

14.2.2 Emerging Context for Cross-Cultural Problems

There is a new and emerging context for resolving cross-cultural problems. The passage of the Civil Rights Act focused on opening opportunities for minorities and women. Other classifications were added later. Waters and Vang (2005) point out that the wave of immigration began with the liberalization of the immigration law in 1965. They further point out that in 1970, the United States was seen as predominately a nation of blacks and whites. Thus race relations in the United States have generally been cast as black and white. To this day, most discussions of race in the media focus on blacks and whites. Waters and Vang claim that in 1970, 88% of people in the United States were white and 11% were blacks. Hispanics can be of any race. In the 40 years since then, the cultural face of the United States and many countries in Europe is changing. The changes have been driven by immigration, family reunification, and high immigrant births.

The main change that has occurred is the realization that in the next 30 to 40 years, there will be no racial or ethnic majority in the United States. The implications of that impending crossing point is brought home to many people in the United States who lived in monocultural communities and are now sharing those communities with people who have emigrated from many other countries. Immigration has increased the diversity of religion, languages, and culture. Vang and Waters (2005) state that two-thirds of immigrants are Christian, with the majority being Catholic. They say that 20% report being of a non-Christian faith. When a U.S. resident of a particular community picks up a telephone and calls a government office, he or she may be asked to choose from two or more languages. Also, it is becoming common for school districts to have children who do not speak fluent English.

Immigrants are not dispersed evenly across the United States but form clusters. Hispanics have spread out from the Southwest into the South, Midwest, and Northeast. Other Latino immigrants from Central and South America have also immigrated to similar locations. There are many immigrant communities from Africa, the Middle East, Russia, and Eastern Europe. Many people for whom diversity was a concept are now experiencing the cultural changes brought about by immigration. They are seeing and interacting with people who speak a different language and have different customs. Immigrant subcommunities, where English is not the dominant language, are springing up in previously monocultural communities. Diversity is no longer a concept but a day-to-day reality. Cultural change of this magnitude is leaving many people uneasy and uncomfortable.

There are economic uncertainties in the United States and Europe as countries struggle with high deficits and unemployment, which add to the insecurities people are already feeling. Thus, many of the discussions of immigration are happening in a very polarized climate. Many people experiencing the cultural changes blame immigration and want all illegal immigration stopped. Arizona, for example, has passed a law targeting illegal immigrants; other states are considering similar legislation. Arizona has also passed legislation banning ethnic studies and is planning to offer legislation to deny citizenship to children of illegal immigrants born in the United States. There are calls for boycotts and buycotts as competing groups react to the actions of the Arizona. There is much e-mail and Internet traffic on the subject.

Although many of these issues have been mentioned before, they bear revisiting to create a context for preventing and resolving employee problems. The point to understand is that a very divisive and acrimonious discussion is happening in society, and what happens in society finds its way into the workplace. There are new and intense sensitivities being created with the discussion happening at the ends of the spectrum. The discussions generate intense feelings in many people, and people will carry those feelings and perspectives into the workplace. Televised and print commentaries on people at public gatherings talking about wanting their America back and anti-immigrant discussions can and will be interpreted by some individuals as code for discriminating against them. Discussions from the ends of the spectrum make it difficult to find the common ground in the middle.

Race and ethnicity and now other cultural diversities such as sexual orientation have always been difficult to discuss in a reasonable way. Because some cultural groups have experienced and in some cases still experience discrimination, any discussions that is not culturally neutral can and sometimes will lead to claims of cultural insensitivity and in some cases discrimination. An employee can claim discrimination, and the other employee will claim that employee is using the race or gender card. This situation can seem like a quagmire of swampland full of quicksand that is impossible to navigate. In reality, it can be difficult but not impossible.

In the same way that managers develop antenna to detect other employee issues, such as employees who always have an excuse and employees who want to curry favor, managers can develop culturally sensitive antenna. Sometimes even discussion of cultural competence can create a tension in the majority group and defensiveness in employees from diverse groups. Most, but not all, employees know that it is prudent not to discuss race, gender, or sexual orientation in a direct way. Doing so can result in language that uses other words but can be seen as code for the real issue—cultural change. Given that sensitivity, it is understandable that many smart managers would want to stay away from any cross-cultural problem. In reality, it is smarter and easier to face the problem and to deal with it directly. Demographics dictate that organizational diversity will increase and cross-cultural issues will increase and sharpen in tone as the United States approaches the crossing point. Awareness of the context makes it easier to resolve these issues.

14.2.3 Start and End with Assistance from the Human Resource Office

Anytime there is a problem between employees who come from different cultures (used in the broadest sense to include, in addition, race or ethnicity, gender, sexual orientation, social class, and other differences), it is sensible to include the human resource (HR) office in the solution.

The HR office's response to employee problems is usually bounded by the policies on discipline, which are designed to provide a process and appeals process for disciplining employees who have violated a rule, policy, or procedure or are performing their duties in an unsatisfactory manner (Dresang 2009). The HR office can ensure that the problem has not been egregious enough to merit some form of discipline. As the resolution efforts proceed, the HR office serves to keep the efforts well within the organization's policies and rules. The resolution should not be worse than the problem. The HR office will have experience in resolving employee problems, and that experience can help a manager and employees reach a reasonable solution.

Human resources being outside the organizational unit can add gravity to the situation. Organizational units have their own miniculture. As long as the process of resolving a dispute stays within the unit, the employees will be in their comfort zone. Once a representative from an outside department joins the process, the employees realize that there is a greater seriousness to their dispute and actions. Under such circumstances, employees may be more amenable to working out their differences.

14.3 Discovering the Real Problem or Issue

Many employee problems have their roots in the multicultural informal organization and the informal cross-cultural relationships. A manager may see only the incident that was precipitated by underlying cultural tensions and may resolve the problem in a way that further exacerbates the underlying tensions. Equity theory (Adams 1965) can be a useful framework in understanding human problems in the workplace.

Equity theory involves two comparisons.

Oneself		Other
Inputs	Equals	Inputs
Outcomes		Outcomes

An employee makes a subjective assessment of the relative inputs he or she has made and the outcomes from those inputs and compares them with the inputs and outcomes of other employees. If an employee concludes that the comparison is equal, there are no problems. If, on the other hand, an employee senses that someone else is getting a similar reward for less effort or a greater reward for similar effort, the employee may experience a sense of unfairness. He or she may feel that the other person does not deserve the rewards he or she is receiving.

On the surface, this dynamic seems to be fairly straightforward and easily understood, but in reality there are subtleties that can mask the real problem. It can be more easily understood in the popular societal expression of the same dynamic—envy. Envy can create a host of employee problems that may not, at first, seem to arise out of envy. There are some cultures whose members are aware of the destructive power of envy. In the Hispanic culture, for example, envy or *envidia*, is well understood. Whereas envy is a feeling, *envidia* also encompasses the actions that accompany envy. Some envious individuals are willing to undertake activities to undercut the successes of others. These dynamics exist in all cultures, but it is easier to resolve these dynamics when there is a language to identify them.

Organizations have their own social culture. Employees may have been in their organizational units for a long time and have, over this period of time, developed a social culture where everyone knows his or her place. A bright new employee of color joins the organizational unit and quickly makes an excellent impression. The managers recognize her abilities, and she becomes a star employee. Some long-time employees may see her as not having paid her dues and become resentful of her success. A period of subtle sabotage can then begin, and the tension builds between the employees. On any given day, an incident can bring the resentments to the surface and the supervisor is now in the position of resolving the incident. The supervisor may not even be aware of the underlying dynamics that created the incident. Resolving that incident does not necessarily resolve the underlying tensions. If tensions persist, a closer look at the underlying dynamics can be informative.

The work of Elton Mayo and Fritz Roethlisberger (Tompkins 2005, Chapter 8), which resulted from the Hawthorne studies, provides an insightful framework for understanding these problems. Mayo saw industrial unrest as arising out of the irrational tendencies of what are otherwise normal people. For Mayo, workplace disputes happen because neither the person who is complaining nor the person who receives the complaint is aware of what lies behind it (Tompkins 2005, 154). Roethlisberger then extended Mayo's work through the concept of organizations as interdependent social systems. Changes in the system can create changes in social relationships, personal relationships, and human behavior (Tompkins 2005, 165). The bank-wiring observation study led to the conclusion that many employee complaints resulted from the social relationships of the employees. Roethlisberger and Dickson (the Chief of the Employee Relations Research Department at the Hawthorne Plant) used the findings that the behavior in the bank-wiring room was socially organized to develop their definitions of the formal and informal organization. The informal organization is composed of several cliques of employees, which can help or oppose management initiatives (Tompkins 2005, 166).

The works of Mayo and Roethlisberger are a useful perspective to examine employee problems as organizations become more diverse. Employee cliques or social groups form in the informal organization. If the social groups form along the lines that determine the diversity, cultural fault lines can be created in the organization. Social distance between employee groups tends to increase when there is relatively little mixing between the groups. The increased social distance among the diverse groups can be a precursor to cultural issues underlying what may on the surface be more traditional employee problems.

In *In Search of Excellence*, Peters and Waterman (1982) popularized the concept of managing by walking around. Even though it has been 30 years since the book's publication, there is still wisdom in managing by walking around. Managers who spend most of their time in their office and attending meetings will see only the formal organization. The manager will see the relationships among employees only in formal settings. He or she will not be aware of the employee relationships that are part of the informal organization. The network of relationships in the informal organization can be a powerful mechanism that affects the formal relationships.

Example 14.1: Sometimes the Answer Is in the Informal Culture

The dean of a college at a university asked one of the faculty who is a minority if he wanted to be an assistant dean. The dean was looking to increase the diversity in his administrative staff. The faculty member politely declined. The dean was disappointed and couldn't understand why the faculty member declined. The person was a member of a department where he was the only minority and the rest of his department was not open to diversity. The department chair and other members of the department had made it known that he was much better off being quiet and remaining in the background. Had the dean been more familiar with the informal culture of the college, he would have understood the culture of the department and known why his offer was declined by the minority faculty member.

Walking around and seeing the employees in their offices and workstations can give managers a very different perspective of the employee relationships than otherwise gained. Formal meetings can restrict employee behavior into rigid organizational roles, whereas informal interaction can show entirely different facets of employee personalities. Managers can be more effective in managing by walking around by keeping conversations informal. Walking around to inquire about work projects can be interpreted as looking over the employees' shoulders.

How a manager walks around can affect the view of the informal culture. A manager of large state agency, for example, commented that he walks around and talks to employees. When he first started walking around, he was impressed and frankly surprised that his employees were always working. Even when other employees were visiting as he walked by or into their offices, they were discussing work projects. The manager, who frequently travels around the state, traded his traditional leather-soled shoes for loafers with rubber soles to make clearing airline security easier; he found the loafers so comfortable that he continued to use them at work. Now as he walked around, the employees were not as engaged in work activities and their conversations were more social than work related. The welcoming looks were replaced by surprised looks. When he wore the leather-soled shoes, they could hear him coming but now they could not.

Walking around can create stronger cross-cultural working relationships. Informal conversations can humanize the more formal organizational relationships. Many employees respond favorably to the attention they are getting from the managers. This dynamic was illustrated in the illumination study of the Hawthorne studies. In the illumination study, researchers were studying the effects of different levels of lighting on worker productivity. They found that regardless of the intensity of the light, worker productivity kept increasing. In one case, the researchers decreased the intensity of the lighting. Nonetheless, productivity kept increasing until the workers could not see, at which point productivity dropped (Tompkins 2005). The workers were evidently responding favorably to the management attention they were receiving.

Managing by walking around can reinforce the messages of cultural competence: respect, inclusion, and teamwork. Walking around and talking with all the employees communicates a powerful message of inclusion. Some employees who are culturally different from their manager may feel a little awkward when a manager stops by their office or workstation. This awkwardness can result when employees are from cultures where great respect and deference are given to figures of authority. Employees who live in communities where everyone is from the same culture that differs from the dominant culture may also be awkward in these informal situations. Graciousness and repetition can change the awkward interactions into more comfortable conversations.

By including all employees, the manager communicates a powerful message about the importance of cultural competence to the effectiveness of the organization. The informal network of employees is a powerful channel of organizational communication. It is not unusual for the employee informal organization to be more informed and cognizant of organizational activities and the decisions of top executives than are many managers. Many top executives and many managers forget that their secretaries and office staff can often hear their discussions and phone conversations. Executive secretaries are usually more discrete than other employees and less likely to reveal what they hear. Other office staff may not be as circumspect.

What the office staff hears can quickly flow into the employee informal network, which can sometimes be a better channel of communication than official organizational communications. During times of change, the informal network can go into overdrive as employees attempt to discern what is going on. For example, a federal manager who oversees regional administrators told the story of how one of the regional administrators, who is white, called him asking for a merit bonus of $5,000. About five minutes after hanging up the phone, the manager walked out of the office to get a cup of coffee from the cafeteria. One of his employees, who is black and works in an office across the hall from his, approached him and asked, "Are you really going to give the regional administrator a $5,000 bonus?" Such instant messaging is not uncommon for members of various social groups keeping track of the way they are treated in comparison with other groups.

Management by walking around implies a method that is effective only in the immediate vicinity of a manager. This method can, however, be modified for managers who manage offices that are geographically distributed. When visiting geographically distant offices, the manager can spend social time with employees. The manager can invite them to lunch and dinner or for coffee for social conversation. Instead of walking around, the manager can check in by telephone, which can serve the same purpose as walking around. E-mail and text messages are convenient, but there is a personal element in talking by phone that cannot be duplicated through e-mails or text messages.

Managers can shape the informal culture and use the informal network to convey the importance of cultural competence. In walking around, a manager can ask employees about how effective they are working as a team. Managers can ask about how culturally competent managers and employees are. Employees are sensitive to the priorities of managers. Many managers are aware of the maxim "What gets measured gets done." Managers express the importance of cultural competence when they check on the progress of employees' cultural competence. Doing so becomes an informal performance management system. Employees will quickly pass on that message using the informal communication network.

This brings us to the point of this section: discovering the real problem or issue. William E. Deming, quoted in part at the start of the chapter, begins with the idea of finding a problem in order to fix it. Deming's sixth point can be added to Point 5: "Institute training and retraining" (Walton 1986, Chapter 10). When these two points from Deming are added to equity theory and the findings of the Hawthorne study, a manager is better equipped to use managing by walking around to understand the real employee problem or issue. He or she gains a better sense of any underlying tensions that exist in the informal organizations and is more likely to see the incident in the context of the underlying tensions. Resolution of the problem creates an opportunity to address the cross-cultural tensions that feed the problem, thereby minimizing the source that creates the problem.

Walking around can be an extension of mentoring and coaching employees. The manager demonstrates the importance of being culturally competent by modeling the behavior. Many multicultural employees are aware that managers are more comfortable with employees who resemble them. The dynamics of equity theory and envy can underlie the perception the employees have of the manager. A manager who makes a point of stopping by the offices and workstations of diverse employees lets all the employees know that he or she is inclusive of all groups. The manager can coach and mentor employees to understand what cultural competence looks like.

Over time, a shared comfort will develop, and that comfort zone will make it easier for employees to discuss any simmering and bubbling tensions that may exist. The manager can act as coach and mentor to guide the employees into resolving tensions before they lead to conflict. Preventing problems is easier before the employees experiencing the problems have let the tension become personal and cut across cultural lines. In this way, managers diminish the informal and social networks' power to create cross-cultural problems that are often the most difficult to resolve.

14.4 Working through Emotionally Charged Issues

Many emotionally charged relationships surface when the debate of societal issues continues into the workplace. The line between freedom of speech and creating a hostile work environment can be very thin and shifting. Indeed, when the media highlight extreme positions on sensitive social issues, some employees feel they may continue the discussion in the workplace. An employee can believe strongly that the United States should have English-only laws, for example. That belief expressed inside the organization can be viewed as simply a discussion of societal issues or as a potentially volatile comment creating a hostile environment, especially where there are many bilingual employees, who may have parents who do not speak English. Another example is an employee who may have a strong opinion on same-sex marriage and may want to express the opinion in the workplace. Employees may discuss this controversial issue for weeks and no one complains. Then one day an employee walks into a manager's office and says that the comments are offensive and wants them to stop. Yet another example concerns the language used in rallies, which may be acceptable to the participants of the rallies but may be considered offensive by fellow employees. Employees may respond to the opinions aired in the workplace, and less-than-reasoned discussion will ensue that will become very emotionally charged. When the employees work together, the emotional context will carry over into their workplace interactions.

Many of the books on HR management and personnel management attempt to use rational methods to resolve problems with difficult employees. Such methods are effective once the employees are not in a highly charged emotional state. Much of the literature and training workshops focus on personality problems and inappropriate behavior. Emotionally charged cross-cultural problems can easily cross the line into charges of discrimination and hostile work environment. Cross-cultural problems will by definition include employees who are from protected classes covered by the Civil Rights Act and other affirmative action or equal employment opportunity legislation with legal liability for the organization.

The problematic part of the process is getting through the emotionally charged state so that the problem can be addressed rationally. Some of the best methods come from managers who have successfully navigated this uncharted territory. Many conversations with managers show commonalities in their success. The managers' methods have commonalities with emotional intelligence and the work on resiliency, even when the managers were unfamiliar with either concept. Those commonalities are the topic of this section.

The commonalities in the methods managers use to work through emotionally charged issues are numerous:

1. Be mindful that emotional employees will create an emotional state in the manager.
2. Do not feed the intensity of the emotion by trying to suppress the emotion.
3. Bleed off the energy by listening dispassionately.
4. Be empathetic and acknowledge that the issue is important to the employee and that the manager understands that the employee is upset.
5. Communicate that the employee is a member of the team (inclusiveness).
6. Once there is a calmer common ground, facilitate a discussion to determine the many facets of the problem.
7. Once the parameters of the problem have been discussed, ask the employee to help solve this problem in a way that reinforces good working relationships and team effectiveness.
   a. Asking the employee to resolve the issue in a way that reinforces the working relationships gives the employee a voice in the solution.
   b. The solution will focus on strengthening the teamwork of the organization.
   c. Most employees want a positive solution once their issue has been heard.
8. Keep in mind that employees want to be heard and that once the manager has listened, there is greater willingness to move beyond the issue.
9. Know that the message of the manager's willingness to treat employee complaints seriously will be spread through the informal and social network.
10. Accept that in those cases where these methods do not work, the problem may be insolvable and will require the assistance of the HR office.

The most difficult aspect of dealing with highly emotional employees is obvious—they are highly emotional! Many employees and managers are uncomfortable when others are highly emotional. Intense emotions seem to generate a resonating energy that can create an intense emotional state in the listener as well. Trying to suppress the emotional energy can actually intensify that energy, in effect acting in the same way as a pressure cooker. Understanding one's own reaction is the first step to moving beyond the emotional situation.

Realizing that one will feel an emotional response makes it easier not to respond in a way that intensifies the employee's emotional state. Employees have only a limited amount of emotional energy. If the manager does not feed their emotional energy, that energy will dissipate in a matter of time. The manager can listen dispassionately and let the employee vent until the energy dissipates. The intensity of the emotion lets a manager gauge how important the event is to the employee. Once the employee has regained some semblance of equilibrium, the manager can empathically acknowledge the importance of the issue to the employee. The manager can say, "I see that this has affected you deeply. I understand that this is very important to you, and I will treat it with that importance. You are a valued team member, and we need to resolve this." This approach assures the employee that the matter is being treated seriously. This message helps the employee become calmer, since he or she knows the situation is being treated seriously.

A special consideration here involves how to handle employees who are crying while they discuss their problems. Tears and sobs make many people uncomfortable, and the employee who is crying is likely uncomfortable with the tears as well. There may be gender differences in the response to the crying, and there may be employees who use crying as form of manipulation. One manager said that what he found effective is keeping a box of tissues on his desk. When he sees an employee crying, he hand out the box of tissues and say, "I'm okay with your crying. Please go ahead." Then he quietly listens. This approach, the manager says, seems to minimize the awkwardness for everyone.

Discussions from the focus groups of the multicultural employees can give managers additional insight into managing diversity. Many executives commented that they were uncomfortable discussing problems with their supervisors. When they could no longer tolerate the problem, their explanation would come out in an angry torrent. Employees from cultures with high deference to and respect for figures of authority may find it difficult to express any concerns they may have. Simmering unaddressed concerns can serve to intensify the feelings of the employee such that any explanation becomes an eruption of words. The manager sees the intense emotion but may not realize that the emotional outburst is a manifestation of the employee's frustration in not knowing how to address issues professionally. The issue itself may be relatively minor, but the employee's frustration may be all that is seen.

Negative interactions and misunderstood interactions across cultural lines can easily reinforce negative group stereotypes. Race and ethnicity are not the only drivers of employees not knowing how to address work-related problems with managers. Social class can also be a factor. The Pew Research Center (U.S.

Population Projections: 2005–2050; Passel and Cohn 2008) found that the proportion of working-age adults who are foreign born will rise from 15% in 2005 to 23% by 2050. The proportion of children who are immigrants or who have an immigrant parent will rise from 23% in 2005 to 34% by 2050. Waters and Vang (2005) see immigrants as being overrepresented in groups with low education and in low-wage jobs.

The emerging available pool of working-age employees will have many individuals with close roots to their countries of origin. With many of the parents working in low-wage jobs, immigrants and their children may not be familiar with the professional culture of government organizations. In the absence of professional role models, the only place that these individuals may learn how to deal with conflict is their families. There are many wonderful families in all groups, but the way some families handle conflict may not work well in the workplace. Even small issues expressed in an inappropriate manner may seem more problematical than they really are. Knowing that there may be a cultural explanation for an employee's unusual response to an issue can help a manager understand how to raise cross-cultural issues properly. Such understanding can create a more open frame-of-mind for employees. Creating an environment where employees can get past their emotions to reach a quieter, more receptive equilibrium can resolve many emotionally charged issues.

14.5 Communicating to Resolve Issues

Today and probably into the near future, intense societal commentary of many cultural issues will continue to increase the possibility of cross-cultural conflict in an organization. There are many societal issues that can carry over into the workplace to create cross-cultural tensions.

One can imagine an employee, having heard about Arizona's push to create legislation denying citizenship to children of undocumented immigrants, expressing agreement and support for that legislation. Perhaps an employee who is a U.S. citizen, but with one parent who is an undocumented immigrant, overhears the conversation. In another scenario, an employee has watched a television program where the host has made the case that the United States is a Christian country. A non-Christian employee walks by and overhears the discussion. Or an employee belongs to a religious denomination that opposes same-sex marriage and expresses an opinion on the subject at work. Another employee, who is gay and in a committed relationship, overhears the conversation. Such situations reflect the reality that even when employees do not engage in an intense discussion of social issues, an underlying tension can easily result, even from casual comments, that will affect workplace relationships. At the first instance that a workplace misunderstanding occurs, the underlying tension will crystallize around relatively mild workplace misunderstandings.

On first hearing the complaint, a manager may consider the matter a simple workplace problem. As the discussion with the manager continues, however, the underlying tensions caused by overhearing unwelcomed remarks from another employee now surface. To be determined is whether the remarks reflect normal workplace conversations that occur in the informal organization or indicate a perceived hostile environment. As many books on HR management explain, once a manager is notified that a behavior or comment is unwelcomed and is, according to one employee, unwanted and hostile, the organization is on notice and must decide if it is, in fact, creating a hostile environment and whether the organization must undertake remedial action. Such problems arising out of the informal organization are now on the verge of becoming part of an organizational response.

An organization that is culturally competent and expects its employees to be culturally competent will have a much lower number of incidents such as those described above. A supportive environment that values diversity and the diverse employees who contribute to the success of the organization creates a fertile field for culturally competent relationships. Coaching and mentoring on cultural competence tends to discourage the behaviors that create cross-cultural misunderstandings, especially in organizations where cultural competence is part of the performance appraisal of all employees. Organizational efforts to prevent and correct the actions that can create a hostile environment can be handled through the performance appraisal process.

In the context of having managers understand the legal requirements of an organization to protect its employees from harassment, a savvy manager will understand that employees may say under emotional stress something that they may reconsider when they are in a calmer frame-of-mind.

Cultural competence can be an ally in helping to guide a manager through a sensitive situation. Having learned how to defuse and lessen the emotional intensity of the initial discussion, the manager now has a calmer and more reasonable environment in which to craft a solution acceptable to employees involved in the dispute. Investing time in learning the facets of the situation that led to the dispute communicates the manager's interest in understanding the employee. Identifying what created the situation can help shift the discussion from the emotional aspects to a more rational perspective. A rational approach is more successful after the emotional intensity has decreased.

Once the parameters of the situation have been understood, the manager can say, "We have two ways to resolve this situation. We can call the HR office to intervene and assure that all employees have a good working environment. Or, we can use this opportunity to learn how to resolve uncomfortable issues in a way that creates or rebuilds good working relationships. We are members of the same team, and we have to be effective to be successful as an organization. We can use this opportunity to further develop culturally competent managerial skills, which can serve to further an employee's career. Would you be willing to have all of us working together to resolve this in a way that helps us all? If you decide that you are willing to work with us so that all of us can learn and grow from this, I will make sure that it is noted in your performance appraisal. I will also let my supervisor know of your willingness and ability to resolve difficult issues."

The manager can have variations of the same conversation with all the affected employees. In conversations with managers who have experience in resolving difficult issues, all the managers reported variations of that conversation. Using this approach gives the employees involved in the issue a positive way to resolve the problem. Having moved beyond the emotional intensity into a more rational problem-solving approach minimizes the likelihood of having the situation regress into an emotional and uncomfortable situation. The affected parties are now members of a team seeking a team solution with support from their supervisor. Instead of a zero-sum game where one of the participants loses, there are incentives for all the parties to be successful and move beyond the awkward situation.

Once an acceptable resolution has been worked out and accepted by the affected employees, the manager acknowledges their effort through formal recognition. The manager will make sure that their success is noted in their performance appraisal. A letter to the manager's supervisor describing the success but not the details, with copies to the employees, lets the employees understand the importance of being culturally competent and can provide an incentive to further improve their abilities. The informal social network will quickly spread the word that even when there are potential incidents that may happen in the course of everyday work conversations, the organization will support employees to resolve tricky and potentially divisive incidents in a way that benefits them and could advance their careers. This knowledge can create cross-cultural comfort and serve to lessen any cross-cultural social distance.

In those rare cases where this strategy fails to work, the HR office can be a last resort; here, the matter goes through the formal organizational process for dealing with these types of employee issues. This is a last resort because though the official organizational involvement can appropriately protect the employees and organization, it can also leave a residue of underlying tensions that reduce team cohesion and effectiveness.

The approach discussed here incorporates some of the work on resilience completed by Karen Reivich and Andrew Shatte (2002) and the work of their mentor, Martin Seligman, on learned helplessness. The researchers make the point that it is resilience that determines who succeeds and fails. They see resilience as more important than education, training, and experience. Some of the factors incorporated into the previous discussion are emotion regulation, empathy, reaching out, causal analysis, self-efficacy, and impulse control. The approach helps managers and employees become more resilient and thereby increase the resilience of the organization.

The approach also incorporates elements from Daniel Goleman's work on emotional intelligence (1995, 2000). The concepts of resiliency and emotional competence have both been adapted to fit in a cultural competence framework. The elements from emotional competence that have been adapted are emotional self-awareness, accurate self-assessment, emotional self-control, adaptability, initiative, empathy, organizational awareness, conflict management, and teamwork and collaboration.

The approach that managers with extensive experience used in successfully resolving difficult employee issues also had elements of emotional competence and resilience. Their approach is rooted in what their mentors taught them and what their experience taught them would be successful. Many of the managers mentioned that they had failures, but the failures were helpful in learning what was successful.

The Hay Group (2004a, 2004b) has instruments to measure resilience and emotional competence, as well as other organizational aspects such as climate and leadership styles. One of the multicultural leadership programs (reported earlier) made extensive use of the Hay Group organizational instruments, and the results were incorporated into the multicultural training. The instruments were administered to the employee, the employee's supervisor, fellow employees, and where appropriate, to their customers. This allowed for a 360-degree view of the employee and not just self-reported data. One advantage of the emotional competence inventory is that the Hay Group validated the instrument by checking with many of the organizations whose employees took the instruments. The emotional competence inventory contains successful levels for each characteristic. The employee can see if he or she is at the level at which successful managers were rated. This is informative and valuable feedback for employees who are looking to enhance their organizational leadership and managerial skills.

One of the authors has been certified and accredited by the Hay Group to administer and interpret the instruments, among them the emotional competence inventory and the resilience factor inventory. The insight gained from the use of these instruments in multicultural leadership training is interwoven throughout this book, and it must be recognized that these instruments are very helpful to organizations.

14.6 Moving beyond the Issues

Much of this chapter has been aimed at the manager. The employee has an important role in moving beyond the issues. For example, Kim, who is a devout Buddhist, overhears Victor talking about the commentators on television expressing their views that the United States is a Christian country. Kim, being a non-Christian, feels that the comments are really aimed at her, and she is offended. She is not comfortable approaching Victor to express her feelings and say that she believes the comments are directed at her and her family to make her feel unwelcome.

Instead, she goes to see Peg, who is her supervisor. How Kim approaches and expresses the problem will determine how easy it will be for everyone to move beyond the issue.

It is common for employees to take their problems to a supervisor, and the implicit role for supervisors is to resolve employee issues. The resulting effects of this common organizational practice merit a closer examination. When an employee hands a problem to a manager, the manager becomes responsible for dealing with the problem. It is the rare manager who relishes being handed problems, especially difficult problems. The employee has just made the manager's life more difficult.

A better approach is using the Problem–Solution–Results (PSR) approach. The authors have been unable to determine who developed PSR, but an Internet search shows that it is extensively used in many different organizations. The PSR approach extends the statement of the problem to include possible solutions and the results of those solutions. Now the manager will see an employee who has a problem and who has the initiative to develop a solution that has positive results. The PSR approach gives the manager an entirely different view of the employee. The PSR approach has a limitation, however. The limitation is that it is a rational approach, and rational approaches work best when everyone is in a calm emotional state. Emotional intelligence (Goleman 2000) and the resilience factor (Reivich and Shatte 2002) provide insights to guide employees and managers through emotional issues and into a more rational situation. Both are considered important for career success, and they share some common concepts.

The emotional competence framework developed by Goleman (2000) has four broad areas that include several competencies. Two broad areas are personal competence and social competence. The Hay Group (2004a) has adapted these competencies into four broad areas: self-awareness, self-management, social awareness, and relationship management. The Hay Group has developed an emotional competency instrument to measure the level of an individual's emotional competency. The emotional competence inventory has the added benefit of having target levels for success in the organization.

There are specific emotional competencies that are appropriate for Kim's situation (Goleman 2002, 26–27):

1. Emotional awareness: understanding one's own emotions and the effect the emotions have on others
2. Self-control: not letting emotions create impulsive behavior
3. Initiative: showing willingness to take advantage of opportunities
4. Understanding others: respecting others' feelings and perspectives
5. Leveraging diversity: creating opportunities from the diversity of employees
6. Conflict management: resolving conflicts
7. Collaboration and cooperation: being an effective team-member

Kim can use emotional intelligence to understand that Victor's comments have affected her deeply and personally. She knows that she is upset and that emotions can create impulsive and reactive behavior. She knows that she will have to assert self-control not to act impulsively and will have to deal with regretting the repercussions of impulsive behavior. She knows that leveraging diversity begins with understanding that diverse employees can see the world differently and that includes respecting other's feelings and perspectives. Kim can now see this as an opportunity to further develop her competencies, which take practice. She can demonstrate her initiative by looking for a way to resolve the conflict in a way that furthers collaboration and cooperation.

The resilience factor (Reivich and Shatte 2002) adds additional insights helpful in moving past difficult issues. Resiliency can be seen as the ability to overcome challenges and setbacks. Shatte and Reivich list seven factors of resilience:

1. Emotion regulation: not letting emotions get in the way
2. Impulse control: having the ability to control inappropriate behaviors
3. Causal analysis: seeing the majority of the causes of the problems
4. Self-efficacy: believing in oneself as being effective
5. Realistic optimism: basing one's optimism on accurate assessment of the situation
6. Empathy: understanding others
7. Reaching out: willingly taking on challenges

Reivich and Shatte (2002) see resilience as determining who succeeds and who fails. They see emotion regulation and impulse control as being highly correlated. Emotion regulation is one of the biggest factors. When emotions do not lead to impulsive and inappropriate behaviors and actions, the situation is not made worse. Reivich and Shatte see congruity between causal analysis and self-efficacy, which can lead to realistic optimism. Kim can see that to be effective, she has to move beyond reacting impulsively and making the situation worse. She proceeds to causal analysis—the determination of the causes of the problems. She knows that she heard Victor say that the United States is a Christian nation. He did not know that she could hear him, and he did not make a point of directly telling her his views. She realizes that she felt as if he was saying that she did not belong in the United States, but he did not really say that. She uses empathy to realize that diversity, by its nature, brings employees together with different beliefs and perspectives. They will not always agree with each other. What she would like as a resolution is to not hear comments that make her feel that she is not welcome, but she wants to reach out in a way that makes the situation better for everyone and does not negatively affect collaboration and teamwork. She believes that she is an effective employee.

Using her understanding of emotional intelligence and the factors that create resiliency, she can apply the cultural competence model to develop the PSR approach when she sees Peg about the problem. As a reminder, the cultural competence model involves:

1. Culture—a respect for diverse viewpoints
2. Communication— a willingness to communicate inclusion and being part of a team
3. Misunderstandings and conflict—a recognition that diversity can create misunderstandings, but the misunderstandings do not have to create conflict
4. Leader–follower dynamics—an understanding that she is working in an organizational culture and so the relationship with her supervisor should conform to the organizational culture and not necessarily to how she would handle the situation when with her family or in her community

Kim walks into Peg's office and tells her she would like to talk with her. Kim dispassionately lays out all the facets of the situation and how she feels about the comment. Kim has explained the problem in a calm and composed manner. She tells Peg that she has thought about the situation for some time before coming in to see her. She tells Peg, "I know that we are a diverse group of employees and that we have different beliefs. I respect Victor's perspective on religion, and I don't want a misunderstanding to create conflict. I would like to resolve this situation in a way that will allow me to maintain a good working relationship with Victor. I know that we are all members of a team here, and I want to do my part in maintaining team effectiveness. I could approach Victor directly to try to resolve the situation between us. I know that religion is a sensitive topic for many people, and I really do not want to make the situation worse. I would like you to work with me to find a way for all of us to move beyond this to enable us to maintain good working relationships so we can continue collaborating and being an effective team."

Kim is using her understanding of emotional competence and resilience to control how she reacts so she does not react impulsively. She uses PSR to demonstrate to Peg that she is not handing her a problem. She has included a possible solution that could result in moving beyond the issues. She is also letting Peg know that she has the initiative and willingness to work on a solution. Furthermore, Kim is enabling Peg to remain in her comfort zone as a supervisor by giving her the opportunity to recommend another solution. She is asking Peg to mentor her so that she can learn from the situation and is interested in not letting the situation create tension or make the situation worse. These are positive attributes for a manager to see in an employee.

14.7 Summary and Conclusion

Where there are employees, there will invariably be employee problems. Managers are inevitably drawn into the resolution of employee problems. Employees can have problems with other employers or with their supervisor. Cross-cultural employee problems can be particularly sensitive to resolve. There is the possibility that an employee will perceive the problem as inciting discrimination or creating a hostile environment. The HR office can serve to guide the manager through the legal and organizational policies aimed at preventing discrimination and workplace hostility.

There is an emerging cultural context that affects the resolution of cross-cultural employee problems. The media has given much exposure to the changes in culture being created by the country's changing demographics. Immigrants and minorities are moving into many communities that were once monocultural. There are growing numbers of schoolchildren in these communities without a good command of the English language. In the former monocultural community, stores now advertise in languages other than English. Subcultures are forming. Such changes can be upsetting to many people.

The media has also highlighted the role of immigration in driving the demographic changes. Much has been said in the media about the United States not having a racial or ethnic majority by 2050. Although Europe has not experienced the immigration levels the United States has been experiencing, there has been enough for many Europeans to feel other cultures in their midst. In the United States, as in Europe, there has been intense discussions of the cultural changes. Much of the discussion centers on immigration, especially illegal immigration. There is a call to stop all illegal immigration and to make localities unfriendly to residents without legal documentation. There are many undocumented immigrants in the United States from many different countries. There are also many individuals with origins in those countries who are citizens or who are legal residents. It is almost impossible to tell who has documentation from appearances.

The Hawthorne studies illuminated the existence and role of the informal and social networks in the organization. Employees do spend time in informal conversations with their colleagues, and their discussions about societal issues may carry over into the workplace and may sometimes be expressed in a less-than-eloquent manner. The topics can include negative perceptions of people like fellow employees who may be minorities protected by the Civil Rights Act and other affirmative action or equal employment opportunity legislation. These employees may overhear the discussions and take umbrage at what they perceive as a personal attack. The groundwork is now laid for a potential flashpoint among employees or, at the very least, a workplace with increased tensions. A simple work problem can be described as discrimination, or the tensions can lead to an aggrieved employee looking for any work-related excuse to express his or her frustrations. A manager may have difficulty understanding the real issue or problem, however. Meanwhile, the employees will be very upset and in a highly charged emotional state.

Conversations with many managers who have successfully coped with myriad difficult employee issues illustrate a commonality in their approach. Discovering the real problem or issue cannot happen while the employee is upset and emotional.

The manager and employees have to move through the emotional state into a quieter, calmer atmosphere, a tricky proposition at best. The approaches used by the successful managers were grounded in emotional intelligence competencies, whether or not the managers were aware of those competencies or understood the concept of emotional intelligence.

Because many of employee problems are rooted in the informal and social networks of the employees, a manager can understand the nature of the problem by understanding the dynamics of the informal culture and social networks. A manager accomplishes this by walking around and visiting employees in their offices and workplaces.

Emotional intelligence and the seven factors of resilience provide competencies for effectively moving beyond intense emotional discussions. The cultural competence model extends the power of emotional intelligence and resilience into the new cultural dynamics that are emerging as demographics drive cultural changes in society and organizations to levels that have never been experienced before.

The employee can make the largest impact in moving beyond the issues in a way that strengthens working relationships and team collaborations. Adding PSR—the Problem–Solution–Results model—to the understandings of emotional intelligence, resiliency, and cultural competence gives employees the competencies to move beyond focusing on the problem to finding solutions and seeing results.

In reality, cultural competence is good management adapted for the unprecedented cultural changes in organizations and society.

Chapter 15

The Human Resource Office: The Last Resort

15.1 Introduction

Every manager should have a textbook on human resource management (HRM) or personnel management. The topics covered in the books may seem aimed at employees who work in human resource (HR) offices. In reality, they are also good management techniques that give managers powerful tools.

HR employees are well steeped in the policies and practices of an organization; however, they may be less well versed in the programs and the requirements of managing those programs. When asked to help, it is likely that their approach will stem from the HR policies and not from the requirements of program management. Consequently, a manager who understands HRM is well prepared to have a collaborative relationship with the HR office.

Managers who understand HRM requirements and language have the tools to restructure organizational units in ways that increase organizational effectiveness. Changes in the environment can sometimes require organizational restructuring, which can involve rearranging the job requirements of existing job positions. The restructuring can allocate the job requirements in ways that address any inequities that may have developed over time. For example, technology has the potential to change the current job description of existing required job duties and skills. In such a case, analysis and job reclassification can legitimately be used to alter the job classification to incorporate the new duties, and job reclassifications can result in pay increases.

The manager who understands the HR office's requirements and can explain his or her proposed organizational and program changes in language understood by HR personnel can develop a truly collaborative relationship with the HR office, whose support is crucial for making organizational changes. HR personnel know that the manager understands their need to minimize and prevent personnel actions that can create a liability for the organization. Having the support of the HR office gives a manager a powerful ally.

Many HR offices are also responsible for overseeing relationships with employee unions. It is also important for a manager to have a good working relationship with the president of any union whose members are employees of the organization. Increasingly, union member reflect the growing diversity in the United States, resulting from demographic changes driven by the immigration of the 1980s and legislation that allowed previously undocumented immigrants to become citizens. A relatively new phenomenon, the increased diversity and cultural changes may result in government agencies where, for example, the managers are predominately white but the lower grades and classifications are made up of multicultural and minority employees. The union members in this circumstance may be mostly minority and employees of color.

Issues that arise in the informal social networks about perceived better treatment of white employees by white managers may surface through union grievances. Having good formal and informal working relationships with the union president and union stewards is important in dealing with such grievances.

Example 15.1: Union Grievances Can Be Indicators of Cross-Cultural Tensions

George, a high-level federal manager, related the conversation he had with the union president, Fred. George and Fred had a good working relationship and worked out many issues informally over lunch and coffee. George had employees who had submitted union grievances. George headed a large agency where many of his managers were white and the majority of the lower-ranked employees were employees of color. There were existing tensions among the employees of color and their white co-workers over cultural issues. The grievances were filed over the problems that resulted from the tension and not from any management actions.

George ran into Fred as he was walking down the hallway. George called out to Fred, "Fred, can you give a couple of minutes? There are a couple of issues I want to run by you."

Fred stopped to say, "Sure, what can I do for you?"

"You filed a couple of grievances against us," George complained to Fred. "The issue is that the employees can't get along with one another, and not an unfair management action. Why are you grieving us because your members can't get along?"

Fred looked at George smilingly and said, "First, we can't grieve ourselves, so we're left with grieving you. Second, you might want to take a closer look at the way your employees treat each other. I wish you luck." Fred then turned around and walked away.

Ideally, there should be an ongoing collaborative relationship with the HR office. There are many management and employee issues where human resources can be a helpful. This chapter will focus on how the HR office can be a powerful ally in cross-cultural employee issues. HR personnel should be the first to consult when there is a cross-cultural employee issue or problem. They should also be the last resort when employee problems seem intractable. Having someone from outside the organizational unit as a partner in resolving employee problems can lend gravitas to the situation. Furthermore, employees may see the outside partner as a signal that resolving the problem is in their best interests, since it is no longer an internal matter.

15.2 When to Use Human Resources in Troubleshooting Difficult Issues

Two perspectives govern how human resources can be used to troubleshoot difficult issues. The first perspective takes a traditional approach, characterized by a low degree of cultural competence. The second requires a culturally competent HR office. A government agency's HR office can actually vary between these ends of the continuum.

15.2.1 Traditional Role of the HR Office in Troubleshooting Difficult Issues

HR employees become the last resort when cross-cultural misunderstandings and conflicts result in an employee's being disciplined. The potential for disciplinary action arises under specific circumstances:

1. The situation is proving to be intractable, and a reasonable solution seems unattainable.
2. It is unclear what the actual details are, and the employees have different descriptions of the episode.
3. Emotions are running high.
4. The language used by the employees borders on creating a hostile environment or suggests discrimination.
5. Discussing the problem increases the tension.

The traditional HR office is defined here as one in which personnel are not well versed in cultural competence. The manager in this situation is relying on the traditional role of HR personnel—namely, to ensure due process for employees. Federal and state legislation creates organizational requirements for the treatment of employees, but it is difficult for managers to keep abreast of all the legislation and its application. (For a list of selected federal legislation, see Berman et al. 2010, 46–47.) HR personnel are, however, required to be familiar with the appropriate legislation and organizational policies and practices for the application of the appropriate legislation.

The HR office will have practices that ensure employees have due process. The practices include the types of documentation necessary for due process or any disciplinary action. When an employee is disciplined, he or she has the right to an appeals process. If either of the employees is a union member, he or she will be accompanied by someone from the union during the appeals hearing. In such cases, it is prudent for a manager to have assistance from human resources.

There are several steps in the disciplinary process:

1. The problem is resolved without requiring any disciplinary action.
2. The employee is given a termination notice.
3. An employee is given a verbal warning containing
   a. What the employee has done wrong.
   b. What the employee needs to do to rectify the problem.
   c. How long the employee has to rectify the problem.
   d. The penalty if there is another incident or if the employee does not rectify the problem.
4. An employee is given a written reprimand containing the same information as in the verbal warning.
   a. The manager can file the written reprimand, and if the problem is rectified, the written reprimand is destroyed.
   b. The manager can insert the written reprimand in the employee's personnel file.
5. The employee has the right to appeal any negative action.

One type of assistance that human resources can provide the manager is serving in a monitoring role. HR personnel know the process and can guide the manager in handling a given situation in a procedurally correct manner. They will be knowledgeable in determining the severity of any disciplinary action required for the problem and can assist the manager in correctly documenting the situation to prepare for the appeals process. Thus the disciplinary action will be suitable to the severity of the problem. The HR office employees can also monitor the discussions so that culturally offensive language is avoided.

As an outside observer to the conflict management, human resources brings a fresh perspective to any discussion. Managers and employees who have worked together for any length of time have developed their own ways of relating to each other. The employees' mutual perceptions have evolved from their formal and informal interactions. Someone who is unfamiliar with the employees' perceptions of each other is not constrained by their previous interactions. So, HR personnel may be able to reframe the situation in ways the involved employees cannot. A new perspective can reset the discussions and create an opportunity for a resolution.

As many experienced managers know, it is not uncommon for an organizational unit to develop its own closely knit miniculture where matters are handled informally. This is a dynamic that evolves in the informal organization, as discussed in the Hawthorne studies. The informal web of relationships can create an informal culture of conducting business and resolving problems. Employees rely on their relationships with each other and the supervisor to handle matters internally. This process relies on established relationships that grow over time. The informal process can successfully resolve many issues internally.

Sometimes problems arise when a new employee joins the organizational unit and has not had time to establish secure relationships with the other employees, the supervisor, and managers. When the agency is not very diverse and the new employee is culturally (in the broadest sense) different than the other employees, the employee's diversity frequently becomes a matter of discussion in the informal social networks. Change, regardless of the type, invariably becomes a subject of discussion in the informal organization. Employees may comment on behaviors, dress, different types of food eaten in the break room, and the employee's speaking in a language other than English. The comments can create an environment of social distance and exclusion, especially when the long-time employees are not culturally competent.

When a problem arises between the new and culturally diverse employee and the long-time employees, the co-workers tend to be more supportive of the employees with whom they have long-established relationships. The informal network can pressure the supervisor, who is also a member of the informal network, to support the established employees. If the new employee understands that he or she is right and refuses to acquiesce, an intractable problem develops. An equitable resolution is difficult under such circumstances because of the pressures of the informal organization.

The manager can change the dynamics of the situation by inviting someone from human resources to assist with the problem resolution. It is unlikely that the individual from human resources is part of the closely knit network, and so the employees in conflict realize they cannot rely on the informal rules and agreements that have grown over time. There is now an authoritative outsider who will rely on the formal organizational structure to settle the conflict. The involvement of the HR office adds seriousness to the situation and a sense that a more formal resolution is forthcoming. That sense of organizational seriousness gives both the manager and the HR employee greater leverage in constructing an equitable solution. The manager now has an organizational reason for not respecting the unwritten agreements. The matter is now out of the manager's hands. The long-time employee may now be more receptive to a reasonable solution.

Diversity, driven by retirements and demographics, will continue to increase. As diverse employees continue to enter the workforce, not all long-standing employees will be culturally competent. The likelihood of not having a culturally competent workforce is higher where there has been no concerted effort to develop cultural competence initiatives. Under such conditions, cross-cultural interactions are likely to lead to misunderstandings. The dynamics of equity theory can easily create issues, especially if envy exacerbates the dynamics.

Discussions of diversity usually center on numbers, percentages, and protected classes of employees. The current diversity in the population of the United States is unprecedented. Whites now make up two-thirds of the total U.S. population, a level unseen since European settlers first came into the United States. The high levels of immigration have also seen the emergence of immigrant communities keeping their native languages and customs. People used to living in monocultural communities now see other cultural communities existing alongside their own. As diversity increases in the workplace, the cultural expressions of the new immigrant communities will be manifested in the organization. This cultural change in the community, now reflected in the organization, can be unsettling to some employees. This point, mentioned before, is stressed here to create a context for discussion.

The dynamics of equity theory now exist in a cross-cultural context that can create new sensitivities. Discussing immigration and immigrants negatively in society can lend tacit support for expressing negative social perceptions of anyone from the same country as the immigrants, even if they are citizens. Those perceptions find their way into and are expressed in the workplace. They provide a cultural context for evaluating others. Often, the result is envy and resentment that color the perceptions of equity.

Increasing diversity leads to more culturally diverse employees. There may now be enough employees with similar cultural characteristics, whether race, ethnicity, or sexual orientation, for example, to create an informal organization that may consist of several culturally different groups coexisting with each other. Each group will have its own culturally shaped lens through which to evaluate others' merits and demerits. How fair the resolution of an employee problem is may easily be judged in different ways by the manager and the employees if they come from different cultural groups. Likewise, diverse social groupings can easily look at the resolution of a cross-cultural problem and judge it differently. When, for example, a manager of color decides that the white employee in a conflict is at fault and the other individual, an employee of color, is the aggrieved party, different cultural groups will see the problem differently from each other. The multicultural employees may see the judgment as equitable, whereas the white employees may not. The same dynamics exist if the manager is white and the employee who is punished is an employee of color whereas the aggrieved employee is white. This fragmented view of equity can create new sensitivities for managers and employees.

When the number of diverse employees was small, the role of different cultures in the workplace was not much of an issue. When enough employees who are culturally similar create their own informal group, there is strength and confidence. The employees may feel more comfortable conversing in their native language;

they also gain power in the informal and formal organization through the force of numbers. Cultural differences are now publicly displayed and evident, and so it is extremely easy for any discussion of cultural differences to become racialized and lead to accusations of discrimination and inappropriate behavior. Without cultural competence to bridge the cultural chasm, manager and employees risk falling into the quagmire of unresolved cultural tensions at the bottom of the gorge.

Managers can understand the underlying tensions from observing the cross-cultural relationships while managing by walking around. For some managers, the process means acquiring new sensibilities. Managers can rely on human resources to help ease cross-cultural tensions. First, managers can explain the situation. Then, they can tell why they require assistance from someone culturally similar to the employee being disciplined. The person being disciplined will interact with someone from human resources who may share cultural, racial, gender, or other characteristics. The culturally diverse social groups in the organization will see a manager who is culturally sensitive, and that observation may serve to bring the cultural lenses into similar focus when determining the equity of situation.

Where a strong organizational emphasis on cultural competence is lacking, human resources assumes a more traditional approach. Even within a traditional approach, the HR office can troubleshoot difficult cross-cultural issues by:

1. Monitoring the process to ensure that proper procedures are followed and the proper documentation is created
2. Bringing a new and fresh perspective that can reset a previously difficult and intractable discussion
3. Bringing an outside formal approach to offset the dynamics of a strong informal organization
4. Reshaping the different cultural lenses through which equity is viewed into a congruent perspective

In many organizations, the assistance the HR office can provide a manager is truly underutilized. It must be recognized that HR personnel can guide a manager through many difficult situations.

15.2.2 Using Human Resources to Troubleshoot Difficult Issues in a Culturally Competent Organization

The HR office in a culturally competent organization is a truly superb resource to minimize cross-cultural issues and reduce problems to a bare minimum. Whereas more formal aspects of the role of human resources in cultural competence have been covered in Chapter 10, "Human Resource Management and Cultural Competence," the emphasis here is in using the HR office as an informal partner in minimizing and troubleshooting difficult issues and problems. The culturally competent organization will require employees and managers to attend cultural competence training and have cultural competency performance measures. Managers have an additional tool: administrative discretion. A manager can develop a collaborative relationship with the HR office and use the relationship to minimize cross-cultural problems.

Managers can request an HR officer to present further training to employees. Even when an organization requires all employees and managers to attend cultural competence training, how seriously the employees and managers have actually incorporated the training into their work routine is debatable. Managers can emphasize the importance of cultural competence by inviting HR officers to conduct training for employees. Managers thereby set the stage for creating an environment with few, if any, cross-cultural issues.

Not all employees view cultural competence as necessary and valuable. Increasing diversity can change the power balance among various cultural groups in the informal organization. An emphasis on diversity and cultural competence can increase these tensions. To sidestep the possibility of adding tension, managers can reinforce how important diversity is to creating a high-performance organization. Diversity can contribute to innovation and engender better solutions, but it can also create misunderstandings and tension. High performance results from high-performing employees and teams. So informal training will emphasize helping employees become better performers and helping them learn to solve any organizational issues. The outcome will be employees who are expected to be more innovative and better at resolving issues that invariably arise. In the process, employees will acquire many career-enhancing competencies they can use to fulfill their career aspirations.

The topics covered in employee training are emotional intelligence, resiliency, Problem–Solution–Response (PSR), and the cultural competence model. Through these topics the manager creates an organizational cultural competence template, which can be used as a checklist to handle employee problems. Both emotional intelligence and resiliency emphasize the importance of emotional self-awareness, self-control, and impulse control. The competencies of understanding others—which according to Goleman (2000, 27) is empathy, or an awareness of others' feelings, needs, and concerns—and political awareness, or reading a group's emotional currents and power relationships, provide the skills to ameliorate and move beyond any intense emotional state. Leveraging diversity, which is also an aspect of empathy (Goleman 2000, 27), provides the transition to the cultural competence model. Employees now understand how to move beyond any emotional reaction to an issue or problem. The HR office now provides instruction on the PSR approach to problem resolution. Examples from *Cultural Competence for Public Managers* or from the actual experiences of the employees and managers can be used to further illustrate the application of these competencies.

Managers who use their administrative discretion and informal relationship with the HR office to provide employees with additional training create the framework for minimizing employee problems, especially problems involving cross-cultural issues. Managers can work together with HR personnel to explain the emerging process for developing employee performance suitable for a high-performance organization and the process for problem resolution. Emotional competence and employee resiliency are career-building competencies, which they now possess. The framework for resolving problems that employees bring to a supervisor will encompass answering the following questions:

1. How is the employee demonstrating emotional self-awareness?
2. How is the employee demonstrating empathy by understanding others?
3. How is the employee using the cultural competence model to understand the dynamics of the situation?
4. How accurate (causal analysis as a factor in resiliency) is the employee in determining the problem's parameters, which also serve to describe the problem in the PSR model?
5. What solutions have the employees developed by working together?
6. How will the solutions result in better working relationships and more effective work teams?

The manager and the HR officer working collaboratively have created an explicit framework for developing high-performance employees with the competencies to solve their own problems. Having to answer the questions lets the employees know that complaining about a problem and expecting the supervisor to rule in their favor is no longer the modus operandi. The framework puts the employees on notice that they have the responsibility not to create cross-cultural or any other organizational problems without explaining how they intend to resolve the conflict. Answering the questions is an informal and yet a very powerful form of performance appraisal. Answering the questions is an assessment of the emotional intelligence, resiliency, and cultural competencies of the employee. The manager can follow through by acknowledging the problem-solving competencies of the employee in the formal employee performance appraisal.

The framework should serve to minimize difficult employee issues. But there is always the possibility that being human, employees will create a difficult situation that cannot be handled using this framework. Employees will sometimes do something that defies rational explanation and may arise from a situation at work, an unknown pressure from the employee's personal life, or sometimes just because they can. If this happens, the HR office, in its more traditional role in handling employee sanctions, can come into play, as noted in the earlier section of this chapter.

15.3 Setting the Stage for Using Human Resources as an Impartial Mediator

Many managers are accustomed to handling issues internally without assistance from the HR office. For many issues, this approach works well. The HR office may be involved in these situations only if the employee appeals the decision.

Cross-cultural issues add an additional layer of complexity, however. In the traditional sense, human resources can be an impartial mediator because it is from outside the immediate work unit. HR personnel do not have a vested interest in a preconceived outcome. They can thus be an added resource in dealing with problems arising out of cross-cultural misunderstandings.

Managers can collaborate with the HR office to create a cross-cultural sense of impartiality. Employees view their manager's interactions with them through a cultural lens. A manager who spends more time with employees who are culturally similar may do so as just a way to get work done. Employees who are culturally different from the manager may interpret the manager's behavior otherwise, however, seeing it as favoring certain employees—those who culturally resemble the manager. There could well be work-related reasons for the increased time spent with similar employees. The perception that the manager favors and supports those who are similar will persist and be reinforced in the employees' informal discussions.

Two culturally diverse employees can easily have a misunderstanding that leads to a conflict in which each claims to be the aggrieved party. The manager who intervenes may see simply two employees having problems. Yet one of the aggrieved parties may see that the manager and the employee with whom she is having a problem are culturally similar. Unsure that she will be treated impartially and just to overcome the perceived partiality, she may become more insistent that the problem really is the other employee. Understanding the cultural context of such a situation allows a manager to use the HR office in a way that conveys a traditional as well as a cultural sense of impartiality. The manager can use an understanding of cultural context to determine the way to interact with employees to create a more culturally balanced perception.

Most of the work on cross-cultural employee problems frames the problem-solving process in terms of better cross-cultural communications. Knowing how to communicate cross-culturally is important, and several examples are included in this book. Culturally competent communication among the employees involved is important. It is just as important to understand the way that employees communicate with each other.

Many cross-cultural problems are rooted in the cultural context of relationships in the informal system. Today, much of the communication among employees is through e-mail, for example. Employees tend to put less thought into writing an e-mail than in writing more formal communications such as letters or memos. One limitation of communicating through e-mails, though, is that the sender cannot observe the reaction of the person reading the memo. In face-to-face communications, one can see the other person's reaction and compensate if the reaction is negative. That interplay is not possible when communicating through e-mails.

A further problem is that the same words may have different connotations in different cultures. Communication, verbal and written, also carries a tone, which gives an additional context to the words. Tone can convey an attitude of respect, sarcasm, dismissal, superiority, and so on. Employees can be very sensitive to the underlying tone in the communication. Yet it is easy for someone writing an e-mail to forget that tone is also conveyed in the message. A message that is curt, because the employee wrote it in a hurry, may be perceived by the employee as insulting. The employee may not have intended an insult and may be horrified to learn that the tone could be interpreted as offensive. Communications across cultural lines require sensitivity, especially in organizations with an underlying cross-cultural tension.

Most people are more comfortable communicating with others who are culturally similar. This is understandable because they are used to the same cultural communication cues. Awkwardness in cross-cultural communications can be inadvertently communicated in an e-mail or conversation.

Example 15.2: Cross-Cultural Miscommunication

Two employees, Raquel and Onuka, who are culturally different, may be working together on a project. Because of their cultural differences, each feels awkward talking informally to the other. The two have no strong informal relationship, and their interactions and communication are limited to the requirements of the formal organization. Onuka is supposed to do a statistical analysis and give the results to Raquel so she can incorporate the analysis into her portion of the report. Raquel thought they had agreed on the date Onuka was to give her the analysis. She awaits delivery.

The due date arrives and passes, however. Raquel sends an e-mail to Onuka saying, "Onuka, you promised me your analysis, yesterday. You're late with your analysis, and you're going to make me late with my report. Raquel."

Onuka reads the e-mail and reacts to the tone by thinking, "She doesn't like me because I'm African, and she wants to blame me for her problems." He responds, "You just want to blame me for your problems. I didn't say I was going to give you the analysis yesterday."

Raquel reads the e-mail and thinks, "He doesn't like me because I'm a woman, and he isn't comfortable working with women. He wants me to look bad." She then fires an angry retort in response. A chain of angry communications has just begun that ends up with both in their supervisor's office angrily blaming each other. Their supervisor has not been aware that any of this has been going on.

This scenario involves many elements of a cross-cultural problem that may be very difficult to resolve. The problem crosses racial and gender lines because of the perception that the problem has to do with race and gender, and the resolution could ensnare the supervisor as favoring one over the other. Both employees are highly angry; they are upset and feeling quite righteous. Whatever the gender of the supervisor, one of the employees will see that the supervisor is of the same gender as the other employee and may therefore favor that employee. Also, if one employee perceives that the supervisor has spent more time with the other employee, that time spent may become a factor. The impartiality of the supervisor can now easily come into question. Keeping in mind these possible perceptions, the supervisor can say to the employees, "This a complicated issue, and I am having trouble understanding it very well. I am going to ask human resources to send someone to help us resolve this. This way, someone from the outside who is impartial can help in resolving this issue. In the meantime, I don't want either of you communicating with each other. If you need something, see me."

The numerous and diverse cultures and cultural characteristics that now exist in any given organization and the country as a whole are creating a need for new perspectives and sensitivities in what were once firmly established but narrow views. Asking, "Can the supervisor be impartial in resolving the problem in the example?" is framing the wrong question. A better question to ask is, "How does the supervisor use organizational resources so that each employee can see impartiality in the process?" Whereas the first question makes sense in a monocultural context, the second question is framed in the context of diverse cultural perceptions in the workplace. In many organizations, a monocultural workplace is quickly evolving into a multicultural workplace.

Supervisors can ask the HR office associate to help create a sense of impartiality in the cultural context of the situation. Cultural balance can restore a sense of balance to the problematic situation. Each of the aggrieved employees can see someone with at least one cultural similarity. Culture in this sense includes race or ethnicity, gender, sexual orientation, and social class.

At a university in the Southwest, a white female faculty member from a major northeastern university was conducting a workshop on mentoring students with their research projects. The workshops were funded by a federal grant that provides assistance to minority students. In attendance were 20 faculty members from the local university. Five of the professors were white, and the other 15 professors were very diverse. There were professors from China, South Korea, India, Pakistan, Peru, Ecuador, and Mexico. There were also Mexican American professors. The various races and ethnicities were fairly evenly distributed throughout the room. The training included several role-playing exercises, which the visiting professor would conduct by pulling her chair close to one of the professors and then role-playing a situation. Over the course of the training day, the faculty of color noticed that she approached only faculty who were white, even when a professor of color was closer. This was noted, and among themselves the faculty of color discussed her behavior during their coffee breaks, when no white colleagues were nearby.

Actions, interactions, decisions, and delegation of assignments may have one interpretation in a monocultural organization. In an organization where several cultures coexist, however, there will be differences in the interpretation of any managerial action. Employees of color will rarely if ever mention their perceptions to a manager who is culturally different. This omission easily creates a blind spot for the manager. Communicating such perceptions will be a new competency for managers, and for many managers it will not be competency that happens naturally.

Emotional intelligence can be adapted to include cultural competence. It starts with acknowledging that employees will use a cultural lens to view the manager's interactions with employees. Goleman (2000, 26–27) divides emotional intelligence into two broad categories, personal competence and social competence. He defines personal competence as the competencies that determine how we manage ourselves. Social competence is defined as how we handle relationships. Emotional intelligence competencies used in a culturally competent context give a manager the tools for personal change and the tools to improve organizational cross-cultural relations.

Under personal competence, the emotional intelligence competencies that can help a manager convey a sense of cross-cultural impartiality are emotional awareness, adaptability, and initiative. Managers can use initiative for self-reflection to ponder whether their interactions with employees are culturally balanced. They can use emotional awareness to determine the cultural effects of their actions and to consider how those actions will affect the emotions of their employees. Adaptability is the willingness to make changes. Seeing their interactions with employees through a cultural lens, managers use empathy to see how their actions may be perceived and if necessary to change the way they interact with employees.

Goleman (2000) classifies empathy, the awareness of others' feelings and perspectives, to group several emotional competencies. His second broad classification under social competence is social skills, that is, being adept at creating desirable responses in others. In the category of social skills are influence, change catalyst, and collaboration, which are helpful for creating a sense of organizational impartiality in collaboration with the HR office.

By being change catalysts, managers initiate or manage changes. Managers can balance their interactions with employees to reflect their organization's cultural diversity. They can be more culturally balanced in publicly recognizing the accomplishments of employees. Regardless of cultural background, each employee should see someone who is culturally similar being given public recognition. Publicly recognizing the accomplishments of employees in a way that includes all the diverse cultural groups can have a secondary effect of increasing cross-cultural relationships in the informal organization.

The way a manager interacts with employees affects the relationships of that individual with others. Using emotional intelligence in a culturally competent manner gives managers a powerful tool to rebalance cross-cultural employee relationships. By first rebalancing their cross-cultural relationships with employees, managers set the stage for using the HR office as an impartial mediator. Managers can use the diversity in human resources to create a cross-cultural balance in their role as impartial mediator. The aggrieved employees can feel more relaxed seeing someone who is culturally similar across the table. Having a culturally similar person from the HR office serve as an impartial mediator enhances the sense of organizational cultural balance. Working together in this cross-cultural environment makes it easier to get to the real issue and to move beyond it.

15.4 Using Human Resources as an Early Warning System

The HR office touches the lives of every employee in the organization. In its organizational role, human resources is the only part of the organization that can track the cultural evolution of the organization. It collects extensive data on the demographics of the employees and their effectiveness. Understanding changing trends and the implications of the changes allows the department to flag potential issues the changes may create. Appropriate training programs can be developed to address possible problems.

Many books on human resources do not address cultural competence and managing diversity. The topics they cover are related to affirmative action and equal employment opportunity, discrimination laws, hostile environments, sexual harassment, and employee sanction and appeal processes. It can be helpful to human resources as well as managers to have an early warning system in place. The HR office has the tools to track the changing diversity of the organization. With an understanding of the new dynamics that diversity creates in the organization, the HR office can guide top managers in successfully becoming culturally competent.

Most HR offices have diversity information in their HRM information systems. Diversity data, if organized by departments and organizational units, show the distribution of cultural diversity. HR offices can perform additional analysis on existing data to obtain useful cultural information, which can help human resources contribute to creating a more culturally competent organization. Understanding how increasing diversity can change the cultural dynamics of an organization and employee relationships can guide the HR office in developing an early warning system. Some of the information that human resources can provide may be obtained by answering the following questions:

1. How diverse is the community the organization serves, and has the diversity been changing rapidly?
2. What is the current diversity in the organization?
3. Are there clusters of diversity, with some organizational units less diverse than others?
4. What percentages of current employees are retirement-eligible in the next 10 years?
5. Are the retirement-eligible employees culturally diverse, or are they mainly from one racial or ethnic group?
6. Are the retirement-eligible employees balanced in terms of gender, or are most of the retirement-eligible employees of one gender?
7. Over the last five years, has the applicant pool been growing more diverse (see data gathered for compliance with affirmative action or equal employment opportunity laws)?
   a. Does the diversity of the applicant pools—that is, the race, ethnicity, or gender—reflect the community the organization serves?

8. Is diversity evenly distributed hierarchically throughout the organization, or are the multicultural employees mostly on the lower rungs of the organization's career ladder?

Given that rapid demographic and cultural changes have been a recent occurrence and have accelerated over the last 30 years, it is understandable that organizations may reflect the great diversity that exists in the community they serve. Organizations increase diversity through filling employee vacancies. There may, however, be insufficient employee retirements and turnover to create the opportunity to increase diversity to more accurately reflect the community. The HR office should interpret employee data in the context of the cultural changes happening in the community its organization serves.

The federal government draws employees from the entire country and has the entire country to attract a diverse applicant pool. States and local governments are experiencing cultural changes at different rates. Some states such as Vermont have very little diversity. Other states such as Texas have become no-majority states, and other states are quickly approaching that crossing point. Some are experiencing a rapid increase in diversity but the diversity is clustered only in small areas of the state with industries that attract immigrant and minority communities. The rest of the state can still be mainly monocultural. The changing demographics are not evenly distributed but are clustered throughout the United States.

Although some communities are experiencing extremely rapid growth in immigrant and minority communities, local government employee turnover rates are not high enough to have the governing body reflect the changing community. As the composition of communities rapidly changes across racial and ethnic lines, however, potential conflicts are created as the new residents want to take their place in local governments.

To be useful as an early warning system, diversity information must be understood in relation to the community served. If the diversity of the community has been stable for several years and the projections show little likelihood of growth, then rapid cultural change will also be unlikely. If, however, the community has been experiencing great and rapid changes in the diversity of its residents, it is only a matter of time that new and diverse members of the community will want local government to address their needs in the same way it addresses the needs of other residents.

Delivering services in a culturally competent manner (described in Chapter 12, "Cultural Competence in Health Care") will almost certainly require hiring employees from among the new residents, because they will understand the cultural requirements of their communities. Residents of these immigrant and minority communities who become the employees will most likely not only understand the culture but also know the language of the new communities. Employees from different cultural backgrounds are now government employees, for example, and the new employees bring with them new cultural characteristics. Through their diverse backgrounds, they create changes in the informal and social networks of the organization. But because the changes are happening rapidly, not all employees are culturally competent; inevitably, cross-cultural issues emerge and have to be resolved. The way the cross-cultural problems are resolved can ameliorate or exacerbate cross-cultural tensions. The HR office is in a position to propose and develop cultural competence training for the employees. Information here can be used to create the cultural competence training to forestall and minimize cross-cultural issues.

The HR office can use the data it gathers on recruitment and retirement to enable the organization to reflect the diversity of the community it serves. First, a profile of the organization's current diversity can be matched against the diversity in the community. The probability is high that any large mismatches will become an issue in the future. So to avoid possible issues, human resources can begin developing recruiting plans to adjust the organization's diversity to align it with the community's diversity. It can also alert the top executives to the political implications of the gaps. Second, the data on employees who are retirement-eligible provide the HR office with information to develop recruitment plans. Analyzing the retirement-eligible data in terms of racial, ethnic, and gender differences provides a profile of possible changes in diversity. If the employees who can retire are predominately white and the applicant pools are becoming more diverse, the organization may be reflecting societal demographic changes. By examining the rate of change, the HR office can determine the probability of future cross-cultural problems within the organization. Major changes happening quickly give employees less time to adjust to the changes, and thus the possibility of cross-cultural problems increases. Human resources can use this information to predict the need for cultural competency training and to have processes in place to resolve cross-cultural problems.

The distribution of diversity inside the organization can provide a useful gauge of the cultural dynamics of an organization. In an organization with diverse and multicultural employees heavily grouped in organizational clusters may have different dynamics than an organization where distribution is more even. In one organization, for example, the information technology (IT) department employees were almost all of Indian background. Some individuals were immigrants from India, and some were children of immigrants. The director originally came to the United States from India on an H1-B visa and then became a legal resident. He was now a U.S. citizen. The talk in the informal and social networks of the informal organization was that he would not hire people unless they were from India. There was no easy way to determine the veracity of the perceptions of the other employees, but the perceptions were a topic of conversation reinforced whenever the other employees talked about information technology.

It is also not uncommon, for instance, for employees of color to express the same sentiments about an organizational unit without diversity. Some of the typical comments are "They don't like minorities over there" and "Don't even think about applying for a position there; they don't hire minorities." Whether what they say is true is very difficult to determine, but cultural perceptions are treated as reality.

Clusters of diversity provide a sharp cultural contrast that is noticed and discussed by employees in their informal conversations. Each group creates its own cultural interpretation of the actions of the managers and employees; whether the actions involve promotions, employee awards, employee recognition, or employee discipline, they can each be seen in a different light through each cultural lens.

Because the large increase in diversity has been a relatively recent phenomenon, it may not be too unusual for multicultural employees to be clustered in the lower ranks of the organization. Organizations located in communities with sizable immigrant communities may have members of those communities overrepresented in clerical and janitorial positions and underrepresented in the professional and managerial ranks. Universities located in cities with large and growing migrant and minority communities, for example, may have most of the physical plant, janitorial jobs, and clerical positions staffed by members of these groups.

An individual walking around university campuses will see the clusters of multicultural employees. A closer look will likely reveal that the employees are speaking the language of their countries of origin and relate to each other in their own culturally determined way. New minicultures are emerging and thriving in the organizational culture. Formal interactions between the multicultural employees and the less-diverse employees are usually polite but constrained. Conversations of employees within their own cultural group are free ranging, with more conversations of their perceived inequities. Social-class differences add another layer of complexity to the dynamics.

Example 15.3: Cross-Cultural and Social Class Miscommunication

Rex, a white professor, works in a university located in a city with a large immigrant population. Many of the lower-ranked university staff are from the immigrant community. There are enough of them at the university to have recreated their own culture within the organization. They have a strong social network within the formal organization, though many of their supervisors are white. Rex has just left the office of Connie, who is white and the department chair. He has spent 20 minutes complaining about a printing project he needs. Rex explains that when he went to the print shop, the employees (from the immigrant community) told him it could not be done.

Connie is puzzled. What Rex wants done is not difficult, and the print shop should be fully capable of doing what he wants. Connie walks to the department's secretary, Nadia, who is from the immigrant community and knows the staff at the print shop. Over the last year, Connie and Nadia have established a very comfortable cross-cultural ground resulting in very good working relationship. Connie relays Rex's complaint to Nadia, and then she says: "You know the staff at the print shop. They do a lot work for us. They should be able to do what he wants. What's going on?"

Nadia looks up at Connie, who is standing, and replies, "Rex gets very arrogant with us, and he always uses a demeaning tone when he talks to us." Then, with a small smile she continues, "We know he thinks we are all dumb and can't do anything. So when he wants something, they will look at him and politely tell him that it can't be done and they don't know how to do what he wants. After he walks out, they'll look at each other and laugh."

Connie just shakes her head and asks Nadia, "How do we fix this?"

"Easy," Nadia replies. "Let me take his printing requests over to them, and don't let him talk to anybody over there. He'll ruin it for all of us."

"Thanks! What would I do without you?" Connie says. She then walks over to Rex's office and tells him: "I've been thinking about what you told me, and I realize how important your research is. You shouldn't waste your time going over to print shop. Tell me what you want, and I'll see that it gets done."

Rex sighs and tells Connie, "Thanks for helping."

One may see the problem as developing across either cultural or social-class lines. A case can be made for either. The dynamics are similar for both. One only needs to observe the interactions between professionals and the blue-collar staff who come in to repair something in the office.

Similar to the dynamics in many communities, new cultures begin appearing in what were once monocultural communities. Those people who are observant will see the beginnings of the change. Others will not notice until there are shops and restaurants communicating in a new language and selling items and foods they do not recognize. By this time, the immigrant community may have defined borders. The original residents will now encounter the new residents throughout the community. Numbers have given the immigrants strength, and so the newly resident may become more outspoken. As invariably happens, some individuals will relish and truly enjoy the new experiences that diversity creates. Others will feel uncomfortable and find themselves embroiled in cross-cultural misunderstandings and conflict. The same process happens in organizations.

Understanding the cultural changes that accompany the growth of diversity prepares the HR office to act as an early warning system. Answering the eight questions identified earlier lets human resources know where in this cultural transition the organization currently resides. Having that knowledge allows human resources to help create a culturally competent organization by developing new diversity policies, rewriting old diversity policies, developing cultural competence training, and anticipating possible cross-cultural issues. By monitoring the changes diversity creates, the HR office has the systems in place to be the early warning system.

15.5 Establishing a Long-Term Relationship with Human Resources

Interestingly enough, one of the best ways to establish a long-term relationship with HR personnel is to treat the HR office as if were a different culture. For many managers who are unfamiliar with the role of human resources, the HR office is indeed a foreign culture with a different language. Many managers see the office as an impediment to doing what they need. They know who they want to hire, so why does human resources demand all this extra paperwork that only adds another to-do item for their already overfilled list? Why can't they just let him hire the best person and leave him alone?

The HR office's contribution to this relationship is that not many of its employees are familiar with the work of the program managers. The conversations between a program manager and an HR employee tends to be one where the employee tells the program manager what process will be used and what documentation is necessary. Rarely will the HR person spend time asking about the work and how it contributes to the organizational mission. The same cross-cultural dynamics occur as if the interaction were happening across cross-cultural lines. The cultural differences now mean different organizational perspectives and technical knowledge.

Managers can now apply the same cultural competencies across different departments just as successfully as across racial and ethnic cultures. Managers begin by having respect for and an understanding of the HR office and its role in the organization. Just as in learning about other cultures, a class about human resources is immensely helpful and becomes a handy management tool. The next best method is to acquire and read a book on human resources. Having read the book (or at least portions of it), managers can find out if someone at the HR office is willing to help them learn more about human resources and the way it can help them become more effective. As one does in being culturally competent, managers are communicating inclusion and "we are part of team."

Managers start with formally scheduled meetings. They can schedule meetings with HR employees responsible for recruitment and selection, hiring, position analysis, disciplinary actions, health and safety, benefits, and training and development. As the relationship develops and managers begin having more social conversations with the employees from human resources, the managers can invite them to lunch or for coffee. The formal relationships is now morphing into a relationship that is part of the informal network, and those social networks open avenues of new support for managers.

As managers encounter situations where the HR office can be helpful, they call for advice on handling the particular situations. They have now developed a collaborative relationship and common ground with the HR office as a member of the team. Now when any misunderstandings happen with the office, managers have common ground from which to resolve the problems and move beyond the issues. Program managers and HR personnel will not always see the situation from the same perspective and misunderstandings will happen.

Being part of the informal network that includes HR employees allows managers to understand the different organizational cultural lens through which the HR office views organizational dynamics. Thereby managers are developing different sources that can make them more successful. The informal culture is the place to explore new approaches. The relationships forged in the informal organization can change the response from "This is the only way we can do this, we can't do it that way," in answer to a formal request, into "Wow, we haven't done that before. There must be a way to get that done. Let me check and give you a call," in answer to an informal request.

Developing a long-term relationship with personnel in human resources does take time. A manager may ask, "Where am I going to get the time to do this?" This is a legitimate question for which the marshmallow example (do you want one marshmallow now or two in an hour?) provides an answer. Investing the time now will have a greater payoff in the future with many more marshmallows.

15.6 Summary and Conclusion

The HR office can be used as a last resort in resolving difficult employee issues—in those rare situations, for example, where employees are so highly upset that they remain unwilling to accept a solution and it is not clear who is really at fault or what the real issue is. Human resources can serve as the last resort in its traditional role as an outsider without a vested interest in either employee.

In a Zen-like way, the HR office is best utilized as a last resort by being the first resort. Emotional intelligence and resiliency show managers and employees how to get beyond the emotional state. Emotional intelligence and the seven factors of resiliency combined with the cultural competence model give managers the tools to resolve seemingly intractable cross-cultural employee problems more effectively.

Most problem-solving techniques and processes are based on a using a rational approach. The rational side of the brain is not always easily accessible when an employee is very upset and highly emotional. Cultural competence shows a manager how cross-cultural issues develop across cultural sensitivities that do not exist in monocultural situations. Cultural competence creates a cultural context for emotional intelligence and resiliency. The combination of the three—that is, of cultural competence, emotional intelligence, and resiliency—can be seen as an emerging new intelligence as the country becomes more multicultural.

Having used cultural competence, emotional intelligence, and resiliency to move beyond the highly charged emotional state, the employees can now use a more rational approach such as Problem–Solution–Results (PSR). The employees having a problem or issue now also have the responsibility to develop a solution that results in better working relationships and a more effective work team.

As a first resort, human resources can provide training on cultural competence, emotional intelligence, resiliency, and PSR. It can explain the six questions that are now the new process for resolving employee issues. Managers reinforce the new process and communicate that bringing in problems to be settled is not enough. Employees will now be responsible for crafting the solution as well. Having that expectation may lead employees to resolve their problems informally; consequently, the manager may see many fewer problems requiring involving the HR office as the last resort.

Using the HR office as a truly impartial mediator requires reexamining the meaning of being impartial. Simply being an outsider without a vested interest in any of the employees may, in many situations, be an indicator of being impartial. Increasing multicultural diversity brings with it new cultural lenses through which we may see many previously accepted concepts in a new light and not necessarily as the same picture. Managers may spend more time with employees culturally similar to them because in doing so they feel comfortable. Yet their doing that will be noticed by and commented on by the employees who are culturally different. Two employees can have an issue wherein one employee is culturally similar to the manager and the other employee is culturally different. These employees can have different perceptions of the manager's ability to be impartial. Here, the manager can best use the HR office to balance the cultural characteristics of the employees. Each employee can see someone across the table who resembles him or her.

Understanding that by its very nature diversity also changes the cultures in the organization, especially the informal culture, which influences the formal culture, allows the HR office to use the employee data it collects to trace the cultural changes happening in the organization. This early warning system can help the organization develop the policies and training programs to have the organization become more culturally competent.

Cultural competence can be used to develop a long-term relationship with human resources. The relationship a manager develops with the HR office brings on board a powerful and helpful team member who can make a manager more successful. Developing this relationship is an investment with a long-term payoff.

WHERE DO WE GO FROM HERE?

Chapter 16

What the Future Holds: More Change

Necessity is the mother of all inventions.

Author unknown, though ascribed to Plato

16.1 Introduction

The United States is still projected to become a no racial/ethnic majority nation sometime between 2040 and 2050 (Ortman and Guarneri 2009). A report by the Pew Hispanic Center on the 2010 census (Passel, Cohn, and Lopez 2011) shows that racial and ethnic minorities accounted for 91.7% of the population growth from 2000 to 2010, Hispanics accounted for 56%, and non-Hispanic whites accounted for 8.3% (see Table 16.1).

One out of every three people in the United States is nonwhite. The same Pew report lists these states as having the largest Hispanic population growth: South Carolina, Alabama, Tennessee, Kentucky, Arkansas, and North Carolina (Passel, Cohn, and Lopez 2011, 2). An indicator of the changes to come is also contained in this report; in 2010, 23.1% of all children age 17 and under are Hispanic (p. 1). These children are making their way through the K–12 school system and will soon be ready to enroll in colleges and universities and then into the workforce. The oldest of the 78 million baby boomers is 65 in 2011 and eligible for Medicare. Because the baby boom is an 18 year phenomenon, all baby boomers should be at least 65 by the end of 2029. One can see in these figures that as the baby boomers retire, their replacements will be employees of color.

Table 16.1 Percentage of U.S. Population by Race and Ethnicity, 2000 and 2010

	2000	2010
Whites	69.1%	63.7%
Hispanics	12.5	16.3
Blacks	12.1	12.2
Asian	3.6	4.7

Source: Data from Passel, J. S., D. Cohn, and M. H. Lopez, *Census 2010: 50 Million Latinos–Hispanics Account for More Than Half of Nation's Growth in Past Decade*, Pew Hispanic Center, Washington, DC, http://pewhispanic.org/files/reports/140.pdf, 2011.

A story in a local paper shows the changing face of the United States. "This Is Our Home Now: Country's Changing Face Emerges in America's Heartland" (Klepper 2010) describes the changes to Garden City, Kansas. Garden City is a meatpacking center with a population of 28,000. The immigrants there are Hispanic, Burmese, and Somali. Klepper describes the town as a Norman Rockwell Main Street, decorated with Fourth of July banners, that also has a Buddhist temple and Mexican grocery stores. Women in *burkas* walk down the street.

The changing face of the community has sparked discussions about assimilation versus multiculturalism as the residents try to adapt to the cultural changes. Klepper sees immigration as one of the reasons for the demographic shift. He sees Arizona legislation, as well as similar legislation being passed in other states and communities, as a reaction to the demographic changes. Klepper quotes the former mayor, Nancy Harness, as saying that the communities that still look as they did in the 1950s and 1960s are dying and that the immigrants are bringing new blood and children.

Cultural diversity has been driven by immigration and the high birthrates of some minority communities. Many cities and towns already include immigrant communities that could easily be mistaken for a community in their country of origin. Some school districts have many students with limited English proficiency. The school districts need teachers proficient in the new students' first languages. School districts in large cities may require teachers who know several different languages. The children live in communities with different cultures and their parents may not speak English or understand the requirements of the U.S. school system. The school districts may require additional staff who knows the language and customs of the immigrant communities to communicate with the students' parents.

When residents of the diverse communities call a government office, they may be asked to choose which language they want to use. When they turn on their television, they may see several channels where the programming is entirely in the language of their immigrant community and the shows reflect their culture. When shopping, they will hear people speaking in languages other than English and they will see items and foods they have never seen before. Diversity is no longer a concept. It is a personal experience that for many people occurs on a daily basis. The way diversity is changing is evident every day. The neighborhood and city look different. The reality that the United States has changed and will continue changing hits home every day. This situation is analogous to a person traveling to a foreign country where he does not know the language or the customs. He is expecting someone to guide him in this new and unfamiliar environment. The guide does not show up, however. Everything he sees is strange and unfamiliar. He begins to feel distressed as his anxiety intensifies.

In many communities, the foreign country has come to their city and neighborhood. Many people are seeing their community being transformed into a culture with which they are unfamiliar. They see the new community growing, and the residents' cultural customs are reflected in their language, stores, and restaurants. As the new communities grow, their economic and political power also increases as they take their place in society. The older residents may not be comfortable visiting the new immigrant community as they see what they consider their own space diminishing as the new cultural communities grow and expand.

Similar scenarios are being replicated across the United States in many communities that had been formerly monocultural.

In response, the media and the Internet have created channels of communication for people uncomfortable with these cultural changes and who want a common forum for their opinions. Their language is at times strident and ugly. The societal debate will likely flow into the school system, universities, and private and public sector organizations. The changes will occur in the center of the societal debate. Successes will likely be uneven. We are in a transitional period where the forces driving the change are growing and strengthening, and the forces opposing the changes are aging and their proportional advantage is decreasing. Transitional periods are usually characterized by the changing dynamics of these opposing forces. The United States is in the transitional period before the tipping point of minority births outnumbering white births. The crossing point where the country becomes a no-majority country is still 30–40 years away. Eventually a new equilibrium is reached, but that can be of little comfort to managers trying to manage diversity in the midst of a contentious debate.

A few months before the 2010 congressional elections, the U.S. Department of Labor issued regulations ordering businesses to extend rights to gay employees under the Family and Medical Leave Act, which previously included only heterosexual couples. This regulation is another small victory for gays in their battle for more equitable rights in the workplace and society. President Obama signed the repeal of the "Don't ask, don't tell" policy in December 2010. Opponents of the repeal predicted that up to 260,000 troops would leave the service (Burns and Krehely 2011). Implementation seems to be proceeding smoothly and even the anticipated resistance from the Marine Corps has been muted. The facts on the Servicemembers Legal Defense Network (SLDN; n.d.) Web site indicate that 92%

of service members responding to surveys said that serving with a gay coworker would be neutral to very good in terms of their ability to work together. The SLDN also sees that the younger generation of service members understand that sexual orientation has nothing to do with job performance.

Diversity, which includes race and ethnicity, gender, sexual orientation, and social class, is changing the culture in the United States in ways that have not been seen before. One commonality for many of the cultural changes is the discussion between those who want the country to remain the way it has always been and those who welcome the changes. Much of the media focus is on the more extreme positions. The media focus and the Internet have allowed many to rally around the discussion on the ends of the continuum. On one end of the discussion one can hear, "I want my America back!" On the other end one can hear, "No one is illegal." There is a similar discussion of sexual orientation.

The media coverage and the ability of the Internet have created rallies where like-minded people can express their views and hear others who agree. In any year there is a congressional election, these rallies attract candidates for office who want to convince them they share their views. In their quest to show the audiences how strongly the candidates support their position, they may make statements that can be considered as extreme by some. On June 15, 2010, CBS News reported that a congressional candidate from a southwestern state suggested that the United States could place land mines along the Mexican border to secure the international boundary. He later backtracked on the comments. This is not an isolated incident. As the tone of the societal debate intensifies and the tone sharpens, it becomes easier for extreme statements to be made in the heat of the moment. Elections can easily politicize societal debates and make congressional action more difficult.

The cultural changes created by diversity are being discussed in sometimes sharp and acrimonious societal debate. Race and ethnicity, gender, sexual orientation, and social classes are topics that are not always easy to discuss in a quiet and dispassionate manner. These have always been awkward and difficult topics to discuss. Common ground and understanding are difficult to find if people shy away from discussing these topics intelligently.

Studies of emotional intelligence have shown the existence and importance of understanding emotions and found that the way we manage our emotions affects how we manage ourselves and determines how we handle relationships with other people. Diversity and cultural competence highlight the need for a diversity consciousness and cultural intelligence.

16.2 What Tomorrow Will Look Like

In 2011, the United States is approaching or already at the tipping point for many cultural changes. In 2009, women were on the verge of becoming the majority of the labor force as they held 49.8% of the nation's jobs (Cauchon 2009). A

U.S. Department of Labor (DOL) report, *Women in the Labor Force: A Databook 2010* (Solis and Hall 2010), shows "women accounted for 51 percent of all people employed in management, professional, and related occupations" (p. 1). The DOL report also shows that in 2008, 27% of married women earned more than their husbands. Minority births are projected to be over 50% in 2010 (Yen 2010). As these children become school age, minorities will be become the majority in the school system. This trend will flow into the universities and the workforce. Communities, cities, states, and the country as a whole will have no majority. The heart of the citizens of the United States, as embedded in the U.S. Constitution, is not changing. The face of those citizens, what they look like, most definitely is changing.

It is highly likely that the gay and lesbian community will continue to acquire the same rights as the heterosexual community. It is also likely that each step will happen in the maelstrom of contentious debate about the gains.

The rivulets of change are becoming a torrent that will create a tsunami of cultural change. We are in the transitional period as the torrents create changes in the cultural landscape. In the same way that torrents gouge out new channels in the landscape, the cultural torrents are gouging and reshaping the landscape. The cultural torrents are reshaping the cultural landscapes in the same way that rushing water recreates the landscape in a battleground between the force of the water and the resistance of the rocks softened by the dirt in which they are embedded.

The role of immigration in changing the face of the United States is becoming the focal point in stopping or slowing down the cultural change. The legislation in Arizona, S.B. 1070, which hopes to make it easier to determine who is in the United States legally and to deport those individuals without documentation, is being considered by other states and communities. The emphasis of the legislation is on undocumented immigration. Other legislation points at the discomfort some find in the changing face of the United States. Legislation has passed that outlaws ethnic studies whose aim is to educate students about the cultural roots, heritage, and accomplishments of diverse peoples. With similar aims, women's studies wants women of accomplishment highlighted in what had been the primary domain of male accomplishments. There are those who would like Arizona to pass legislation denying U.S. citizenship to babies born in the United States even when citizenship is guaranteed by the Fourteenth Amendment.

Cindy Barks and Paula Rhoden report in their column in the *Prescott Daily Courier* (June 2, 2010) of the controversy created when a mural showing children of several races was being painted at Miller Valley Elementary School. The artists used pictures of actual students. The artists reported that they received many comments during the two months they were painting the mural. People in passing cars verbally assailed the artists with shouted racial slurs. The people in the cars would shout, "Get the [racial slurs of blacks and Latinos] off the wall!" The artists were pressured to lighten the face of the student who was most prominently displayed. The student is Latino, but he was also mistaken for being black. The reporters said that while many of the comments on their Web site were positive, there were also comments that described the mural as tacky, ugly, and ghetto. An arguable case can be made that the motivation for all this antagonism is a discomfort and resistance to the changing face of the United States. The changing face of the country also reflects a changing culture, and cultural change is difficult for some people. Change does not come easily or without resistance.

Counterbalancing these forces are those of people who see opportunity in the changing cultural face of the United States. Marisa Guthrie, in her 2010 article "How the Census Will Change Your Business," for *A Q&A with Telemundo's Don Browne* says she believes the 2010 Census will show that the Hispanic population increased by 40% and accounted for one-half the growth of the U.S. population. An analysis by Passel and Cohn (2011) shows that there were nearly 1 million more Hispanics counted in the 2010 census than were expected. Day (n.d.) estimates that Hispanics would contribute 45% of the country's growth from 2010 to 2030 and 60% from 2030 to 2050. Almost one in six people in the United States is a Latino, and together they have a purchasing power of $1.3 trillion and growing. Guthrie uses data from the Telemundo Research Solutions Group to illustrate that the growth of the Hispanic population is coming in many unlikely states, as shown in Table 16.2.

Table 16.2 shows both the opportunities and the challenges of the increasing cultural changes. The opportunities of the new markets are being counterbalanced by rapid cultural changes in new and unexpected places.

Don Browne says in Guthrie's article (2010) that "probably the single fastest way to grow any business is to understand and embrace the growth. And if you don't, it's at your own peril" (p. 2). In some ways this is a culturally competent observation. The rapid increase in the Hispanic and Asian populations with their increased purchasing power is attracting the attention of businesses wanting to market to these

Table 16.2 Growth Rates of the Hispanic Population in the United States from 2000 to 2008

State	Percentage Increase in Hispanic Population (2000–2008)
South Carolina	94%
South Dakota	93%
Tennessee	87%
Kansas	59%
Oregon	38%
Oklahoma	32%

Source: Data from Guthrie, M., How the census will change your business: A Q&A with Telemundo's Don Browne, *Broadcasting and Cable*, http://www .broadcastingcable.com/article/453938-How_the_Census_Will_Change_Your_ Business_A_Q_A_With_Telemundo_s_Don_Browne.php, 2010.

fast-growing communities. Their marketing incentive suggests why in some areas the private sector may be ahead of the government in addressing cultural changes.

Many organizations still do not fully reflect the diversity of the communities they serve. There are many reasons for this disconnect. Much of the literature on diversity, social equity, and cultural competence reflects the need for such diversity, however. Successes in increasing an organization's diversity mean many new employees with different cultural characteristics join the organization. The increasing internal diversity allows groups of culturally similar individuals to reinforce and recreate their own cultural closeness within the organization. Affinity groups are growing in number and in size. The cultural borders that exist in society are being recreated in the organization. In some organizations, the societal tensions over cultural differences now find a home within the organization itself. Thus managers are facing a changing organizational environment as the societal cultural tensions emerge in the workplace. Managerial techniques successful in more monocultural environments may not be as effective in a multicultural setting; they may instead actually make the situation worse.

The next 5 to 15 years seem they will be a tumultuous period of uneasy change. Whether one looks globally or locally, there are many ongoing changes. It is still too early in this phase to determine whether the transition will end in strengthening the current institutions, weakening them, or lead to structural change that reorders the institutions. Regardless of which outcomes results, the changing demographics will create a new face for the emerging institutions.

16.3 The Changing Face of Organizations

The year 2010 can be considered a tipping point for the United States in terms of the growth of minority communities. It is the year that minority births are expected to outnumber white births (Yen 2010). In five years, this minority cohort will enter the school system. In the 2020s, the minority will become the majority in the school system, and many individuals in this group will then find their way into universities and the workplace. The demographic changes in the changing composition of many communities are moving through the school systems on their way to redoing the face of the workplace. Births are evidently overtaking immigration as the driving force behind cultural change. Even were it possible to stop all immigration, legal and illegal, the crossing point will still occur. It may happen a few years later, but it will happen.

Speaking about changes that will occur in the future masks the fact that reaching the crossing point where there is no racial or ethnic majority is not a step but a gradually elevating ramp. A homeowner wishing to work on his roof does not jump up on the roof but uses a ladder. The journey from the ground to the roof is incremental, and the distance from the ground to the roof increases with each step the homeowner takes. Conjecturing what will be happening 20 to 30 years from now may not be particularly helpful to a manager or employee who is looking forward to being retired by then. Understanding the ramp up to that crossing point can, however, be very helpful to today's manager and employees.

When you consider moving to a new location, whether to another part of the state, another state, or even another country, making the decision to move is easier if you know someone there or have friends there. Having contacts in the new location will reassure you that when you arrive, there will be someone familiar to you who can help you find a place to live and a job. With the encouragement of people you know, you may choose to move in anticipation of having a better life. With friends and contacts in place, you can be hopeful of successfully integrating into the new community.

The same dynamics are at play for many immigrants. They move knowing that at their destination will be many friends and maybe family members. Where the economic opportunities are growing, whether they be on farms, in packing plants, or at processing plants, there will be many jobs. As new plants are built and need employees to do difficult jobs, opportunities arise for migrants to move in to take advantage of them. Many times, the wages for the type of work immigrants do are not very attractive to the local residents. As the community grows, a critical mass is reached where enterprises aimed at the community's members can be successful. A culturally different community now exists where there was none before. A cultural but porous border is formed. Even with a porous border, the flow will be mainly one way; the members of the immigrant community will go into the established community because their children attend schools there and major purchases are available only there.

Most of the residents of the immigrant community will likely be U.S. citizens, but a few may be undocumented. They will all have cultural and language similarities. Cultural misunderstandings will occur nonetheless, and the frequency will increase as the community grows. A cultural divide will start to develop within the community. Although many communities adapt successfully, in others, the cultural misunderstandings fuel a movement to stop the cultural changes. There may be local legislation passed to make residence in the community difficult for those without documentation. The debate leading to the legislation may be acrimonious and, on occasion, even hateful. The acrimony makes it difficult to establish friendly personal and social relationships between the two groups. The discussions follow people into their workplaces, where tensions between culturally different groups of employees result and complicate the life of a public manager.

On the other end of the spectrum are communities that see the racial and ethnic composition of the city changing but initiate efforts to respond to the changing demographics in a more integrative manner. Public officials and managers who would like to replicate their efforts can learn much by contacting leaders who take a positive, integrative approach to cross-cultural issues. (For contact information, see this book's Appendix.)

Any given community in the United States will fit somewhere on a spectrum of diversity: the community can be a place with little or no diversity, at one end of the spectrum, or it can be one where there is a racial or ethnic majority, at the other end. It is self-evident that racial and ethnic groups can vary widely in size and type. Large cities may be home to several different, thriving immigrant and minority communities who are from diverse racial and ethnic groups. The members of the immigrant and minority communities may or may not get along with each other, their interactions thereby adding another layer of complexity to their situation.

The city organizations will likely see their city's ethnic and racial tensions carry over into the workplace as employees with diverse backgrounds compete for the same positions. The dynamics of equity theory exist for groups as well. These tensions and dynamics contribute to making the life of a public manager and the employees more culturally complex.

It is easy to default into discussing the coming changes in terms of broad groups: racial and ethnic groups, male and female, gay and straight, or blue collar and white collar. The emerging reality is much more complex. A gay son of an immigrant from a Middle Eastern country whose parents sought asylum in the United States will experience the world quite differently than a white lesbian whose parents have been professionally successful. Racial and ethnic perspectives have usually been related to the background of the individual. Discussions of people characterized by gender, sexual orientations, and social class have not generally been discussed in terms of race and ethnicity. Does a U.S. citizen who is an immigrant from Nigeria and works in an assembly plant share a common perspective with a U.S. citizen who is from Cambodia? Do they both share a perspective in common with a white person who works at the same assembly plant?

Race and ethnicity are infusing almost all the diversity categories and creating racial and ethnic subcategories within those diverse areas. Research on women of color and gays of color is increasing (see, for example, the publications listed in this book's Appendix). Race and ethnicity are introducing new cultural flavors to formerly monocultural communities. Race and ethnicity are also adding new cultural dimensions to what had once been areas not linked to racial and ethnic classifications of diversity. Race and ethnicity are becoming a prism through which one light becomes refracted into different colors. Managers seeing all this diversity can easily get overwhelmed by the implications of what all this diversity means in terms of their ability to manage it. The diffusion of race and ethnicity into what were once race-neutral categories is bringing to the forefront a topic that has been difficult for many to discuss—race. Pretending that race does not exist only keeps the tensions under the surface and simmering until an incident occurs that raises the emotional temperature and brings the issue to a boil.

Much of the efforts on diversity have been on having the diversity of the organization reflect the diversity of the community. The size of the baby-boomer generation who are now beginning to retire points to the coming need for replacements in the workplace. The large numbers of baby boomers relative to the generation replacing them presages a coming labor shortage in the near future. According to

Carnevale, Smith, and Strohl (2010), the economy will be creating 46.8 million new openings by 2018. Of these new job openings, 33 million will be the consequence of workers retiring and workers leaving their jobs—an impact made by the retiring baby boomers over the next several years. The researchers see the economy creating 13.8 million new openings. One-third of the job openings will require a college degree, and another 30% will require some college. Carnevale, Smith, and Strohl project that universities will produce 3 million fewer college graduates than the job market requires.

Many immigrants are overrepresented in the groups with low levels of education. There are also the different languages their children speak, as well as issues of health and well-being. The delivery of health care to these growing immigrant and minority communities has provided the impetus for the federal government and various foundations in mandating culturally competent health care. Many school districts are developing similar programs to provide education for the rising growth of multicultural children.

Universities will be recruiting from the multicultural high school graduates. Being a first-generation college student and having parents who do not have a high school diploma are risk factors for educational achievement (Arbona 2005). Many universities already have programs to assist this population in graduating within a reasonable time frame. The universities with the better culturally competent programs will be more successful. This multicultural wave is finding its way into the workplace and bringing with it an increasing need for culturally competent managers.

The labor shortage is hard to see when unemployment is almost 10%, as of this writing, and there are millions unemployed, but the labor shortage is on the way. Managers and human resource departments will find themselves in a fierce competition between many public and private organizations for multicultural applicants. Managers and human resources can use the same cultural competencies for managing diversity inside an organization to become more competitive in attracting the best and brightest from an increasingly diverse applicant pool.

In the same way that humankind has always managed to adapt to a changing environment, successful managers will develop a cultural consciousness, intelligence, and competence to adapt. Time will help. There seems to be a generational difference in the acceptance of a multicultural society. The younger generations seems more accepting of multiculturalism, as shown by the responses of the college students mentioned earlier in the book. Cultural competence will find its way into the educational system and into organizational training programs.

16.4 Remaining a Step Ahead

Don Browne's words on the changing demographics of the country (Guthrie 2010), mentioned earlier in this chapter, are good advice for remaining a step ahead. Recall that he said, "Probably the single fastest way to grow any business is to understand

and embrace this growth. And if you don't, it's at your own peril" (p. 2). Success for public managers is similar. A public manager will be successful by understanding and embracing the change. Many managers already are.

Harvard's Center for Public Leadership (CPL), under the direction of David Gergen, and Harvard's Kennedy School are in the planning stages for a Latino Leadership Initiative (LLI) titled "Preparing to Lead: An Initiative for Next Generation Latino Leadership." The beginning sentence of the flyer for the LLI states, "It is estimated that the Latino community will double in size over the next 40 years and will comprise more than 30% of the United States population by 2050" (Collado 2010).

The program intends to bring together 50 college juniors who come from or are committed to serving the Latino community. The program coordinators anticipate that many of the participants will be first-generation college students. The students will attend classes for a week and receive a week of executive education. The classes will be at the Kennedy School and taught by Harvard faculty. (If interested, see this book's Appendix for contact information.)

In 2010, the Center for Progressive Leadership in Washington, D.C., conducted a five-month program for talented young people working in or desiring to work in progressive organizations. The ongoing program aims to help talented young people of color, women, and people from the lesbian, gay, bisexual, and transgender community. The e-mail soliciting applicants for this program lists the goals of the program as providing leadership training, coaching, networking, and community building. (See this book's Appendix for contact information.)

There are many similar programs in the women's community, Asian community, African American community, and other diverse communities. Many universities also have programs aimed at the emerging multicultural students. Many public and private organizations have programs to develop multicultural leaders. In common, they recognize the changing face of the United States and are capitalizing on the changing demographics. There are many efforts to cultivate a cadre of talented multicultural leaders for the future. They are attempting to fill the coming labor shortages with a talented multicultural leadership. The competition for these multicultural leaders will be fierce. Culturally competent managers and HR offices can be at the front of the line in attracting this talent into their organizations.

This book, by its very nature, has focused on the difficulties, problems, and issues that accompany the increasing diversity and cultural change. It is important to highlight the many people and programs that understand the demographic changes and are embracing the growth. These people and programs do not receive the same media exposure as do the acrimonious discussions aired on television or found on the Internet. Yet there are many examples of people who are successfully adapting to the changing environment. These are the efforts that lead not only to culturally competent organization but to a thriving and successful culturally competent country.

16.5 Culturally Competent Leadership for Tomorrow

That the demographic changes are creating an unprecedented cultural change should be evident by now. Regardless of the sentiments of some individuals in the public debate on the changing culture of the country, the question is not "How do we stop this cultural change?" but "How do we best take advantage of the innovation that diversity brings and minimize the problems that cultural change can create?"

Residents of states that experience frequent tornadoes or hurricanes know that the time to prepare for the coming storms is well before they arrive. The perspective of affirmative action programs and equal education opportunity laws and initiatives springs from a time when the white population was much larger than the minority population. As the demographics change the proportions to a no-majority population, the perspective shifts from the dominant population needing to be sensitive to the needs of the minority community to a perspective that regardless of which racial or ethnic group we identify with, there will be many other co-workers, whether top executives, managers, supervisors, or employees, who are culturally different. Each will have to be culturally competent to succeed in this new and unprecedented cultural milieu.

As evolution has taught us, those who best survive and thrive in changing environments are those with the flexibility to adapt to new environment. Those who do not adapt, in the case of organizations, will retire at the first opportunity rather than change. Those who successfully navigate the changing cultural landscape will emerge as the new leaders. Employees become supervisors and managers by being promoted. Culturally competent leadership for tomorrow begins with today's young employees entering the workplace. In a changing environment, the best way to be promoted today is to be seen as the person who can solve tomorrow's problems.

In many ways, cultural competence is emerging as a new intelligence. Howard Gardner (1983) from Harvard led the development of the concept of multiple intelligences. Gardner proposed eight different intelligences: linguistic, logical-mathematical, spatial, bodily kinesthetic, musical, interpersonal, intrapersonal, and naturalist. Goleman (1995, 2000) added emotional intelligence into the lexicon. Emotional intelligence has become a necessity for employees and managers who want to be successful. Cultural competence may be seen as an emerging new intelligence. In the same way that the field of management incorporated emotional intelligence, it is now incorporating cultural competence. Necessity is the mother of all inventions, and the necessity for cultural competence is here.

Appendix

Cultural Competence Literature and Legislation

The theoretical roots of cultural competence are in the federal requirements for culturally competent delivery of services to immigrant and minority communities (Johnson, Lenartowicz, and Apud 2004). The federal requirements were a response to the health disparities in immigrant and minority communities. The various cultural differences were creating misunderstandings and problems across the cultural barriers. Cultural competence arose as a mechanism to bridge those cultural gaps in health care delivery.

Legislation and Its Contribution to Cultural Competence

Bailey (2010), in her chapter titled "Cultural Competency and the Practice of Public Administration" in *Diversity and Public Administration: Theory, Issues, and Perspectives,* ed. Mitchell Rice, 174–175, lists the relevant legislation:

1. The 1946 Hospital Survey and Construction Act (Hill-Burton Act) requires community hospitals and health centers that receive funds to agree to a general principle of nondiscrimination. This has been interpreted as providing language assistance.
2. The 1964 Civil Rights Act bans discrimination and exclusion on the grounds of race, color, or national origin for any recipient of federal financial assistance.
3. The 1965 Social Security Act that established Medicare and Medicaid requires Medicaid to provide "culturally and linguistically appropriate services." Medicare reimburses hospitals for the cost of providing bilingual services.

4. The 1988 Hawaiian Health Care Improvement Act requires "culturally based health care and health education" for Native Hawaiians.
5. The 1990 Disadvantaged Minority Health Improvement Act requires the U.S. Department of Health and Human Services and the Office of Minority Health to develop the ability of health care professionals to address the cultural and linguistic barriers to the delivery of health care to minority populations. It also includes increasing the participation of limited-English-speaking participants. The Office of Minority Health is required to support research, demonstrations, and evaluations to assess innovative models that better understand the delivery of health services to minority communities. This has fueled much of the research on cultural competence.
6. The 1994 Developmental Disabilities Assistance and Bill of Rights Act defines cultural competence as "services, supports or other assistance that are provided in a manner that is responsive to the beliefs, interpersonal styles, attitudes, language and behaviors of individuals who are receiving services, and in a manner that has the greatest likelihood of ensuring their maximum participation in the program."

The federal agencies responsible for implementing much of this legislation are the Office of Minority Health and Health Resources and Services Administration in the U.S. Department of Health and Human Services. The work of these offices is discussed in greater detail in Chapter 12, "Cultural Competence in Health Care."

Federal Agencies and Cultural Competence

The following agencies are a rich depository of information on cultural competence information.

Health Resources and Human Services Administration (HRSA), U.S. Department of Health and Human Services

http://www.hrsa.gov/culturalcompetence

The HRSA Web site is the major source for information and a Web-based delivery system on cultural competence in health care. The site contains assessment tools, presentations, training curricula, and highlights of funded projects designed to meet the needs of special population groups, including African Americans; Hispanics; Native Americans and Alaska Natives; and gay, lesbian, bisexual, transgender, and HIV/AIDS groups.

The Office of Minority Health (OMH), U.S. Department of Health and Human Services

http://minorityhealth.hhs.gov

The Office of Minority Health has developed five reports. This office has also designed national standards on culturally and linguistically appropriate services (CLAS) for health care organizations. There are three levels of standards: mandatory, guidelines, and recommendations. They are classified as culturally competent care, language-access services, and organizational supports for cultural competence. Standards 6 and 7 are mandatory for all recipients of federal funds. Standards 1, 2, 3, 8, 9, 10, 11, 12, and 13 are guidelines recommended for adoption as mandates by federal and national accrediting agencies. Standard 14 is suggested for voluntary adoption by health care organizations. The 14 standards are as follows:

1. Health care organizations should ensure that patients/consumers receive from all staff members effective, understandable, and respectful care that is provided in a manner compatible with the cultural health beliefs and practices and preferred language.
2. Health care organizations should implement strategies to recruit, retain, and promote at all levels of the organization a diverse staff and leadership that are representative of the demographic characteristics of the service area.
3. Health care organizations should ensure that staff at all levels and across all disciplines receive education and training in culturally and linguistically appropriate service delivery.
4. Health care organizations must offer and provide language assistance services, including bilingual and interpreter services, at no cost to each patient/consumer with limited English proficiency, points of contact, in a timely manner during all hours or operation.
5. Health care organizations must provide to patients/consumers in their preferred language offers and written notices informing them of their right to receive language assistance services.
6. Health care organizations must assure the competence of language assistance provided to the limited English proficient patients/consumers by interpreters and bilingual staff. Family and friends should be used to provide interpretation services (except on request by the patient/consumer).
7. Health care organizations must make available easily understood patient-related materials and signage in the languages of the commonly encountered groups and/or groups represented in the service area.
8. Health care organizations should develop, implement, and promote a written strategic plan that lists clear goals, policies, operational plans, and management accountability/oversight mechanism to provide culturally and linguistically appropriate services.
9. Health care organizations should conduct initial and ongoing organizational self-assessments and CLAS-related activities and are encouraged to integrate cultural and linguistic competence-related measures into their internal audits, performance improvement programs, patient satisfaction assessments, and outcomes-based evaluations.

10. Health care organizations should ensure that data on the individual patient's/consumer's race and spoken and written language are collected in health records, integrated into the organization's management information systems, and periodically updated.
11. Health care organizations should maintain a current demographic, cultural, and epidemiological profile of the community as well as a needs assessment to accurately plan for and implement services that respond to the cultural and linguistic characteristics of the service area.
12. Health care organizations should develop participatory, collaborative partnerships with communities and utilize a variety of formal and informal mechanisms to facilitate community and patient/consumer involvement in designing and implementing CLAS-related activities.
13. Health care organizations should ensure that conflict and grievance resolution processes are provided and linguistically sensitive and capable of identifying, preventing, and resolving cross-cultural problems or complaints by patients/consumers.
14. Health care organizations are encouraged to regularly make available to the public information about their progress and successful innovations in implementing CLAS standards and to provide notice in their communities about the availability of this information.

Samples of Cultural Competence Information Found on Government Web Sites

U.S. Department of Health and Human Services Administration on Aging. n.d. *A Toolkit for Serving Diverse Communities.* http://www.aoa.gov/AoARoot/AoA_Programs/Tools_Resources/DOCS/AoA_DiversityToolkit_Full.pdf

U.S. Department of Health and Human Services, Health Resources and Services Administration. 2002. *Indicators of Cultural Competence in Health Care Delivery Organizations: An Organizational Cultural Competence Assessment Profile.* http://www.hrsa.gov/CulturalCompetence/healthdlvr.pdf

U.S. Department of Health and Human Services, Office of Minority Health. 2001. *National Standards for Culturally and Linguistically Appropriate Services in Health Care* (Final Report). http://minorityhealth.hhs.gov/assets/pdf/checked/finalreport.doc

U.S. Department of Health and Human Services, Office of Minority Health. 2004. *Setting the Agenda for Research on Cultural Competence in Health Care.* http://www.ahrq.gov/research/cultural/pdf

The Concept of Cultural Competence

Rice (2010) sees the study and practice of public administration as supporting culture-blind services and programs and the focus on cultural competency evolving slowly. He sees that the concept is still not accepted and understood by scholars and administrators in public administration and the delivery of public services. For Rice, the definition of cultural competency comes from the literature of other professions and fields. Much of that literature comes from the federally legislated requirements for the delivery of health care to minority communities (Johnson, Lenartowicz, and Apud 2004).

The 1990 Disadvantaged Minority Health Improvement Act requires the Office of Minority Health (see above legislation) to support research, demonstrations, and evaluations to assess innovative models that better understand the delivery of health services to minority communities. The better understanding refers to addressing the cultural and linguistic barriers to the delivery of health care to these populations. It also includes increasing the participation of limited-English-speaking participants. Although there had been research before the legislation (Gutierrez et al. 1988; Hardy-Fanta and MacMahon-Herrera 1981; Inclan 1985; Rogler et al. 1987; Sabogal et al. 1987; Zayas 1987; Zayas and Bryant 1984; Zayas and Palleja 1988), the legislation led to an increase in research and a focus on the delivery of health services to minority communities and their cultures.

Research Focus on Health Care for Minority Communities

One focus of research was the delivery and utilization of health care in minority communities. Herrick and Brown (1998) and Leong and Lau (2001) examined the underutilization of mental health services and the barriers in mental health delivery to Asian Americans. Johnson and Cameron (2001) looked at the barriers to providing effective mental health services to American Indians. Hurdle (2002) examined culturally based interventions in Native Hawaiian healing. The delivery of health care to Hispanics also received attention from researchers. Several researchers (Rodriguez 1986, 1987; Rodriguez, Lessinger, and Guarnaccia 1992; Zayas 1987; Zayas and Bryant 1984; Zayas et al. 1997) examined the cultural barriers and delivery of mental health services to Hispanics. Harris, Andrews, and Elixhauser (1997) looked at the difference in the use of medical procedures between blacks and whites. Snowden (2001) examined the barriers African Americans were experiencing in the delivery of mental health services.

There is a plethora of research on cultural competence in health care. One of the influential works on cultural competence is that of Cross et al. (1989), "Towards a Culturally Competent System of Care," which is referenced by many authors (Applewhite 1998; Bailey 2010; Chang 2007; Goode, Dunne, and Bronheim 2006; Johnson, Lenartowicz, and Apud 2006; Mathews 2010; Rice 2010; Siegel, Haugland, and Chambers 2003). The effects of race and ethnicity on various medical treatments were studied by a variety of researchers (Bach et al. 1999; Byrd 1990; Harris, Andrews, and Elixhauser 1997; Peterson et al. 1997; Schulman et al. 1999). Betancourt et al. (2003) see that there are racial and ethnic disparities in health care even when patients are covered by insurance. They see cultural competence as a way to overcome the racial and ethnic disparities in health care. They see sociocultural barriers in the delivery of health care at three levels: organizational (leadership and workforce), structural (processes of care), and clinical (provider-patient encounter). They see a cultural competence framework in the delivery of health care as including minority recruitment into the health professions, development of interpreter services, and language-appropriate health education materials, and provider education on cross-cultural issues.

Parker and Geron (2007) in their qualitative study of 56 nursing home focus group transcripts found five cultural competence concerns:

1. Not all the staff were aware of cultural differences among the residents.
2. Nursing home staff experienced challenges in both verbal and nonverbal communication.
3. Staff tended to minimize cultural differences.
4. There were discriminatory actions and comments.
5. The organizations did not always respond in an adequate manner.

Starr and Wallace (2009) noted in their descriptive and exploratory study using a cultural competence assessment tool that public health nurse participants had a moderate level of cultural competence. However, cultural awareness and sensitivity scores were higher than scores for culturally competent behaviors.

Mental health services also received attention from researchers. Marin and Gamba (2003) explored acculturation, and Sue and Zane (1987) looked at the role that culture and cultural values play in psychotherapy. Ridley (1995) wrote on overcoming unintentional racism in counseling and therapy. In 2003, the American Psychological Association (APA) came out with guidelines on multicultural education, training, research, and practice for psychologists (*American Psychologist* 2003). The U.S. Department of Health and Human Services, Substance Abuse and Mental Health Services, Center for Mental Health Services (2009), defines cultural and linguistic competence as "an integrated pattern of human behavior that includes thoughts, communications, languages, practices, beliefs, values, customs, courtesies, rituals, manners of interacting, roles, relationships and expected behaviors of a racial, ethnic, religious or social group; the ability to transmit the above to succeeding generations; is dynamic in nature" (p. 10).

Cultural Intelligence and Business

Globalization is creating more collaborative international ventures (Johnson, Lenartowiz, and Apud 2006). Globalization is creating a competitive advantage for employees with international assignments (Kumar, Rose, and Subramaniam 2008). Tan (2004, 19) sees the global workplace as requiring individuals "to be sensitive to different cultures and to interact appropriately with people from different cultures, and to analyze new cultures as they are encountered." Amiri, Moghimi, and Kazemi (2010) see globalization as increasing cultural diversity, which is creating challenges for individuals and organizations. Thomas and Inkson (2004) see the globalization of people with global business involving interactions and relationships with people who are culturally different.

Johnson, Lenartowicz, and Apud (2006) see many international business failures blamed on the lack of cultural competence of the practitioners. They see globalization as increasing collaborative ventures with foreign firms. Many of the ventures do not succeed, for which they see two reasons emerging from the literature: the failure of expatriates and the inability of managers to understand the cultural challenges of working in other countries. Thomas and Inkson (2004) see the globalization of people creating new and major challenges because of the difficulty of bridging cultural boundaries.

Johnson, Lenartowicz, and Apud (2006) find in their literature review that cultural competence is widely used in the United States in the fields of health care, medicine, psychology, and education in the context of minorities and governmental agencies and systems. Cultural competence is also used in the context of workforce diversity referring to cultural subgroups classifieds by gender, ethnic origin, religion, sexual orientation, and age. They see the definitions as specific but not applicable to international business. Earley (2002) and Earley and Ang (2003) introduced the concept of cultural intelligence as "a person's capability to adapt as s/he interacts with others from different cultural regions" (2002, 283).

Cultural intelligence is defined by Thomas and Inkson (2004, 14) as meaning "being skilled and flexible about understanding a culture, learning more about it from your ongoing interactions with it, and gradually reshaping your thinking to be more sympathetic to the culture and your behavior to be more skilled and appropriate when interacting with others from the culture." They define cultural intelligence as having three components:

1. Knowledge of the culture and principles of cross-cultural interactions
2. Mindfulness practice that pays attention to cross-cultural cues
3. Culturally correct behaviors

Tan (2004) suggests that cultural intelligence be viewed in the context of emotional or social intelligence. Emotional intelligence assumes that people use culturally familiar situations in interacting with others. Cultural intelligence involves interacting with others in unfamiliar situations. Tan defines three key parts of cultural intelligence:

1. Cultural strategic thinking: Thinking and solving problems in particular ways
2. Motivational focus: Being energized and persistent in one's actions
3. Behavioral aspect: Acting in certain ways

Kumar, Rose, and Subramaniam (2008, 320) define cultural intelligence as representing "an individual's capability for successful adaptation to new and unfamiliar cultural settings and ability to function easily and effectively in situations characterized by cultural diversity." They define cultural intelligence as being composed of three aspects:

1. Mental (metacognitive and cognitive)
2. Motivational
3. Behavioral

The mental aspect is the ability to conceptualize, acquire, and understand cultural knowledge. The motivational aspect is the willingness to interact with others and to adapt to the other's culture. The behavioral aspect is having the adaptive behaviors in line with the mental and motivational aspects.

Amiri, Moghimi, and Kazemi (2010) studied the correlation between cultural intelligence and employee performance. They see cultural diversity creating problems for individuals and organizations. Globalization has created a need for more culturally diverse organizations. Cultural intelligence is emerging as an important factor in an employee's performance inside and among various cultural environments (p. 418). Their study found significant correlation between cultural intelligence (metacognitive, cognitive, and motivational aspects) and employee behavior.

Cultural intelligence has been used in the context of leadership as well. Northouse (2007) includes a chapter on culture and leadership in his book *Leadership: Theory and Practice*. It is interesting to note that his third edition, published in 2004, did not include the chapter on culture and leadership. This may be seen in the context of globalization and increasing diversity generating more interest in cultural intelligence and cultural competence. Northouse (2007, 302) defines culture as the "learned beliefs, values, rules, norms, symbols, and traditions that are common to a people." He views culture as being dynamic. He defines multiculturalism as taking more than one culture into account and also classified by race, gender, ethnicity, sexual orientation, and age. Diversity is different cultures or ethnicities within a group or organization. He sees the work of Hofstede (1980, 2001) as probably being the most referenced work on cultural dimensions and the benchmark for much of the research on world cultures. Hofstede analyzed the responses from 100,000 respondents in more than 50 countries. He identified five major dimensions where cultures differ: power distance, uncertainty avoidance, individualism-collectivism, masculinity-femininity, and long-term and short-term orientation. The work of Hall (1976) on the primary characteristics of culture is also cited.

In the context of culture and leadership, Northouse (2007) references the work of House and Javidan (2004) as offering the strongest findings. These studies are called the GLOBE studies. The studies covered 62 societies. The GLOBE researchers used their own research as well as the work of others (Hofstede 1980, 2001;

Kluckhohn and Strodtbeck 1961; Triandis 1995). The researchers identified nine dimensions of culture:

1. Uncertainty avoidance
2. Power distance
3. Institutional collectivism
4. In-group collectivism
5. Gender egalitarianism
6. Assertiveness
7. Future orientation
8. Performance orientation
9. Humane orientation

They also described leadership behaviors as they are viewed in different cultures. The six global leadership behaviors are these:

1. Charismatic or value-based leadership
2. Team-oriented leadership
3. Participative leadership
4. Humane-oriented leadership
5. Autonomous leadership
6. Self-protective leadership

Yukl (2002) includes a chapter titled "Ethical Leaderships and Diversity" in his book *Leadership in Organizations*. He sees the importance of cross-cultural research on leadership because of increasing globalization. Similar to Northouse, he describes the works of Hofstede (1980, 1993) and the GLOBE Project.

Thomas and Inkson (2004) include a chapter titled "Leadership across Cultures" in their book *Cultural Intelligence*. The leadership styles of several countries are described. Leadership in Arab countries is referred to as a "sheikhocracy," a blend of personal autocracy and conformity to rules and regulation. The respect is for those who made the rules and not for the rationality of the rules themselves. Leadership in Japan is based on a combination of *amae*, defined as indulgent love with obligation and the moral obligation to pay the debt. Leadership in France is characterized as being paternalistic and charismatic. Russian leaders are characterized as being powerful autocrats.

Thomas and Inkson (2004) see culturally intelligent leadership as focusing on the culture and expectations of the followers. They classify the cultural characteristics as those of individualistic and collectivistic. Individualistic cultures expect the individual to make decisions. Collectivist cultures expect decisions to be made by consensus. They also use Hofstede's classifications: power distance, uncertainty avoidance, and masculinity and femininity. Chin and Gaynier (2006) bring into the discussion of culture and leadership the concept of the organizational culture.

They attribute to globalization an increasing diverse workforce and, along with the diversity, a more complex social environment within the organization. They argue that the 21st-century leaders also need cultural intelligence in addition to intellectual intelligence and emotional intelligence. They attribute the lack of understanding of the organizational and ethnic cultures of the workplace as leading to the failure, confusion, and frustration of leaders. They see the Western value of color-blindness as being well meaning but misguided. They believe that "managing cultural differences is a key factor in building and sustaining organizational competitiveness and vitality" (p. 5). They discuss British, Japanese, Italian, and American corporate leaders as leveraging their cultural strengths to create competitive advantages. The process is described as:

1. Having a shared management philosophy
2. Creating a cultural environment
3. Developing human resources strategies that include cultural diversity

Cultural competence is also encountered in human resources. Logging on to Society for Human Resources Management (SHRM) Web site (http://www.shrm .org) and entering *cultural competence* in the search function shows several Web pages of references to material on cultural competence. Some of the topics include health care leads the way in cultural competence; cultural competence is key for marketing and sales; how to help cultural minorities advance; cultural training is a key element for global assignments; cultural intelligence: a new approach to international management training; executive coaching: cross-cultural perspective; the right balance: aligning cultural fit with diversity goals; culturally competent performance discussions; realizing the full potential of diversity and inclusion as a core business strategy; and homeland security uses DVDs for cultural awareness training.

Toward a Definition of Cultural Competence

The 1994 Developmental Disabilities Assistance and Bill of Rights Act defines cultural competence as "services, supports or other assistance that are provided in a manner that is responsive to the beliefs, interpersonal styles, attitudes, language and behaviors of individuals who are receiving services, and in a manner that has the greatest likelihood of ensuring their maximum participation in the program" (Bailey 2010). The legislation provided a legislative definition of cultural competence. In effect, the 1994 Act legislates the delivery of services in a culturally relevant manner. The services are to be delivered in a manner consistent with the culture of the recipient.

The Department of Health and Human Services, Substance Abuse and Mental Health Services Administration, Center for Mental Health Services, defines cultural and linguistic competence as "an integrated pattern of human behavior that includes thoughts, communications, languages, practices, beliefs, values, customs, courtesies, rituals, manners of interacting, roles, relationships and expected behaviors of a racial, ethnic, religious or social group; the ability to transmit the above to succeeding generations: is dynamic in nature." The definition is listed on page 10 of the Cooperative Agreements for the Comprehensive Community Health Services for Children and Their Families Program, Child Mental Health Initiative (CMHI), FY 2005 Request for Applications (RFA).

The 1994 Developmental Disabilities Assistance and Bill of Rights Act was not the first attempt to define cultural competence. Cross et al. (1989) of the Georgetown University Child Development Center published "Towards a Culturally Competent System of Care." The authors define cultural competency as a "set of cultural behaviors and attitudes integrated into the practice methods of a system, agency, or its professionals that enables them to work effectively in cross cultural situations" (1989, 2). For Cross et al., cultural competency is a cultural development process that has a negative-to-positive continuum. They list six stages:

1. Cultural destructiveness
2. Cultural incapacity
3. Cultural blindness
4. Cultural precompetence
5. Cultural competency
6. Cultural proficiency (1989, 6–8)

The definition of cultural competence used by the National Center for Cultural Competence, Georgetown University, was adapted from the work of Cross et al.

Gallegos (1982) published "The Ethnic Competence Model for Social Work Education" in *Color in White Society*, ed. B. W. White. Gallegos sees ethnic competence as the acquiring of culturally relevant understanding of the problems of minorities that can be used to deliver culturally appropriate interventions. The National Association of Social Workers (NASW 2007, 10) defines culture as "the integrated pattern of human behavior that includes thoughts, communications, actions, customs, and institutions of a racial, ethnic, religious, or social group." This definition is consistent with the definition of cultural competence in the 1994 legislation.

Sue (2006) and Sue, Ivey, and Pedersen (1996) define cultural competence for mental health providers as:

1. Cultural awareness and beliefs: Provider's sensitivity to her or his own personal values and how these may influence perceptions of the client, client's problem, and the counseling relationship
2. Cultural knowledge: Counselor's knowledge of the client's culture, worldview, and expectations for the counseling relationship
3. Cultural skills: Counselor's ability to intervene in a manner that is culturally sensitive and relevant (Sue 2006, 238)

This cultural competence framework was adopted by the American Psychological Association's *Multicultural Guidelines* (Sue 2006).

Betancourt et al. (2003, 118) see a culturally competent health care system as "one that acknowledges and incorporates—at all levels—the importance of culture, assessment of cross-cultural relations vigilance toward the dynamics of cultural differences, expansion of cultural knowledge, and adaptation of services to meet culturally unique needs." They see three barriers to a culturally competent health care system:

1. Organizational barriers: The lack of minority representation in the leadership and workforce that does not reflect the racial or ethnic composition of the population.
2. Structural barriers: The lack of cross-cultural communication capabilities, including the lack of interpreter services or culturally and linguistically appropriate health education information
3. Clinical barriers: Cross-cultural differences between client and provider, with the cultural and linguistic barriers leading to poorer health outcomes

Zayas et al. (1997, 406) define cultural competence as "the knowledge and interpersonal skills to understand, appreciate, and work with families from cultures other than one's own and using the knowledge and skills effectively to employee therapeutic techniques in achieving behavioral and emotional change."

Davis and Donald (1997) develop an operational definition of cultural competence that includes transforming cultural knowledge into organizational standards, policies, practices, and attitudes to better serve culturally diverse clients. For them, competence includes learning new behaviors and using them appropriately.

Brach and Fraser (2000) see cultural competence in an organizational context of incorporating the appropriate practices and policies to address cultural diversity. The Cultural Institute of Canada also defines cultural competency in an organizational context as the behaviors, attitudes, and policies that allow organizations to work with culturally diverse populations. Associations, university centers, and foundations also play a large role in defining cultural competence. Their role is described in a later section.

The Cultural Diversity Institute, University of Calgary (2001, 1) defines cultural competence as being "a set of congruent behaviors, attitudes, and policies that enable the organization or agency to work effectively with various racial, ethnic, religious, and linguistic groups."

Taylor (1994, 54) sees intercultural competence as "an adaptive capacity based on an inclusive and integrative world view which allows participants to effectively accommodate the demands of living in a host culture."

Cross et al. (1989) define cultural competence as congruent behaviors, attitudes, and policies that come together in a system, in an agency, or among professionals and enable them to work effectively in cross-cultural situations.

Chang (2007) sees cultural competence as integrative and transformative and as attained through the experience of discovery of internal discovery and external adjustment. In his study of international humanitarian aid workers, their experience of cultural competence is divided into three levels:

1. Peripheral level: Encounter and recognize
2. Cognitive level: Familiarize and adjust
3. Reflective level: Transform and enlighten (2007, 193)

The contributions of Cross et al. (1989) and Gallegos (1982) signal a shift in the delivery of health services to minority communities. There is now a focus on the awareness, understanding, and practice (competency) of the role that culture plays in the delivery of health services. There is now a cultural context for the delivery of health services to minority communities. Cross et al.'s inclusion of cultural competence as "practice" creates an organizational component. Cultural competence is now a structural component of organizations. In essence, to deliver culturally relevant services, organizations need to be culturally competent.

Criticisms of Cultural Competence

Carpenter-Song, Schwallie, and Longhofer (2007) take an anthropological perspective in the use of the culture in the cultural competence models. The models frequently view culture as static, confuse culture with race and ethnicity, and do not describe diversity within a group. Culture is viewed as the property of certain individuals belonging to racial or ethnic minority groups. When definitions of culture are based on race and differences in ethnic groups, they do not allow for diversity and cultural change that members of the groups may undergo. Such other factors as class, gender, generation, age, and geography may be as or more important to the identity of an individual.

Wu and Martinez (2006) see most of the work on cultural competency focusing on defining what it means and very little work on taking cultural competence into action. Sue (2006) also sees a similar problem. For him, the critical issue is moving from the definitional phase into a practice or research phase. The philosophical definition does not have operational specificity. Sue raises the following questions:

1. What cultural knowledge is important, and can one know all cultures?
2. Do different cultural groups have different competencies?
3. Does the treatment process require different competencies at different times?
4. Is cultural competency one-dimensional or multidimensional?

The criticisms raise two important considerations: one, determining what are the important aspects of culture that one needs to learn to be culturally competent; two, recognizing that there has been little effort to practice of cultural competence.

Additional Resources
Culturally Competent Leadership

Cultural Competency and Leadership, Chancellor's Diversity Initiative, University of Missouri, http://diversity.missouri.edu/cultural-competency

Latino Leadership Initiative, Harvard Kennedy School, Center for Public Leadership, Dario Collado, Program Manager, Telephone: 617-496-0280, E-mail: Dario_collado@hks.harvard.edu

Self-Assessment for Cultural Competence, American Speech-Language-Hearing Association, http://www.asha.org/practice/multicultural/self.htm

Mentoring and Career Advancement

Ambrose, L. 2008. *Common sense mentoring.* Deerfield, IL: Perrone-Ambrose Associates.

Brown, S. D., and R. W. Lent, eds. 2005. *Career development and counseling: Putting theory and research to work.* Hoboken, NJ: John Wiley.

Career Advancement. http://www.fedcareer.info

Elliott, A. J., and C. S. Dweck, eds. 2005. *Handbook of competence and motivation.* New York: Guilford Press.

London, M. 1998. *Career barriers: How people experience, overcome, and avoid failure.* Mahwah, NJ: Lawrence Erlbaum.

Picou, J. S., and R. E. Campbell, eds. 1975. *Career behavior of special groups.* Columbus, OH: Charles E. Merrill.

Stoddard, D., with R. J. Tomasy. 2003. *The heart of mentoring: Ten proven principles for developing people to their fullest potential.* Colorado Springs, CO: NavPress.

International Protocols

French, M., Ambassador. 2010. *United States protocol: The guide to official diplomatic etiquette.* Lanham, MD: Rowman and Littlefield.

Nelson, C. A. 1998. *Protocol for profit: A manager's guide to competing worldwide.* Vol. 1. New York: International Thomson Business Press.

Transition Center, Foreign Service Institute, U.S. Department of State. 2005. *Protocol for the modern diplomat.* http://www.au.af.mil/au/awc/awcgate/state/protocol_for_diplomats.pdf

Students and Higher Education

Gloria, A. M., J. Castellanos, and V. Orozco. 2005. Perceived educational barriers, cultural fit, coping responses, and psychological well-being of Latina undergraduates. *Hispanic Journal of Behavioral Sciences* 27 (2): 161–183.

Hurtado, S., and L. Ponjuan. 2005. Latino educational outcomes and the campus climate. *Journal of Hispanic Higher Education* 4 (3): 235–251.

Pajares, F. 1996, Winter. Self-efficacy beliefs in academic settings. *Review of Educational Research* 66 (4): 543–578.

Saunders, M., and I. Serna. 2004. Making college happen: The college experiences of first-generation Latino students. *Journal of Hispanic Higher Education* 3 (2): 146–163.

Strage, A. A. (1999). Social and academic integration and college success: Similarities and differences as a function of ethnicity and family educational background. *College Student Journal* 33 (2): 198–205.

Zwick, R., and J. C. Sklar. 2005. Predicting college grades and degree completion using high school grades and SAT scores: The role of student ethnicity and first language. *American Educational Research Journal* 42 (3): 439–464.

References

Adams, J. S. 1965. Inequity in social exchange. In *Advances in experimental social psychology*, ed. L. Berkowitz, 267–299. Vol. 2. New York: Academic Press.

Adebowale, A. 2009. The self-perception and cultural dimensions: Cross-cultural comparison. *Educational Studies* 35 (1): 81–92.

Albrecht, M. H., ed. 2001. Chapter 14, International HRM: Managing diversity in the workplace. *The yin & yang of managing in Asia*. Oxford: Blackwell.

American Management Organization (AMA). 2007. *How to build a high-performance organization: A global study of current trends and future possibilities, 2007–2017*. http://www.gsu.edu.images/HR/HRI-high-performance07.pdf (accessed July 18, 2010).

American Psychological Association (APA). 2003. Guidelines in multicultural education, training, research, practice, and organizational change for psychologists. *American Psychologist* 58: 377–402.

Amiri, A., S. Moghimi, and M. Kazemi. 2010. Studying the relationship between cultural intelligence and employee's performance. *European Journal of Scientific Research* 42 (3): 418–427.

Applewhite, S. 1995. Curanderismo: Demystifying the health beliefs and practices of elderly Mexican-Americans. *Health and Social Work* 20 (4): 247–253.

Applewhite, S. 1997. Qualitative research in educational gerontology. *Educational Gerontology* 23 (1): 15–27.

Applewhite, S. 1998. Culturally competent practice with elderly Latinos. *Journal of Gerontological Social Work* 30 (1/2): 1–15.

Arbona, C. 2005. Promoting the career development and academic achievement of at-risk youth: College access programs. In *Career development and counseling: Putting theory and research to work*, ed. S. D. Brown and R. W. Lent, 441–465. Hoboken, NJ: John Wiley.

Archibold, R. 2010. Arizona enacts stringent law on immigration. *New York Times*, Politics section.

Arizona House of Representatives. 2010. HB 2281. Committee on Education.

Assemi, M., S. Mutha, and K. Hudmon. 2007. Evaluation of a train-the-trainer program for cultural competence. *American Journal of Pharmaceutical Education* 71 (6): 1–8.

Associated Press. 2010, December. Obama signs repeal of "don't ask, don't tell." http://www.msnbc.msn.com/id/40777922/ns/politics-white_house (accessed April 8, 2011).

Baby Boomer Headquarters. n.d. The boomer stats. http://bbhq.com/boomrstat.htm (accessed April 4, 2010).

Bach, P., L. Cramer, J. Warren, and C. Begg. 1999. Racial differences in the treatment of early-stage lung cancer. *New England Journal of Medicine* 341: 1198–1205.

Bailey, M. 2005. Diversity and public administration: Cultural competency and the practices of public administration. In *Diversity and public administration: Theory, issues, and perspectives*, ed. M. F. Rice, 177–196. Armonk, NY: M. E. Sharpe.

Bailey, M. 2010. Cultural competency and the practice of public administration. In *Diversity and public administration: Theory, issues, and perspectives*, 2nd ed., ed. M. F. Rice, 171–188. Armonk, NY: M. E. Sharpe.

Baldridge, L. 1993. *Complete guide to executive manners*. New York: Simon & Schuster.

Barak, M., and A. Levin. 2002. Outside the corporate mainstream and excluded from the work community: A study of diversity, job satisfaction, and well being. *Community, Work & Family* 5 (2): 133–157.

Barks, C., and P. Rhoden. 2010. Art attack: Elementary school mural getting a "lighter" facelift. *Prescott Daily Courier*. http://www.prescottaz.com/print.asp?SectionID=1 (accessed June 21, 2010).

Barr, S. 2006. Next generation of hires must be cultivated quickly and differently, OPM chief says. *Washington Post*. http://www.washingtonpost.com/wp-dyn/content/article/2006/01/31/AR2006013101952 (accessed September 20, 2008).

Beach, M., S. Saha, and L. Cooper. 2006. *The role and relationship of cultural competence and patient-centeredness in health care quality*. Commonwealth Fund Report. http//www.commonwealthfund.org/Content/Publications/Fund-Reports (accessed May 22, 2010).

Berman, E. M., J. S. Bowman, J. P. West, and R. Van Wart. 2010. *Human resource management in public service*. Thousand Oaks, CA: Sage.

Betancourt, J. 2004. Cultural competence: Magical or mainstream movement? *New England Journal of Medicine* 10 (351): 953–955.

Betancourt, J. R., A. R. Green, J. E. Carrillo, and O. Ananeh-Firempong. 2003, July/August. Defining cultural competence: A practical framework for addressing racial/ethnic disparities in health and health care. *Public Health Reports* 118 (4): 293–302.

Black, J. S., and M. Mendenhall. 1990. Cross-cultural training, effectiveness: A review and a theoretical framework for future research. *Academy of Management Review* 15 (1): 113–136.

Blitz, J. 2010. Five European states back burka ban. *FT.com*. http://www.ft.com/cms/s/e0c0e732-254d-11df-9cdb (accessed March 15, 2010).

Bonder, B. R., L. Martin, and A. Miracle. 2001. Achieving cultural competence: The challenge for clients and healthcare workers in a multicultural society. *Generations* 25 (1): 35–44.

Borrego, E. 2009. Transitional cultural competence models for a no racial/ethnic majority in the U.S. American Society for Public Administration (ASPA) National Conference, Miami, March 23.

Borrego, E., P. Cruise, S. Parsons, and J. Melendez. 2009. The globalization of health care: Is health tourism the next wave? American Society for Public Administration (ASPA) National Conference, Miami, March 24.

Borrego, E., P. Cruise, S. Parsons, G. Perez, and A. Sousa. 2007, March. Crossing bridges for health care: U.S.–Mexico transborder interdependence and collaboration. Paper presented at the annual meeting of the American Society for Public Administration (ASPA), Washington, DC.

Borrego, V. J. 1980. A conceptual framework of organizational stress. PhD diss. University of Southern California, School of Public Administration.

Brach, C., and I. Fraser. 2000. Can cultural competency reduce racial and ethnic disparities? A review and conceptual model. *Medicare Care Research and Review* 57 (Suppl. 1): 181–217.

Bucher, R. D. 2010. *Diversity consciousness: Opening our minds to people, cultures, and opportunities.* 3rd ed. Upper Saddle River, NJ: Prentice Hall.

Burkett, L. 2007. *Medical tourism: Concerns, benefits, and the American legal perspective. Journal of Legal Medicine* 28: 223–245.

Burns, C., and J. Krehely. 2011. "Don't ask, don't tell" repeal moves forward–Gay men and women will serve openly this year. *Center for American Progress.* http://www.americanprogress.org/issues/2011/03/repeal_moves_forward.html (accessed April 24, 2011).

Bush, C. T. 2000. Cultural competence: Implications of the surgeon general's report on mental health. *Journal of Child and Adolescent Psychiatric Nursing* 13 (4): 177–178.

Byrd, W. 1990. Race, biology, and health care: Reassessing a relationship. *Journal of Health Care for the Poor and Underserved* 1: 278–296.

California Association of Public Hospitals and Health Systems (CAPH). n.d. http://www.caph.org/content/FastFacts.htm (accessed August 12, 2010).

Campaign for Youth. 2010. Demographics of America's future workforce. http://www.campaignforyouth.org/admin/fact/files/Demographics-of-Americas-Future-Workforce-pdf (accessed May 3, 2010).

Carnevale, A. P., N. Smith, and J. Strohl. 2010, June. Help wanted: Projections of jobs and education requirements through 2018. Washington, DC: Georgetown University Center on Education and the Workforce.

Carpenter-Song, E., M. Schwallie, and J. Longhofer. 2007. Cultural competence reexamined: Critique and directions for the future. *Psychiatric Services* 58 (10): 1362–1365.

Cauchon, D. 2009. Women gain as men lose jobs. *USA Today.* http://www.usatoday.com/news/nation/2009-09-02-womenwork_N.htm (accessed March 7, 2010).

Chang, W. 2007. Cultural competence of international humanitarian workers. *Adult Education Quarterly* 57 (3): 187–204.

Charan, R., S. Drotter, and J. Noel. 2001a. *How to build the leadership-powered company.* New York: John Wiley.

Charan, R., S. Drotter, and J. Noel. 2001b. *The leadership pipeline.* San Francisco: Jossey-Bass.

Chase, B. 2002. Teacher: School thyself. *Oakland Post* 38 (93): 4.

Cheney, K. 2009. Eight myths about health care reform, *AARP* 52 (4B): 26–27.

Chin, C., and L. Gaynier. 2006. Global leadership competence: A cultural intelligence perspective. Paper presented at the 2006 MBAA Conference. http://www.csuohio.edu/sciences/dept/psychology/graduate/diversity/GlobalLeadership%2011206.pdf (accessed September 12, 2010).

City of Seattle Race and Social Justice Initiative. 2008. *Report 2008: Looking back, moving forward.* http://www.seattle.gov/rsji/090120rsjiReport.pdf

Clinton, H. n.d. Quote from BrainyQuote. http://www.brainyquote.com/quotes/authors/h/hillary_clinton_3.html

CNN Wire Staff. 2011. 2 arrested as France's ban on burqas, niqabs takes effect. *CNNWorld.* http://articles.cnn.com/2011-04-11/world/france.burqa.ban_1_france-s-islamic-burqas-french-muslim?_s=PM:WORLD (accessed April 28, 2011).

Coleman, D. 2006, September. Immigration and ethnic change in low-fertility countries: A third demographic transition. *Population and Development Review* 32 (3): 401–406.

Collado, D. 2010. Harvard's center for public leadership unveils effort to support young Latino leaders. *Harvard Kennedy School.* http://www.hks.harvard.edu/new-events/news/press-releases/cpl-latino-leaders-jun10 (accessed October 8, 2010).

Collins, J. 2001. *Good to great.* New York: HarperCollins.

Connolly, C. 2008. Organizational culture: Is it a plus or minus in your organization? *National Executive Institute Associates.* http://www.neiassociates.org/connolly.pdf (accessed May 8, 2010).

Cook, E. P., M. J. Heppner, and K. M. O'Brien. 2002. Career development of women of color and white women: Assumptions, conceptualizations, and interventions from an ecological perspective. *Career Development Quarterly* 50: 291–304.

Cooper, A. 2009. Sotomayor: Judicial record. Anderson Cooper 360°. http://ac360.blogs.cnn.com/2009/07/10/sotomayor-judicial-record (accessed November 18, 2009).

Cooper, J. J. 2010. Arizona ethnic studies law signed by Governor Brewer, condemned by UN human rights experts. *Huffington Post.* http://www.huffingtonpost.com/2010/05/12/arizona-ethnic-studies-la_n_572864.html

Coyner, T. 2008. Working as expatriate businessman in Korea. http://www.koreatimes.co.kr/www/news/include/print.asp?newsIdx=31663 (accessed February 21, 2010).

Cross, T., B. Bazron, K. Dennis, and M. Issacs. 1989. *Towards a culturally competent system of care.* Vol. 1. Washington, DC: Georgetown University Child Development Center, CASSP Technical Assistance Center.

Cross, W. E., Jr. 1971. The Negro-to-Black conversion experience. *Black World* 20 (9): 13–27.

Crumley, B. 2010. Halal burgers? Another French brouhaha over Islam. *TIME.* http://www.time.com/time/world/article/0,8599,1967299,00.html (accessed May 19, 2011).

Cultural Diversity Institute, University of Calgary. 2000. *Cultural competency: A self-assessment guide for human service organizations.* http://www.calgary.ca/docgallery/bu/cns/fcss/cultural_competency_self_assesment_guide.pdf

Curtis, C. 1998. Creating culturally responsive curriculum: Making race matter. *The Clearing House* 71 (3): 135–140.

Dana, R., and J. Allen. 2008. *Cultural competency training in a global society.* London: Springer.

Day, J. n.d. *Population profile of the United States: National population projections.* Washington, DC: U.S. Census Bureau. http://www.census.gov/population/www/pop-profile/natproj.html (accessed April 21, 2011).

Dede, M. 2002. Building a public personnel system for the City of Freedonia: A new approach to teaching human resources management in an MPA program. *Journal of Public Affairs Education* 8 (4): 275–286.

Delgado Godoy, L. 2002. Immigration in Europe: Realities and policies (Working paper 02-18). Washington, DC: Institute of Public Goods & Policies. http://www.Kent.ac.uk/wramsoc/workingpapers/firstyearreports/backgroundreports/immigrationbackgroundreport.pdf (accessed March 3, 2009).

Deming, W. E. 1986. *Out of the crisis.* Cambridge, MA: MIT Press.

Dewitt, K. 1992. Minority college attendance rose in late 80's, report says. NYTimes.com. http://www.nytimes.com/1992/01/20/us/minority-college-attendance-rose-in-late80-s-report-says.html (accessed October 7, 2009)

Dodd, J., F. Garcia, R. G. Johnson III, and E. Morales. 2000. Collaborating for equity in diversity. In *Multicultural collaboration guide for early career educators,* ed. M. S. Fishbaugh, 165–188. Baltimore: Paul H. Brooks.

Dohm, A. 2000. Gauging the labor force effects of retiring baby-boomers. *Monthly Labor Review*, July, 17–25.

Dolan, J., and D. Rosenbloom. 2003. *Representative bureaucracy: Classic readings and continuing controversies.* Armonk, NY: M. E. Sharpe.

Dresang, D. L. 2009. *Personnel management in government agencies and nonprofit organizations.* 5th ed. New York: Pearson Longman.

Earley, P. 2002. Redefining interactions across cultures and organizations: Moving forward with cultural intelligence. *Research in organizational behavior* 24: 271–299.

Earley, P., and S. Ang. 2003. *Cultural intelligence: Individual interactions across cultures.* Stanford, CA: Stanford Business Books.

Earnest, F., and F. Shawnta. 2003. Managing diversity using a strategic planned change approach. *Journal of Management Development* 22 (10): 863–881.

Elliott, P. 2010. Gay workers to get family leave, *Yahoo! News*. Associated Press. http://news .yahoo.com/s/ap/20100622/ap_on_bi_ge/us_obama (accessed June 21, 2010).

Embrick, D., and M. Rice. 2010. Diversity ideology in the United States: Historical, contemporary, and sociological perspectives. *Diversity and public administration.* 2nd ed. Armonk, NY: M. E. Sharpe.

Erlanger, S. 2010. Top French schools, asked to diversify, fear for standards. *New York Times*. http://www.nytimes.com/2010/07/01/world/europe/01ecoles (accessed July 1, 2010).

European Commission, Employment, Social Affairs and Equal Opportunities. n.d. For diversity—Against discrimination. http://www.stop-discrimination.info

Fadiman, A. 1998. *The Spirit catches you and you fall down: A Hmong child, her American doctors, and the collision of two cultures.* New York: Farrar, Strauss & Giroux.

Fain, P. 2010. Gay college presidents to meet in Chicago. *Chronicle of Higher Education.* http://chronicle.com/article/Gay-College-Presidents-to-Meet/65719/

Farley, C., and S. Ang. 2003. *Cultural intelligence: Individual interactions across cultures.* Stanford, CA: Stanford Business Books.

Fayol, H. 1949. *General and industrial management.* London: Pitman & Sons.

Feagin, J., and H. Vera. 1995. *White racism.* New York: Routledge.

Fernandez, V. 2010. Arizona's ban on ethnic studies worries more than Latinos. *La Prensa San Diego.* http://laprensa-sandiego.org/stories/arizona%E2%80%99s-ban-on-ethnic-studies-worries-more-than-latinos/ (accessed August 6, 2010)

Fisher, C. D., L. F. Schoenfeldt, and J. B. Shaw. 2003. *Human resource management.* 5th ed. New York: Houghton Mifflin.

Frederickson, G. 2005. The state of social equity in American public administration. *National Civic Review* 94 (4): 31–38.

Freedom House. 2005. *Women's rights in the Middle East and North Africa,* ed. S. Nazir and L. Tomppert. Lanham, MD: Rowman & Littlefield.

Fry, R. 2010. Minorities and the recession-era college enrollment boom. Pew Research Center. http://pewresearch.org/pubs/1629/recession-era-increase-post-secondary-minority-enrollment

Gallegos, J. 1982. The ethnic competence model for social work education. In *Color in white society*, ed. B. W. White, 1–9. Silver Spring, MD: NASW.

Galloway, F. A. 2010. New immigration law in Arizona reminiscent of King Holiday repeal. http://www.Blackvoicesnews.com

Gardner, H. 1983. *Frames of mind: The theory of multiple intelligences.* New York: Basic Books.

Georgetown University Center for Child and Human Development, National Center for Cultural Competence. 2009. *Foundations of cultural & linguistic competence.* http://www11.georgetown.edu/research/gucchd/nccc/foundations (accessed April 4, 2009).

Geron, S. M. 2002. Cultural competency: How is it measured? Does it make a difference? *Generations* 26 (3): 39–45.

Golden Gate University. 2010. http://www.ggu.edu

Goleman, D. 1995. *Emotional intelligence: Why it can matter more than IQ.* New York: Bantam Books.

Goleman, D. 2000. *Working with emotional intelligence.* New York: Bantam Books.

Golembiewski, R. 1995. *Managing diversity in organizations.* Tuscaloosa: University of Alabama Press.

Goode, T., M. Dunne, and S. Bronheim. 2006. Cultural competence in primary health care: Partnerships for a research agenda. *National Center for Cultural Competence Policy Brief 3.* Vol. 37. http://www.dml.georgetown.edu/depts/pediatrics/gucdc/cultural.html (accessed May 23, 2010).

Goodsell, C. 2003. *The case for the bureaucracy: A public administration polemic.* 4th ed. Chatham, NJ: Chatham House.

Goodwin, L. 2010. Author of Arizona immigration law wants to end birthright citizenship. *Yahoo! News.* http:news.yahoo.com.s/ynews/20100521/pl_ynews/ (accessed June 11, 2010).

Guthrie, M. 2010. How the census will change your business: A Q&A with Telemundo's Don Browne. *Broadcasting and Cable,* June 21. http://www.broadcastingcable.com/article/453938-How_the_Census_Will_Change_Your_Business_A_Q_A_With_Telemundo_s_Don_Browne.php

Gutierrez, J., A. Sameroff, and B. Karrer. 1988. Acculturation and SES effects on Mexican-American parents' concepts of development. *Child Development* 59: 250–255.

Hall, B. 2000. Immigration in the European Union: Problem or solution? *OECD Observer,* Summer. http://www.oecdobserver.org/news/fullstory.php/aid/337/

Hall, E. 1959. *The silent language.* New York: Doubleday.

Hall, E. 1976. *Beyond culture.* New York: Anchor Press.

Hall, E. 1983. *The dance of life: The other dimension of time.* New York: Doubleday/Anchor.

Hall, E., and M. Hall. 1987. *Hidden differences: Doing business with the Japanese.* New York: Doubleday/Anchor.

Hardy-Fanta, C., and E. MacMahon-Herrera. 1981. Adapting family therapy to the Hispanic family. *Social Casework* 62: 250–255.

Harris, D., R. Andrews, and A. Elixhauser. 1997. Racial and gender differences in use of procedures for black and white hospitalized adults. *Ethnicity and Disease* 7: 91–105.

Hawking, S. 1998. *A brief history of time.* 10th anniversary ed. New York: Bantam Books.

Hay Group. 2004a. Emotional and social competency inventory accreditation program. http://www.haygroup.com/leadershipandtalentondemand/downloadfiles/misc/esci_-_accreditation_.pdf (accessed April 29, 2011).

Hay Group. 2004b. The resilience factor inventory accreditation. http://www.adaptivlearning.com (accessed April 29, 2011)

Hayes, B. C., S. A. Bartle, and D. A. Major. 2002. Climate for opportunity: A conceptual model. *Human Resources Review* 12 (3): 445–469.

Health Resources and Human Services Administration (HRSA), U.S. Department of Health and Human Services. 2002. *Other definitions of cultural competence.* http://www.hrsa.gov/culturalcompetence/

Herrick, D. 2007. *Medical tourism: Global competition in health care* (Policy report 304). Dallas, TX: National Center for Policy Analysis.

Herrick, C., and H. Brown. 1998. Underutilization of mental health services by Asian-Americans residing in the United States. *Issues in Mental Health Nursing* 19: 225–240.

Hofstede, G. 1980. *Culture's consequences: International differences in work-related values.* Thousand Oaks, CA: Sage.

Hofstede, G. 1993. Cultural constraints in management theories. *Academy of Management Executive* 7: 81–90.

Hofstede, G. 2001. *Culture's consequences: Comparing values, behaviors, institutions, and organizations across nations.* 2nd ed. Thousand Oaks, CA: Sage.

Homedes, N., and A. Ugalde. 2003. *Public health matters: Globalization and health at the United States–Mexico Border, American Journal of Public Health* 93 (12): 2016–2022.

Hope, C. 2008. UK migration: Answers are needed. *The Telegraph.* http://blogs.telegraph .co.uk/news/christopherhope/3655821 (accessed October 18, 2009).

House, R., P. Hanges, M. Javidan, P. Dorfman, V. Gupta, et al., eds. 2004. *Culture, leadership, and organizations: The GLOBE study of 62 societies.* Thousand Oaks, CA: Sage.

House, R., and M. Javidan. 2004. Overview of GLOBE. In *Culture, leadership, and organizations: The GLOBE study of 62 societies*, ed. R. House, P. Hanges, M. Javidan, P. Dorfman, V. Gupta, et al., 9–28. Thousand Oaks, CA: Sage.

Hume, J. 1998, December 10. Nobel Peace Prize lecture, Oslo, Norway. http://nobelprize .org/nobel_prizes/peace/laureates/1998/hume-lecture.html

Hurdle, D. 2002. Native Hawaiian traditional healing: Culturally-based interventions for social work practice. *Social Work* 47 (2): 183–192.

ICPA. 2010. Public administration challenges and opportunities: Serving citizens in a globalised world. Sixth International Conference on Public Administration (ICPA), Canberra, Australia, October 22–24.

Inclan, J. 1985. Variations in value orientation in mental health work with Puerto Ricans. *Psychotherapy* 22: 324–334.

Johnson, J. L., and M. C. Cameron. 2001. Barriers to providing effective mental health services to American Indians. *Mental Health Services Research* 3 (4): 181–187.

Johnson, J., T. Lenartowicz, and S. Apud. 2006. Cross-cultural competence in international business: Toward a definition and a model. *Journal of International Business Studies* 37: 525–543.

Johnson III, R. G. 2004. Has public administration grown up? A case for class-related education and research. *International Journal of Public Administration* 27 (7): 509–517.

Johnson III, R. G., ed. 2009a. *The queer community: Continuing the struggle for social justice.* San Diego: Birkdale.

Johnson III, R. G. 2009b. Still invisible: The African American gay male experience in the 21st century. In *The queer community: Continuing the struggle for social justice*, ed. R. G. Johnson III, 155–173. San Diego: Birkdale.

Johnson III, R. G., and E. Borrego. 2009. Public administration and the increased need for cultural competencies in the twenty-first century. *Administrative Theory & Praxis* 31 (2): 207–224.

Johnson III, R. G., and G. L. A. Harris, eds. 2010. *Women of color in leadership: Taking their rightful place.* San Diego: Birkdale.

Johnson III, R. G., C. Reyes, and S. Smith. 2009. Repositioning the culture of power: Advocating for systemic change in higher education. *Journal of Public Affairs Education* 15 (1): 33–45.

Johnson III, R. G., and Rivera, M. 2007. Refocusing graduate public affairs education: A need for diversity competencies in human resource management. *Journal of Public Affairs Education* 13 (1): 15–27.

Johnston, P. 2005. Immigration is altering Britain's ethnic mix. *The Telegraph.* http://www.telegraph.co.uk/news/1481880 (accessed July 11, 2008).

Jones, G. 2010. Italy in racism debate as migrants quit riot town. Reuters news service. http://www.reuters.com/article/idUSLDE60906 (accessed April 21, 2010).

Kabat-Zinn, J. 1990. *Full catastrophe living: using the wisdom of your body and mind to face stress, pain, and illness.* 15th anniversary ed. New York: Bantam Dell.

Kareem, N. 2009. The history of Martin Luther King Jr. holiday. About.com: Race Relations.

Kelts, R. 2010. Toyota and trust: Was the Akio Toyoda apology lost in translation? *Christian Science Monitor.* http://new.yahoo.com/s/scm/20100225/cm_csm/282844_1 (accessed March 7, 2010).

Kennedy, J. F. 1963, June 10. Commencement address, American University, Washington, DC.

King, K. 2009. Resilience: Queer professors from the working class. Book review in *New Horizon in Adult Education & Resource Development* 23 (4): 94.

Klepper, D. 2010. "This is our home now": Country's changing face emerges in America's heartland. *The Monitor*, July 4, p. 15A.

Klimecki, R., and S. Litz. 2004. Human resources management as intervention in the evolution of human services. Paper presented at the International Federation of Scholarly Associations of Management, World Conference, Gohteborg, Sweden.

Klingner, D., and J. Nalbandian. 2003. *Public personnel management: Contexts and strategies.* Upper Saddle River, NJ: Prentice Hall.

Klingner, D., J. Nalbandian, and J. Llorens. 2010. *Public personnel management: Contexts and strategies.* 6th ed. New York: Longman.

Kluckhohn, R., and F. Strodtbeck. 1961. *Variations in value orientations.* New York: HarperCollins.

Korn/Ferry International. 1998. *Diversity in the executive suite: Creating successful career paths and strategies.* Los Angeles: Korn/Ferry International.

Kumar, N., R. Rose, and Subramaniam. 2008. The effects of personality and cultural intelligence on international assignment effectiveness: A review. *Journal of Social Sciences* 4 (4): 320–328.

Lavizzo-Mourey, R., and E. Mackenzie. 1996. Cultural competence: Essential measurement of quality for managed care organizations. *Annals of Internal Medicine* 124: 919–921.

Lawler, J. J. 1996. Diversity issues in South-East Asia: The case of Thailand. *International Journal of Manpower* 17 (4/5): 152–167.

LeBaron, M. 2003. Cross-cultural communication. In *Beyond intractability*, ed. G. Burgess and H. Burgess. Boulder: Conflict Research Consortium, University of Colorado. http://www.beyondintractability.org/essay/cross-cultural_communication/

Le-Doux, C., and F. E. Montalvo. 1999. Multicultural content in social work graduate programs: A national survey. *Journal of Multicultural Social Work* 7 (1–2): 37–55.

Lecca, P. 1998. *Cultural competency in health, social, and human services: Directions for the twenty-first century.* New York: Garland.

Lehrer, J. 2009. Don't! The secret of self-control. *The New Yorker.* http://www.newyorker.com/reporting/2009/ (accessed May 16, 2010).

Leong, F. T. L., and A. S. L. Lau. 2001. Barriers to effective mental health services to Asia Americans. *Mental Health Services Research* 3 (4): 215–223.

Lindquist, J., and C. Kaufman-Scarborough. 2007. The polychronic-monochronic tendency model. *Time & Society* 16 (2/3): 269–301.

Marin, G., and R. Gamba. 2003. Acculturation and changes in cultural behavior. In *Acculturaltion: Advances in theory, measurement, and applied research*, ed. K. Chun, P. Organista, and G. Marin, 83–94. Washington, DC: American Psychological Association.

Martinez, K., C. Green, and F. Sanundo. 2004. The CLAS challenge: Promoting culturally and linguistically appropriate services in health care. *International Journal of Public Administration* 27 (1/2): 39–61.

Mathews, A. 2010. Diversity management and cultural competency. In *Diversity and public administration: Theory, issues, and perspectives*, 2nd ed., ed. M. F. Rice, 210–263. Armonk, NY: M. E. Sharpe.

McClellan, S. 2006. Dynamics of racially diverse workplaces: Directions for preparing effective leaders. Paper presented at the 2006 NASPAA Annual Conference: The Future of the Public Sector, Minneapolis, October 19.

McIntosh, P. 1998. White privilege and male privilege: Personal account of coming to see correspondences through work in women's studies (Working paper No. 189). Wellesley, MA: Wellesley College Center for Research on Women.

McPhatter, A. 1997. Cultural competence in child welfare: What is it? How do we achieve it? What happens with it? *Child Welfare* 82 (2): 103–125.

MediaMatters staff. 2010, May 14. Buchanan complains that with Kagan, Supreme Court will have too many Jews. *MediaMatters for America*. http://mediamatters.org/pring/blog/201005140037 (accessed June 21, 2010).

Mianecki, J. 2011, April. Don't ask don't tell going better than expected. *Latimes.com*. http://latimes.com/news/nationworld/nation/wire/sc-dc-0408-don't-ask-20110408,0,6541937.story (accessed April 8, 2001).

Michaels, A. 2009. Muslim Europe: The demographic time bomb transforming our continent. *The Telegraph*. http://www.telegraph.co.uk/news/worldnews/europe/5994047 (accessed October 18, 2009).

Miller, M. 2010. Predicting kid's success ... with marshmallows. *CBS News*. http://cbsnews.com/stories/2010/04/21/eveningnews/ (accessed May 16, 2010).

Milner, R. 2005. Developing a multicultural curriculum in a predominantly white teaching context: Lessons from an African American teacher in a suburban English classroom. *Curriculum Inquiry* 35 (4): 391–394.

Mischel, W., Y. Shoda, and M. L. Rodriguez. 1989. Delay of gratification in children. *Science* 244: 933–938.

Morello, C., and D. Keating. 2009. Number of foreign-born U.S. residents drops. *The Washington Post*. http://www.washingtonpost.com/wp-dyn/content/article/2009/09/21/AR2009092103251.html (accessed July 28, 2010)

National Association of Social Workers (NASW). 2007. *Indicators for the achievement of the NASW Standards for Cultural Competence in Social Work Practice*. Washington, DC: NASW.

Nelson, C. 2004. The diversity challenge in rural education. *English Journal* 93 (6): 22–24.

Nelson, S., and G. Pellett, producers, directors, writers. 1997. *Shattering the silences*. Film available from Public Broadcasting Service (PBS).

North Carolina Council of Churches. n.d. To cure every disease, equal access to healthcare, proper 6, year A. http://www.actsoffaith.org/Acts_of_Faith/Acts_of_Faith_Year_A/Year_A_Part_1/healthcare_quotes.htm (accessed October 20, 2010).

Northouse, P. 2007. *Leadership: Theory and practice.* 4th ed. Thousand Oaks, CA: Sage.

Oldfield, K., and R. G. Johnson III. 2008. *Resilience: Queer professors from the working class.* Albany, NY: SUNY Press.

Ortman, J., and C. Guarneri. 2009. *United States population projections.* http://www.census.gov/population/www/projections/analytical-documents09.pdf (accessed April 21, 2011).

Parker, V., and S. Geron. 2007. Cultural competence in nursing homes: Issues and implications for education. *Gerontology & Geriatrics Education* 28 (2): 37–54.

Passel, J. S., and D. Cohn. 2008. *U.S. population projections: 2005–2050.* Washington, DC: Pew Research Center.

Passel, J. S., and D. Cohn. 2011. *How many Hispanics? Comparing new census counts with the latest census estimates.* Washington, DC: Pew Hispanic Center. http://www.pewhispanic.org/files/reports/139.pdf

Passel, J. S., D. Cohn, and M. H. Lopez. 2011, March 24. *Census 2010: 50 million Latinos– Hispanics account for more than half of nation's growth in past decade.* Washington, DC: Pew Hispanic Center. http://pewhispanic.org/files/reports/140.pdf (accessed April 23, 2011).

Peace Corps Wiki. http://www.peacecorpswiki.org/Diversity_and_cross-cultural_issues

Peake, P. K., M. Hebl, and W. Mischel. 2002. Strategic attention deployment for delay of gratification in working and waiting situations. *Developmental Psychology* 38 (2): 313.

Peters, T. J., and R. H. Waterman. 1982. *In search of excellence: Lessons from America's best-run companies.* New York: Harper.

Peterson, E., L. Shaw, E. DeLong, D. Pryor, R. Califf, and D. Mark. 1997. Racial variation in the use of coronary-revascularization procedures. Are the differences real? Do they matter? *New England Journal of Medicine* 336 (7): 480–486.

Pew Hispanic Center. 2006, August. Pew Hispanic Center tabulations of 2000 Census and 2005 American Community Survey. http://pewhispanic.org/reports/middecade/ (accessed July 18, 2008).

Pitts, D. W., and E. M. Jarry. 2005. Ethnic diversity and organizational performance: Assessing diversity effects at the managerial and street levels. Paper presented at the Eighth Public Management Research Conference, Los Angeles, September 29–October 1. http://pmranet.org/conference/USC2005papers/pmra.pitts.jarry.2005.doc

Pope-Davis, D., and H. Coleman, eds. 1997. *Multicultural counseling competencies: Assessment, education and training and supervision* (Multicultural Aspects of Counseling and Psychotherapy series). Thousand Oaks, CA: Sage.

Primm, A., F. Osher, and M. Gomez. 2005. Race and ethnicity, mental health services and cultural competence in the criminal justice system: Are we ready to change? *Community Mental Health Journal* 41 (5): 557–569.

Provencher, D. 2008. One in ten: Teaching tolerance for (class) difference, ambiguity and queerness in the culture classroom. In *Resilience: Queer professors from the working class,* ed. K. Oldfield and R. G. Johnson III, 115–130. Albany, NY: SUNY Press.

Qureshi, A., F. Collazos, M. Ramos, and M. Casas. 2008. Cultural competency training in psychiatry. *European Psychiatry* 23 (1): 49–58.

Race: The power of an illusion. 2003. San Francisco: California Newsreel.

Random House Webster's college dictionary. 1997. 2nd ed. New York: Random House.

Reimann, J., G. Talavera, M. Salmon, J. Nunez, and R. Velasquez. 2004. Cultural competence among physicians treating Mexican Americans who have diabetes: A structural model. *Social Science & Medicine* 59 (11): 2195–2205.

Reivich, K., and A. J. Shatte. 2002. *The resilience factor.* New York: Broadway Books.

Reuters. 2010, September 27. Employer health costs to rise in 2011. http:// http://www.reuters .com/article/2010/09/27/us-usa-healthcare-costs-idUSTRE68Q3N520100927 (accessed November 14, 2010).

Reuters. 2011, April 11. France begins ban on niqab and burqa–Women wearing a face veil in public could now be fined or given lessons in French citizenship. *Guardian. co.uk.* http://www.guardian.co.uk/world/2011/apr/11/france-begins-burqa-niqab-ban (accessed April 28, 2011).

Riccucci, N. 2003. *Managing diversity in public sector workforces.* Boulder, CO: Westview Press.

Rice, M. 2007. A post-modern cultural competency framework for public administration and public service delivery. *International Journal of Public Sector Management* 20 (7): 622–637.

Rice, M. F. 2008. A primer for developing a public agency service ethos of cultural competency. *Journal of Public Affairs and Education* 14 (1): 21–28.

Rice, M. F., ed. 2010. *Diversity and public administration: Theory, issues, and perspectives.* Armonk, NY: M. E. Sharpe.

Rice, M. F., and D. Arekere. 2005. Workforce diversity initiatives and best practices in business and governmental organizations: Developments, approaches, and issues. In *Diversity and public administration: Theory, issues, and perspectives,* ed. M. F. Rice, 22–44. Armonk, NY: M. E. Sharpe.

Ridley, C. 1995. *Overcoming unintentional racism in counseling and therapy.* Thousand Oaks, CA: Sage.

Rio Grande Valley Health Training Alliance. 2006. *Growing our own: The Rio Grande Valley's strategy for coping with the nursing shortage* (Final report). http://www.harlingen.tstc .edu/.../RGVAlliedHealthTrainingAlliance.ppt

Rodriguez, O. 1986. *Overcoming barriers to clinical services among chronically mentally ill Hispanics: Lessons for the evaluation of Project COPA demonstration* (Research bulletin 9). New York: Fordham University, Hispanic Research Center.

Rodriguez, O. 1987. *Hispanics and human services: Help seeking in the inner city* (Monograph 13). New York: Fordham University, Hispanic Research Center.

Rodriguez, O., J. Lessinger, and P. Guarnaccia. 1992. The societal and organizational contexts of culturally sensitive mental health services: Findings from an evaluation of bilingual/bicultural psychiatric programs. *Journal of Mental Health Administration* 19: 213–223.

Rogler, L., R. Malgady, G. Costantino, and R. Blumenthal. 1987. What do culturally sensitive mental health services mean? The case of Hispanics. *American Psychologist* 42: 565–570.

Rosado, C. 2006. What do we mean by "managing diversity"? In *Workforce diversity,* Vol. 3, *Concepts and cases,* ed. S. Reddy. Andhra Pradesh, India: ICAFAI University. http://www.edchange.org/multicultural/papers/rosado_managing_diversity.pdf (accessed January 12, 2010).

Rouson, B., B. Applegate, V. Asakura, M. Moss, P. St. Onge, and A. Vergara-Lobo. 2009. *Cultural competency in the nonprofit sector: Starting the conversation.* St. Paul, MN: Fieldstone Alliance.

Ruth-Sahd, L. 2003. Intuition: A multicultural nursing curriculum. *Nursing Education Perspectives* 24 (3): 129–135.

Sabogal, F., G. Marin, M. VanOss, and E. Perez-Stable. 1987. Hispanic familism and acculturation: What changes and what doesn't? *Hispanic Journal of Behavioral Sciences* 9: 397–412.

Sanchez, T. 1996. Multiculturalism: Practical consideration for curricular change. *The Clearing House* 69 (3): 171–174.

Savage, C. 2009. A judge's view of judging is on the record. *Nytimes.com*. http://www.nytimes.com/2009/05/15/us/15judge.html (accessed January 12, 2010).

Schulman, K., J. Berlin, W. Harless, J. Kerner, and S. Sistrunk. 1999. The effect of race and sex on physicians' recommendations for cardiac catherization. *New England Journal of Medicine* 340: 618–626.

Servicemembers Legal Defense Network (SLDN). n.d. *About "Don't ask, don't tell"* (Factsheet). http://www.sldn.org/pages/about-dadt (accessed April 24, 2011).

Seurkamp, M. P. 2007. *Changing student demographics.* http://universitybusiness.com/viewarticlepf.aspx?articleid=905 (accessed October 27, 2009).

Seyed-Mahmoud, A. 2004. Managing workforce diversity as an essential resources for improving organizational performance. *Work Study* 53 (6): 521–532.

Shin, R., and D. Mesch. 1996. The changing workforce issues and challenges. *International Journal of Public Administration* 19 (3): 291–298.

Shin, R. Q. 2008. Advocating for social justice in academia through recruitment, retention, admissions and professional survival. *Journal of Multicultural Counseling and Development* 36 (3): 180.

Shore, E., S. Viji, and V. Po. 2009. Traditional healers choose to fight H1N1 naturally. *New America Media*. http://newsameriamedia.org/news/view_article.html (accessed February 17, 2010).

Siegel, C., G. Haugland, and E. Chambers. 2003. Performance measures and their benchmarks for assessing organizational cultural competency in behavioral health care service delivery. *Administration and Policy in Mental Health* 31 (2): 141–170.

Snowden, L. 2001. Barriers to effective health services for African Americans. *Mental Health Services Research* 3 (4): 181–187.

Society for Human Resources Management (SHRM). 2010. Global diversity readiness index. http://www.shrm.org/hrdisciplines/Diversity/gdri/pages/default.aspx (accessed April 16, 2011).

Solis, H. (Secretary), and K. Hall (Commissioner). 2010, December. *Women in the labor force: A databook* (Report 1026). Washington, DC: U.S. Department of Labor, Bureau of Labor Statistics. http://www.bls.gov/cps/wlf-databook.2010.htm (accessed April 23, 2011).

Starr, S., and D. Wallace. 2009. Self-reported cultural competence of public health nurses in a southeastern U.S. public health hospital. *Public Health Nursing* 26 (1): 48–57.

Sterling, T. 2010. Dutch anti-immigration party gains ground in vote. *Yahoo! News*. Associated Press report. http://news.yahoo.com/s/ap/20100304/ap_on_re_eu_netherlands (accessed March 3, 2020).

Strickland, B. R. 2008. No more rented rooms. In *Resilience: Queer professors from the working class*, ed. K. Oldfield and R. G. Johnson III, 115–130. Albany, NY: SUNY Press.

Sue, D., A. Ivey, and P. Pedersen. 1996. *A theory of multicultural counseling and therapy.* San Francisco: Brooks/Cole.

Sue, S. 2003. In defense of cultural competency in psychotherapy and treatment. *American Psychologist* 58 (11): 964–970.

Sue, S. 2006. Cultural competency: From philosophy to research and practice. *Journal of Community Psychology* 34 (2): 237–245.

Sue, S., and N. Zane. 1987. The role of culture and cultural techniques in psychotherapy: A critique and reformulation. *American Psychologist* 42: 37–45.

Sum, A., P. Harrington, and I. Khatiwada. 2005. *New foreign immigrants and the U.S. labor market: The unprecedented effects of the nation's labor force and its employed populations, 2000–2004.* Report prepared for the House Subcommittee on Immigration, Border Security, and Claims. Boston: Center for Labor Market Studies, Northeastern University.

Tan, J. 2004. Cultural intelligence and the global economy. *Leadership in Action* 24 (5): 19–21.

Tan, J. S., and Chua, R. Y. 2003. Training and developing cultural intelligence. In *Cultural intelligence: Individual interactions across cultures,* ed. C. Earley and S. Ang, 258–303. Stanford, CA: Stanford Business Books.

Tatum, B. 2003. *Why are all the black kids together in the cafeteria?* New York: Basic Books.

Taylor, E. 1994. Intercultural competency: A transformative learning process. *Adult Education Quarterly* 44 (3): 154–174.

Taylor, F. W. 1967. *The principles of scientific management.* New York: Harper & Row.

Taylor, M. 2006. Under the green oak, an old elite takes root in Tories. *Guardian Newspaper,* August 12. http://www.guardian.co.uk/politics/2006/aug/12/uk.conservatives

Tervalon, M., and J. Murray-Garcia. 1998. Cultural humility versus cultural competence: A critical discussion in defining physician training outcomes in multicultural education. *Journal of Health Care for the Poor and Underserved* 9 (2): 117–125.

Theim, R. 2010. Kaiser survey of people who purchase their own insurance finds rates increasing. *HealthQuote 360.* http://www.healthquote360.com/featured-health-insurance-articles/kaiser-survey-of-people-who-purchase-their-own-insurance-finds-rates-increasing.php (accessed November 14, 2010).

Thomas, D., and K. Inkson. 2004. *Cultural intelligence: People skills for global business.* San Francisco: Berrett-Koehler.

Tilford Group. 2004. *Multicultural competency development: Preparing students to live and work in a diverse world.* Manhattan: Kansas State University.

Tombros, A., B. Jordan, and M. Monterroso. 2007. Cultural competence: An international perspective. *Contraception* 75 (5): 325–327.

Tompkins, J. 2005. *Organization theory and public management.* Belmont, CA: Thomson Wadsworth.

Triandis, H. 1995. *Individualism and collectivism.* Boulder, CO: Westview Press.

Trower, C. A., and R. P. Chait. 2002. Faculty diversity: Too little for too long. *Harvard Magazine,* March/April, 1–12.

Tshikwatamba, N. E. 2003. The challenge of managing diversity in South Africa: More inclusive personnel policies and approaches. *The Public Manager* 32 (3): 36–39.

Tutu, D. 1999. *No future without forgiveness.* New York: Doubleday.

Ukpokodu, O. N. 2003. The challenges of teaching a social studies methods course from a transformative and social reconstructionist framework. *Social Studies* 94 (2): 75–81.

University of Vermont. 2010. http://www.uvm.edu

University of Vermont, Office of Institutional Research. 2009a. *Institutional studies report.* http://www.uvm.edu/~isis/?Page=facstaff0.html

University of Vermont, Office of the President. 2009b. *Diversity.* http://www.uvm.edu/president/?Page=whydiversity_statement.html

U.S. Census Bureau. 2004, March 18. Census Bureau projects tripling of Hispanic and Asian populations in 50 years; non-Hispanic whites may drop to half of total population. http://www.census.gov/Press-Release/www/releases/archives/population/001720 .html (accessed July 9, 2008).

U.S. Census Bureau. 2006. Selected characteristics of baby boomers 42 to 60 years old in 2006 (PowerPoint). U.S. Census Bureau, Population Estimates as of July 1, 2006. Washington, DC: Age and Special Populations Branch, Population Division, U.S. Census Bureau. http://www.census.gov/population/socdemo/age/2006%Baby%Boomers.pdf (accessed April 21, 2011).

U.S. Census Bureau. 2010, January. Race and Hispanic origin of the foreign-born population in the United States: 2007. *American Community Survey Reports.* http://search .census.gov/search?q=U.S.+Census+Bureau.+2010%2C+January.+Race+and+Hisp anic+origin+of+the+foreign-born+population+in+the+Un&Submit.x=7&Submit .y=10&entqr=0&ud=1&output=xml_no_dtd&oe=UTF-8&ie=UTF-8&client=default_ frontend&proxystylesheet=default_frontend&site=census (accessed April 8, 2011).

U.S. Census Bureau News. 2008, August 14. An older and more diverse nation by midcentury .http://www.census.gov/Press-Release/www/releases/archives/population/012496 .html (accessed August 15, 2008).

U.S. Department of Commerce and Vice President Al Gore's National Partnership for Reinventing Government Benchmarking Study. 1999. *Best practices in achieving workforce diversity.* http://govinfo.library.unt.edu/npr/library/workforce-diversity.pdf

U.S. Department of Health and Human Services, Administration on Aging. 2001. *Achieving cultural competence: A guidebook for providers of services to older Americans and their families.* http://www.aoa.prof/addive/culturally/addiv_cult.asp

U.S. Department of Health and Human Services, Office of Minority Health (OMH) (2001). *National standards for culturally and linguistically appropriate services in health care.* http://www.omhrc.gov/assets/pdf/checked/executive.pdf

U.S. Department of Health and Human Services, Substance Abuse and Mental Health Services Administration, Center for Mental Health Services (2009). Request for applications: Cooperative agreements for Comprehensive Community Mental Health Services for Children and Their Families Program, Child Mental Health Initiative (CMHI). http://www.samhsa.gov/Grants/2010/SM-10-005.aspx

U.S. Office of Personnel Management. 2010a. *Guide to senior executive service qualifications.* http://www.opm.gov/ses/references/GuidetoSESQuals_2010.pdf

U.S. Office of Personnel Management. 2010b. *A new day for federal service: Strategic plan 2010–2015.* http://www.opm.gov/strategicplan/pdf/StrategicPlan_20100310.pdf

U.S. Office of Personnel Management, Employment Service Diversity Office. 2000. *Building and maintaining a diverse, high-quality workforce: A guide for federal agencies.* http:// www.opm.gov/diversity/guide.htm

Uttal, L. 2006. Organizational cultural competency: Shifting programs for Latino immigrants from a client-centered to a community-based orientation. *American Journal of Community Psychology* 38 (3/4): 251–262.

Vandiver, B. J., W. Cross, F. Worrell, and P. E. Fhagen-Smith. 2002. Validating the cross racial identity scale. *Journal of Counseling Psychology* 49 (1): 71–85.

Vidu, S. 2004. From crisis to opportunity: Human resource challenges for the public sector in the twenty-first century. *Review of Policy Research* 21 (2): 157–178.

Vijaykar, M. 2001. The new Americans: A universal curriculum can counter racism. *India Currents* 15 (8): 12.

Walton, M. 1986. *The Deming management method.* New York: Perigree.

Warner, D. C., and Scheider, P. G. 2004. *Cross-border health insurance: Options for Texas* (U.S.-Mexican Policy Report Series no. 12). Austin: University of Texas, Inter-American Policy Studies Program, Lyndon B. Johnson School of Public Affairs, Teresa Lozano Long Institute of Latin American Studies.

Waters, M. C., and Z. M. Vang. 2005. The challenges of immigration to race based diversity policies in the United States, Paper presented at the Conference on the Art of the State III: Diversity and Canada's Future, Montebello, Quebec, Canada, October 14.

White, B., ed. 1982. *Color in a white society.* Silver Spring, MD: NASW.

White, H., and M. Rice. 2005. The multiple dimensions of diversity and culture. In *Diversity and public administration: Theory, issues, and perspectives,* ed. M. F. Rice, 3–22. Armonk, NY: M. E. Sharpe.

Williams, D. n.d. Quote from Wisdom Quotes. http://www.wisdomquotes.com/authors/donald-williams/ (accessed January 27, 2010).

Workpermit.com. 2008. Europe needs 56 million immigrant workers by 2050. http://www.workpermit.com/news/2008-01-14/europe/eu-needs-56-million-migrants-2050.htm (accessed July 19, 2009).

Worthington, R., L. Flores, and R. Navarro. 2005. Career development in context: Research with people of color. In *Career development and counseling: Putting theory and research to work,* ed. S. Brown and R. Lent, 225–252. Hoboken, NJ: John Wiley.

Wu, E., and M. Martinez. 2006, October. *Taking cultural competency from theory to action.* New York: The Commonwealth Fund. http://www.commonwealthfund.org/Content/Publications/Fund-Reports/2006/Oct/Taking-Cultural-Competency-from-Theory-to-Action.aspx

Yen, H. 2010. Minority births on track to outnumber white births in U.S. *The Denver Post.* http://www.denverpost.com/fdcp?unique=1302630589416 (accessed July 8, 2010).

Yukl, G. 2002. *Leadership in organizations.* Upper Saddle River, NJ: Prentice Hall.

Zayas, L. 1987. Towards an understanding of suicide risks in young Hispanic females. *Journal of Adolescent Research* 2: 1–11.

Zayas, L., and Z. Bryant. 1984. Culturally sensitive treatment of adolescent Puerto Rican girls and their families. *Child and Adolescent Social Work Journal* 1 (4): 235–253.

Zayas, L., M. Evans, L. Meijia-Maya, and O. Rodriguez. 1997. Cultural competency training for staff serving Hispanic families with a child in psychiatric crisis. *Families in Society: Journal of Contemporary Human Services* 78 (4): 405–412.

Zayas, L., and J. Palleja. 1988. Puerto Rican familism: Considerations for family therapy. *Family Relations* 37 (3): 260–264.

Zayas, L., and F. Solari. 1994. Early childhood socialization in Hispanic families: Context, culture, and practice implications. *Professional Psychology: Research and Practice* 25 (3): 200–206.

Index